EIGHTH EDITION

SOUND AND SENSE

An Introduction to Poetry

True ease in writing comes from art, not chance,
As those move easiest who have learned to dance.
'Tis not enough no harshness gives offense,
The sound must seem an echo to the sense.

Alexander Pope
from *An Essay on Criticism*

EIGHTH EDITION

SOUND AND SENSE

An Introduction to Poetry

LAURENCE PERRINE

THOMAS R. ARP

Southern Methodist University

HARCOURT BRACE COLLEGE PUBLISHERS

Fort Worth Philadelphia San Diego New York Orlando Austin San Antonio
Toronto Montreal London Sydney Tokyo

Acquisitions Editor: Stephen T. Jordan
Manuscript Editor: Helen Triller
Production Editor: Katherine Watson
Designer: Lori J. McThomas
Production Manager: Lynne Bush
Permissions Editor: Eleanor Garner

ISBN: 0-15-582610-7
Library of Congress Catalog Card Number: 91-73099
Printed in the United States of America
Copyrights and Acknowledgments appear on pages 383–89, which constitute a continuation of the copyright page.
7 8 9 0 1 2 016 15 14 13 12 11 10 9

Preface

The eighth edition of *Sound and Sense*, like the previous editions, is written for the college student who is beginning a serious study of poetry. It seeks to give that student a sufficient grasp of the nature and variety of poetry, some reasonable means for reading it with appreciative understanding, and a few primary ideas of how to evaluate it. The separate chapters gradually introduce the student to the elements of poetry, putting the emphasis always on *how* and *why*: *How* can the reader use these elements to get at the meaning of the poem, to interpret it correctly, and to respond to it adequately? *Why* does the poet use these elements? What values have they for the poet and the reader?

In matters of theory, some issues are undoubtedly simplified, but I hope none seriously. The purpose has always been to give the beginning student something to understand and use. The first assumptions of *Sound and Sense* are that poetry needs to be read carefully and thought about considerably and that, when so read, poetry gives its readers continuing rewards in experience and understanding.

Each chapter is divided into two parts: a discussion of the topic indicated by the chapter title, with illustrative poems, and a relevant selection of poems with study questions, for further illustration of the topic. The division between the two parts is visually indicated by a row of asterisks. The whole book is similarly divided into two parts: Part One consists of the sixteen discussion chapters; Part Two contains poems for further reading, without study questions.

As in previous editions, three poets (Dickinson, Donne, and Frost) are represented by a sufficient number of poems to support study of them as individual artists.

The eighth edition differs from the seventh chiefly in the following respects: the number of poems by women and by members of ethnic minorities (and the number of poets representing those groups) has again been increased; there has been a 15% increase in the total number of poems, most of them by contemporary poets; and a section on "Writing about Poetry" has been added as an appendix at the request of readers of the seventh edition.

With this edition Thomas R. Arp, my able and marvelously efficient assistant in the sixth and seventh editions, is elevated in status and duties to coauthor. Tom has clearly seen the intent of each part of the book and how it integrates with other parts. In this edition he has participated fully in the selection of poems, construction of study questions, correspondence with the publishers, and direction of copyediting. He also has rewritten and improved parts of the text itself. He fully deserves this new position and in future editions will carry forward the traditions that began with the first edition (1956), but he will also be open to new ideas, new questions, and new poems.

A book of this kind inevitably owes something to all who have thought and written about poetry. It would be impossible to express all indebtedness, but for personal advice, criticism, and assistance I wish especially to thank my wife, Catherine Perrine, and M. L. Lawhon and the late Margaret Morton Blum of Southern Methodist University.

L. P.

Professional Acknowledgments

The following instructors have offered helpful reactions and suggestions for this eighth edition of *Sound and Sense*.

Dr. Mary K. Allen
Cameron University

A. Leon Arksey
Seattle Pacific University

M. F. Austin
Columbia State Community College

Irene A. Bania
Erie Community College

Craig Barrow
University of Tennessee, Chattanooga

Cheri Beth Beasley
University of North Carolina, Charlotte

Betty J. Beckley
University of Maryland, College Park

Dr. A. M. Belmont, Jr.
Southern Arkansas University

Louise D. Bentley
Union University

Lois Birky
Illinois Central College

Don Blankenship
West Valley College

Arnold J. Bradford
Northern Virginia Community College, Manassas

Elaine Brookshire
Northeast Alabama State Jr. College

Devin Brown
Brevard College

Susan M. Butler
Thomas Nelson Community College

Warren J. Carson
University of South Carolina, Spartanburg

Carol Cauthen
Jacksonville State University

Nathan Anthony Cervo
Franklin Pierce College

Ray Cichon
Fitchburg State College

Michael M. Clarke
Loyola University of Chicago

Betty Cochran
Beaufort Community College

Matthew W. Cooney
Salem State College

Charlotte C. Crittenden
Georgia Southern College

Margaret DeHart
Trinity Valley Community College

Robert Douglas
University of Alaska, Anchorage

Richard Downing
Pasco-Hernando Community College

Shirley Duffy
North Shore Community College

Bart Edelman
Glendale College

Lawrence Fine
Wentworth Institute of Technology

Georgegeen Gaertner
Lake Superior State University

C. Herbert Gilliland
U.S. Naval Academy

Alan Goodell
Mt. Hood Community College

Dr. Darlene J. Gravett
Gardner-Webb College

Janet Hill Gregory
Shelton State Jr. College

Alice Griffin
Lehman College, Cuny

John D. Hain
Tennessee Temple University

Minon A. Hamm
Union College

John Hanes
Duquesne University

Ruth M. Harrison
Arkansas Tech University

Anne M. Haselkorn
York College, Cuny

Wayne E. Haskin
North Carolina State University

Patty Ray Hawkins
Tennessee Temple University

Jane N. Heymann
Mitchell Community College

Judith R. Hiltner
Christian Brothers College

Harland Hoffman
Kearney State College

W. M. Hagen
Oklahoma Baptist University

Robert M. Hogge
Weber State College

John B. Humma
Georgia Southern University

Bernetta Jackson
Washington University, St. Louis

Randolph J. Jackson
Brevard College

Karla Jay
Pace University

Ruby T. Johnson
Wallace Community College

Ruth Johnston
Pace University

James L. Jolly, Jr.
Shelton State Community College

Joyce Jolly
Shelton State Community College

M. Jean Jones
Columbia State Community College

Mary Jordon
Illinois Central College

Harvey Kassebaum
Cuyahoga Community College

Marilyn King
Northeast Alabama State Jr. College

David Kelly
Dyersburg State Community College

Patricia C. Knight
Amarillo College

Al Krahn
Milwaukee Area Technical College

Mary Kramer
University of Lowell

Val Larsen
Virginia Tech

Kenneth P. Leisch
Danville Area Community College

Howard F. Livingston
Pace University

Elizabeth Bergmann Loizeaux
University of Maryland, College Park

Gary W. Longrie
Milwaukee Area Technical College

Nelda J. Lott
Mississippi Gulf Coast Community College

Gerald F. Luboff
County College of Morris

Jo Marshall
Jefferson State Community College

Alexander J. Maxwell
Shoreline Community College

Dr. Terry Miller
Indian River Community College

Virginia Ramey Mollenkott
William Paterson College of New Jersey

Clara Lee R. Moodie
Central Michigan University

Nancy Moore
University of South Carolina, Spartanburg

John Morressy
Franklin Pierce College

Paul E. McClure
North Georgia College

Mary McCauley
Dyersburg State Community College

Jo McDougall
Pittsburg State University

Jane Neuberger
Cazenovia College

Larry O'Hanlon
Fullerton College

David M. Packard
John A. Logan College

Dan Peterson
Southern University, Baton Rouge

Dr. Helmuth C. Poggemiller
Liberty University

Norman Prinsky
Augusta College

Barbara Read
Kilgore College

Paul F. Rellinger
Eric Community College

Thomas C. Renzi
Canisius College

Noel Robinson
County College of Morris

Joseph E. Roesch
Onondaga Community College

Mardee M. Rose
University of Wisconsin, Stevens Point

Paula Ross
Gadsden State Community College

Emma L. Roth
St. Mary's College

Karen Rowe
Bob Jones University

Donald N. Schweda
Quincy College

Linda Jo Scott
Olivet College

J. R. Scrutchins
Oklahoma Baptist University

Linda R. Selman
Southern Arkansas University

Robert V. Shaver
Danville Community College

Kathleen A. Sherfick
Albion College

Craig L. Shurtleff
Illinois Central College

Lynne M. Shuster
Erie Community College

Keith Slocum
Montclair State College

Ethel M. Smeak
Mary Baldwin College

LeNita Beetem Smith
Northwestern Oklahoma State University

John Steele
Salem State College

C. Ralph Stephens
Essex Community College

William Studebaker
College of Southern Idaho

Mali Subbiah
Weber State College

Mitchell E. Summerlin
Calhoun Community College

Elizabeth Tentarelli
Merrimack College

Richard J. Thompson
Canisius College

S. Gregory Tiernan
Mission College

David Toor
SUNY at Cortland

Mikel Vause
Weber State College

Gene Washington
Utah State University

Evelyn E. J. Webb
Mississippi Gulf Coast Community College

John P. Weber
Cypress College

David W. Wickham
Mountain View College

CONTENTS

CHAPTER FIVE *Figurative Language 1* Simile, Metaphor, Personification, Apostrophe, Metonymy 60

CHAPTER SIX *Figurative Language 2* Symbol, Allegory 79

CHAPTER THIRTEEN *Sound and Meaning* 197

CHAPTER FOURTEEN *Pattern* 214

PART 1

The Elements of Poetry

CHAPTER ONE

What Is Poetry?

Poetry is as universal as language and almost as ancient. The most primitive peoples have used it, and the most civilized have cultivated it. In all ages and in all countries, poetry has been written, and eagerly read or listened to, by all kinds and conditions of people — by soldiers, statesmen, lawyers, farmers, doctors, scientists, clergy, philosophers, kings, and queens. In all ages it has been especially the concern of the educated, the intelligent, and the sensitive, and it has appealed, in its simpler forms, to the uneducated and to children. Why? First, because it has given pleasure. People have read it, listened to it, or recited it because they liked it — because it gave them enjoyment. But this is not the whole answer. Poetry in all ages has been regarded as important, not simply as one of several alternative forms of amusement, as one person might choose bowling, another chess, and another poetry. Rather, it has been regarded as something central to existence, something having unique value to the fully realized life, something that we are better off for having and without which we are spiritually impoverished. To understand the reasons for this, we need to have at least a provisional understanding of what poetry is — provisional, because people have always been more successful at appreciating poetry than at defining it.

Initially, poetry might be defined as a kind of language that says *more* and says it *more intensely* than does ordinary language. To understand this fully, we need to understand what poetry "says." For language is employed on different occasions to say quite different kinds of things; in other words, language has different uses.

Perhaps the commonest use of language is to communicate *information*. We say that it is nine o'clock, that we liked a certain movie, that George Washington was the first president of the United States, that bromine and iodine are members of the halogen group of chemical elements. This we might call the *practical* use of language; it helps us with the ordinary business of living.

But it is not primarily to communicate information that novels, short stories, plays, and poems are written. These exist to bring us a sense and a perception of life, to widen and sharpen our contacts with existence. Their concern is with *experience*. We all have an inner need to live more deeply and fully and with greater awareness, to know the experience of others, and to understand our own experience better. Poets, from their own store of felt, observed, or imagined experiences, select, combine, and reorganize. They create significant new experiences for their readers — significant because focused and formed — in which readers can participate and from which they may gain a greater awareness and understanding of their world. Literature, in other words, can be used as a gear for stepping up the intensity and increasing the range of our experience and as a glass for clarifying it. This is the *literary* use of language, for literature is not only an aid to living but a means of living.*

Suppose, for instance, that we are interested in eagles. If we want simply to acquire information about eagles, we may turn to an encyclopedia or a book of natural history. There we find that the family Falconidae, to which eagles belong, is characterized by imperforate nostrils, legs of medium length, a hooked bill, the hind toe inserted on a level with the three front ones, and the claws roundly curved and sharp; that land eagles are feathered to the toes and sea-fishing eagles halfway to the toes; that their length is about three feet and their wingspan seven feet; that they usually build their nests on some inaccessible cliff; that the eggs are spotted and do not exceed three; and perhaps that the eagle's "great power of vision, the vast height to which it soars in the sky, the wild grandeur of its abode, have . . . commended it to the poets of all nations."†

But unless we are interested in this information only for practical purposes, we are likely to feel a little disappointed, as though we had grasped the feathers of the eagle but not its soul. True, we have learned many facts about the eagle, but we have missed somehow its lonely majesty, its power, and the "wild grandeur" of its surroundings that would make the eagle a living creature rather than a mere museum specimen. For the living eagle we must turn to literature.

*A third use of language is as an instrument of persuasion. This is the use we find in advertisements, propaganda bulletins, sermons, and political speeches. These three uses of language — the practical, the literary, and the hortatory — are not sharply divided. They may be thought of as three points of a triangle; most actual specimens of written language fall somewhere within the triangle. Most poetry conveys some information, and some poetry has a design on the reader. But language becomes *literature* when the desire to communicate experience predominates.

†*Encyclopedia Americana* IX (1955) 473–74.

1. The Eagle

He clasps the crag with crooked hands;
Close to the sun in lonely lands,
Ringed with the azure world, he stands.

The wrinkled sea beneath him crawls;
He watches from his mountain walls,
And like a thunderbolt he falls.

Alfred, Lord Tennyson (1809–1892)

QUESTIONS

1. What is peculiarly effective about the expressions "crooked hands," "close to the sun," "ringed with the azure world," "wrinkled," "crawls," and "like a thunderbolt"?
2. Notice the formal pattern of the poem, particularly the contrast of "he stands" in the first stanza and "he falls" in the second. Is there any other contrast between the two stanzas?

When "The Eagle" has been read well, readers will feel that they have enjoyed a significant experience and understand eagles better, though in a different way, than they did from the encyclopedia article alone. For while the article *analyzes* our experience of eagles, the poem in some sense *synthesizes* such an experience. Indeed, we may say the two approaches to experience — the scientific and the literary — complement each other. And we may contend that the kind of understanding we get from the second is at least as valuable as the kind we get from the first.

Literature, then, exists to communicate significant experience — significant because concentrated and organized. Its function is not to tell us *about* experience but to allow us imaginatively to *participate* in it. It is a means of allowing us, through the imagination, to live more fully, more deeply, more richly, and with greater awareness. It can do this in two ways: by *broadening* our experience — that is, by making us acquainted with a range of experience with which, in the ordinary course of events, we might have no contact — or by *deepening* our experience — that is, by making us feel more poignantly and more understandingly the everyday experiences all of us have.

We can avoid two mistaken approaches to poetry if we keep this conception of literature firmly in mind. The first approach always looks for a lesson or a bit of moral instruction. The second expects to find poetry always beautiful. Let us consider one of the songs from Shakespeare's *Love's Labor's Lost* (5.2).

2. Winter

When icicles hang by the wall,
And Dick the shepherd blows his nail,
And Tom bears logs into the hall,
And milk comes frozen home in pail,
When blood is nipped and ways be foul,
Then nightly sings the staring owl,
"Tu-whit, tu-who!"
    A merry note,
    While greasy Joan doth keel° the pot. skim

When all aloud the wind doth blow,
And coughing drowns the parson's saw,
And birds sit brooding in the snow,
And Marian's nose looks red and raw,
When roasted crabs° hiss in the bowl, crab apples
Then nightly sings the staring owl,
"Tu-whit, tu-who!"
    A merry note,
    While greasy Joan doth keel the pot.

William Shakespeare (1564–1616)

QUESTIONS

1. Vocabulary: *nail* (2), *saw* (11).
2. Is the owl's cry really a "merry" note? How are this adjective and the verb "sings" employed?
3. In what way does the owl's cry contrast with the other details of the poem?

In this poem Shakespeare communicates the quality of winter life around a sixteenth-century English country house. But he does not do so by telling us flatly that winter in such surroundings is cold and in many respects unpleasant, though with some pleasant features too (the adjectives *cold, unpleasant*, and *pleasant* are not even used in the poem). Instead, he provides a series of concrete homely details that suggest these qualities and enable us, imaginatively, to experience this winter life ourselves. The shepherd blows on his fingernails to warm his hands; the milk freezes in the pail between the cowshed and the kitchen; the cook is slovenly and unclean; the roads are muddy; the folk listening to the parson have colds; the birds "sit brooding in the snow"; and the servant girl's nose is raw from cold. But pleasant things are in prospect. Tom is bringing in logs for the fire, the hot cider or ale is ready for drinking, and the cook is preparing the soup or stew. In contrast to all these familiar details of country life is the mournful and eerie note of the owl.

Obviously the poem contains no moral. Readers who always look in poetry for some lesson, message, or noble truth about life are bound to be disappointed. Moral-hunters see poetry as a kind of sugar-coated pill—a wholesome truth or lesson made palatable by being put into pretty words. What they are really after is a sermon—not a poem, but something inspirational. Yet "Winter," which has appealed to readers now for nearly four centuries, is not inspirational and contains no moral preachment.

Neither is the poem "Winter" beautiful. Though it is appealing in its way and contains elements of beauty, there is little that is really beautiful in red raw noses, coughing in chapel, nipped blood, foul roads, and greasy cooks. Yet some readers think that poetry deals exclusively with beauty—with sunsets, flowers, butterflies, love, God—and that the one appropriate response to any poem is, after a moment of awed silence, "Isn't that beautiful!" For such readers poetry is a precious affair, the enjoyment only of delicate souls, removed from the heat and sweat of ordinary life. But theirs is too narrow an approach to poetry. The function of poetry is sometimes to be ugly rather than beautiful. And poetry may deal with common colds and greasy cooks as legitimately as with sunsets and flowers. Consider another example:

3. Dulce et Decorum Est

Bent double, like old beggars under sacks,
Knock-kneed, coughing like hags, we cursed through sludge,
Till on the haunting flares we turned our backs,
And towards our distant rest began to trudge.
Men marched asleep. Many had lost their boots,
But limped on, blood-shod. All went lame, all blind;
Drunk with fatigue; deaf even to the hoots
Of gas-shells dropping softly behind.

Gas! GAS! Quick, boys!—An ecstasy of fumbling,
Fitting the clumsy helmets just in time,
But someone still was yelling out and stumbling
And flound'ring like a man in fire or lime.—
Dim through the misty panes and thick green light,
As under a green sea, I saw him drowning.

In all my dreams before my helpless sight
He plunges at me, guttering, choking, drowning.

If in some smothering dreams, you too could pace
Behind the wagon that we flung him in,

And watch the white eyes writhing in his face,
His hanging face, like a devil's sick of sin,
If you could hear, at every jolt, the blood
Come gargling from the froth-corrupted lungs
Bitter as the cud
Of vile, incurable sores on innocent tongues,—
My friend, you would not tell with such high zest
To children ardent for some desperate glory,
The old lie: *Dulce et decorum est*
Pro patria mori.

Wilfred Owen (1893–1918)

QUESTIONS

1. The Latin quotation, from the Roman poet Horace, means "It is sweet and becoming to die for one's country." What is the poem's comment on this statement?
2. List the elements of the poem that seem not beautiful and therefore "unpoetic." Are there any elements of beauty in the poem?
3. How do the comparisons in lines 1, 14, 20, and 23–24 contribute to the effectiveness of the poem?

Poetry takes all life as its province. Its primary concern is not with beauty, not with philosophical truth, not with persuasion, but with experience. Beauty and philosophical truth are aspects of experience, and the poet is often engaged with them. But poetry as a whole is concerned with all kinds of experience—beautiful or ugly, strange or common, noble or ignoble, actual or imaginary. One of the paradoxes of human existence is that all experience—even painful experience—is, for the good reader, enjoyable when transmitted through the medium of art. In real life, death and pain and suffering are not pleasurable, but in poetry they may be. In real life, getting soaked in a rainstorm is not pleasurable, but in poetry it can be. In actual life, if we cry, usually we are unhappy; but if we cry in a movie, we are manifestly enjoying it. We do not ordinarily like to be terrified in real life, but we sometimes seek movies or books that will terrify us. We find some value in all intense living. To be intensely alive is the opposite of being dead. To be dull, to be bored, to be imperceptive is in one sense to be dead. Poetry comes to us bringing life and therefore pleasure. Moreover, art focuses and organizes experience so as to give us a better understanding of it. And to understand life is partly to be master of it.

There is no sharp distinction between poetry and other forms of imaginative literature. Although some beginning readers may believe that poetry can be recognized by the arrangement of its lines on the page or by its use of rime and meter, such superficial signs are of little worth. The Book of Job in the Bible and Melville's *Moby Dick* are highly poetical, but the familiar verse that begins: "Thirty days hath September, / April, June, and November . . . " is not. The difference between poetry and other literature is one only of degree. Poetry is the most condensed and concentrated form of literature. It is language whose individual lines, either because of their own brilliance or because they focus so powerfully what has gone before, have a higher voltage than most language. It is language that grows frequently incandescent, giving off both light and heat.

Ultimately, therefore, poetry can be recognized only by the response made to it by a good reader, someone who has acquired some sensitivity to poetry. But there is a catch here. We are not all good readers. To a poor reader, poetry will often seem dull and boring, a fancy way of writing something that could be said more simply. So might a color-blind man deny that there is such a thing as color.

The act of communication involved in reading poetry is like the act of communication involved in receiving a message by radio. Two devices are required: a transmitting station and a receiving set. The completeness of the communication depends on both the power and clarity of the transmitter and the sensitivity and tuning of the receiver. When a person reads a poem and no experience is received, either the poem is not a good poem or the reader is a poor reader or not properly tuned. With new poetry, we cannot always be sure which is at fault. With older poetry, if it has acquired critical acceptance—has been enjoyed by generations of good readers—we may assume that the receiving set is at fault. Fortunately, the fault is not irremediable. Though we cannot all become expert readers, we can become good enough to find both pleasure and value in much good poetry, or we can increase the amount of pleasure we already find in poetry and the number of kinds of poetry in which we find it. The purpose of this book is to help you increase your sensitivity and range as a receiving set.

Poetry, finally, is a kind of multidimensional language. Ordinary language—the kind that we use to communicate information—is one-dimensional. It is directed at only part of the listener, the understanding. Its one dimension is intellectual. Poetry, which is language used to communicate experience, has at least four dimensions. If it is to communicate experience, it must be directed at the *whole* person, not just at your understanding. It must involve not only your intelligence but also your senses, emotions, and imagination. To the intellectual dimension, poetry adds a sensuous dimension, an emotional dimension, and an imaginative dimension.

Poetry achieves its extra dimensions—its greater pressure per word and its greater tension per poem—by drawing more fully and more consistently than does ordinary language on a number of language resources, none of which is peculiar to poetry. These various resources form the subjects of a number of the following chapters. Among them are connotation, imagery, metaphor, symbol, paradox, irony, allusion, sound repetition, rhythm, and pattern. Using these resources and the materials of life, the poet shapes and makes a poem. Successful poetry is never effusive language. If it is to come alive it must be as cunningly put together and as efficiently organized as a tree. It must be an organism whose every part serves a useful purpose and cooperates with every other part to preserve and express the life that is within it.

* * *

4. Spring

When daisies pied and violets blue,
   And lady-smocks all silver-white,
And cuckoo-buds of yellow hue
   Do paint the meadows with delight,
The cuckoo then, on every tree,
Mocks married men; for thus sings he,
                "Cuckoo!
Cuckoo, cuckoo!" O word of fear,
Unpleasing to a married ear!

When shepherds pipe on oaten straws,
   And merry larks are plowmen's clocks,
When turtles tread, and rooks, and daws,
   And maidens bleach their summer smocks,
The cuckoo then, on every tree,
Mocks married men; for thus sings he,
                "Cuckoo!
Cuckoo, cuckoo!" O word of fear,
Unpleasing to a married ear!

William Shakespeare (1564–1616)

QUESTIONS

1. Vocabulary: *pied* (1), *lady-smocks* (2), *oaten straws* (10), *turtles* (12), *tread* (12), *rooks* (12), *daws* (12).
2. This song is a companion piece to "Winter." In what respects are the two poems similar? How do they contrast? What details show that this poem, like "Winter," was written by a realist, not simply by a man carried away with the beauty of spring?
3. The word "cuckoo" is "unpleasing to a married ear" because it sounds like *cuckold*. Cuckolds were a frequent butt of humor in earlier English literature. If you do not know the meaning of the word, look it up. How does this information help to shape the tone of the poem? Is it solemn? Light and semihumorous?

5. The Whipping

The old woman across the way
is whipping the boy again
and shouting to the neighborhood
her goodness and his wrongs.

Wildly he crashes through elephant-ears,
pleads in dusty zinnias,
while she in spite of crippling fat
pursues and corners him.

She strikes and strikes the shrilly circling
boy till the stick breaks
in her hand. His tears are rainy weather
to woundlike memories:

My head gripped in bony vise
of knees, the writhing struggle
to wrench free, the blows, the fear
worse than blows that hateful

Words could bring, the face that I
no longer knew or loved . . .
Well, it is over now, it is over,
and the boy sobs in his room,

And the woman leans muttering against
a tree, exhausted, purged—
avenged in part for lifelong hidings
she has had to bear.

Robert Hayden (1913–1980)

QUESTIONS

1. What similarities connect the old woman, the boy, and the speaker? Can you say that one of them is the main subject of the poem?
2. Does this poem express any beauty? What human truth does it embody? Could you argue against the claim that "it is over now, it is over" (19)?

6. The Computation

For the first twenty years since yesterday
  I scarce believed thou couldst be gone away;
For forty more I fed on favors past,
  And forty on hopes that thou wouldst they might last.
Tears drowned one hundred, and sighs blew out two;
  A thousand, I did neither think nor do,
Or not divide, all being one thought of you.
  Or, in a thousand more, forgot that too.
Yet call not this long life; but think that I
  Am, by being dead, immortal. Can ghosts die?

John Donne (1572–1631)

QUESTIONS

1. Who is the "I" of the poem? Who is the "thou" or "you"? How long have they been separated—literally? Figuratively?
2. Are the numbers in this "mathematical" poem used vaguely or precisely? What reasons can you find for their choice and arrangement?
3. Explain how, in the last two lines, the speaker undermines the series of overstatements just completed with another equally hyperbolic claim. Is he really dead? Of what did he "die"?

7. The Two Ravens

As I was walking all alone
I heard two ravens making a moan;
The one unto the other did say,
"Where shall we go and dine today?"

"In behind yon old turf dike
I know there lies a new-slain knight;
And nobody knows that he lies there
But his hawk, his hound, and his lady fair.

"His hound is to the hunting gone,
His hawk to fetch the wild-fowl home,
His lady's taken another mate,
So we may make our dinner sweet.

"You'll sit on his white neck-bone,
And I'll pick out his bonny blue eyes;
With one lock of his golden hair
We'll thatch our nest when it grows bare.

"Many a one for him makes moan,
But none shall know where he is gone;
O'er his white bones, when they are bare,
The wind shall blow forevermore."

Anonymous (c. 15th century)

QUESTIONS

1. This is a modernized version of a **folk ballad**, a narrative poem composed before Gutenberg's invention of movable type (c. 1436). Such ballads were meant to be recited or sung, and they were composed in simple stanzaic form (usually in quatrains riming *abcb* or in couplets riming *aa bb cc* and so forth) to make them easier to remember. They often concerned events of the day and served therefore as primitive newspapers. They usually contained a good deal of dialogue and frequently had refrains that listeners could sing in unison.
   This poem tells an implied story of false love, murder, and disloyalty. What purpose does the ballad serve by having the story told from the point of view of the two scavenging birds? How do they emphasize the atmosphere of the poem?
2. The poem presents few details about the knight, his lady, or his followers. Is there enough information for the reader (or listener) to form a plausible theory about what has happened? How does the lady know that the knight lies dead behind the dike? What is implied by the facts that "Many a one for him makes moan" but no one knows what has become of him except his hawk, his hound, and his lady? That he is "new-slain" but his lady has already "taken another mate"? Does the poem lose or gain in effect by not being entirely clear?
3. Below is the traditional version of the poem. The language of old English and Scottish folk ballads may present a considerable initial obstacle, but if you accept it, you may find that it contributes a unique flavor. A British critic, T. R. Henn, writing of this poem in his book *The Apple and the Spectroscope* (London: Methuen, 1951, 11) said, "Modernize the spelling [of the last stanza], and you have destroyed . . . the key of the poem: the thin high music of the lament, the endlessly subtle variations on the *a* sound, the strange feeling that all things have been unified with the shrillness of the wind through the heather." Does this seem to you a valid comment?

The Twa Corbies

As I was walking all alane,
I heard twa corbies making a mane;
The tane unto the t'other say,
"Where sall we gang and dine to-day?"

"In behint yon auld fail dike,
I wot there lies a new slain knight;
And naebody kens that he lies there,
But his hawk, his hound, and lady fair.

"His hound is to the hunting gane,
His hawk to fetch the wild-fowl hame,
His lady's ta'en another mate,
So we may mak our dinner sweet.

"Ye'll sit on his white hause-bane,
And I'll pike out his bonny blue een;
Wi' ae lock o' his gowden hair
We'll theek our nest when it grows bare.

"Many a one for him makes mane,
But nane sall ken where he is gane;
O'er his white banes, when they are bare,
The wind sall blaw for evermair."

8. Ballad of Birmingham

(On the bombing of a church in Birmingham, Alabama, 1963)

"Mother dear, may I go downtown
Instead of out to play,
And march the streets of Birmingham
In a Freedom March today?"

"No, baby, no, you may not go,
For the dogs are fierce and wild,
And clubs and hoses, guns and jails
Aren't good for a little child."

"But, mother, I won't be alone.
Other children will go with me,
And march the streets of Birmingham
To make our country free."

"No, baby, no, you may not go,
For I fear those guns will fire.

But you may go to church instead
And sing in the children's choir."

She has combed and brushed her night-dark hair,
And bathed rose petal sweet,
And drawn white gloves on her small brown hands,
And white shoes on her feet.

The mother smiled to know her child
Was in the sacred place,
But that smile was the last smile
To come upon her face.

For when she heard the explosion,
Her eyes grew wet and wild.
She raced through the streets of Birmingham
Calling for her child.

She clawed through bits of glass and brick,
Then lifted out a shoe.
"O, here's the shoe my baby wore,
But, baby, where are you?"

Dudley Randall (b. 1914)

QUESTIONS

1. This poem is based on a historical incident. Throughout 1963, Birmingham, Alabama, was the site of demonstrations and marches protesting the racial segregation of schools and other public facilities. Although they were intended as peaceful protests, these demonstrations often erupted in violence as police attempted to disperse them with fire hoses and police dogs. On the morning of September 15, 1963, a bomb exploded during Sunday School at the 16th Street Baptist Church. Four children were killed and 14 were injured. How does the poem differ from what you would expect to find in a newspaper account of such an incident? In an encyclopedia entry? In a speech calling for the elimination of racial injustice?
2. What do the details in the fifth stanza (17–20) contribute to the effect of the poem? Is "she" (17) the mother or the child?
3. What characteristics does this poem share with "The Two Ravens" (No. 7) and "Edward" (No. 182), which are traditional folk ballads? Why do you think this twentieth-century poet chose to write in a form that alludes to that tradition?
4. What purpose does the poem have beyond simply telling a story? How does the irony help achieve that purpose?

9. The Red Wheelbarrow

so much depends
upon

a red wheel
barrow

glazed with rain
water

beside the white
chickens.

William Carlos Williams (1883–1963)

QUESTIONS

1. The speaker asserts that "so much depends upon" the objects he refers to, leading the reader to ask *how much* and *why*. This glimpse of a farm scene implies one kind of answer. What is the importance of wheelbarrow, rain, and chicken to a farmer? To all of us?
2. What further importance can you infer from the references to color, shape, texture, and the juxtaposition of objects? Does the poem itself have a shape? What two ways of observing and valuing the world does the poem imply?

10. Terence, this is stupid stuff*

"Terence, this is stupid stuff:
You eat your victuals fast enough;
There can't be much amiss, 'tis clear,
To see the rate you drink your beer.
But oh, good Lord, the verse you make,
It gives a chap the belly-ache.
The cow, the old cow, she is dead;
It sleeps well the horned head:
We poor lads, 'tis our turn now
To hear such tunes as killed the cow.
Pretty friendship 'tis to rhyme
Your friends to death before their time
Moping melancholy mad:
Come, pipe a tune to dance to, lad."

Why, if 'tis dancing you would be,
There's brisker pipes than poetry.
Say, for what were hop-yards meant,

*Whenever a heading duplicates the first line of the poem or a substantial portion thereof, with only the first word capitalized, it is probable that the poet left the poem untitled and that the anthologist has substituted the first line or part of it as an editorial convenience. Such a heading is not referred to as the title of the poem.

Or why was Burton built on Trent?
Oh many a peer of England brews
Livelier liquor than the Muse,
And malt does more than Milton can
To justify God's ways to man.
Ale, man, ale's the stuff to drink
For fellows whom it hurts to think:
Look into the pewter pot
To see the world as the world's not.
And faith, 'tis pleasant till 'tis past:
The mischief is that 'twill not last.
Oh I have been to Ludlow fair
And left my necktie God knows where,
And carried half-way home, or near,
Pints and quarts of Ludlow beer:
Then the world seemed none so bad,
And I myself a sterling lad;
And down in lovely muck I've lain,
Happy till I woke again.
Then I saw the morning sky:
Heigho, the tale was all a lie;
The world, it was the old world yet,
I was I, my things were wet,
And nothing now remained to do
But begin the game anew.

Therefore, since the world has still
Much good, but much less good than ill,
And while the sun and moon endure
Luck's a chance, but trouble's sure,
I'd face it as a wise man would,
And train for ill and not for good.
'Tis true, the stuff I bring for sale
Is not so brisk a brew as ale:
Out of a stem that scored the hand
I wrung it in a weary land.
But take it: if the smack is sour,
The better for the embittered hour;
It should do good to heart and head
When your soul is in my soul's stead;
And I will friend you, if I may,
In the dark and cloudy day.

There was a king reigned in the East:
There, when kings will sit to feast,
They get their fill before they think

With poisoned meat and poisoned drink.
He gathered all that springs to birth
From the many-venomed earth;
First a little, thence to more,
He sampled all her killing store;
And easy, smiling, seasoned sound,
Sate the king when healths went round.
They put arsenic in his meat
And stared aghast to watch him eat;
They poured strychnine in his cup
And shook to see him drink it up:
They shook, they stared as white's their shirt:
Them it was their poison hurt.
—I tell the tale that I heard told.
Mithridates, he died old.

A. E. Housman (1859–1936)

QUESTIONS

1. The poem has two speakers. Who are they? Where are they? Of what does the first speaker complain? What request does he make of the second speaker?
2. Hops (17) and "malt" (21) are principal ingredients of beer and ale. Burton-upon-Trent (18) is an English city famous for its breweries. Milton (21), in the invocation of his epic poem *Paradise Lost*, declares that his purpose is to "justify the ways of God to men." What, in Terence's eyes, is the efficacy of liquor in helping one live a difficult life? What is the "stuff" *he* brings "for sale" (49)?
3. Essentially, Terence assesses the value of three possible aids for worthwhile living. What are they? Which does Terence consider the best? What six lines of the poem best sum up his philosophy?
4. This poem is the second last in Housman's book *A Shropshire Lad*. The last poem also concerns poetry and its place in the world. May we consider Terence in this poem a surrogate for Housman?
5. Most people like reading material that is cheerful and optimistic; they argue that "there's enough suffering and unhappiness in the world already." What, for Housman, is the value of pessimistic and tragic literature?
6. "Mithridates" (76) was a king of Pontus and a contemporary of Julius Caesar; his "tale" is told in Pliny's *Natural History*. The poem is structured by its line spacing into four verse paragraphs. What is the connection of this last verse paragraph with the rest of the poem? What is the function of each of the other three?

11. Ars Poetica

A poem should be palpable and mute
As a globed fruit,

Dumb
As old medallions to the thumb,

Silent as the sleeve-worn stone
Of casement ledges where the moss has grown—

A poem should be wordless
As the flight of birds.

*

A poem should be motionless in time
As the moon climbs,

Leaving, as the moon releases
Twig by twig the night-entangled trees,

Leaving, as the moon behind the winter leaves,
Memory by memory the mind—

A poem should be motionless in time
As the moon climbs.

*

A poem should be equal to:
Not true.

For all the history of grief
An empty doorway and a maple leaf.

For love
The leaning grasses and two lights above the sea—

A poem should not mean
But be.

Archibald MacLeish (1892–1982)

QUESTIONS

1. How can a poem be "wordless" (7)? How can it be "motionless in time" (15)?
2. The Latin title, literally translatable as "The Art of Poetry," is a traditional title for works on the philosophy of poetry. What is *this* poet's philosophy of poetry? What does he mean by saying that a poem should not "mean" and should not be "true"?

CHAPTER TWO

Reading the Poem

The primary purpose of this book is to develop your ability to understand and appreciate poetry. Here are some preliminary suggestions:

1. Read a poem more than once. A good poem will no more yield its full meaning on a single reading than will a Beethoven symphony on a single hearing. Two readings may be necessary simply to let you get your bearings. And if the poem is a work of art, it will repay repeated and prolonged examination. One does not listen to a good piece of music once and forget it; one does not look at a good painting once and throw it away. A poem is not like a newspaper, to be hastily read and cast into the wastebasket. It is to be hung on the wall of one's mind.

2. Keep a dictionary by you and use it. It is futile to try to understand poetry without troubling to learn the meanings of the words of which it is composed. You might as well attempt to play tennis without a ball. One of your primary purposes while in college should be to build a good vocabulary, and the study of poetry gives you an excellent opportunity. A few other reference books also will be invaluable. Particularly desirable are a good book on mythology (your instructor can recommend one) and a Bible.

3. Read so as to hear the sounds of the words in your mind. Poetry is written to be heard: its meanings are conveyed through sound as well as through print. Every word is therefore important. The best way to read a poem is just the opposite of the best way to read a newspaper. One reads a newspaper as rapidly as possible; one should read a poem as slowly as possible. When you cannot read a poem aloud, lip-read it: form the words with your tongue and mouth even though you do not utter them. With ordinary reading material, lip-reading is a bad habit; with poetry, it is a good habit.

4. Always pay careful attention to what the poem is saying. Though you should be conscious of the sounds of the poem, you should never be so exclusively conscious of them that you pay no attention to what the

poem means. For some readers, reading a poem is like getting on board a rhythmical roller coaster. The car starts, and off they go, up and down, paying no attention to the landscape flashing past them, arriving at the end of the poem breathless, with no idea of what it has been about.* This is the wrong way to read a poem. One should make the utmost effort to follow the thought continuously and to grasp the full implications and suggestions. Because a poem says so much, several readings may be necessary, but on the very first reading you should determine the subjects of the verbs and the antecedents of the pronouns.

5. Practice reading poems aloud. When you find one you especially like, make friends listen to it. Try to read it to them in such a way that they will like it too. (a) Read it affectionately, but not affectedly. The two extremes oral readers often fall into are equally deadly. One is to read as if one were reading a tax report or a railroad timetable, unexpressively, in a monotone. The other is to elocute, with artificial flourishes and vocal histrionics. It is not necessary to put emotion into reading a poem. The emotion is already there. It only wants a fair chance to get out. It will express *itself* if the poem is read naturally and sensitively. (b) Of the two extremes, reading too fast offers greater danger than reading too slow. Read slowly enough that each word is clear and distinct and that the meaning has time to sink in. Remember that your friends do not have the advantage, as you do, of having the text before them. Your ordinary rate of reading will probably be too fast. (c) Read the poem so that the rhythmical pattern is felt but not exaggerated. Remember that poetry, with few exceptions, is written in sentences, just as prose is, and that punctuation is a signal as to how it should be read. Give all grammatical pauses their full due. Do not distort the natural pronunciation of words or a normal accentuation of the sentence to fit into what you have decided is its metrical pattern. One of the worst ways to read a poem is to read it ta-*dum* ta-*dum* ta-*dum* with an exaggerated emphasis on every other syllable. On the other hand, it should not be read as if it were prose. An important test of your reading will be how you handle the end of a line that lacks line-ending punctuation. A frequent mistake of the beginning reader is to treat each line as if it were a complete thought, whether grammatically complete or not, and to drop the voice at the end of it. A frequent mistake of the sophisticated reader is to take a running start upon approaching the end of a line and fly over it as if it were not there.

*Some poems encourage this type of reading. When this is so, usually the poet has not made the best use of rhythm to support sense.

The line is a rhythmical unit, and its end should be observed whether there is punctuation or not. If there is no punctuation, you ordinarily should observe the end of the line by the slightest of pauses or by holding on to the last word in the line just a little longer than usual, without dropping your voice. In line 12 of the following poem, you should hold on to the word "although" longer than if it occurred elsewhere in the line. But do not lower your voice on it: it is part of the clause that follows in the next stanza.

12. The Man He Killed

Had he and I but met
By some old ancient inn,
We should have sat us down to wet
Right many a nipperkin!° half-pint cup

But ranged as infantry,
And staring face to face,
I shot at him as he at me,
And killed him in his place.

I shot him dead because—
Because he was my foe,
Just so: my foe of course he was;
That's clear enough; although

He thought he'd 'list, perhaps,
Off-hand-like—just as I—
Was out of work—had sold his traps—° belongings
No other reason why.

Yes; quaint and curious war is!
You shoot a fellow down
You'd treat, if met where any bar is,
Or help to half-a-crown.

Thomas Hardy (1840–1928)

QUESTIONS

1. In informational prose the repetition of a word like "because" (9–10) would be an error. What purpose does the repetition serve here? Why does the speaker repeat to himself his "clear" reason for killing a man (10–11)? The word "although" (12) gets more emphasis than it ordinarily would because it comes not only at the end of a line but at the end of a stanza. What purpose does this emphasis serve? Can the redundancy of "old ancient" (2) be poetically justified?

2. Someone has defined poetry as "the expression of elevated thought in elevated language." Comment on the adequacy of this definition in the light of Hardy's poem.

One starting point for understanding a poem at the simplest level, and for clearing up misunderstanding, is to paraphrase its content or part of its content. To **paraphrase** a poem means to restate it in different language, so as to make its prose sense as plain as possible. The paraphrase may be longer or shorter than the poem, but it should contain all the ideas in the poem in such a way as to make them clear to a puzzled reader, and to make the central idea, or **theme**, of the poem more accessible.

13. A Study of Reading Habits

When getting my nose in a book
Cured most things short of school,
It was worth ruining my eyes
To know I could still keep cool,
And deal out the old right hook
To dirty dogs twice my size.

Later, with inch-thick specs,
Evil was just my lark:
Me and my cloak and fangs
Had ripping times in the dark.
The women I clubbed with sex!
I broke them up like meringues.

Don't read much now: the dude
Who lets the girl down before
The hero arrives, the chap
Who's yellow and keeps the store,
Seem far too familiar. Get stewed:
Books are a load of crap.

Philip Larkin (1922–1985)

QUESTIONS

1. The three stanzas delineate three stages in the speaker's life. Describe each.
2. What kind of person is the speaker? What kind of books does he read? May we identify him with the poet?
3. Contrast the speaker's advice in stanza 3 with Terence's counsel in "Terence, this is stupid stuff" (No. 10). Are A. E. Housman and Philip Larkin at odds in their attitudes toward drinking and reading? Discuss.

Larkin's poem may be paraphrased as follows:

> There was a time when reading was one way I could avoid almost all my troubles — except for school. It seemed worth the danger of ruining my eyes to read stories in which I could imagine myself maintaining my poise in the face of threats and having the boxing skill and experience needed to defeat bullies who were twice as big as I.
>
> Later, already having to wear thick glasses because my eyesight had become so poor, I found my delight in stories of sex and evil: imagining myself with Dracula cloak and fangs, I relished vicious nocturnal adventures. I fancied myself a rapist who beat and tortured his delectable, vulnerable victims, leaving them broken and destroyed!
>
> I don't read much any more, because now I can identify myself only with the flawed secondary characters, such as the flashy dresser who wins the heroine's confidence and then betrays her in a moment of crisis before the cowboy hero comes to her rescue, or the cowardly storekeeper who cringes behind the counter at the first sign of danger. Getting drunk is better than reading — books are just full of useless lies.

Notice that in a paraphrase, figurative language gives way to literal language; similes replace metaphors and normal word order supplants inverted syntax. But a paraphrase retains the speaker's use of first, second, and third person, and the tenses of verbs. Though it is neither necessary nor possible to avoid using some of the words found in the original, a paraphrase should strive for plain, direct diction. And since a paraphrase is prose, it does not maintain the length and position of poetic lines.

A paraphrase is useful only if you understand that it is the barest, most inadequate approximation of what the poem really "says" and is no more equivalent to the poem than a corpse is to a person. After you have paraphrased a poem, you should endeavor to see how far short of the poem it falls, and why. In what respects does Larkin's poem say more, and say it more memorably, than the paraphrase? Does the phrase "full of useless lies" capture the impact of "a load of crap"? Furthermore, a paraphrase may fall far short of revealing the theme of a poem. "A Study of Reading Habits" represents a man summing up his reading experience and evaluating it — but in turn the poem itself evaluates *him* and his defects. A statement of the theme of the poem might be this: A person who turns to books as a source of self-gratifying fantasies may, in the course of time, discover that escapist reading no longer protects him from his awareness of his own reality, and he may out of habit have to find other, more potent, and perhaps more self-destructive means of escaping.

To aid us in the understanding of a poem, we may ask ourselves a number of questions about it. Two of the most important are *Who is the speaker?* and *What is the occasion?* A cardinal error of some readers is to assume that a speaker who uses the first person pronouns (*I, my, mine, me*) is always the poet. A less risky course would be to assume always that the speaker is someone other than the poet. Poems, like short stories, novels, and plays, belong to the world of fiction, an imaginatively conceived world that at its best is "truer" than the factually "real" world that it reflects. When poets put themselves or their thoughts into a poem, they present a *version* of themselves; that is, they present a person who in many ways is *like* themselves but who, consciously or unconsciously, is shaped to fit the needs of the poem. We must be very careful, therefore, about identifying anything in a poem with the biography of the poet.

However, caution is not prohibition. Sometimes events or ideas in a poem will help us to understand some episodes in the poet's life. More importantly for us, knowledge of the poet's life may help us understand a poem. There can be little doubt, when all the evidence is in, that "Terence, this is stupid stuff" (No. 10) is Housman's defense of the kind of poetry he writes, and that the six lines in which Terence sums up his beliefs about life and the function of poetry are Housman's own beliefs. On the other hand, it would be folly to suppose that Housman ever got drunk at Ludlow fair and once lay down in "lovely muck" and slept all night in a roadside ditch.

We may well think of every poem, therefore, as being to some degree *dramatic*—that is, the utterance of a fictional character rather than of the person who wrote the poem. Many poems are expressly dramatic. The fact that Philip Larkin was a poet and novelist, and for many years the chief administrator of a university library, underscores the wide gap between the author and speaker of "A Study of Reading Habits."

In "The Man He Killed" the speaker is a soldier; the occasion is his having been in battle and killed a man—obviously for the first time in his life. We can tell a good deal about him. He is not a career soldier: he enlisted only because he was out of work. He is a workingman: he speaks a simple and colloquial language ("nipperkin," "'list," "off-hand-like," "traps"). He is a friendly, kindly sort who enjoys a neighborly drink of ale in a bar and will gladly lend a friend a half crown when he has it. He has known what it is to be poor. In any other circumstances he would have been horrified at taking a human life. It gives him pause even now.

He is trying to figure it out. But he is not a deep thinker and thinks he has supplied a reason when he only has supplied a name: "I killed the man . . . because he was my foe." The critical question, of course, is *why* was the man his "foe." Even the speaker is left unsatisfied by his answer, though he is not analytical enough to know what is wrong with it. Obviously this poem is expressly dramatic. We need know nothing about Thomas Hardy's life (he was never a soldier and never killed a man) to realize that the poem is dramatic. The internal evidence of the poem tells us so.

A third important question that we should ask ourselves upon reading any poem is *What is the central purpose of the poem?** The purpose may be to tell a story, to reveal human character, to impart a vivid impression of a scene, to express a mood or an emotion, or to convey vividly some idea or attitude. Whatever the purpose is, we must determine it for ourselves and define it mentally as precisely as possible. Only by relating the various details in the poem to the central purpose or theme can we fully understand their function and meaning. Only then can we begin to assess the value of the poem and determine whether it is a good one or a poor one. In "The Man He Killed" the central purpose is quite clear: it is to make us realize more keenly the irrationality of war. The puzzlement of the speaker may be our puzzlement. But even if we are able to give a more sophisticated answer than his as to why men kill each other, we ought still to have a greater awareness, after reading the poem, of the fundamental irrationality in war that makes men kill who have no grudge against each other and who might under different circumstances show each other considerable kindness.

14. Is my team plowing

"Is my team plowing,
  That I was used to drive
And hear the harness jingle
  When I was man alive?"

*Our only reliable evidence of the poem's purpose, of course, is the poem itself. External evidence, when it exists, though often helpful, also may be misleading. Some critics have objected to the use of such terms as "purpose" and "intention" altogether; we cannot know, they maintain, what was *attempted* in the poem; we can know only what was *done*. We are concerned, however, not with the *poet's* purpose, but with the *poem's* purpose; that is, with the theme (if it has one), and this is determinable from the poem itself.

Aye, the horses trample,
  The harness jingles now;
No change though you lie under
  The land you used to plow.

"Is football playing
  Along the river shore,
With lads to chase the leather,
  Now I stand up no more?"

Aye, the ball is flying,
  The lads play heart and soul;
The goal stands up, the keeper
  Stands up to keep the goal.

"Is my girl happy,
  That I thought hard to leave,
And has she tired of weeping
  As she lies down at eve?"

Aye, she lies down lightly,
  She lies not down to weep:
Your girl is well contented.
  Be still, my lad, and sleep.

"Is my friend hearty,
  Now I am thin and pine;
And has he found to sleep in
  A better bed than mine?"

Yes, lad, I lie easy,
  I lie as lads would choose;
I cheer a dead man's sweetheart,
  Never ask me whose.

A. E. Housman (1859–1936)

QUESTIONS

1. What is meant by "whose" in line 32?
2. Is Housman cynical in his observation of human nature and human life?
3. The word "sleep" in the concluding stanzas suggests three different meanings. What are they? How many meanings are suggested by the word "bed"?

Once we have answered the question *What is the central purpose of the poem?* we can consider another question, equally important to full understanding: *By what means is that purpose achieved?* It is important to distinguish means from ends. A student on an examination once used the poem "Is my team plowing" as evidence that A. E. Housman believed in immortality, because in it a man speaks from the grave. This is as much a misconstruction as to say that Thomas Hardy in "The Man He Killed" joined the army because he was out of work. The purpose of Housman's poem is to communicate poignantly a certain truth about human life: life goes on after our deaths pretty much as it did before—our dying does not disturb the universe. The poem achieves this purpose by means of a fanciful dramatic framework in which a dead man converses with his still-living friend. The framework tells us nothing about whether Housman believed in immortality (as a matter of fact, he did not). It is simply an effective means by which we *can* learn how Housman felt a man's death affected the life he left behind. The question *By what means is the purpose of the poem achieved?* is partially answered by describing the poem's dramatic framework, if it has any. The complete answer requires an accounting of various resources of communication that we will discuss in the rest of this book.

The most important preliminary advice we can give for reading poetry is to maintain always, while reading it, the utmost mental alertness. The most harmful idea one can get about poetry is that its purpose is to soothe and relax and that the best place to read it is lying in a hammock with a cool drink while low music plays in the background. You *can* read poetry lying in a hammock, but only if you refuse to put your mind in the same attitude as your body. Its purpose is not to soothe and relax but to arouse and awake, to shock us into life, to make us more alive. Poetry is not a substitute for a sedative.

An analogy can be drawn between reading poetry and playing tennis. Both offer great enjoyment if the game is played hard. Good tennis players must be constantly on the tips of their toes, concentrating on their opponent's every move. They must be ready for a drive to the right or left, a lob overhead, or a drop shot barely over the net. They must be ready for topspin or underspin, a ball that bounces crazily to the left or right. They must jump for the high ones and run for the far ones. And they will enjoy the game almost exactly in proportion to the effort they put into it. The same is true of reading poetry. Great enjoyment is there, but this enjoyment demands a mental effort equivalent to the physical effort one puts into tennis.

The reader of poetry has one advantage over the tennis player. Poets are not trying to win matches. They may expect the reader to stretch for their shots, but they *want* the reader to return them.

GENERAL QUESTIONS FOR ANALYSIS AND EVALUATION

Most of the poems in this book are accompanied by study questions that are by no means exhaustive. The following is a list of questions that you may apply to any poem. You may be unable to answer many of them until you have read further into the book.

1. Who is the speaker? What kind of person is the speaker?
2. Is there an identifiable audience for the speaker? What can we know about it (her, him, or them)?
3. What is the occasion?
4. What is the setting in time (hour, season, century, and so on)?
5. What is the setting in place (indoors or out, city or country, land or sea, region, nation, hemisphere)?
6. What is the central purpose of the poem?
7. State the central idea or theme of the poem in a sentence.
8. What is the tone of the poem? How is it achieved?
9. a. Outline the poem so as to show its structure and development, or
   b. Summarize the events of the poem.
10. Paraphrase the poem.
11. Discuss the diction of the poem. Point out words that are particularly well chosen and explain why.
12. Discuss the imagery of the poem. What kinds of imagery are used? Is there a structure of imagery?
13. Point out examples of metaphor, simile, personification, and metonymy, and explain their appropriateness.
14. Point out and explain any symbols. If the poem is allegorical, explain the allegory.
15. Point out and explain examples of paradox, overstatement, understatement, and irony. What is their function?
16. Point out and explain any allusions. What is their function?
17. Point out significant examples of sound repetition and explain their function.
18. a. What is the meter of the poem?
    b. Copy the poem and mark its scansion.
19. Discuss the adaptation of sound to sense.
20. Describe the form or pattern of the poem.
21. Criticize and evaluate the poem.

* * *

15. Break of Day

'Tis true, 'tis day; what though it be?
Oh, wilt thou therefore rise from me?
Why should we rise because 'tis light?
Did we lie down because 'twas night?
Love which in spite of darkness brought us hither
Should, in despite of light, keep us together.

Light hath no tongue, but is all eye;
If it could speak as well as spy,
This were the worst that it could say:
That, being well, I fain would stay,
And that I loved my heart and honor so,
That I would not from him that had them go.

Must business thee from hence remove?
Oh, that's the worst disease of love;
The poor, the foul, the false, love can
Admit, but not the busied man.
He which hath business and makes love, doth do
Such wrong as when a married man doth woo.

John Donne (1572–1631)

QUESTIONS

1. Who is the speaker? Who is addressed? What is the situation? Can the speaker be identified with the poet?
2. Explain the comparison in line 7. To whom does "I" (10–12) refer? Is "love" (15) the subject or object of "can admit"?
3. Summarize the arguments used by the speaker to keep the person addressed from leaving. What is the speaker's scale of value?
4. Are the two persons married or unmarried? Justify your answer.

16. There's been a death in the opposite house

There's been a death in the opposite house
As lately as today.
I know it by the numb look
Such houses have alway.

The neighbors rustle in and out,
The doctor drives away.
A window opens like a pod,
Abrupt, mechanically;

Somebody flings a mattress out—
The children hurry by;
They wonder if it died on that—
I used to when a boy.

The minister goes stiffly in
As if the house were his,
And he owned all the mourners now,
And little boys besides;

And then the milliner, and the man
Of the appalling trade,
To take the measure of the house.
There'll be that dark parade

Of tassels and of coaches soon;
It's easy as a sign—
The intuition of the news
In just a country town.

Emily Dickinson (1830–1886)

QUESTIONS

1. What can we know about the speaker in the poem?
2. By what signs does the speaker recognize that a death has occurred? Explain them stanza by stanza.
3. Comment on the words "appalling" (18) and "dark" (20).
4. What is the speaker's attitude toward death?

17. When in Rome

Mattie dear
the box is full
take
whatever you like
to eat
(an egg
or soup
. . . there ain't no meat.)
there's endive there
and
cottage cheese
(whew! if I had some
black-eyed peas . . .)
there's sardines
on the shelves
and such
but
don't
get my anchovies
they cost
too much!
(me get the
anchovies indeed!
what she think, she got—
a bird to feed?)

there's plenty in there
to fill you up.
(yes'm. just the
sight's
enough!

Hope I lives till I get
home
I'm tired of eatin'
what they eats in Rome . . .)

Mari Evans

QUESTIONS

1. Who are the two speakers? What is the situation? Why are the second speaker's words enclosed in parentheses?
2. What are the attitudes of the two speakers toward one another?
3. What implications have the title and the last two lines?

18. The Mill

The miller's wife had waited long,
The tea was cold, the fire was dead;
And there might yet be nothing wrong
In how he went and what he said:
"There are no millers any more,"
Was all that she had heard him say;
And he had lingered at the door
So long that it seemed yesterday.

Sick with a fear that had no form
She knew that she was there at last;
And in the mill there was a warm
And mealy fragrance of the past.
What else there was would only seem
To say again what he had meant;
And what was hanging from a beam
Would not have heeded where she went.

And if she thought it followed her,
She may have reasoned in the dark
That one way of the few there were
Would hide her and would leave no mark:

Black water, smooth above the weir
  Like starry velvet in the night,
Though ruffled once, would soon appear
  The same as ever to the sight.

Edwin Arlington Robinson (1869–1935)

QUESTIONS

1. What is the meaning of the husband's remark in line 5? What has the husband's occupation been, and what historical developments would lead him to make that remark?
2. What does the miller's wife find in the mill in stanza 2? What does she do in stanza 3? Why?
3. Poets, especially modern poets, are often accused of being perversely obscure. Certainly this poem tells its story in a roundabout way—by hints and implications rather than by direct statements. Is there any justification for this "obscurity" or has the poet indeed been needlessly unclear?
4. What details of the poem especially bring it to life as experience?

19. Mirror

I am silver and exact. I have no preconceptions.
Whatever I see I swallow immediately
Just as it is, unmisted by love or dislike.
I am not cruel, only truthful—
The eye of a little god, four-cornered.
Most of the time I meditate on the opposite wall.
It is pink, with speckles. I have looked at it so long
I think it is a part of my heart. But it flickers.
Faces and darkness separate us over and over.

Now I am a lake. A woman bends over me,
Searching my reaches for what she really is.
Then she turns to those liars, the candles or the moon.
I see her back, and reflect it faithfully.
She rewards me with tears and an agitation of hands.
I am important to her. She comes and goes.
Each morning it is her face that replaces the darkness.
In me she has drowned a young girl, and in me an old woman
Rises toward her day after day, like a terrible fish.

Sylvia Plath (1932–1963)

QUESTIONS

1. Who is the speaker? Distinguish means from ends.
2. In what ways is the mirror like and unlike a person (stanza 1)? In what ways is it like a lake (stanza 2)?
3. What is the meaning of the last two lines?

20. I wandered lonely as a cloud

I wandered lonely as a cloud
That floats on high o'er vales and hills,
When all at once I saw a crowd,
A host, of golden daffodils;
Beside the lake, beneath the trees,
Fluttering and dancing in the breeze.

Continuous as the stars that shine
And twinkle on the milky way,
They stretched in never-ending line
Along the margin of a bay:
Ten thousand saw I at a glance,
Tossing their heads in sprightly dance.

The waves beside them danced; but they
Outdid the sparkling waves in glee;
A poet could not but be gay,
In such a jocund company;
I gazed—and gazed—but little thought
What wealth the show to me had brought:

For oft, when on my couch I lie
In vacant or in pensive mood,
They flash upon that inward eye
Which is the bliss of solitude;
And then my heart with pleasure fills,
And dances with the daffodils.

William Wordsworth (1770–1850)

QUESTIONS

1. Vocabulary: *jocund* (16), *pensive* (20). What different emotional suggestions do the following pairs of words exhibit: *lonely* (1) and *solitude* (22), *crowd* (3) and *host* (4)?
2. What is the speaker's mood in lines 1–2? Where is that mood echoed later in the poem? What was his changed mood when he saw the daffodils? Is this identical to his mood when he later remembers them?

3. What one word—though in four different grammatical forms—occurs once in each stanza of the poem? How is that word related to the words of motion or immobility that the speaker uses to describe himself in lines 1–2 and 19–20?
4. Characterize the speaker. What aspects of this poem make it seem a true, personal experience?

21. The Solitary Reaper

Behold her, single in the field,
Yon solitary Highland lass!
Reaping and singing by herself;
Stop here, or gently pass!
Alone she cuts and binds the grain,
And sings a melancholy strain;
O listen! for the vale profound
Is overflowing with the sound.

No nightingale did ever chaunt
More welcome notes to weary bands
Of travelers in some shady haunt
Among Arabian sands.
A voice so thrilling ne'er was heard
In springtime from the cuckoo-bird,
Breaking the silence of the seas
Among the farthest Hebrides.

Will no one tell me what she sings?—
Perhaps the plaintive numbers° flow — measures
For old, unhappy, far-off things,
And battles long ago.
Or is it some more humble lay,° — song
Familiar matter of today?
Some natural sorrow, loss, or pain
That has been, and may be again?

Whate'er the theme, the maiden sang
As if her song could have no ending;
I saw her singing at her work,
And o'er the sickle bending—
I listened, motionless and still;
And, as I mounted up the hill,
The music in my heart I bore
Long after it was heard no more.

William Wordsworth (1770–1850)

QUESTIONS

1. In how many ways is the girl's song like birdsong?
2. Why does the poet place the birds in stanza 2 in Arabia and the Hebrides rather than in Scotland or England?
3. In what way does the suggested range of subject matter for the reaper's song (stanza 3) parallel the geographical references in stanza 2?
4. Why does the music have such a profound effect on the speaker? Does the beauty of the song explain this effect, or are additional factors involved?
5. In the last stanza the speaker turns from present to past tense. Why?
6. Of the poems in this chapter, one ("Mirror," No. 19) has an object for its speaker. A second ("A Study of Reading Habits," No. 13) has a speaker who is demonstrably the opposite of his creator. A third ("Break of Day," No. 15), though written by a male poet, has a female speaker. A fourth ("There's been a death in the opposite house," No. 16), though written by a woman, has a male speaker. In this poem, however, there are no signs of a speaker who is different from the poet, and in the preceding poem ("I wandered lonely as a cloud," No. 20) there is a speaker who resembles in thought and feeling the speaker in this poem, and who, moreover, speaks of himself as "a poet." Is there any reason not to identify the speakers in these two poems as the poet himself?

EXERCISE

Here are three definitions of poetry, all framed by poets themselves. Which definition best fits the poems you have so far read? Discuss.

1. Poetry is Transfiguration, the transfiguration of the Actual or the Real into the Ideal, at a lofty elevation, through the medium of melodious or nobly sounding verse. *Alfred Austin*
2. The art of poetry is simply the art of electrifying language with extraordinary meaning. *Lascelles Abercrombie*
3. A poem consists of all the purest and most beautiful elements in the poet's nature, crystalized into the aptest and most exquisite language, and adorned with all the outer embellishment of musical cadence or dainty rhyme. *Grant Allen*

CHAPTER THREE

Denotation and Connotation

A primary distinction between the practical use of language and the literary use is that in literature, especially in poetry, a *fuller* use is made of individual words. To understand this, we need to examine the composition of a word.

The average word has three component parts: sound, denotation, and connotation. It begins as a combination of tones and noises, uttered by the lips, tongue, and throat, for which the written word is a notation. But it differs from a musical tone or a noise in that it has a meaning attached to it. The basic part of this meaning is its **denotation** or denotations: that is, the dictionary meaning or meanings of the word. Beyond its denotations, a word also may have connotations. The **connotations** are what it suggests beyond what it expresses: its overtones of meaning. It acquires these connotations from its past history and associations, from the way and the circumstances in which it has been used. The word *home*, for instance, by denotation means only a place where one lives, but by connotation it suggests security, love, comfort, and family. The words *childlike* and *childish* both mean "characteristic of a child," but *childlike* suggests meekness, innocence, and wide-eyed wonder, while *childish* suggests pettiness, willfulness, and temper tantrums. If we list the names of different coins—nickel, peso, lira, shilling, sen, doubloon—the word *doubloon*, to four out of five readers, immediately will suggest pirates, though a dictionary definition includes nothing about pirates. Pirates are part of its connotation.

Connotation is very important in poetry, for it is one of the means by which the poet can concentrate or enrich meaning—say more in fewer words. Consider, for instance, the following short poem:

22. There is no frigate like a book

There is no frigate like a book
To take us lands away,
Nor any coursers like a page
Of prancing poetry.
This traverse may the poorest take
Without oppress of toll.
How frugal is the chariot
That bears the human soul!

Emily Dickinson (1830–1886)

In this poem Emily Dickinson is considering the power of a book or of poetry to carry us away, to take us from our immediate surroundings into a world of the imagination. To do this she has compared literature to various means of transportation: a boat, a team of horses, a wheeled land vehicle. But she has been careful to choose kinds of transportation and names for them that have romantic connotations. "Frigate" suggests exploration and adventure; "coursers," beauty, spirit, and speed; "chariot," speed and the ability to go through the air as well as on land. (Compare "Swing Low, Sweet Chariot" and the myth of Phaëthon, who tried to drive the chariot of Apollo, and the famous painting of Aurora with her horses, once hung in almost every school.) How much of the meaning of the poem comes from this selection of vehicles and words is apparent if we try to substitute *steamship* for "frigate," *horses* for "coursers," and *streetcar* for "chariot."

QUESTIONS

1. What is lost if *miles* is substituted for "lands" (2) or *cheap* for "frugal" (7)?
2. How is "prancing" (4) peculiarly appropriate to poetry as well as to coursers? Could the poet without loss have compared a book to coursers and poetry to a frigate?
3. Is this account appropriate to all kinds of poetry or just to certain kinds? That is, was the poet thinking of poems like Wilfred Owen's "Dulce et Decorum Est" (No. 3) or of poems like Coleridge's "Kubla Khan" (No. 214) and Keats's "La Belle Dame sans Merci" (No. 242)?

Just as a word has a variety of connotations, so may it have more than one denotation. If we look up the word *spring* in the dictionary, for instance, we will find that it has between twenty-five and thirty distinguishable meanings: It may mean (1) a pounce or leap, (2) a season of the year, (3) a natural source of water, (4) a coiled elastic wire, and so forth.

This variety of denotation, complicated by additional tones of connotation, makes language confusing and difficult to use. Any person using words must be careful to define precisely by context the meaning that is desired. But the difference between the writer using language to communicate information and the poet is this: the practical writer will always attempt to confine words to one meaning at a time; the poet will often take advantage of the fact that the word has more than one meaning by using it to mean more than one thing at the same time. Thus when Edith Sitwell in one of her poems writes, "This is the time of the wild spring and the mating of the tigers,"* she uses the word *spring* to denote both a season of the year and a sudden leap (and she uses *tigers* rather than *lambs* or *birds* because it has a connotation of fierceness and wildness that the other two lack).

23. When my love swears that she is made of truth

When my love swears that she is made of truth,
I do believe her, though I know she lies,
That she might think me some untutored youth,
Unlearnèd in the world's false subtleties.
Thus vainly thinking that she thinks me young,
Although she knows my days are past the best,
Simply I credit her false-speaking tongue;
On both sides thus is simple truth suppressed.
But wherefore says she not she is unjust?° unfaithful
And wherefore say not I that I am old?
Oh, love's best habit is in seeming trust,
And age in love loves not to have years told:
Therefore I lie with her and she with me,
And in our faults by lies we flattered be.

William Shakespeare (1564–1616)

QUESTIONS

1. How old is the speaker in the poem? How old is his beloved? What is the nature of their relationship?
2. How is the contradiction in line 2 to be resolved? How is the one in lines 5–6 to be resolved? Who is lying to whom?
3. How do "simply" (7) and "simple" (8) differ in meaning? The words "vainly" (5), "habit" (11), "told" (12), and "lie" (13) all have double denotative meanings. What are they?

**Collected Poems* (New York: Vanguard, 1954) 392.

4. What is the tone of the poem—that is, the attitude of the speaker toward his situation? Should line 11 be taken as an expression of (a) wisdom, (b) conscious rationalization, or (c) self-deception? In answering these questions, consider both the situation and the connotations of all the important words beginning with "swears" (1) and ending with "flattered" (14).

A frequent misconception of poetic language is that poets seek always the most beautiful or noble-sounding words. What they really seek are the most *meaningful* words, and these vary from one context to another. Language has many levels and varieties, and poets may choose from all of them. Their words may be grandiose or humble, fanciful or matter-of-fact, romantic or realistic, archaic or modern, technical or everyday, monosyllabic or polysyllabic. Usually a poem will be pitched pretty much in one key: the words in Emily Dickinson's "There is no frigate like a book" (No. 22) and those in Thomas Hardy's "The Man He Killed" (No. 12) are chosen from quite different areas of language, but both poets have chosen the words most meaningful for their own poetic context. Sometimes a poet may import a word from one level or area of language into a poem composed mostly of words from a different level or area. If this is done clumsily, the result will be incongruous and sloppy; if it is done skillfully, the result will be a shock of surprise and an increment of meaning for the reader. In fact, the many varieties of language open to poets provide their richest resource. Their task is one of constant exploration and discovery. They search always for the secret affinities of words that allow them to be brought together with soft explosions of meaning.

24. The Naked and the Nude

For me, the naked and the nude
(By lexicographers construed
As synonyms that should express
The same deficiency of dress
Or shelter) stand as wide apart
As love from lies, or truth from art.

Lovers without reproach will gaze
On bodies naked and ablaze;
The Hippocratic eye will see
In nakedness, anatomy;
And naked shines the Goddess when
She mounts her lion among men.

The nude are bold, the nude are sly
To hold each treasonable eye.
While draping by a showman's trick
Their dishabille in rhetoric,
They grin a mock-religious grin
Of scorn at those of naked skin.

The naked, therefore, who compete
Against the nude may know defeat;
Yet when they both together tread
The briary pastures of the dead,
By Gorgons with long whips pursued,
How naked go the sometime nude!

Robert Graves (1895–1985)

QUESTIONS

1. Vocabulary: *lexicographers* (2), *construed* (2), *art* (6), *Hippocratic* (9), *dishabille* (16), *Gorgons* (23), *sometime* (24).
2. What kind of language is used in lines 2–5? Why? (For example, why is "deficiency" more appropriate than *lack*? Purely because of meter?)
3. What is meant by "rhetoric" (16)? Why is the word "dishabille" in this line preferable to some less fancy word?
4. Explain why the poet's words are better than these hypothetical substitutes: *brave* for "bold" (13), *clever* for "sly" (13), *clothing* for "draping" (15), *smile* for "grin" (17).
5. What, for the poet, is the difference in connotation between "naked" and "nude"? Try to explain reasons for the difference. If your own sense of the two words differs from that of Graves, state the difference and give reasons to support your sense of them.
6. Explain the reversal in the last line.

People using language only to convey information are usually indifferent to the sound of the words and are hampered by their connotations and multiple denotations. They would rather confine each word to a single, exact meaning. They use, one might say, a fraction of the word and throw the rest away. Poets, on the other hand, use as much of the word as possible. They are interested in connotation and use it to enrich and convey meaning. And they may rely on more than one denotation.

The purest form of practical language is scientific language. Scientists need a precise language to convey information precisely. The existence of multiple denotations and various overtones of meaning hinders them in accomplishing their purpose. Their ideal language would be a language with a one-to-one correspondence between word and meaning;

that is, every word would have one meaning only, and for every meaning there would be only one word. Since ordinary language does not fulfill these conditions, scientists have invented languages that do. A statement in one of these languages may look like this:

$$SO_2 + H_2O = H_2SO_3$$

In such a statement the symbols are entirely unambiguous; they have been stripped of all connotation and of all denotations but one. The word *sulfurous*, if it occurred in poetry, might have all kinds of connotations: fire, smoke, brimstone, hell, damnation. But H_2SO_3 means one thing and one thing only: sulfurous acid.

The ambiguity and multiplicity of meanings possessed by words are an obstacle to the scientist but a resource to the poet. Where the scientist wants singleness of meaning, the poet wants richness of meaning. Where the scientist requires and has invented a strictly one-dimensional language in which every word is confined to one denotation, the poet needs a multidimensional language and creates it partly by using a multidimensional vocabulary, in which the dimensions of connotation and sound are added to the dimension of denotation.

The poet, we may say, plays on a many-stringed instrument and sounds more than one note at a time.

The first task in reading poetry, therefore, as in reading any kind of literature, is to develop a sense of language, a feeling for words. One needs to become acquainted with their shape, their color, and their flavor. There are two ways of doing this: extensive use of the dictionary and extensive reading.

EXERCISES

1. Which word in each group has the most "romantic" connotations? (a) horse, steed, nag; (b) king, ruler, tyrant, autocrat; (c) Chicago, Pittsburgh, Samarkand, Birmingham.
2. Which word in each group is the most emotionally connotative? (a) female parent, mother, dam; (b) offspring, children, progeny; (c) brother, sibling.
3. Arrange the words in each group from most positive to most negative in connotation: (a) skinny, thin, gaunt, slender; (b) prosperous, loaded, moneyed, opulent; (c) brainy, intelligent, eggheaded, smart.
4. Which of the following should you be less offended at being accused of? (a) having acted foolishly, (b) having acted like a fool.
5. In any competent piece of writing, the possibly multiple denotations and connotations of the words used are controlled by context. The context screens out irrelevant meanings while allowing the relevant meanings to pass through. What denotation has the word *fast* in the following contexts: fast

runner, fast color, fast living, fast day? What are the varying connotations of these four denotations of *fast*?

6. In the following examples the denotation of the word *white* remains the same, but the connotations differ. Explain. (a) The young princess had blue eyes, golden hair, and a breast as white as snow. (b) Confronted with the evidence, the false princess turned as white as a sheet.

* * *

25. The Sheaves

Where long the shadows of the wind had rolled,
Green wheat was yielding to the change assigned;
And as by some vast magic undivined
The world was turning slowly into gold.
Like nothing that was ever bought or sold
It waited there, the body and the mind;
And with a mighty meaning of a kind
That tells the more the more it is not told.

So in a land where all days are not fair,
Fair days went on till on another day
A thousand golden sheaves were lying there,
Shining and still, but not for long to stay—
As if a thousand girls with golden hair
Might rise from where they slept and go away.

Edwin Arlington Robinson (1869–1935)

QUESTIONS

1. Are the words "gold" and "golden" employed primarily for their denotative or their connotative meanings? Explain.
2. Explain the multiple denotations of "tells" and "told" (8) and of "fair" and "fair" (9–10). What connotations are attached to those denotations?
3. What kind of literary experience or context is connoted by the following: "vast magic," "turning . . . into gold," "in a land," and the action described in lines 13–14?
4. Trace the contrasts between the material and nonmaterial values implied in the poem. Which set of values does the speaker prefer? How attainable is the nonmaterial value? Can you explain the regretful tone of the last two lines?
5. Why are the poet's words more effective than these possible alternatives: "green wheat" rather than *unripe grain*? "yielding to the change assigned" rather than *naturally ripening*? "undivined" rather than *unexplained*? "land" rather than *nation*? "thousand girls" rather than *countless females*? "golden hair" rather than *blonde*?

26. Naming of Parts

To-day we have naming of parts. Yesterday,
We had daily cleaning. And to-morrow morning,
We shall have what to do after firing. But to-day,
To-day we have naming of parts. Japonica
Glistens like coral in all of the neighboring gardens,
And to-day we have naming of parts.

This is the lower sling swivel. And this
Is the upper sling swivel, whose use you will see,
When you are given your slings. And this is the piling swivel,
Which in your case you have not got. The branches
Hold in the gardens their silent, eloquent gestures,
Which in our case we have not got.

This is the safety-catch, which is always released
With an easy flick of the thumb. And please do not let me
See anyone using his finger. You can do it quite easy
If you have any strength in your thumb. The blossoms
Are fragile and motionless, never letting anyone see
Any of them using their finger.

And this you can see is the bolt. The purpose of this
Is to open the breech, as you see. We can slide it
Rapidly backwards and forwards: we call this
Easing the spring. And rapidly backwards and forwards
The early bees are assaulting and fumbling the flowers:
They call it easing the Spring.

They call it easing the Spring: it is perfectly easy
If you have any strength in your thumb: like the bolt,
And the breech, and the cocking-piece, and the point of balance,
Which in our case we have not got; and the almond-blossom
Silent in all of the gardens and the bees going backwards and forwards,
For to-day we have naming of parts.

Henry Reed (1914–1986)

QUESTIONS

1. Who is the speaker (or who are the speakers) in the poem, and what is the situation?
2. What basic contrasts are represented by the trainees and by the gardens?
3. What is it that the trainees "have not got" (28)? How many meanings have the phrases "easing the Spring" (22) and "point of balance" (27)?
4. What differences in language and rhythm do you find between the lines that involve the "naming of parts" and those that describe the gardens?

5. Does the repetition of certain phrases throughout the poem have any special function or does it merely create a kind of refrain?
6. What statement does the poem make about war as it affects men and their lives?

27. Pathedy of Manners

At twenty she was brilliant and adored,
Phi Beta Kappa, sought for every dance;
Captured symbolic logic and the glance
Of men whose interest was their sole reward.

She learned the cultured jargon of those bred
To antique crystal and authentic pearls,
Scorned Wagner, praised the Degas dancing girls,
And when she might have thought, conversed instead.

She hung up her diploma, went abroad,
Saw catalogues of domes and tapestry,
Rejected an impoverished marquis,
And learned to tell real Wedgwood from a fraud.

Back home her breeding led her to espouse
A bright young man whose pearl cufflinks were real.
They had an ideal marriage, and ideal
But lonely children in an ideal house.

I saw her yesterday at forty-three,
Her children gone, her husband one year dead,
Toying with plots to kill time and re-wed
Illusions of lost opportunity.

But afraid to wonder what she might have known
With all that wealth and mind had offered her,
She shuns conviction, choosing to infer
Tenets of every mind except her own.

A hundred people call, though not one friend,
To parry a hundred doubts with nimble talk.
Her meanings lost in manners, she will walk
Alone in brilliant circles to the end.

Ellen Kay (b. 1931)

QUESTIONS

1. The title alludes to the type of drama called "comedy of manners" and coins a word combining the suffix *-edy* with the Greek root *path-* (as in *pathetic, sympathy, pathology*). How does the poem narrate a story with both comic and

pathetic implications? What might the central character be blamed for? What arouses our pity for her?

2. Explore the multiple denotations, and the connotations attached to each denotation, of "brilliant" (both in 1 and 28), "interest" and "reward" (4), "cultured" and "jargon" (5), "circles" (28).
3. Why are the poet's words more effective than these possible synonyms: "captured" rather than *learned*? "conversed" rather than *chatted*, *gossiped*, or *talked*? "catalogues" rather than *volumes* or *multitudes*? "espouse" rather than *marry*?
4. At what point in the poem does the speaker shift from language that represents the way the woman might have talked about herself to language that reveals how the speaker judges her? Point out examples of both kinds of language.

28. Cross

My old man's a white old man
And my old mother's black.
If ever I cursed my white old man
I take my curses back.

If ever I cursed my black old mother
And wished she were in hell,
I'm sorry for that evil wish
And now I wish her well.

My old man died in a fine big house.
My ma died in a shack.
I wonder where I'm gonna die,
Being neither white nor black?

Langston Hughes (1902–1967)

QUESTIONS

1. What different denotations does the title have? Explain.
2. The language in this poem, such as "old man" (1, 3, 9), "ma" (10), and "gonna" (11), is plain, and even colloquial. Is it appropriate to the subject? Why?

29. The world is too much with us

The world is too much with us; late and soon,
Getting and spending, we lay waste our powers:
Little we see in nature that is ours;
We have given our hearts away, a sordid boon!
This sea that bares her bosom to the moon,
The winds that will be howling at all hours,

And are up-gathered now like sleeping flowers,
For this, for everything, we are out of tune;
It moves us not.—Great God! I'd rather be
A pagan suckled in a creed outworn;
So might I, standing on this pleasant lea,
Have glimpses that would make me less forlorn;
Have sight of Proteus rising from the sea;
Or hear old Triton blow his wreathèd horn.

William Wordsworth (1770–1850)

QUESTIONS

1. Vocabulary: *boon* (4), *Proteus* (13), *Triton* (14). What two relevant denotations has "wreathèd" (14)?
2. Explain why the poet's words are more effective than these possible alternatives: *earth* for "world" (1), *selling and buying* for "getting and spending" (2), *exposes* for "bares" (5), *dozing* for "sleeping" (7), *posies* for "flowers" (7), *nourished* for "suckled" (10), *visions* for "glimpses" (12), *sound* for "blow" (14).
3. Should "Great God!" (9) be considered as a vocative (term of address) or an expletive (exclamation)? Or something of both?
4. State the theme (central idea) of the poem in a sentence.

30. A Hymn to God the Father

Wilt thou forgive that sin where I begun,
Which is my sin though it were done before?
Wilt thou forgive those sins through which I run,° ran
And do them still, though still I do deplore?
When thou hast done, thou hast not done,
For I have more.

Wilt thou forgive that sin by which I won
Others to sin, and made my sin their door?
Wilt thou forgive that sin which I did shun
A year or two, but wallowed in a score?
When thou hast done, thou has not done,
For I have more.

I have a sin of fear, that when I have spun
My last thread, I shall perish on the shore;
Swear by thyself that at my death thy Sun
Shall shine as it shines now, and heretofore;
And having done that, thou hast done.
I have no more.

John Donne (1572–1631)

QUESTIONS

1. In 1601, John Donne at 29 secretly married Anne More, aged 17, infuriating her upper-class father, who had him imprisoned for three days. Because of the marriage, Donne lost his job as private secretary to an important official at court, and probably ruined his chances for the career at court that he wanted. It was, however, a true love match. In 1615 Donne entered the church. In 1617 his wife, then 33, died after bearing him twelve children. In 1621 he was appointed Dean of St. Paul's Cathedral in London and quickly won a reputation for his eloquent sermons. His religious poems differ markedly in tone from the often cynical, sometimes erotic poems of his youth. The foregoing poem was written during a severe illness in 1623. Is this information of any value to a reader of the poem?
2. What sin is referred to in lines 1–2? What is meant by "when I have spun / My last thread" (13–14)? By "I shall perish on the shore" (14)?
3. Puns on what three different words give structure and meaning to the poem? Explain the relevance of each.

31. Base Details

If I were fierce, and bald, and short of breath,
   I'd live with scarlet Majors at the Base,
And speed glum heroes up the line to death.
   You'd see me with my puffy petulant face,
Guzzling and gulping in the best hotel,
   Reading the Roll of Honor. "Poor young chap,"
I'd say—"I used to know his father well;
   Yes, we've lost heavily in this last scrap."
And when the war is done and youth stone dead,
I'd toddle safely home and die—in bed.

Siegfried Sassoon (1886–1967)

QUESTIONS

1. Vocabulary: *petulant* (4). "Up the line" (3) was a British slang phrase in World War I meaning "into action."
2. In what ways should the title be interpreted? (Both words have two pertinent denotative meanings with varying connotations attached to them.) What applications has "scarlet" (2)? What is the force of "fierce" (1)? Explain why the poet's words are preferable to these possible alternatives: *fleshy* for "puffy" (4), *eating and drinking* for "guzzling and gulping" (5), *battle* for "scrap" (8), *totter* for "toddle" (10).
3. Who evidently is the speaker? (Is he in the military? How familiar is he with the language and attitudes of majors? How much does he identify with their values?) Does he mean what he says? What is the purpose of the poem?

CHAPTER FOUR

Imagery

Experience comes to us largely through the senses. My experience of a spring day, for instance, may consist partly of certain emotions I feel and partly of certain thoughts I think, but most of it will be a cluster of sense impressions. It will consist of *seeing* blue sky and white clouds, budding leaves and daffodils; of *hearing* robins and bluebirds singing in the early morning; of *smelling* damp earth and blossoming hyacinths; and of *feeling* a fresh wind against my cheek. A poet seeking to express the experience of a spring day must therefore provide a selection of sense impressions. So in "Spring" (No. 4) Shakespeare gives us "daisies pied" and "lady-smocks all silver-white" and "merry larks" and the song of the cuckoo and maidens bleaching their summer smocks. Had he not done so, he probably would have failed to evoke the emotions that accompanied his sensations. The poet's language, then, must be more *sensuous* than ordinary language. It must be more full of imagery.

Imagery may be defined as the representation through language of sense experience. Poetry appeals directly to our senses, of course, through its music and rhythms, which we actually hear when it is read aloud. But indirectly it appeals to our senses through imagery, the representation to the imagination of sense experience. The word *image* perhaps most often suggests a mental picture, something seen in the mind's eye—and *visual* imagery is the kind of imagery that occurs most frequently in poetry. But an image may also represent a sound (*auditory imagery*); a smell (*olfactory imagery*); a taste (*gustatory imagery*); touch, such as hardness, softness, wetness, or heat and cold (*tactile imagery*); an internal sensation, such as hunger, thirst, fatigue, or nausea (*organic imagery*); or movement or tension in the muscles or joints (*kinesthetic imagery*). If we wished to be scientific, we could extend this list further, for psychologists no longer confine themselves to five or even six senses, but for purposes of discussing poetry the preceding classification should ordinarily be sufficient.

32. Meeting at Night

The gray sea and the long black land;
And the yellow half-moon large and low;
And the startled little waves that leap
In fiery ringlets from their sleep,
As I gain the cove with pushing prow,
And quench its speed i' the slushy sand.

Then a mile of warm sea-scented beach;
Three fields to cross till a farm appears;
A tap at the pane, the quick sharp scratch
And blue spurt of a lighted match,
And a voice less loud, through its joys and fears,
Than the two hearts beating each to each!

Robert Browning (1812–1889)

"Meeting at Night" is a poem about love. It makes, one might say, a number of statements about love: being in love is a sweet and exciting experience; when one is in love everything seems beautiful, and the most trivial things become significant; when one is in love one's sweetheart seems the most important thing in the world. But the poet actually *tells* us none of these things directly. He does not even use the word *love* in his poem. His business is to communicate experience, not information. He does this largely in two ways. First, he presents us with a specific situation, in which a lover goes to meet his sweetheart. Second, he describes the lover's journey so vividly in terms of sense impressions that the reader virtually sees and hears what the lover saw and heard and seems to share his anticipation and excitement.

Every line in the poem contains some image, some appeal to the senses: the gray sea, the long black land, the yellow half-moon, the startled little waves with their fiery ringlets, the blue spurt of the lighted match—all appeal to our sense of sight and convey not only shape but also color and motion. The warm sea-scented beach appeals to the senses of both smell and touch. The pushing prow of the boat on the slushy sand, the tap at the pane, the quick scratch of the match, the low speech of the lovers, and the sound of their hearts beating—all appeal to the sense of hearing.

33. Parting at Morning

Round the cape of a sudden came the sea,
And the sun looked over the mountain's rim:
And straight was a path of gold for him,
And the need of a world of men for me.

Robert Browning (1812–1889)

QUESTIONS

1. This poem is a sequel to "Meeting at Night." "Him" (3) refers to the sun. Does the last line mean that the lover needs the world of men or that the world of men needs the lover? Or both?
2. Does the sea *actually* come suddenly around the cape or *appear* to? Why does Browning mention the *effect* before its *cause* (the sun looking over the mountain's rim)?
3. Do these poems, taken together, suggest any larger truths about love? Browning, in answer to a question, said that the second part is the man's confession of "how fleeting is the belief (implied in the first part) that such raptures are self-sufficient and enduring—as for the time they appear."

The sharpness and vividness of any image will ordinarily depend on how specific it is and on the poet's use of effective detail. The word *hummingbird*, for instance, conveys a more definite image than does *bird*, and *ruby-throated hummingbird* is sharper and more specific still. However, to represent something vividly a poet need not describe it completely. One or two especially sharp and representative details will often serve, allowing the reader's imagination to fill in the rest. Tennyson in "The Eagle" (No. 1) gives only one detail about the eagle itself—that he clasps the crag with "crooked hands"—but this detail is an effective and memorable one. Robinson in "The Mill" (No. 18) withholds specific information about the life that the miller and his wife had shared, but the fact that she smells "a warm / And mealy fragrance of the past" when she enters the mill speaks volumes about her sense of loss. Browning, in "Meeting at Night," calls up a whole scene with "A tap at the pane, the quick sharp scratch / And blue spurt of a lighted match."

Since imagery is a peculiarly effective way of evoking vivid experience, and since it may be used to convey emotion and suggest ideas as well as to cause a mental reproduction of sensations, it is an invaluable resource of the poet. In general, the poet will seek concrete or image-bearing words in preference to abstract or non-image-bearing words. We cannot evaluate a poem, however, by the amount or quality of its imagery alone. Sense impression is only one of the elements of experience. Poetry may attain its ends by other means. We should never judge any single element of a poem except in reference to the total intention of that poem.

* * *

34. A Late Aubade

You could be sitting now in a carrel
Turning some liver-spotted page,
Or rising in an elevator-cage
Toward Ladies' Apparel.

You could be planting a raucous bed
Of salvia, in rubber gloves,
Or lunching through a screed of someone's loves
With pitying head,

Or making some unhappy setter
Heel, or listening to a bleak
Lecture on Schoenberg's serial technique.
Isn't this better?

Think of all the time you are not
Wasting, and would not care to waste,
Such things, thank God, not being to your taste.
Think what a lot

Of time, by woman's reckoning,
You've saved, and so may spend on this,
You who had rather lie in bed and kiss
Than anything.

It's almost noon, you say? If so,
Time flies, and I need not rehearse
The rosebuds-theme of centuries of verse.
If you *must* go,

Wait for a while, then slip downstairs
And bring us up some chilled white wine,
And some blue cheese, and crackers, and some fine
Ruddy-skinned pears.

Richard Wilbur (b. 1921)

QUESTIONS

1. Vocabulary: *aubade* (see Glossary of Poetic Terms), *carrel* (1), *raucous* (5), *screed* (7), *Schoenberg* (11).
2. Who is the speaker? What is the situation? What plea is the speaker making?

3. As lines 22–23 suggest, this poem treats an age-old theme of poetry. What is it? In what respects is this an original treatment of it? Though line 23 is general in reference, it alludes specifically to a famous poem by Robert Herrick (No. 63). In what respects are these two poems similar? In what respects are they different?
4. What clues are there in the poem as to the characters and personalities of the two people involved?
5. How does the last stanza provide a fitting conclusion to the poem?

35. After Apple-Picking

My long two-pointed ladder's sticking through a tree
Toward heaven still,
And there's a barrel that I didn't fill
Beside it, and there may be two or three
Apples I didn't pick upon some bough.
But I am done with apple-picking now.
Essence of winter sleep is on the night,
The scent of apples: I am drowsing off.
I cannot rub the strangeness from my sight
I got from looking through a pane of glass
I skimmed this morning from the drinking trough
And held against the world of hoary grass.
It melted, and I let it fall and break.
But I was well
Upon my way to sleep before it fell,
And I could tell
What form my dreaming was about to take.
Magnified apples appear and disappear,
Stem end and blossom end,
And every fleck of russet showing clear.
My instep arch not only keeps the ache,
It keeps the pressure of a ladder-round.
I feel the ladder sway as the boughs bend.
And I keep hearing from the cellar bin
The rumbling sound
Of load on load of apples coming in.
For I have had too much
Of apple-picking: I am overtired
Of the great harvest I myself desired.
There were ten thousand thousand fruit to touch,
Cherish in hand, lift down, and not let fall.
For all
That struck the earth,
No matter if not bruised or spiked with stubble,

Went surely to the cider-apple heap
As of no worth.
One can see what will trouble
This sleep of mine, whatever sleep it is.
Were he not gone,
The woodchuck could say whether it's like his
Long sleep, as I describe its coming on,
Or just some human sleep.

Robert Frost (1874–1963)

QUESTIONS

1. How does the poet convey so vividly the experience of "apple-picking"? Point out effective examples of each kind of imagery used. What emotional responses do the images evoke?
2. How does the speaker regard his work? Has he done it well or poorly? Does he find it enjoyable or tedious? Is he dissatisfied with its results?
3. The speaker predicts what he will dream about in his sleep. Why does he shift to the present tense (18) when he begins describing a dream he has not yet had? How sharply are real experience and dream experience differentiated in the poem?
4. The poem uses the word "sleep" six times. Does it, through repetition, come to suggest a meaning beyond the purely literal? If so, what attitude does the speaker take toward this second signification? Does he fear it? Does he look forward to it? What does he expect of it?
5. If sleep is symbolic (both literal and metaphorical), other details also may take on additional meaning. If so, how would you interpret (a) the ladder, (b) the season of the year, (c) the harvesting, (d) the "pane of glass" (10)? What denotations has the word "Essence" (7)?
6. How does the woodchuck's sleep differ from "just some human sleep"?

36. A narrow fellow in the grass

A narrow fellow in the grass
Occasionally rides—
You may have met him? Did you not,
His notice instant is:

The grass divides as with a comb,
A spotted shaft is seen,
And then it closes at your feet
And opens further on.

He likes a boggy acre,
A floor too cool for corn,
But when a boy, and barefoot,
I more than once at noon

Have passed, I thought, a whip-lash
Unbraiding in the sun,
When, stooping to secure it,
It wrinkled, and was gone.

Several of nature's people
I know, and they know me;
I feel for them a transport
Of cordiality;

But never met this fellow,
Attended or alone,
Without a tighter breathing
And zero at the bone.

Emily Dickinson (1830–1886)

QUESTIONS

1. The subject of this poem is never named. What is it? How does the imagery identify it?
2. The last two lines might be paraphrased as "without being frightened." Why is Dickinson's wording more effective?
3. Who is the speaker?

37. Living in Sin

She had thought the studio would keep itself;
no dust upon the furniture of love.
Half heresy, to wish the taps less vocal,
the panes relieved of grime. A plate of pears,
a piano with a Persian shawl, a cat
stalking the picturesque amusing mouse
had risen at his urging.
Not that at five each separate stair would writhe
under the milkman's tramp; that morning light
so coldly would delineate the scraps
of last night's cheese and three sepulchral bottles;
that on the kitchen shelf among the saucers
a pair of beetle-eyes would fix her own—
envoy from some village in the moldings . . .
Meanwhile, he, with a yawn,
sounded a dozen notes upon the keyboard,
declared it out of tune, shrugged at the mirror,
rubbed at his beard, went out for cigarettes;
while she, jeered by the minor demons,

pulled back the sheets and made the bed and found
a towel to dust the table-top,
and let the coffee-pot boil over on the stove.
By evening she was back in love again,
though not so wholly but throughout the night
she woke sometimes to feel the daylight coming
like a relentless milkman up the stairs.

Adrienne Rich (b. 1929)

QUESTIONS

1. Explain the grammatical structure and meaning of the sentence in lines 4–7. What are its subject and verb? What kind of life do its images conjure up? To whom or what does "his" (7) refer?
2. On what central contrast is the poem based? What is its central mood or emotion?
3. Discuss the various kinds of imagery and their function in conveying the experience of the poem.

38. Those Winter Sundays

Sundays too my father got up early
and put his clothes on in the blueblack cold,
then with cracked hands that ached
from labor in the weekday weather made
banked fires blaze. No one ever thanked him.

I'd wake and hear the cold splintering, breaking.
When the rooms were warm, he'd call,
and slowly I would rise and dress,
fearing the chronic angers of that house,

Speaking indifferently to him,
who had driven out the cold
and polished my good shoes as well.
What did I know, what did I know
of love's austere and lonely offices?

Robert Hayden (1913–1980)

QUESTIONS

1. Vocabulary: *offices* (14).
2. What kind of imagery is central to the poem? How is this imagery related to the emotional concerns of the poem?

3. How do the subsidiary images relate to the central images?
4. From what point in time does the speaker view the subject matter of the poem? What has happened to him in the interval?

39. The Widow's Lament in Springtime

Sorrow is my own yard
where the new grass
flames as it has flamed
often before but not
with the cold fire
that closes round me this year.
Thirtyfive years
I lived with my husband.
The plumtree is white today
with masses of flowers.
Masses of flowers
load the cherry branches
and color some bushes
yellow and some red
but the grief in my heart
is stronger than they
for though they were my joy
formerly, today I notice them
and turned away forgetting.
Today my son told me
that in the meadows,
at the edge of the heavy woods
in the distance, he saw
trees of white flowers.
I feel that I would like
to go there
and fall into those flowers
and sink into the marsh near them.

William Carlos Williams (1883–1963)

QUESTIONS

1. Why is springtime so poignant a time for this lament? What has been the speaker's previous experience at this time of year?
2. Why does the speaker's son tell her of the flowering trees "in the distance"? What does he want her to do? Contrast the two locations in the poem—"yard" versus "meadows," "woods," and "marsh." What does the widow desire?

3. Imagery may have degrees of vividness, depending on its particularity, concreteness, and specific detail. Where is the most vivid visual imagery in this poem? What other senses does the imagery evoke?

40. Spring

Nothing is so beautiful as spring—
  When weeds, in wheels, shoot long and lovely and lush;
  Thrush's eggs look little low heavens, and thrush
Through the echoing timber does so rinse and wring
The ear, it strikes like lightnings to hear him sing;
  The glassy peartree leaves and blooms, they brush
  The descending blue; that blue is all in a rush
With richness; the racing lambs too have fair their fling.

What is all this juice and all this joy?
  A strain of the earth's sweet being in the beginning
In Eden garden.—Have, get, before it cloy,

  Before it cloud, Christ, lord, and sour with sinning,
Innocent mind and Mayday in girl and boy,
  Most, O maid's child, thy choice and worthy the winning.

Gerard Manley Hopkins (1844–1889)

QUESTIONS

1. The first line makes an abstract statement. How is this statement brought to carry conviction?
2. The sky is described as being "all in a rush / With richness" (7–8). In what other respects is the poem "rich"?
3. To what two things does the speaker compare the spring in lines 9–14? In what ways are the comparisons appropriate?
4. Lines 11–14 might be made clearer by paraphrasing them thus: "Christ, lord, child of the virgin: save the innocent mind of girl and boy before sin taints it, since it is most like yours and worth saving." Why are Hopkins's lines more effective, both in imagery and in syntax?

41. To Autumn

Season of mists and mellow fruitfulness,
  Close bosom-friend of the maturing sun;
Conspiring with him how to load and bless
  With fruit the vines that round the thatch-eaves run;
To bend with apples the mossed cottage-trees,
  And fill all fruit with ripeness to the core;

To swell the gourd, and plump the hazel shells
With a sweet kernel; to set budding more,
And still more, later flowers for the bees,
Until they think warm days will never cease,
For summer has o'er-brimmed their clammy cells.

Who hath not seen thee oft amid thy store?
Sometimes whoever seeks abroad may find
Thee sitting careless on a granary floor,
Thy hair soft-lifted by the winnowing wind;
Or on a half-reaped furrow sound asleep,
Drowsed with the fume of poppies, while thy hook
Spares the next swath and all its twinèd flowers:
And sometimes like a gleaner thou dost keep
Steady thy laden head across a brook;
Or by a cider-press, with patient look,
Thou watchest the last oozings hours by hours.

Where are the songs of spring? Ay, where are they?
Think not of them, thou hast thy music too,—
While barred clouds bloom the soft-dying day,
And touch the stubble-plains with rosy hue;
Then in a wailful choir the small gnats mourn
Among the river sallows, borne aloft
Or sinking as the light wind lives or dies;
And full-grown lambs loud bleat from hilly bourn;
Hedge-crickets sing; and now with treble soft
The red-breast whistles from a garden-croft;
And gathering swallows twitter in the skies.

John Keats (1795–1821)

QUESTIONS

1. Vocabulary: *hook* (17), *barred* (25), *sallows* (28), *bourn* (30), *croft* (32).
2. How many kinds of imagery do you find in the poem? Give examples of each.
3. Are the images arranged haphazardly or are they carefully organized? In answering this question, consider (a) what aspect of autumn each stanza particularly concerns, (b) what kind of imagery dominates each stanza, and (c) what time of the season each stanza presents. Is there any progression in time of day?
4. What is autumn personified as in stanza 2? Is there any suggestion of personification in the other two stanzas?
5. Although the poem is primarily descriptive, what attitude toward transience and passing beauty is implicit in it?

CHAPTER FIVE

Figurative Language 1

Simile, Metaphor, Personification, Apostrophe, Metonymy

Poetry provides the one permissible way of saying one thing and meaning another.
ROBERT FROST

Let us assume that your brother has just come in out of a rainstorm and you say to him, "Well, you're a pretty sight! Got slightly wet, didn't you?" And he replies, "Wet? I'm drowned! It's raining cats and dogs, and my raincoat's like a sieve!"

You and your brother probably understand each other well enough; yet if you examine this conversation literally, that is to say unimaginatively, you will find that you have been speaking nonsense. Actually you have been speaking figuratively. You have been saying less than what you mean, or more than what you mean, or the opposite of what you mean, or something other than what you mean. You did not mean that your brother was a pretty sight but that he was a wretched sight. You did not mean that he got slightly wet but that he got very wet. Your brother did not mean that he got drowned but that he got drenched. It was not raining cats and dogs; it was raining water. And your brother's raincoat is so unlike a sieve that not even a child would confuse them.

If you are familiar with Molière's play *Le Bourgeois Gentilhomme*, you will remember how delighted M. Jourdain was to discover that he had been speaking prose all his life. Many people might be equally surprised to learn that they have been speaking a kind of subpoetry all their lives. The difference between their figures of speech and the poet's is that theirs are probably worn and trite, the poet's fresh and original.

On first examination, it might seem absurd to say one thing and mean another. But we all do it—and with good reason. We do it because we can say what we want to say more vividly and forcefully by figures than we can by saying it directly. And we can say more by figurative statement than we can by literal statement. Figures of speech offer another way of adding extra dimensions to language.

Broadly defined, **a figure of speech** is any way of saying something other than the ordinary way, and some rhetoricians have classified as many as 250 separate figures. For our purposes, however, a figure of speech is more narrowly definable as a way of saying one thing and meaning another, and we need to be concerned with no more than a dozen. **Figurative language**—language using figures of speech—is language that cannot be taken literally (or should not be taken literally only).

Metaphor and **simile** are both used as a means of comparing things that are essentially unlike. The only distinction between them is that in simile the comparison is *expressed* by the use of some word or phrase, such as *like, as, than, similar to, resembles*, or *seems*; in metaphor the comparison is *implied*—that is, the figurative term is *substituted for* or *identified with* the literal term.

42. The Guitarist Tunes Up

With what attentive courtesy he bent
Over his instrument;
Not as a lordly conqueror who could
Command both wire and wood,
But as a man with a loved woman might,
Inquiring with delight
What slight essential things she had to say
Before they started, he and she, to play.

Frances Cornford (1886–1960)

QUESTION

Explore the comparisons. Do they principally illuminate the guitarist or the lovers or both? What one word brings the figurative and literal terms together?

43. The Hound

Life the hound
Equivocal
Comes at a bound
Either to rend me
Or to befriend me.

I cannot tell
The hound's intent
Till he has sprung
At my bare hand
With teeth or tongue.
Meanwhile I stand
And wait the event.

Robert Francis (1901–1987)

QUESTION

What does "equivocal" (2) mean? Show how this is the key word in the poem. What is the effect of placing it on a line by itself?

Metaphors may take one of four forms, depending on whether the literal and figurative terms are respectively *named* or *implied*. In the first form of metaphor, as in simile, *both* the literal *and* figurative terms are *named*. In Francis's poem, for example, the literal term is "life" and the figurative term is "hound." In the second form, the literal term is *named* and the figurative term is *implied*.

44. Bereft

Where had I heard this wind before
Change like this to a deeper roar?
What would it take my standing there for,
Holding open a restive door,
Looking downhill to a frothy shore?
Summer was past and day was past.
Somber clouds in the west were massed.
Out in the porch's sagging floor
Leaves got up in a coil and hissed,
Blindly struck at my knee and missed.
Something sinister in the tone
Told me my secret must be known:
Word I was in the house alone
Somehow must have gotten abroad,
Word I was in my life alone,
Word I had no one left but God.

Robert Frost (1874–1963)

QUESTIONS

1. Describe the situation precisely. What time of day and year is it? Where is the speaker? What is happening to the weather?
2. To what are the leaves in lines 9–10 compared?
3. The word "hissed" (9) is onomatopoetic (see Glossary of Poetic Terms). How is its effect reinforced in the lines following?
4. Though lines 9–10 present the clearest example of the second form of metaphor, there are others. To what is the wind ("it") compared in line 3? Why is the door (4) "restive" and what does this do (figuratively) to the door? To what is the speaker's "life" compared (15)?
5. What is the tone of the poem? How reassuring is the last line?

In the third form of metaphor, the literal term is *implied* and the figurative term is *named*. In the fourth form, *both* the literal *and* figurative terms are *implied*. The following poem exemplifies both forms:

45. It sifts from leaden sieves

It sifts from leaden sieves,
It powders all the wood.
It fills with alabaster wool
The wrinkles of the road.

It makes an even face
Of mountain and of plain—
Unbroken forehead from the east
Unto the east again.

It reaches to the fence,
It wraps it rail by rail
Till it is lost in fleeces;
It deals celestial veil

To stump and stack and stem—
A summer's empty room—
Acres of joints where harvests were,
Recordless,° but for them. unrecorded

It ruffles wrists of posts
As ankles of a queen,
Then stills its artisans like ghosts,
Denying they have been.

Emily Dickinson (1830–1886)

QUESTIONS

1. This poem consists essentially of a series of metaphors having the same literal term identified only as "It." What is "It"?
2. In several of these metaphors the figurative term is named—"alabaster wool" (3), "fleeces" (11), "celestial veil" (12). In two of them, however, the figurative term as well as the literal term is left unnamed. To what is "It" compared in lines 1–2? In lines 17–18?
3. Comment on the additional metaphorical expressions or complications contained in "leaden sieves" (1), "alabaster wool" (3), "even face" (5), "unbroken forehead" (7), "a summer's empty room" (14), "artisans" (19).

Metaphors of the fourth form, as one might guess, are comparatively rare. An extended example, however, is provided by Dickinson's "I like to see it lap the miles" (No. 161).

Personification consists in giving the attributes of a human being to an animal, an object, or a concept. It is really a subtype of metaphor, an implied comparison in which the figurative term of the comparison is always a human being. When Sylvia Plath makes a mirror speak and think (No. 19), she is personifying an object. When Keats describes autumn as a harvester "sitting careless on a granary floor" or "on a half-reaped furrow sound asleep" (No. 41), he is personifying a season. Personifications differ in the degree to which they ask the reader actually to visualize the literal term in human form. In Keats's comparison, we are asked to make a complete identification of autumn with a human being. In Sylvia Plath's, though the mirror speaks and thinks, we continue to visualize it as a mirror; similarly, in Frost's "Bereft" (No. 44), the "restive" door remains in appearance a door tugged by the wind. In Browning's reference to "the startled little waves" (No. 32), a personification is barely suggested; we would make a mistake if we tried to visualize the waves in human form or even, really, to think of them as having human emotions.*

*The various figures of speech blend into each other, and it sometimes is difficult to classify a specific example as definitely metaphor or symbol, symbolism or allegory, understatement or irony, irony or paradox. Often a given example may exemplify two or more figures at once. In "The Guitarist Tunes Up" (No. 42), "wire and wood" are metonymies (see page 65) for a guitar and are personified as subjects, slaves, or soldiers who could be commanded by a lordly conqueror. In "The world is too much with us" (No. 29), when the winds are described as calm, "like sleeping flowers," the flowers function as part of a simile and are personified as something that can sleep. The important consideration in reading poetry is not that we classify figures definitively but that we construe them correctly.

46. Joy and Temperance

Joy and Temperance and Repose
Slam the door on the doctor's nose.

Anonymous

QUESTION

Compare this poem with the widely known "An apple a day / Keeps the doctor away." How are they alike? How do they differ? Which do you prefer, and why?

Closely related to personification is **apostrophe**, which consists in addressing someone absent or dead or something nonhuman as if that person or thing were present and alive and could reply to what is being said. The speaker in A. E. Housman's "To an Athlete Dying Young" (No. 238) apostrophizes a dead runner. William Blake apostrophizes a tiger throughout his famous poem (No. 209) but does not otherwise personify it. Keats apostrophizes *and* personifies autumn (No. 41). Personification and apostrophe are both ways of giving life and immediacy to one's language, but since neither requires great imaginative power on the part of the poet—apostrophe especially does not—they may degenerate into mere mannerisms and are to be found as often in bad and mediocre poetry as in good. We need to distinguish between their effective use and their merely conventional use.

47. Western Wind

Western wind, when wilt thou blow,
The small rain down can rain?
Christ! if my love were in my arms,
And I in my bed again!

Anonymous (c. 1500)

QUESTIONS

1. Paraphrase the first two lines. What do you conceive to be the speaker's situation?
2. What is the connection between the first two lines and the last two?

Synecdoche (the use of the part for the whole) and **metonymy** (the use of something closely related for the thing actually meant) are alike in that both substitute some significant detail or aspect of an experience for the experience itself. Thus Shakespeare uses synecdoche when he says that the cuckoo's song is unpleasing to a "married ear" (No. 4), for he means a married *man*. Kay uses synecdoche when she refers to "catalogues of domes" (No. 27), because what she means is "enough domed buildings to fill a catalogue." Robert Graves uses synecdoche in "The Naked and the Nude" (No. 24) when he refers to a doctor as a "Hippocratic eye," and Housman's Terence (No. 10) uses synecdoche when he declares that "malt does more than Milton can / To justify God's ways to man," for "malt" means beer or ale, of which malt is an essential ingredient. On the other hand, when Terence advises "fellows whom it hurts to think" to "Look into the pewter pot / To see the world as the world's not," he is using metonymy, for by "pewter pot" he means the ale *in* the pot, not the pot itself, and by "world" he means human life and the conditions under which it is lived. Shakespeare uses metonymy when he says that the yellow cuckoo-buds "paint the meadows with delight" (No. 4), for he means with bright color that produces delight. Robert Frost uses metonymy in "'Out, Out—'" (No. 91) when he describes an injured boy holding up his cut hand "as if to keep / The life from spilling," for literally he means to keep the blood from spilling. In each case, however, the poem gains in vividness, meaning, or compactness. Kay, by substituting one architectural detail for whole buildings, suggests the superficiality and boredom of a person who looks at many but appreciates none. Shakespeare, by referring to bright color as "delight," evokes not only the visual effect but the emotional response it arouses. Frost tells us both that the boy's hand is bleeding and that his life is in danger.

Many synecdoches and metonymies, of course, like many metaphors, have become so much a part of the language that they no longer strike us as figurative; this is the case with *redhead* for a red-haired person, *hands* for manual workers, *highbrow* for a sophisticate, *tongues* for languages, and a boiling *kettle* for the water *in* the kettle. Such figures are often referred to as *dead metaphors* (where the word *metaphor* is itself a metonymy for all figurative speech). Synecdoche and metonymy are so much alike that it is hardly worthwhile to distinguish between them, and the latter term is increasingly used for both. In this book metonymy will be used for both figures—that is, for any figure in which a part or something closely related is substituted for the thing literally meant.

We said at the beginning of this chapter that figurative language often provides a more effective means of saying what we mean than does direct statement. What are some of the reasons for that effectiveness?

First, figurative language affords us imaginative pleasure. Imagination might be described in one sense as that faculty or ability of the mind that proceeds by sudden leaps from one point to another, that goes up a stair by leaping in one jump from the bottom to the top rather than by climbing up one step at a time.* The mind takes delight in these sudden leaps, in seeing likenesses between unlike things. We all probably have taken pleasure in staring into a fire and seeing castles and cities and armies in it, or in looking into the clouds and shaping them into animals or faces, or in seeing a man in the moon. We name our plants and flowers after fancied resemblances: jack-in-the-pulpit, babies'-breath, Queen Anne's lace. Figures of speech are therefore satisfying in themselves, providing us with a source of pleasure in the exercise of the imagination.

Second, figures of speech are a way of bringing additional imagery into verse, of making the abstract concrete, of making poetry more sensuous. When Tennyson's eagle falls "like a thunderbolt" (No. 1), his swooping down for his prey is charged with energy, speed, and power; the simile also recalls that the Greek god Zeus was accompanied by an eagle and armed with lightning. When Emily Dickinson compares poetry to prancing coursers (No. 22), she objectifies imaginative and rhythmical qualities by presenting them in visual terms. When Robert Browning compares the crisping waves to "fiery ringlets" (No. 32), he starts with one image and transforms it into three. Figurative language is a way of multiplying the sense appeal of poetry.

Third, figures of speech are a way of adding emotional intensity to otherwise merely informative statements and of conveying attitudes along with information. If we say, "So-and-so is a rat" or "My feet are killing me," our meaning is as much emotional as informative. When Philip Larkin's pathetic escapist compares books to "a load of crap" (No. 13), the vulgar language not only expresses his distaste for reading, but intensifies the characterization of him as a man whose intellectual growth was stunted. When Wilfred Owen compares a soldier caught in a gas attack to a man drowning under a green sea (No. 3), he conveys a feeling of despair and suffocation as well as a visual image.

Fourth, figures of speech are an effective means of concentration, a way of saying much in brief compass. Like words, they may be multidimensional. Consider, for instance, the merits of comparing life to a candle, as Shakespeare does in a passage from *Macbeth* (No. 92). Life is

*It is also the faculty of mind that is able to "picture" or "image" absent objects as if they were present. It was with imagination in this sense that we were concerned in the chapter on imagery.

like a candle in that it begins and ends in darkness; in that while it burns, it gives off light and energy, is active and colorful; in that it gradually consumes itself, gets shorter and shorter; in that it can be snuffed out at any moment; in that it is brief at best, burning only for a short duration. Possibly your imagination can suggest other similarities. But at any rate, Macbeth's compact, metaphorical description of life as a "brief candle" suggests certain truths about life that would require dozens of words to state in literal language. At the same time it makes the abstract concrete, provides imaginative pleasure, and adds a degree of emotional intensity.

Obviously, if we are to read poetry well, we must be able to interpret figurative language. Every use of figurative language involves a risk of misinterpretation, though the risk is well worth taking. For the person who can translate the figure, the dividends are immense. Fortunately all people have imagination to some degree, and imagination can be cultivated. By practice, one's ability to interpret figures of speech can be increased.

EXERCISE

Identify each of the following quotations as literal or figurative. If figurative, explain what is being compared to what and explain the appropriateness of the comparison. EXAMPLE: "Talent is a cistern; genius is a fountain." ANSWER: Metaphor. Talent = cistern; genius = fountain. Talent exists in finite supply; it can be used up. Genius is inexhaustible, ever renewing.

1. O tenderly the haughty day
   Fills his blue urn with fire. — *Ralph Waldo Emerson*
2. It is with words as with sunbeams—the more
   they are condensed, the deeper they burn. — *Robert Southey*
3. The pen is mightier than the sword. — *Edward Bulwer-Lytton*
4. The strongest oaths are straw
   To the fire i' the blood. — *William Shakespeare*
5. The Cambridge ladies . . . live in furnished souls. — *e. e. cummings*
6. Dorothy's eyes, with their long brown lashes,
   looked very much like her mother's. — *Laetitia Johnson*
7. The tawny-hided desert crouches watching her. — *Francis Thompson*
8. Let us eat and drink, for tomorrow we shall die. — *Isaiah 22:13*
9. Let us eat and drink, for tomorrow we may die.
   Common misquotation of the above

*　　　*　　　*

48. Mind

Mind in its purest play is like some bat
That beats about in caverns all alone,
Contriving by a kind of senseless wit
Not to conclude against a wall of stone.

It has no need to falter or explore;
Darkly it knows what obstacles are there,
And so may weave and flitter, dip and soar
In perfect courses through the blackest air.

And has this simile a like perfection?
The mind is like a bat. Precisely. Save
That in the very happiest intellection
A graceful error may correct the cave.

Richard Wilbur (b. 1921)

QUESTIONS

1. A poet may use a variety of metaphors and similes in developing a subject or may, as Wilbur does here, develop a single figure at length (this poem is an example of an **extended simile**). Identify in this chapter a poem containing a variety of figures and define the advantages of each type of development.
2. Explore the similarities between the two things compared in this poem. What is meant by "a graceful error" and by "correct the cave"?

49. I felt a funeral in my brain

I felt a funeral in my brain,
And mourners to and fro
Kept treading—treading—till it seemed
That sense was breaking through.

And when they all were seated,
A service, like a drum,
Kept beating—beating—till I thought
My mind was going numb.

And then I heard them lift a box
And creak across my soul
With those same boots of lead again.
Then space began to toll,

As all the heavens were a bell
And being, but an ear,
And I and silence, some strange race,
Wrecked, solitary, here.

And then a plank in reason broke
And I dropped down, and down,
And hit a world at every plunge,
And finished knowing, then.

Emily Dickinson (1830–1886)

QUESTIONS

1. What senses are evoked by the imagery? What important sense is missing from the poem?
2. In sequence, what aspects of a funeral constitute this **extended metaphor**? Is it possible to discover the sequence of mental events that are being compared to them? With respect to the funeral activities in stanzas 1–3, where is the speaker imaginatively located?
3. What finally happens to the speaker?

50. Metaphors

I'm a riddle in nine syllables,
An elephant, a ponderous house,
A melon strolling on two tendrils,
O red fruit, ivory, fine timbers!
This loaf's big with its yeasty rising.
Money's new-minted in this fat purse.
I'm a means, a stage, a cow in calf.
I've eaten a bag of green apples,
Boarded the train there's no getting off.

Sylvia Plath (1932–1963)

QUESTIONS

1. Like its first metaphor, this poem is a riddle to be solved by identifying the literal terms of its metaphors. After you have identified the speaker ("riddle," "elephant," "house," "melon," "stage," "cow"), identify the literal meanings of the related metaphors ("syllables," "tendrils," "fruit," "ivory," "timbers," "loaf," "yeasty rising," "money," "purse," "train"). How do you interpret line 8?
2. How does the form of the poem relate to its content?

51. Toads

Why should I let the toad *work*
   Squat on my life?
Can't I use my wit as a pitchfork
   And drive the brute off?

Six days of the week it soils
   With its sickening poison—
Just for paying a few bills!
   That's out of proportion.

Lots of folk live on their wits:
  Lecturers, lispers,
Losels,° loblolly-men,° louts— scoundrels; bumpkins
  They don't end as paupers;

Lots of folk live up lanes
  With fires in a bucket,
Eat windfalls and tinned sardines—
  They seem to like it.

Their nippers° have got bare feet, children
  Their unspeakable wives
Are skinny as whippets—and yet
  No one actually *starves*.

Ah, were I courageous enough
  To shout *Stuff your pension!*
But I know, all too well, that's the stuff
  That dreams are made on;

For something sufficiently toad-like
  Squats in me, too;
Its hunkers° are heavy as hard luck, haunches
  And cold as snow,

And will never allow me to blarney
  My way to getting
The fame and the girl and the money
  All at one sitting.

I don't say, one bodies the other
  One's spiritual truth;
But I do say it's hard to lose either,
  When you have both.

Philip Larkin (1922–1985)

QUESTIONS

1. Two "toads" are described in the poem. Where is each located? How are they described? What are the antecedents of the pronouns "one" and "the other / one" (33–34) respectively?
2. What characteristics in common have the people mentioned in lines 9–12? Those mentioned in lines 13–20?
3. Explain the pun in lines 22–23 and the literary allusion it leads into. (If you don't recognize the allusion, check Shakespeare's *The Tempest*, Act 4, scene 1, lines 156–58).

4. The first "toad" is explicitly identified as "work" (1). The literal term for the second "toad" is not named. Why not? What do you take it to be?
5. What kind of person is the speaker? What are his attitudes toward work?

52. A Valediction: Forbidding Mourning

As virtuous men pass mildly away,
  And whisper to their souls to go,
While some of their sad friends do say,
  The breath goes now, and some say, no:

So let us melt, and make no noise,
  No tear-floods, nor sigh-tempests move;
'Twere profanation of our joys
  To tell the laity our love.

Moving of th' earth brings harms and fears,
  Men reckon what it did and meant,
But trepidation of the spheres,
  Though greater far, is innocent.

Dull sublunary lovers' love
  (Whose soul is sense) cannot admit
Absence, because it doth remove
  Those things which elemented it.

But we by a love so much refined,
  That ourselves know not what it is,
Inter-assurèd of the mind,
  Care less, eyes, lips, and hands to miss.

Our two souls therefore, which are one,
  Though I must go, endure not yet
A breach, but an expansion,
  Like gold to airy thinness beat.

If they be two, they are two so
  As stiff twin compasses are two;
Thy soul the fixed foot, makes no show
  To move, but doth, if th' other do.

And though it in the center sit,
  Yet when the other far doth roam,
It leans, and hearkens after it,
  And grows erect, as that comes home.

Such wilt thou be to me, who must
  Like th' other foot, obliquely run;
Thy firmness makes my circle just,
  And makes me end, where I begun.

John Donne (1572–1631)

QUESTIONS

1. Vocabulary: *valediction* (title), *mourning* (title), *profanation* (7), *laity* (8), *trepidation* (11), *innocent* (12), *sublunary* (13), *elemented* (16). Line 11 is a reference to the spheres of the Ptolemaic cosmology, whose movements caused no such disturbance as does a movement of the earth—that is, an earthquake.
2. Is the speaker in the poem about to die? Or about to leave on a journey? (The answer may be found in a careful analysis of the simile in the last three stanzas.)
3. The poem is organized around a contrast of two kinds of lovers: the "laity" (8) and, as their implied opposite, the "priesthood." Are these terms literal or metaphorical? What is the essential difference between their two kinds of love? How, according to the speaker, does their behavior differ when they must separate from each other? What is the motivation of the speaker in this "valediction"?
4. Find and explain three similes and one metaphor used to describe the parting of true lovers. The figure in the last three stanzas is one of the most famous in English literature. Demonstrate its appropriateness by obtaining a drawing compass or by using two pencils to imitate the two legs.
5. What kind of language is used in the poem? Is the language consonant with the figures of speech?

53. To His Coy Mistress

Had we but world enough, and time,
This coyness, lady, were no crime.
We would sit down, and think which way
To walk, and pass our long love's day.
Thou by the Indian Ganges' side
Shouldst rubies find; I by the tide
Of Humber would complain. I would
Love you ten years before the Flood,
And you should, if you please, refuse
Till the conversion of the Jews.
My vegetable love should grow
Vaster than empires, and more slow;
An hundred years should go to praise
Thine eyes, and on thy forehead gaze;

Two hundred to adore each breast,
But thirty thousand to the rest;
An age at least to every part,
And the last age should show your heart.
For, lady, you deserve this state,
Nor would I love at lower rate.
  But at my back I always hear
Time's wingèd chariot hurrying near;
And yonder all before us lie
Deserts of vast eternity.
Thy beauty shall no more be found,
Nor, in thy marble vault, shall sound
My echoing song; then worms shall try
That long-preserved virginity,
And your quaint honor turn to dust,
And into ashes all my lust:
The grave's a fine and private place,
But none, I think, do there embrace.
  Now therefore, while the youthful hue
Sits on thy skin like morning dew,
And while thy willing soul transpires
At every pore with instant fires,
Now let us sport us while we may,
And now, like amorous birds of prey,
Rather at once our time devour
Than languish in his slow-chapped power.
Let us roll all our strength and all
Our sweetness up into one ball,
And tear our pleasures with rough strife
Thorough° the iron gates of life. — through
Thus, though we cannot make our sun
Stand still, yet we will make him run.

Andrew Marvell (1621–1678)

QUESTIONS

1. Vocabulary: *coy* (title), *Humber* (7), *transpires* (35). "Mistress" (title) has the now archaic meaning of *sweetheart*; "slow-chapped" (40) derives from *chap*, meaning *jaw*.
2. What is the speaker urging his sweetheart to do? Why is she being "coy"?
3. Outline the speaker's argument in three sentences that begin with the words *If*, *But*, and *Therefore*. Is the argument valid?
4. Explain the appropriateness of "vegetable love" (11). What simile in the third section contrasts with it and how? What image in the third section contrasts

with the distance between the Ganges and the Humber? Of what would the speaker be "complaining" by the Humber (7)?

5. Explain the figures in lines 22, 24, and 40 and their implications.
6. Explain the last two lines. For what is "sun" a metonymy?
7. Is this poem principally about love or about time? If the latter, what might making love represent? What philosophy is the poet advancing here?

54. Song: Go, lovely rose!

Go, lovely rose!
Tell her that wastes her time and me
That now she knows,
When I resemble her to thee,
How sweet and fair she seems to be.

Tell her that's young
And shuns to have her graces spied
That hadst thou sprung
In deserts where no men abide,
Thou must have uncommended died.

Small is the worth
Of beauty from the light retired.
Bid her come forth,
Suffer herself to be desired
And not blush so to be admired.

Then die! that she
The common fate of all things rare
May read in thee,
How small a part of time they share
That are so wondrous sweet and fair!

Edmund Waller (1607–1687)

QUESTIONS

1. Vocabulary: *resemble* (4), *suffer* (14).
2. The speaker addresses a rose, but his message is to a beautiful young woman. How might this indirect means of speaking to her increase the effect of his message? What is he asking her to do? What part does "time" play in the poem?
3. Rather than using apostrophe to compare his love to a rose, the speaker might have addressed her directly, making the comparison in a simile or a metaphor ("you are like a rose" or "you are a rose"), or he might have used an abstract third-person form ("she is like a rose" or "she is a rose"). What does the poem gain from apostrophe?

55. In the Museum

Small and emptied woman you lie here a thousand years dead
your hands on your diminished loins flat in this final bed
teeth jutting from your unwound head your spiced bones black and dried,
who knew you and kissed you and kept you and wept when you died;
died you young had you grace? Risus sardonicus replied.
Then quick I seized my husband's hand while he stared at his bride.

Isabella Gardner (b. 1915)

QUESTIONS

1. Vocabulary: *Risus sardonicus* (5) is a coined Latin phrase such as might appear on the identification label for a specimen in a natural history museum; it means "sardonic laughter." What different denotations has *quick* (6)?
2. The speaker apostrophizes a mummy, as indicated by "emptied" (1), "unwound" (3), and "spiced" (3). What point does she make by doing so? What are the possible sardonic replies to her question? What feelings are expressed in the last line?
3. What meaning has the last line? Who is the "bride"?

56. Loveliest of Trees

Loveliest of trees, the cherry now
Is hung with bloom along the bough,
And stands about the woodland ride
Wearing white for Eastertide.

Now, of my threescore years and ten,
Twenty will not come again,
And take from seventy springs a score,
It only leaves me fifty more.

And since to look at things in bloom
Fifty springs are little room,
About the woodlands I will go
To see the cherry hung with snow.

A. E. Housman (1859–1936)

QUESTIONS

1. Very briefly, this poem presents a philosophy of life. In a sentence, what is it?
2. How old is the speaker? Why does he assume that his life will be seventy years in length? What is surprising about the words "only" (8) and "little" (10)?
3. A good deal of ink has been spilt over whether "snow" (12) is literal or figurative. What do you say? Justify your answer.

57. Names of Horses

All winter your brute shoulders strained against collars, padding
and steerhide over the ash hames, to haul
sledges of cordwood for drying through spring and summer,
for the Glenwood stove next winter, and for the simmering range.

In April you pulled cartloads of manure to spread on the fields,
dark manure of Holsteins, and knobs of your own clustered with oats.
All summer you mowed the grass in meadow and hayfield, the mowing machine
clacketing beside you, while the sun walked high in the morning;

and after noon's heat, you pulled a clawed rake through the same acres,
gathering stacks, and dragged the wagon from stack to stack,
and the built hayrack back, uphill to the chaffy barn,
three loads of hay a day from standing grass in the morning.

Sundays you trotted the two miles to church with the light load
of a leather quartertop buggy, and grazed in the sound of hymns.
Generation on generation, your neck rubbed the windowsill
of the stall, smoothing the wood as the sea smooths glass.

When you were old and lame, when your shoulders hurt bending to graze,
one October the man who fed you and kept you, and harnessed you every morning,
led you through corn stubble to sandy ground above Eagle Pond,
and dug a hole beside you where you stood shuddering in your skin,

and lay the shotgun's muzzle in the boneless hollow behind your ear,
and fired the slug into your brain, and felled you into your grave,
shoveling sand to cover you, setting goldenrod upright above you,
where by next summer a dent in the ground made your monument.

For a hundred and fifty years, in the pasture of dead horses,
roots of pine trees pushed through the pale curves of your ribs,
yellow blossoms flourished above you in autumn, and in winter
frost heaved your bones in the ground—old toilers, soil makers:

O Roger, Mackerel, Riley, Ned, Nellie, Chester, Lady Ghost.

Donald Hall (b. 1928)

QUESTIONS

1. Halfway through, the poem shifts its focus from what had seemed to be *one* horse to generations of them, yet it maintains a singular form of address until the last two lines. What does this mixing of plural and singular add to the meaning? What feelings for the horse(s) does the speaker display?

2. With the exception of the metaphor in line 8, the only figure in the poem is apostrophe. Why is it important that the poem maintains its literalness? How does that add to the effect of the apostrophe?

58. Dream Deferred

What happens to a dream deferred?

Does it dry up
like a raisin in the sun?
Or fester like a sore—
And then run?
Does it stink like rotten meat?
Or crust and sugar over—
like a syrupy sweet?

Maybe it just sags
like a heavy load.

Or does it explode?

Langston Hughes (1902–1967)

QUESTIONS

1. Of the six images, five are similes. Which is a metaphor? Comment on its position and its effectiveness.
2. Since the dream could be any dream, the poem is general in its implication. What happens to your understanding of it on learning that its author was a black American?

EXERCISES

1. Robert Frost has said that "poetry is what evaporates from all translations." Why might this be true? How much of a word can be translated?
2. Ezra Pound has defined great literature as "simply language charged with meaning to the utmost possible degree." Would this be a good definition of poetry? The word "charged" is roughly equivalent to *filled*. Why is "charged" a better word in Pound's definition?

CHAPTER SIX

Figurative Language 2

Symbol, Allegory

59. The Road Not Taken

Two roads diverged in a yellow wood,
And sorry I could not travel both
And be one traveler, long I stood
And looked down one as far as I could
To where it bent in the undergrowth;

Then took the other, as just as fair,
And having perhaps the better claim,
Because it was grassy and wanted wear;
Though as for that the passing there
Had worn them really about the same,

And both that morning equally lay
In leaves no step had trodden black.
Oh, I kept the first for another day!
Yet knowing how way leads on to way,
I doubted if I should ever come back.

I shall be telling this with a sigh
Somewhere ages and ages hence:
Two roads diverged in a wood, and I—
I took the one less traveled by,
And that has made all the difference.

Robert Frost (1874–1963)

QUESTIONS

1. Does the speaker feel that he has made the wrong choice in taking the road "less traveled by"? If not, why will he sigh? What does he regret?
2. Why will the choice between two roads that seem very much alike make such a big difference many years later?

A **symbol** may be roughly defined as something that means *more* than what it is. "The Road Not Taken," for instance, concerns a choice made between two roads by a person out walking in the woods. He would like to explore both roads. He tells himself that he will explore one and then come back and explore the other, but he knows that he will probably be unable to do so. By the last stanza, however, we realize that the poem is about something more than the choice of paths in a wood, for that choice would be relatively unimportant, while this choice, the speaker believes, is one that will make a great difference in his life and is one that he will remember with a sigh "ages and ages hence." We must interpret his choice of a road as a symbol for any choice in life between alternatives that appear almost equally attractive but will result through the years in a large difference in the kind of experience one knows.

Image, metaphor, and symbol shade into each other and are sometimes difficult to distinguish. In general, however, an image means only what it is; the figurative term in a metaphor means something other than what it is; and a symbol means what it is and something more, too. A symbol, that is, functions literally and figuratively at the same time.* If I say that a shaggy brown dog was rubbing its back against a white picket fence, I am talking about nothing but a dog (and a picket fence) and am therefore presenting an image. If I say, "Some dirty dog stole my wallet at the party," I am not talking about a dog at all and am therefore using a metaphor. But if I say, "You can't teach an old dog new tricks," I am talking not only about dogs but about living creatures of any species and am therefore speaking symbolically. Images, of course, do not cease to be images when they become incorporated in metaphors or symbols. If we are discussing the sensuous qualities of "The Road Not Taken," we should refer to the two leaf-strewn roads in the yellow wood as an image; if we are discussing the significance of the poem, we talk about the roads as symbols.

The symbol is the richest and at the same time the most difficult of the poetic figures. Both its richness and its difficulty result from its imprecision. Although the poet may pin down the meaning of a symbol to something fairly definite and precise, more often the symbol is so general in its meaning that it can suggest a great variety of specific meanings. It is like an opal that flashes out different colors when slowly turned in the light. The choice in "The Road Not Taken," for instance, concerns some

*This account does not hold for nonliterary symbols such as the letters of the alphabet and algebraic signs (the symbol ∞ for infinity or $=$ for equals). With these, the symbol is meaningless except as it stands for something else, and the connection between the sign and what it stands for is purely arbitrary.

choice in life, but what choice? Was it a choice of profession? A choice of residence? A choice of mate? It might be any, all, or none of these. We cannot determine what particular choice the poet had in mind, if any, and it is not important that we do so. It is enough if we see in the poem an expression of regret that the possibilities of life experience are so sharply limited. The speaker in the poem would have liked to explore both roads, but he could explore only one. The person with a craving for life, whether satisfied or dissatisfied with the choices he has made, will always long for the realms of experience that he had to forego. Because the symbol is a rich one, the poem suggests other meanings too. It affirms a belief in the possibility of choice and says something about the nature of choice — how each choice narrows the range of possible future choices, so that we make our lives as we go, both freely choosing and being determined by past choices. Though not a philosophical poem, it obliquely comments on the issue of free will and determinism and indicates the poet's own position. It can do all these things, concretely and compactly, by its use of an effective symbol.

Symbols vary in the degree of identification and definition given them by their authors. In this poem Frost forces us to interpret the choice of roads symbolically by the degree of importance he gives it in the last stanza. Sometimes poets are much more specific in identifying their symbols. Sometimes they do not identify them at all. Consider, for instance, the next two poems.

60. A Noiseless Patient Spider

A noiseless patient spider,
I marked where on a little promontory it stood isolated,
Marked how to explore the vacant vast surrounding,
It launched forth filament, filament, filament, out of itself,
Ever unreeling them, ever tirelessly speeding them.

And you, O my soul where you stand,
Surrounded, detached, in measureless oceans of space,
Ceaselessly musing, venturing, throwing, seeking the spheres to connect
 them,
Till the bridge you will need be formed, till the ductile anchor hold,
Till the gossamer thread you fling catch somewhere, O my soul.

Walt Whitman (1819–1892)

In the first stanza the speaker describes a spider's apparently tireless effort to attach its thread to some substantial support so that it can begin constructing a web. The speaker reveals his attentive interest by the hinted personification of the spider, and his sympathy with it is expressed in the overstatement of size and distance—he is trying to perceive the world as a spider sees it from a "promontory" surrounded by vast space. He even attributes a human motive to the spider: exploration, rather than instinctive web-building. Nevertheless, the first stanza is essentially literal—the close observation of an actual spider at its task. In the second stanza the speaker explicitly interprets the symbolic meaning of what he has observed: his soul (personified by apostrophe and by the capabilities assigned to it) is like the spider in its constant striving. But the soul's purpose is to find spiritual or intellectual certainties in the vast universe it inhabits. The symbolic meaning is richer than a mere comparison; while a spider's actual purpose is limited to its instinctive drives, the human soul strives for much more, in a much more complex "surrounding." And of course, the result of the soul's symbolized striving is much more open-ended than is the attempt of a spider to spin a web, as the paradoxical language ("surrounded, detached," "ductile anchor") implies. *Can* the human soul connect the celestial spheres?

QUESTIONS

1. In "The Hound" (No. 43) Robert Francis compares unpredictable human life to a hound. Whitman compares the striving human soul to a spider. Why is Francis's comparison a metaphor and Whitman's a symbol? What additional comparison does Whitman make to the soul's quest? What figure of speech is it?
2. In what ways are the spider and the soul contrasted? What do the contrasts contribute to the meaning of the symbol?
3. Can the questing soul represent human actions other than the search for spiritual certainties?

61. The Sick Rose

O Rose, thou art sick!
The invisible worm
That flies in the night,
In the howling storm,

Has found out thy bed
Of crimson joy,
And his dark secret love
Does thy life destroy.

William Blake (1757–1827)

QUESTIONS

1. What figures of speech do you find in the poem in addition to symbol? How do they contribute to its force or meaning?
2. Several symbolic interpretations of this poem are given below. Do you think of others?
3. Should symbolic meanings be sought for the night and the storm? If so, what meanings would you suggest?

In "A Noiseless Patient Spider" the symbolic meaning of the spider is identified and named. By contrast, in "The Sick Rose" no meanings are explicitly indicated for the rose and the worm. Indeed, we are not *compelled* to assign them specific meanings. The poem is validly read as being about a rose that has been attacked on a stormy night by a cankerworm.

The organization of "The Sick Rose" is so rich, however, and its language so powerful that the rose and the worm refuse to remain *merely* a flower and an insect. The rose, apostrophized and personified in the first line, has traditionally been a symbol of feminine beauty and of love, as well as of sensual pleasures. "Bed" can refer to a woman's bed as well as to a flower bed. "Crimson joy" suggests the intense pleasure of passionate lovemaking as well as the brilliant beauty of a red flower. The "dark secret love" of the "invisible worm" is more strongly suggestive of a concealed or illicit love affair than of the feeding of a cankerworm on a plant, though it fits that too. For all these reasons the rose almost immediately suggests a woman and the worm her secret lover—and the poem suggests the corruption of innocent but physical love by concealment and deceit. But the possibilities do not stop there. The worm is a common symbol or metonymy for death; and for readers steeped in Milton (as Blake was) it recalls the "undying worm" of *Paradise Lost*, Milton's metaphor for the snake (or Satan in the form of a snake) that tempted Eve. Meanings multiply also for the reader who is familiar with Blake's other writings. Thus "The Sick Rose" has been variously interpreted as referring to the destruction of joyous physical love by jealousy, deceit, concealment, or the possessive instinct; of innocence by experience; of humanity by Satan; of imagination and joy by analytic reason; of life by death. We cannot say what specifically the poet had in mind, nor need we do so. A symbol defines an *area* of meaning, and any interpretation that falls within that area is permissible. In Blake's poem the rose stands for something beautiful, or desirable, or good. The worm stands for some corrupting agent. Within these limits, the meaning is largely "open." And because the meaning is open, the reader is justified in bringing personal experience to its interpretation. Blake's poem, for instance, might remind someone of a gifted friend whose promise has been destroyed by drug addiction.

Between the extremes exemplified by "A Noiseless Patient Spider" and "The Sick Rose" a poem may exercise all degrees of control over the range and meaning of its symbolism. Consider another example.

62. You, Andrew Marvell

And here face down beneath the sun
And here upon earth's noonward height
To feel the always coming on
The always rising of the night:

To feel creep up the curving east
The earthly chill of dusk and slow
Upon those under lands the vast
And ever-climbing shadow grow

And strange at Ecbatan the trees
Take leaf by leaf the evening strange
The flooding dark about their knees
The mountains over Persia change

And now at Kermanshah the gate
Dark empty and the withered grass
And through the twilight now the late
Few travelers in the westward pass

And Baghdad darken and the bridge
Across the silent river gone
And through Arabia the edge
Of evening widen and steal on

And deepen on Palmyra's street
The wheel rut in the ruined stone
And Lebanon fade out and Crete
High through the clouds and overblown

And over Sicily the air
Still flashing with the landward gulls
And loom and slowly disappear
The sails above the shadowy hulls

And Spain go under and the shore
Of Africa the gilded sand
And evening vanish and no more
The low pale light across that land

Nor now the long light on the sea:
And here face downward in the sun
To feel how swift how secretly
The shadow of the night comes on . . .

Archibald MacLeish (1892–1982)

QUESTIONS

1. We ordinarily speak of *nightfall*. Why does MacLeish speak of the "rising" of the night? What implicit metaphorical comparison is suggested by phrases like "rising of the night" (4), "the flooding dark" (11), "the bridge / Across the silent river gone" (17–18), "deepen on Palmyra's street" (21), "Spain go under" (29), and so on?
2. Does the comparative lack of punctuation serve any function? What is the effect of the repetition of "and" throughout the poem?
3. Ecbatan was founded in 700 B.C. and is associated in history with Cyrus the Great, founder of the Persian Empire, and with Alexander the Great. Kermanshah was another ancient city of Persia. Where are Baghdad, Palmyra, Lebanon, Crete?

On the literal level, "You, Andrew Marvell" is about the coming on of night. The speaker, lying at noon full length in the sun somewhere in the United States,* pictures in his mind the earth's shadow, halfway around the world, moving silently westward over Persia, Syria, Crete, Sicily, Spain, Africa, and finally the Atlantic—approaching swiftly, in fact, the place where he himself lies. But the title of the poem tells us that, though particularly concerned with the passage of a day, it is more generally concerned with the swift passage of time; for the title is an allusion to a famous poem on this subject by Andrew Marvell ("To His Coy Mistress," No. 53) and especially to two lines of that poem:

But at my back I always hear
Time's wingèd chariot hurrying near.

Once we are aware of this larger concern of the poem, two symbolic levels of interpretation open to us. Marvell's poem is primarily concerned with the swift passing of man's life; and the word *night*, we know from our experience with other literature, is a natural and traditional metaphor or symbol for death. Thus, the speaker in "You, Andrew Marvell" is thinking not only about the passing of a day but also about the passing of his life. He is at present "upon earth's noonward height"—

*MacLeish has identified the fixed location of the poem as Illinois on the shore of Lake Michigan.

in the full flush of manhood — but he is acutely conscious of the declining years ahead and of "how swift how secretly" his death comes on.

If we are to account fully for all the data of the poem, however, a third level of interpretation is necessary. What has dictated the poet's choice of geographical references? The places named, of course, progress from east to west; but they have a further linking characteristic. Ecbatan, Kermanshah, Baghdad, and Palmyra are all ancient or ruined cities, the relics of past empires and crumbled civilizations. Lebanon, Crete, Sicily, Spain, and North Africa are places where civilization once flourished more vigorously than it does at present. On a third level, then, the poet is concerned, not with the passage of a day nor with the passage of a lifetime, but with the passage of historical epochs. The poet's own country — the United States — now shines "upon earth's noonward height" as a favored nation in the sun of history, but its civilization, too, will pass.

Meanings ray out from a symbol, like the corona around the sun or like connotations around a richly suggestive word. But the very fact that a symbol may be so rich in meanings requires that we use the greatest tact in its interpretation. Although Blake's "The Sick Rose" might, because of personal association, remind us of a friend destroyed by drug addiction, it would be unwise to say that Blake uses the rose to symbolize a gifted person succumbing to drug addiction, for this interpretation is private, idiosyncratic, and narrow. The poem allows it, but does not itself suggest it.

Moreover, we should never assume that because the meaning of a symbol is more or less open, we may make it mean anything we choose. We would be wrong, for instance, in interpreting the choice in "The Road Not Taken" as some choice between good and evil, for the poem tells us that the two roads are much alike and that both lie "in leaves no step had trodden black." Whatever the choice is, it is a choice between two goods. Whatever our interpretation of a symbolic poem, it must be tied firmly to the facts of the poem. We must not let loose of the string and let our imaginations go ballooning up among the clouds. Because the symbol is capable of adding so many dimensions to a poem, it is a peculiarly effective resource for the poet, but it is also peculiarly susceptible to misinterpretation by the incautious reader.

Accurate interpretation of the symbol requires delicacy, tact, and good sense. The reader must maintain balance while walking a tightrope between too little and too much — between underinterpretation and overinterpretation. If the reader falls off, however, it is much more desirable to fall off on the side of too little. Someone who reads "The Road Not Taken" as being only about a choice between two roads in a wood has at least understood part of the experience that the poem communicates, but the reader who reads into it anything imaginable might as well discard the poem and simply daydream.

Above all, we should avoid the disease of seeing symbols everywhere, like a person with hallucinations, whether there are symbols there or not. It is better to miss a symbol now and then than to walk constantly among shadows and mirages.

63. To the Virgins, to Make Much of Time

Gather ye rosebuds while ye may,
  Old Time is still a-flying;
And this same flower that smiles today
  Tomorrow will be dying.

The glorious lamp of heaven, the Sun,
  The higher he's a-getting,
The sooner will his race be run,
  And nearer he's to setting.

That age is best which is the first,
  When youth and blood are warmer;
But being spent, the worse, and worst
  Times still succeed the former.

Then be not coy, but use your time;
  And while ye may, go marry;
For having lost but once your prime,
  You may forever tarry.

Robert Herrick (1591–1674)

QUESTIONS

1. The first two stanzas might be interpreted literally if the third and fourth stanzas did not force us to interpret them symbolically. What do the rosebuds symbolize (stanza 1)? What does the course of a day symbolize (stanza 2)? Does the poet narrow the meaning of the rosebud symbol in the last stanza or merely name *one* of its specific meanings?
2. How does the title help us interpret the meaning of the symbol? Why is "virgins" a more meaningful word than, for example, *maidens*?
3. Why is such haste necessary in gathering the rosebuds? True, the blossoms die quickly, but they are replaced by others. Who *really* is dying?
4. What are "the worse, and worst" times (11)? Why?
5. Why is the wording of the poem better than these possible alternatives: *blooms* for "smiles" (3), *course* for "race" (7), *used* for "spent" (11), *spend* for "use" (13)?

Allegory is a narrative or description that has a second meaning beneath the surface. Although the surface story or description may have its own interest, the author's major interest is in the ulterior meaning. When Pharaoh in the Bible, for instance, has a dream in which seven fat kine are devoured by seven lean kine, the story does not really become significant until Joseph interprets its allegorical meaning: that Egypt is to enjoy seven years of fruitfulness and prosperity followed by seven years of famine. Allegory has been defined sometimes as an extended metaphor and sometimes as a series of related symbols. But it is usually distinguishable from both of these. It is unlike extended metaphor in that it involves a *system* of related comparisons rather than one comparison drawn out. It differs from symbolism in that it puts less emphasis on the images for their own sake and more on their ulterior meanings. Also, these meanings are more fixed. In allegory there is usually a one-to-one correspondence between the details and a single set of ulterior meanings. In complex allegories the details may have more than one meaning, but these meanings tend to be definite. Meanings do not ray out from allegory as they do from a symbol.

Allegory is less popular in modern literature than it was in medieval and Renaissance writing, and it is much less often found in short poems than in long narrative works such as *The Faerie Queene*, *Everyman*, and *Pilgrim's Progress*. It has sometimes, especially with political allegory, been used to disguise meaning rather than reveal it (or, rather, to disguise it from some people while revealing it to others). Though less rich than the symbol, allegory is an effective way of making the abstract concrete and has occasionally been used effectively even in fairly short poems.

64. Peace

Sweet Peace, where dost thou dwell? I humbly crave,
Let me once know.
I sought thee in a secret cave,
And asked if Peace were there.
A hollow wind did seem to answer, "No,
Go seek elsewhere."

I did, and going did a rainbow note.
"Surely," thought I,
"This is the lace of Peace's coat;
I will search out the matter."
But while I looked, the clouds immediately
Did break and scatter.

Then went I to a garden, and did spy
A gallant flower,
The Crown Imperial. "Sure," said I,
"Peace at the root must dwell."
But when I digged, I saw a worm devour
What showed so well.

At length I met a reverend good old man,
Whom when for Peace
I did demand, he thus began:
"There was a prince of old
At Salem dwelt, who lived with good increase
Of flock and fold.

"He sweetly lived; yet sweetness did not save
His life from foes.
But after death out of his grave
There sprang twelve stalks of wheat;
Which many wondering at, got some of those
To plant and set.

"It prospered strangely, and did soon disperse
Through all the earth,
For they that taste it do rehearse
That virtue lies therein,
A secret virtue, bringing peace and mirth
By flight of sin.

"Take of this grain, which in my garden grows,
And grows for you;
Make bread of it; and that repose
And peace, which everywhere
With so much earnestness you do pursue,
Is only there."

George Herbert (1593–1633)

QUESTIONS

1. Vocabulary: *gallant* (14), *rehearse* (33), *virtue* (34). "Crown Imperial" (15) is a garden flower, fritillary; "Salem" (23) is Jerusalem.
2. Identify the "prince" (22), his "flock and fold" (24), the "twelve stalks of wheat" (28), the "grain" (37), and the "bread" (39).
3. Should the "secret cave" (stanza 1), the "rainbow" (stanza 2), and the "flower garden" (stanza 3) be understood merely as places where the speaker searched or do they have more precise meanings?
4. Who is the "reverend good old man" (19), and what is *his* garden (37)?

* * *

65. Fire and Ice

Some say the world will end in fire,
Some say in ice.
From what I've tasted of desire
I hold with those who favor fire.

But if it had to perish twice,
I think I know enough of hate
To say that for destruction ice
Is also great
And would suffice.

Robert Frost (1874–1963)

QUESTIONS

1. Who are "some" (1–2)? To what two theories do lines 1–2 refer? (In answering, it might help you to know that the poem was published in 1920.)
2. What do "fire" and "ice" respectively symbolize? What two meanings has "the world"?
3. The poem ends with an *understatement* (see Chapter 7). How does it affect the tone of the poem?

66. Sea-Fever

I must go down to the seas again, to the lonely sea and the sky,
And all I ask is a tall ship and a star to steer her by,
And the wheel's kick and the wind's song and the white sail's shaking,
And a gray mist on the sea's face and a gray dawn breaking.

I must go down to the seas again, for the call of the running tide
Is a wild call and a clear call that may not be denied;
And all I ask is a windy day with the white clouds flying,
And the flung spray and the blown spume, and the sea-gulls crying.

I must go down to the seas again, to the vagrant gypsy life,
To the gull's way and the whale's way where the wind's like a whetted knife;
And all I ask is a merry yarn from a laughing fellow-rover,
And quiet sleep and a sweet dream when the long trick's over.

John Masefield (1878–1967)

QUESTIONS

1. The prose statement made by this poem might be expressed thus: "A man who has been a sailor and known the sea feels forever afterwards a desire to return to the life of ships and sailing." What are some of the means Masefield employs to transform this information into poetry?
2. Is the last line entirely literal, or does it suggest more than it expressly states? What is "the long trick"?

67. Ulysses

It little profits that an idle king,
By this still hearth, among these barren crags,
Matched with an agèd wife, I mete and dole
Unequal laws unto a savage race,
That hoard, and sleep, and feed, and know not me.
I cannot rest from travel; I will drink
Life to the lees. All times I have enjoyed
Greatly, have suffered greatly, both with those
That loved me, and alone; on shore, and when
Through scudding drifts the rainy Hyades
Vext the dim sea. I am become a name;
For always roaming with a hungry heart
Much have I seen and known,—cities of men,
And manners, climates, councils, governments,
Myself not least, but honored of them all;
And drunk delight of battle with my peers,
Far on the ringing plains of windy Troy.
I am a part of all that I have met;
Yet all experience is an arch wherethrough
Gleams that untraveled world, whose margin fades
For ever and for ever when I move.
How dull it is to pause, to make an end,
To rust unburnished, not to shine in use!
As though to breathe were life! Life piled on life
Were all too little, and of one to me
Little remains; but every hour is saved
From that eternal silence, something more,
A bringer of new things; and vile it were
For some three suns to store and hoard myself,
And this gray spirit yearning in desire
To follow knowledge like a sinking star,
Beyond the utmost bound of human thought.

This is my son, mine own Telemachus,
To whom I leave the scepter and the isle—
Well-loved of me, discerning to fulfil
This labor, by slow prudence to make mild
A rugged people, and through soft degrees
Subdue them to the useful and the good.
Most blameless is he, centered in the sphere
Of common duties, decent not to fail
In offices of tenderness, and pay
Meet adoration to my household gods,
When I am gone. He works his work, I mine.

There lies the port; the vessel puffs her sail:
There gloom the dark, broad seas. My mariners,
Souls that have toiled, and wrought, and thought with me—
That ever with a frolic welcome took
The thunder and the sunshine, and opposed
Free hearts, free foreheads—you and I are old;
Old age hath yet his honor and his toil.
Death closes all; but something ere the end,
Some work of noble note, may yet be done,
Not unbecoming men that strove with Gods.
The lights begin to twinkle from the rocks;
The long day wanes; the slow moon climbs; the deep
Moans round with many voices. Come, my friends,
'Tis not too late to seek a newer world.
Push off, and sitting well in order smite
The sounding furrows; for my purpose holds
To sail beyond the sunset, and the baths
Of all the western stars, until I die.
It may be that the gulfs will wash us down;
It may be we shall touch the Happy Isles,
And see the great Achilles, whom we knew.
Though much is taken, much abides; and though
We are not now that strength which in old days
Moved earth and heaven, that which we are, we are:
One equal temper of heroic hearts,
Made weak by time and fate, but strong in will
To strive, to seek, to find, and not to yield.

Alfred, Lord Tennyson (1809–1892)

QUESTIONS

1. Vocabulary: *lees* (7), *Hyades* (10), *meet* (42).
2. Ulysses, king of Ithaca, is a legendary Greek hero, a major figure in Homer's *Iliad*, the hero of Homer's *Odyssey*, and a minor figure in Dante's *Divine Comedy*. After ten years at the siege of Troy, Ulysses set sail for home but, having incurred the wrath of the god of the sea, he was subjected to storms and vicissitudes and was forced to wander for another ten years, having many adventures and seeing most of the Mediterranean world before again reaching Ithaca, his wife, and his son. Once back home, according to Dante, he still wished to travel and "to follow virtue and knowledge." In Tennyson's poem, Ulysses is represented as about to set sail on a final voyage from which he will not return. Locate Ithaca on a map. Where exactly, in geographical terms, does Ulysses intend to sail (59–64)? (The Happy Isles were the Elysian fields, or Greek paradise; Achilles was another Greek prince, the hero of the *Iliad*, who was killed at the siege of Troy.)

3. Ulysses's speech is divided into three sections, beginning at lines 1, 33, and 44. What is the topic or purpose of each section? To whom, specifically, is the third section addressed? To whom, would you infer, are sections 1 and 2 addressed? Where do you visualize Ulysses as standing during his speech?
4. Characterize Ulysses. What kind of person is he as Tennyson represents him?
5. What way of life is symbolized by Ulysses? Find as many evidences as you can that Ulysses's desire for travel represents something more than mere wanderlust and wish for adventure.
6. Give two symbolic implications of the westward direction of Ulysses's journey.
7. Interpret lines 18–21 and 26–29. What metaphor is implied in line 23? What is symbolized by "the thunder and the sunshine" (48)? What do the two metonymies in line 49 stand for?

68. Curiosity

may have killed the cat; more likely
the cat was just unlucky, or else curious
to see what death was like, having no cause
to go on licking paws, or fathering
litter on litter of kittens, predictably.

Nevertheless, to be curious
is dangerous enough. To distrust
what is always said, what seems,
to ask odd questions, interfere in dreams,
leave home, smell rats, have hunches
do not endear cats to those doggy circles
where well-smelt baskets, suitable wives, good lunches
are the order of things, and where prevails
much wagging of incurious heads and tails.

Face it. Curiosity
will not cause us to die—
only lack of it will.
Never to want to see
the other side of the hill
or that improbable country
where living is an idyll
(although a probable hell)
would kill us all.
Only the curious
have, if they live, a tale
worth telling at all.

Dogs say cats love too much, are irresponsible,
are changeable, marry too many wives,

desert their children, chill all dinner tables
with tales of their nine lives.
Well, they are lucky. Let them be
nine-lived and contradictory,
curious enough to change, prepared to pay
the cat price, which is to die
and die again and again,
each time with no less pain.
A cat minority of one
is all that can be counted on
to tell the truth. And what cats have to tell
on each return from hell
is this: that dying is what the living do,
that dying is what the loving do,
and that dead dogs are those who do not know
that dying is what, to live, each has to do.

Alastair Reid (b. 1926)

QUESTIONS

1. On the surface this poem is a dissertation on cats. What deeper comments does it make? Of what are cats and dogs, in this poem, symbols?
2. In what different senses are the words "death," "die," and "dying" here used?
3. Compare and contrast this poem in meaning and manner with "Ulysses."

69. Discovery of the New World

The creatures that we met this morning
marveled at our green skins
and scarlet eyes.
They lack antennae
and can't be made to grasp
your proclamation that they are
our lawful food and prey and slaves,
nor can they seem to learn
their body-space is needed to materialize
our oxygen absorbers—
which they conceive are breathing
and thinking creatures whom they implore
at first as angels or (later) as devils
when they are being snuffed out
by an absorber swelling
into their space.

Their history bled from one this morning
while we were tasting his brain
in holographic rainbows
which we assembled into quite an interesting
set of legends—
that's all it came to, though
the colors were quite lovely before we
poured them into our time;
the blue shift bleached away
meaningless circumstance and they would not fit
any of our truth-matrices—
there was, however,
a curious visual echo in their history
of our own coming to their earth;
a certain General Sherman
had said concerning a group of them
exactly what we were saying to you
about these creatures:
it is our destiny to asterize this planet,
and they will not be asterized,
so they must be wiped out.
We need their space and oxygen
which they do not know how to use,
yet they will not give up their gas unforced,
and we feel sure,
whatever our "agreements" made this morning,
we'll have to kill them all:
the more we cook this orbit,
the fewer next time around.
We've finished burning all their crops
and killed their cattle.
They'll have to come into our pens
and then we'll get to study
the way our heart attacks and cancers spread among them,
since they seem not immune to these.
If we didn't have this mission it might be sad
to see such helpless creatures die,
but never fear,
the riches of this place are ours
and worth whatever pain others may have to feel.
We'll soon have it cleared
as in fact it is already, at the poles.
Then we will be safe, and rich, and happy here forever.

Carter Revard (b. 1931)

QUESTIONS

1. Vocabulary: *Asterize* (35) is a word coined from the common prefix *aster-* or *astro-*; what would you surmise it to mean? "Materialize / our oxygen absorbers" (9–10) and "truth-matrices" (27) are similarly devised terms whose meanings you should easily infer. What does the poem gain from this stretching of normal language?
2. Who (or what) is the speaker? Who (or what) is being addressed, and for what purpose?
3. "A certain General Sherman," some of whose attitudes are adapted beginning in line 35, was William Tecumseh Sherman (1820–1891), the Union general who after the Civil War was sent on a mission to control the native Americans in the West. Sherman was both praised and criticized for his accomplishment but took pride in having confined so many "Indians" to reservations. How does this poem allegorize that aspect of American history?
4. Does this allegory have meaning beyond its reflection of history and its fanciful imagination of a future?

70. Hymn to God My God, in My Sickness

Since I am coming to that holy room
  Where, with thy choir of saints for evermore,
I shall be made thy music, as I come
  I tune the instrument here at the door,
  And what I must do then, think now before.

Whilst my physicians by their love are grown
  Cosmographers, and I their map, who lie
Flat on this bed, that by them may be shown
  That this is my southwest discovery,
  Per fretum febris,° by these straits to die,   through the raging of fever

I joy that in these straits I see my west;
  For though those currents yield return to none,
What shall my west hurt me? As west and east
  In all flat maps (and I am one) are one,
  So death doth touch the resurrectiön.

Is the Pacific Sea my home? Or are
  The eastern riches? Is Jerusalem?
Anyan° and Magellan and Gibraltar,   Bering Strait
  All straits, and none but straits, are ways to them,
  Whether where Japhet dwelt, or Cham, or Shem.

We think that Paradise and Calvary,
  Christ's cross and Adam's tree, stood in one place;

Look, Lord, and find both Adams met in me;
As the first Adam's sweat surrounds my face,
May the last Adam's blood my soul embrace.

So, in his purple wrapped receive me, Lord;
By these his thorns give me his other crown;
And as to others' souls I preached thy word,
Be this my text, my sermon to mine own:
Therefore that he may raise, the Lord throws down.

John Donne (1572–1631)

QUESTIONS

1. Vocabulary: *cosmographers* (7).
2. For the last ten years of his life John Donne was Dean of St. Paul's Cathedral in London, and he is famous for his sermons (see lines 28–30) as well as his poems. According to his earliest biographer (though some scholars disagree), this poem was written eight days before Donne's death. What are "that holy room" (1) and "the instrument" (4)? What is the speaker doing in stanza 1?
3. During Donne's lifetime such explorers as Henry Hudson and Martin Frobisher sought for a Northwest Passage to the East Indies to match Magellan's discovery in 1520 of a southwest passage through the straits that bear his name. Why is "southwest" more appropriate to the speaker's condition than "northwest"? In what ways is his raging fever like a strait? What different meanings of the word "straits" (10) are operative here? What do the straits symbolize?
4. In what ways does the speaker's body resemble a map?
5. Although the map is metaphorical, its parts are symbolic. What does the west symbolize? The east? The fact that west and east are one?
6. What meanings has the word "return" (12)? (Compare line 17.)
7. Japhet, Cham (or Ham), and Shem (20)—the sons of Noah—are in Christian legend the ancestors of the three races of man, roughly identifiable with the populations of Europe, Africa, and Asia. What must one go through, according to the speaker, to reach any place important? In what ways are the Pacific Ocean, the East Indies, and Jerusalem (16–17) each a fitting symbol for the speaker's own destination?
8. The locations of the garden of Eden and of Calvary (21) were identical according to early Christian scholars. How does this tie in with the poem's geographical symbolism? What connection is there between Adam's "sweat" (24) and Christ's "blood" (25)? Because Adam is said in the Bible to prefigure Christ (Romans 5:12–21), Christ is sometimes called the second Adam. How do the two Adams meet in the speaker? What do blood and sweat (together and separately) symbolize?
9. For what are "eastern riches" (17), "his purple" (26), and "his thorns" (27) respectively metonymies? What do "purple" and "thorns" symbolize? What is Christ's "other crown" (27)?

10. With what earlier paradoxes (see Chapter 7) in the poem does the paradox in the final line (very roughly paraphrased from Psalms 146:8) tie in? How does the poem explain human suffering and give it meaning?

71. Our journey had advanced

Our journey had advanced.
Our feet were almost come
To that odd fork in Being's road
"Eternity" by term.

Our pace took sudden awe.
Our feet reluctant led.
Before were cities, but between
The forest of the dead.

Retreat was out of hope,
Behind, a sealed route,
"Eternity's" white flag before,
And God at every gate.

Emily Dickinson (1830–1886)

QUESTIONS

1. Identify the "journey" (1), the "road" (3), the "forest" (8), and the speaker's destination in this allegory. What literal human experience is the subject of the poem?
2. Explain the implications of the plural forms: "our" (1–2, 3–4), "cities" (7), "every gate" (12).
3. What is the underlying metaphor implied in the last stanza by "retreat" (9), "flag" (11), "gate" (12)? Does the "white flag" signify surrender?

72. Dust of Snow

The way a crow
Shook down on me
The dust of snow
From a hemlock tree

Has given my heart
A change of mood
And saved some part
Of a day I had rued.

Robert Frost (1874–1963)

73. Soft Snow

I walked abroad in a snowy day;
I asked the soft snow with me to play;
She played and she melted in all her prime,
And the winter called it a dreadful crime.

William Blake (1757–1827)

QUESTION

In what respects are the two preceding poems alike? In what respects are they essentially different?

EXERCISES

1. Determine whether "sleep," in the following poems, is literal, a symbol, or a metaphor (or simile).
   a. "Stopping by Woods on a Snowy Evening" (No. 104)
   b. "The Chimney Sweeper" (No. 78)
   c. "Is my team plowing" (No. 14)
   d. "The Second Coming" (No. 303)
2. Shapiro's "The Fly" (No. 276) and Shaw's "Shut In" (No. 277) deal with a common subject. Which of them is symbolic? Explain your choice.
3. What does Blake's tiger symbolize (No. 209)?
4. Determine whether the following poems are predominantly symbolic or literal.
   a. "Because I could not stop for Death" (No. 217)
   b. "The Snow Man" (No. 286)
   c. "The Darkling Thrush" (No. 234)
   d. "Song: Go and catch a falling star" (No. 222)
   e. "Blackberry Eating" (No. 245)
   f. "Musée des Beaux Arts" (No. 204)
   g. "Richard Cory" (No. 271)
   h. "The Wild Swans at Coole" (No. 304)
   i. "Poem: As the cat" (No. 298)
   j. "To Waken an Old Lady" (No. 299)
   k. "Desert Places" (No. 228)
   l. "Never Again Would Birds' Song Be the Same" (No. 230)
   m. "Constantly risking absurdity" (No. 225)

CHAPTER SEVEN

Figurative Language 3

Paradox, Overstatement, Understatement, Irony

Aesop tells the tale of a traveler who sought refuge with a Satyr on a bitter winter night. On entering the Satyr's lodging, he blew on his fingers, and was asked by the Satyr why he did it. "To warm them up," he explained. Later, on being served a piping hot bowl of porridge, he blew also on it, and again was asked why he did it. "To cool it off," he explained. The Satyr thereupon thrust him out of doors, for he would have nothing to do with a man who could blow hot and cold with the same breath.

A **paradox** is an apparent contradiction that is nevertheless somehow true. It may be either a situation or a statement. Aesop's tale of the traveler illustrates a paradoxical situation. As a figure of speech, paradox is a statement. When Alexander Pope wrote that a literary critic of his time would "damn with faint praise," he was using a verbal paradox, for how can a man damn by praising?

When we understand all the conditions and circumstances involved in a paradox, we find that what at first seemed impossible is actually entirely plausible and not strange at all. The paradox of the cold hands and hot porridge is not strange to anyone who knows that a stream of air directed upon an object of different temperature will tend to bring that object closer to its own temperature. And Pope's paradox is not strange when we realize that *damn* is being used figuratively, and that Pope means only that a too reserved praise may damage an author with the public almost as much as adverse criticism. In a paradoxical statement the contradiction usually stems from one of the words being used figuratively or in more than one sense.

The value of paradox is its shock value. Its seeming impossibility startles the reader into attention and, by the fact of its apparent absurdity, underscores the truth of what is being said.

74. Much madness is divinest sense

Much madness is divinest sense
To a discerning eye,
Much sense, the starkest madness.
'Tis the majority
In this, as all, prevail:
Assent, and you are sane;
Demur, you're straightway dangerous
And handled with a chain.

Emily Dickinson (1830–1886)

QUESTIONS

1. This poem presents the two sides of a paradoxical proposition: that insanity is good sense, and that good sense is insane. How do the concepts implied by the words "discerning" (2) and "majority" (4) provide the resolution of this paradox?
2. How do we know that the speaker does not believe that the majority is correct? How do the last five lines extend the subject beyond a contrast between sanity and insanity?

Overstatement, understatement, and verbal irony form a continuous series, for they consist, respectively, of saying more, saying less, and saying the opposite of what one really means.

Overstatement, or *hyperbole*, is simply exaggeration, but exaggeration in the service of truth. It is not the same as a fish story. If you say, "I'm starved!" or "You could have knocked me over with a feather!" or "I'll die if I don't pass this course!" you do not expect to be taken literally; you are merely adding emphasis to what you really mean. (And if you say, "There were literally millions of people at the beach!" you are merely piling one overstatement on top of another, for you really mean, "There were figuratively millions of people at the beach," or, literally, "The beach was very crowded.") Like all figures of speech, overstatement may be used with a variety of effects. It may be humorous or grave, fanciful or restrained, convincing or unconvincing. When Tennyson says of his eagle (No. 1) that it is "*Close* to the sun in lonely lands," he says what appears to be literally true, though we know from our study of astronomy that it is not. When Wordsworth reports of his golden daffodils in "I wandered lonely as a cloud" (No. 20) that they "stretched *in never-ending line*" along the margin of a bay, he too reports faithfully a visual appearance. When Frost says, at the conclusion of "The Road Not Taken" (No. 59),

> I shall be telling this with a sigh
> Somewhere *ages and ages hence,*

we are scarcely aware of the overstatement, so quietly is the assertion made. Unskillfully used, however, overstatement may seem strained and ridiculous, leading us to react as Gertrude does to the player-queen's speeches in *Hamlet*: "The lady doth protest too much."

It is paradoxical that one can emphasize a truth either by overstating it or by understating it. **Understatement**, or saying less than one means, may exist in what one says or merely in how one says it. If, for instance, upon sitting down to a loaded dinner plate, you say, "This looks like a nice snack," you are actually stating less than the truth; but if you say, with Artemus Ward, that a man who holds his hand for half an hour in a lighted fire will experience "a sensation of excessive and disagreeable warmth," you are stating what is literally true but with a good deal less force than the situation warrants.

75. The Sun Rising

Busy old fool, unruly sun,
Why dost thou thus
Through windows and through curtains call on us?
Must to thy motions lovers' seasons run?
Saucy pedantic wretch, go chide
Late schoolboys and sour 'prentices,
Go tell court-huntsmen that the king will ride,
Call country ants to harvest offices;
Love, all alike, no season knows, nor clime,
Nor hours, days, months, which are the rags of time.

Thy beams so reverend and strong
Why shouldst thou think?
I could eclipse and cloud them with a wink,
But that I would not lose her sight so long;
If her eyes have not blinded thine,
Look, and tomorrow late tell me
Whether both th' Indias of spice and mine
Be where thou left'st them, or lie here with me.
Ask for those kings whom thou saw'st yesterday,
And thou shalt hear, "All here in one bed lay."

She's all states, and all princes I;
Nothing else is.
Princes do but play us; compared to this,
All honor's mimic, all wealth alchemy.
Thou, sun, art half as happy as we,
In that the world's contracted thus;
Thine age asks ease, and since thy duties be
To warm the world, that's done in warming us.
Shine here to us, and thou art everywhere;
This bed thy center is, these walls thy sphere.

John Donne (1572–1631)

QUESTIONS

1. Vocabulary: *offices* (8), *alchemy* (24).
2. As precisely as possible, identify the time of day and the locale. What three "persons" does the poem involve?
3. What is the speaker's attitude toward the sun in stanzas 1 and 2? How and why does it change in stanza 3?
4. Does the speaker understate or overstate the actual qualities of the sun? Point out specific examples. Identify the overstatements in lines 9–10, 13, 15, 16–20, 21–24, 29–30. What do these overstatements achieve?
5. Line 17 introduces a geographical image referring to the East and West Indies, sources respectively of spices and gold. What relationship between the lovers and the rest of the world is expressed in lines 15–22?
6. Who is actually the intended listener for this extended apostrophe? What is the speaker's purpose? What is the poem's purpose?

76. Incident

Once riding in old Baltimore
Heart-filled, head-filled with glee,
I saw a Baltimorean
Keep looking straight at me.

Now I was eight and very small,
And he was no whit bigger,
And so I smiled, but he poked out
His tongue, and called me, "Nigger."

I saw the whole of Baltimore
From May until December;
Of all the things that happened there
That's all that I remember.

Countee Cullen (1903–1946)

QUESTION

What accounts for the effectiveness of the last stanza? Comment on the title. Is it in key with the meaning of the poem?

Like paradox, *irony* has meanings that extend beyond its use merely as a figure of speech.

Verbal irony, saying the opposite of what one means, is often confused with sarcasm and with satire, and for that reason it may be well to look at the meanings of all three terms. Sarcasm and satire both imply ridicule, one on the colloquial level, the other on the literary level. **Sarcasm** is simply bitter or cutting speech, intended to wound the feelings (it comes from a Greek word meaning to tear flesh). **Satire** is a more formal term, usually applied to written literature rather than to speech and ordinarily implying a higher motive: it is ridicule (either bitter or gentle) of human folly or vice, with the purpose of bringing about reform or at least of keeping other people from falling into similar folly or vice. Irony, on the other hand, is a literary device or figure that may be used in the service of sarcasm or ridicule or may not. It is popularly confused with sarcasm and satire because it is so often used as their tool; but irony may be used without either sarcastic or satirical intent, and sarcasm and satire may exist (though they do not usually) without irony. If, for instance, one of the members of your class raises his hand on the discussion of this point and says, "I don't understand," and your instructor replies, with a tone of heavy disgust in his voice, "Well, I wouldn't expect *you* to," he is being sarcastic but not ironic; he means exactly what he says. But if, after you have done particularly well on an examination, your instructor brings your test papers into the classroom saying, "Here's some *bad* news for you: you all got A's and B's!" he is being ironic but not sarcastic. Sarcasm, we may say, is cruel, as a bully is cruel: it intends to give hurt. Satire is both cruel and kind, as a surgeon is cruel and kind: it gives hurt in the interest of the patient or of society. Irony is neither cruel nor kind: it is simply a device, like a surgeon's scalpel, for performing any operation more skillfully.

Though verbal irony always implies the opposite of what is said, it has many gradations, and only in its simplest forms does it mean *only* the opposite of what is said. In more complex forms it means both what is said and the opposite of what is said, at once, though in different ways and with different degrees of emphasis. When Terence's critic, in "Terence, this is stupid stuff" (No. 10) says, "*Pretty* friendship 'tis to rhyme / Your friends to death before their time" (11–12), we may substitute the literal *sorry* for the ironic "pretty" with little or no loss of meaning. When Terence speaks in reply, however, of the pleasure of drunkenness — "And down in *lovely* muck I've lain, / Happy till I woke again" (35–36) — we cannot substitute *loathsome* for "lovely" without considerable loss of meaning, for, while muck is actually extremely unpleasant to lie in, it may *seem* lovely to an intoxicated person. Thus two meanings — one the opposite of the other — operate at once.

Like all figures of speech, verbal irony runs the danger of being misunderstood. With irony the risks are perhaps greater than with other figures, for if metaphor is misunderstood, the result may be simply bewilderment; but if irony is misunderstood, the reader goes away with exactly the opposite idea from what the user meant to convey. The results of misunderstanding if, for instance, you ironically called someone a villain, might be calamitous. For this reason the user of irony must be very skillful in its use, conveying by an altered tone, or by a wink of the eye or pen, that irony is intended; and the reader of literature must be always alert to recognize the subtle signs of irony.

No matter how broad or obvious the irony, a number of people in any large audience always will misunderstand. The humorist Artemus Ward used to protect himself against these people by writing at the bottom of his newspaper column, "This is writ ironical." But irony is most delightful and most effective when it is subtlest. It sets up a special understanding between writer and reader that may add either grace or force. If irony is too obvious, it sometimes seems merely crude. But if effectively used, it, like all figurative language, is capable of adding extra dimensions to meaning.

77. The Adversary

A mother's hardest to forgive.
Life is the fruit she longs to hand you,
Ripe on a plate. And while you live,
Relentlessly she understands you.

Phyllis McGinley (1905–1978)

QUESTION

What word in the poem is nearest to the title in its connotations?

The term *irony* always implies some sort of discrepancy or incongruity. In verbal irony the discrepancy is between what is said and what is meant. In other forms the discrepancy may be between appearance and reality or between expectation and fulfillment. These other forms of irony are, on the whole, more important resources for the poet than is verbal irony. Two types are especially important.

In **dramatic irony*** the discrepancy is not between what the speaker says and what the speaker means but between what the speaker says and what the poem means. The speaker's words may be perfectly straightforward, but the author, by putting these words in a particular speaker's mouth, may be indicating to the reader ideas or attitudes quite opposed to those the speaker is voicing. This form of irony is more complex than verbal irony and demands a more complex response from the reader. It may be used not only to convey attitudes but also to illuminate character, for the author who uses it is indirectly commenting not only upon the value of the ideas uttered but also upon the nature of the person who utters them. Such comment may be harsh, gently mocking, or sympathetic.

78. The Chimney Sweeper

When my mother died I was very young,
And my father sold me while yet my tongue
Could scarcely cry "'weep! 'weep! 'weep! 'weep!"
So your chimneys I sweep, and in soot I sleep.

There's little Tom Dacre, who cried when his head,
That curled like a lamb's back, was shaved; so I said,
"Hush, Tom! never mind it, for, when your head's bare,
You know that the soot cannot spoil your white hair."

And so he was quiet, and that very night,
As Tom was asleeping, he had such a sight!
That thousands of sweepers, Dick, Joe, Ned, and Jack,
Were all of them locked up in coffins of black.

*The term *dramatic irony*, which stems from Greek tragedy, often connotes something more specific and perhaps a little different from what I am developing here. It describes a speech or an action in a story that has much greater significance to the audience than to the character who speaks or performs it, because the audience possesses knowledge the character does not have, as when the enemies of Ulysses, in the *Odyssey*, wish good luck and success to a man who the reader knows is Ulysses himself in disguise, or as when Oedipus, in the play by Sophocles, bends every effort to discover the murderer of Laius so that he may avenge the death, not knowing, as the audience does, that Laius is the man whom he himself once slew. I have appropriated the term for a perhaps slightly different situation, because no other suitable term exists. Both uses have the common characteristic—that the author conveys to the reader something different, or at least something more, than the character himself intends or understands.

And by came an Angel who had a bright key,
And he opened the coffins and set them all free;
Then down a green plain leaping, laughing, they run,
And wash in a river, and shine in the sun.

Then naked and white, all their bags left behind,
They rise upon clouds and sport in the wind;
And the Angel told Tom, if he'd be a good boy,
He'd have God for his father, and never want joy.

And so Tom awoke, and we rose in the dark,
And got with our bags and our brushes to work.
Though the morning was cold, Tom was happy and warm;
So if all do their duty they need not fear harm.

William Blake (1757–1827)

QUESTIONS

1. In the eighteenth century small boys, sometimes no more than four or five years old, were employed to climb up the narrow chimney flues and clean them, collecting the soot in bags. Such boys, sometimes sold to the master sweepers by their parents, were miserably treated by their masters and often suffered disease and physical deformity. Characterize the boy who speaks in this poem. How do his and the poet's attitudes toward his lot in life differ? How, especially, are the meanings of the poet and the speaker different in lines 3, 7–8, and 24?
2. The dream in lines 11–20, besides being a happy dream, can be interpreted allegorically. Point out possible significances of the sweepers' being "locked up in coffins of black" (12) and the Angel's releasing them with a bright key to play upon green plains.

A third type of irony, **irony of situation**, occurs when a discrepancy exists between the actual circumstances and those that would seem appropriate or between what one anticipates and what actually comes to pass. If a man and his second wife, on the first night of their honeymoon, are accidentally seated at the theater next to the man's first wife, we should call the situation ironic. When, in O. Henry's famous short story "The Gift of the Magi" a poor young husband pawns his most prized possession, a gold watch, in order to buy his wife a set of combs for her hair for Christmas, and his wife sells her most prized possession, her long brown hair, in order to buy a fob for her husband's watch, we call the situation ironic. When King Midas, in the famous fable, is granted his fondest wish, that anything he touch turn to gold, and then finds that he cannot eat because even his food turns to gold, we call the situation

ironic. When Coleridge's Ancient Mariner finds himself in the middle of the ocean with "Water, water, everywhere," but not a "drop to drink," we call the situation ironic. In each case the circumstances are not what would seem appropriate or what we would expect.

Dramatic irony and irony of situation are powerful devices for poetry, for, like symbol, they enable a poem to suggest meanings without stating them — to communicate a great deal more than is said. We have seen one effective use of irony of situation in "The Widow's Lament in Springtime" (No. 39). Another is in "Ozymandias," which follows.

Irony and paradox may be trivial or powerful devices, depending on their use. At their worst they may degenerate into mere mannerism and mental habit. At their best they may greatly extend the dimensions of meaning in a work of literature. Because irony and paradox demand an exercise of critical intelligence, they are particularly valuable as safeguards against sentimentality.

79. Ozymandias

I met a traveler from an antique land
Who said: Two vast and trunkless legs of stone
Stand in the desert . . . Near them, on the sand,
Half sunk, a shattered visage lies, whose frown,
And wrinkled lip, and sneer of cold command,
Tell that its sculptor well those passions read
Which yet survive, stamped on these lifeless things,
The hand that mocked them, and the heart that fed;
And on the pedestal these words appear:
"My name is Ozymandias, king of kings;
Look on my works, ye Mighty, and despair!"
Nothing beside remains. Round the decay
Of that colossal wreck, boundless and bare
The lone and level sands stretch far away.

Percy Bysshe Shelley (1792–1822)

QUESTIONS

1. "Survive" (7) is a transitive verb with "hand" and "heart" as direct objects. Whose hand? Whose heart? What figure of speech is exemplified in "hand" and "heart"?
2. Characterize Ozymandias.
3. Ozymandias was an ancient Egyptian tyrant. This poem was first published in 1817. Of what is Ozymandias a *symbol*? What contemporary reference might the poem have had in Shelley's time?
4. What is the theme of the poem and how is it "stated"?

EXERCISE

Identify the figure in each of the following quotations as paradox, overstatement, understatement, or irony—and explain the use to which the figure is put (emotional emphasis, humor, satire, etc.).

1. Poetry is a language that tells us, through a more or less emotional reaction, something that cannot be said. *Edwin Arlington Robinson*
2. Christians have burnt each other, quite persuaded
   That all the Apostles would have done as they did. *Lord Byron*
3. A man who could make so vile a pun would not scruple to pick a pocket. *John Dennis*
4. Last week I saw a woman flayed, and you will hardly believe how much it altered her person for the worse. *Jonathan Swift*
5. . . . Where ignorance is bliss, / 'Tis folly to be wise. *Thomas Gray*
6. All night I made my bed to swim; with my tears I dissolved my couch. *Psalms 6:6*
7. Believe him, he has known the world too long,
   And seen the death of much immortal song. *Alexander Pope*
8. Cowards die many times before their deaths;
   The valiant never die but once. *William Shakespeare*
9. . . . all men would be cowards if they durst. *John Wilmot, Earl of Rochester*

* * *

80. Batter my heart, three-personed God

Batter my heart, three-personed God; for you
As yet but knock, breathe, shine, and seek to mend;
That I may rise and stand, o'erthrow me, and bend
Your force to break, blow, burn, and make me new.
I, like an usurped town, to another due,
Labor to admit you, but oh, to no end;
Reason, your viceroy in me, me should defend,
But is captived, and proves weak or untrue.
Yet dearly I love you and would be lovèd fain,° gladly
But am betrothed unto your enemy;
Divorce me, untie or break that knot again,
Take me to you, imprison me, for I,
Except° you enthrall me, never shall be free, unless
Nor ever chaste, except you ravish me.

John Donne (1572–1631)

QUESTIONS

1. In this sonnet (one in a group called "Holy Sonnets") the speaker addresses God in a series of metaphors and paradoxes. What is the paradox in the first

quatrain? To what is the "three-personed God" metaphorically compared? To what is the speaker compared? Can the first three verbs of the parallel lines 2 and 4 be taken as addressed to specific "persons" of the Trinity (Father, Son, Holy Spirit)? If so, to which are "knock" and "break" addressed? "breathe" and "blow"? "shine" and "burn"? (What concealed pun helps in the attribution of the last pair? What etymological pun in the attribution of the second pair?)

2. To what does the speaker compare himself in the second quatrain? To what is God compared? Who is the usurper? What role does Reason play in this political metaphor, and why is it a weak one?
3. To what does the speaker compare himself in the sestet (lines 9–14)? To what does he compare God? Who is the "enemy" (10)? Resolve the paradox in lines 12–13 by explaining the double meaning of "enthrall." Resolve the paradox in line 14 by explaining the double meaning of "ravish."

81. Sorting Laundry

Folding clothes,
I think of folding you
into my life.

Our king-sized sheets
like tablecloths
for the banquets of giants,

pillowcases, despite so many
washings, seams still
holding our dreams.

Towels patterned orange and green,
flowered pink and lavender,
gaudy, bought on sale,

reserved, we said, for the beach,
refusing, even after years,
to bleach into respectability.

So many shirts and skirts and pants
recycling week after week, head over heels
recapitulating themselves.

All those wrinkles
to be smoothed, or else
ignored; they're in style.

Myriad uncoupled socks
which went paired into the foam
like those creatures in the ark.

And what's shrunk
is tough to discard
even for Goodwill.

In pockets, surprises:
forgotten matches,
lost screws clinking on enamel;

paper clips, whatever they held
between shiny jaws, now
dissolved or clogging the drain;

well-washed dollars, legal tender
for all debts public and private,
intact despite agitation;

and, gleaming in the maelstrom,
one bright dime,
broken necklace of good gold

you brought from Kuwait,
the strangely tailored shirt
left by a former lover. . . .

If you were to leave me,
if I were to fold
only my own clothes,

the convexes and concaves
of my blouses, panties, stockings, bras
turned upon themselves,

a mountain of unsorted wash
could not fill
the empty side of the bed.

Elisavietta Ritchie (b. 1932)

QUESTIONS

1. Explain the metaphor in the first stanza. Where does the poem explicitly return to it? What psychological association connects line 41 to lines 42–43?
2. Explain how the length of the poem supports the overstatement in line 49. What is the speaker's attitude toward the "you" in the poem, and toward her role as housekeeper?

82. I'm Not Complaining

It isn't as if I never enjoyed good wine
or walked along the Hudson in moonlight,

I have poignant friends & a decent job,
I read good books even if they're about
miserable people but who's perfectly happy,
I didn't go hungry as a kid & I'm not constantly
oppressed by fascists, what if my apartment
never recovered from its ferocious beating,
no one ever said city life was easy, I admit
my hands turn to cardboard during love-making
& I often sweat through two wool blankets—
but anxiety is good for weight-loss, listen,
who isn't frightened of late night humming
in the walls, I don't live in a police state,
I own a passport & can travel even if I can't
afford to, almost everyone is insulted daily,
what if love is a sentence to hard labor &
last year I couldn't pay my taxes, I didn't
go to prison, yes, I've lost friends to alcohol
& cancer but life is an adventure & I enjoy
meeting new people, sure it's hard getting older
& mysteriously shorter but insomnia & depression
afflict even the rich & famous, okay, my folks
were stingy with affection & my pets didn't live long,
believe me, sympathy isn't what I'm after, I'm basically
almost happy, God in all His wisdom knows that at heart
I'm really not complaining . . .

Philip Schultz (b. 1945)

QUESTIONS

1. What is the function of the trite language? What speech impression results from the run-on sentences and use of "&"? Is it possible to infer a circumstance or setting for this speech?
2. Point out where the speaker is understating. What is the purpose of this poem?

83. The Unknown Citizen

(To JS/07/M/378 This Marble Monument Is Erected by the State)

He was found by the Bureau of Statistics to be
One against whom there was no official complaint,
And all the reports on his conduct agree
That, in the modern sense of an old-fashioned word, he was a saint,
For in everything he did he served the Greater Community.
Except for the War till the day he retired

He worked in a factory and never got fired,
But satisfied his employers, Fudge Motors Inc.
Yet he wasn't a scab or odd in his views,
For his Union reports that he paid his dues
(Our report on his Union shows it was sound),
And our Social Psychology workers found
That he was popular with his mates and liked a drink.
The Press are convinced that he bought a paper every day
And that his reactions to advertisements were normal in every way.
Policies taken out in his name prove that he was fully insured,
And his Health-card shows he was once in hospital but left it cured.
Both Producers Research and High-Grade Living declare
He was fully sensible to the advantages of the Installment Plan
And had everything necessary to the Modern Man,
A phonograph, a radio, a car and a frigidaire.
Our researchers into Public Opinion are content
That he held the proper opinions for the time of year;
When there was peace, he was for peace; when there was war, he went.
He was married and added five children to the population,
Which our Eugenist says was the right number for a parent of his
  generation,
And our teachers report that he never interfered with their education.
Was he free? Was he happy? The question is absurd:
Had anything been wrong, we should certainly have heard.

W. H. Auden (1907–1973)

QUESTIONS

1. Vocabulary: *scab* (9), *Eugenist* (26).
2. Explain the allusion and the irony in the title. Why was the citizen "unknown"?
3. This obituary of an unknown state "hero" was apparently prepared by a functionary of the state. Give an account of the citizen's life and character from Auden's own point of view.
4. What trends in modern life and social organization does the poem satirize?

84. Departmental

An ant on the tablecloth
Ran into a dormant moth
Of many times his size.
He showed not the least surprise.
His business wasn't with such.
He gave it scarcely a touch,
And was off on his duty run.

Yet if he encountered one
Of the hive's enquiry squad
Whose work is to find out God
And the nature of time and space,
He would put him onto the case.
Ants are a curious race;
One crossing with hurried tread
The body of one of their dead
Isn't given a moment's arrest—
Seems not even impressed.
But he no doubt reports to any
With whom he crosses antennae,
And they no doubt report
To the higher up at court.
Then word goes forth in Formic:
"Death's come to Jerry McCormic,
Our selfless forager Jerry.
Will the special Janizary
Whose office it is to bury
The dead of the commissary
Go bring him home to his people.
Lay him in state on a sepal.
Wrap him for shroud in a petal.
Embalm him with ichor of nettle.
This is the word of your Queen."
And presently on the scene
Appears a solemn mortician;
And taking formal position
With feelers calmly atwiddle,
Seizes the dead by the middle,
And heaving him high in air,
Carries him out of there.
No one stands round to stare.
It is nobody else's affair.

It couldn't be called ungentle.
But how thoroughly departmental.

Robert Frost (1874–1963)

QUESTIONS

1. Vocabulary: *dormant* (2), *Formic* (22), *Janizary* (25), *commissary* (27), *sepal* (29), *ichor* (31).
2. The poem is ostensibly about ants. Is it ultimately about ants? Give reasons to support your view that it is or is not.

3. What is the author's attitude toward the "departmental" organization of ant society? How is it indicated? Could this poem be described as "gently satiric"? If so, in what sense?
4. Compare and contrast this poem with "The Unknown Citizen" in content and manner.

85. The State

When they killed my mother it made me nervous;
I thought to myself, it was *right*:
Of course she was crazy, and how she ate!
And she died, after all, in her way, for the State.
But I minded: how queer it was to stare
At one of them not sitting there.

When they drafted Sister I said all night,
"It's healthier there in the fields";
And I'd think, "Now I'm helping to win the War,"
When the neighbors came in, as they did, with my meals.
And I was, I was; but I was scared
With only one of them sitting there.

When they took my cat for the Army Corps
Of Conservation and Supply,
I thought of him there in the cold with the mice
And I cried, and I cried, and I wanted to die.
They were there, and I saw them, and that is my life.
Now there's nothing. I'm dead, and I want to die.

Randall Jarrell (1914–1965)

QUESTIONS

1. Point out examples of overstatement and understatement. Do they create verbal irony, or dramatic irony? Resolve the paradox in line 18.
2. Compare the purpose of this poem to that of "The Unknown Citizen" and "Departmental." In what ways are they similar? In what ways are they dissimilar?

86. Mr. Z

Taught early that his mother's skin was the sign of error,
He dressed and spoke the perfect part of honor;
Won scholarships, attended the best schools,
Disclaimed kinship with jazz and spirituals;

Chose prudent, raceless views of each situation,
Or when he could not cleanly skirt dissension,
Faced up to the dilemma, firmly seized
Whatever ground was Anglo-Saxonized.

In diet, too, his practice was exemplary:
Of pork in its profane forms he was wary;
Expert in vintage wines, sauces and salads,
His palate shrank from cornbread, yams and collards.

He was as careful whom he chose to kiss:
His bride had somewhere lost her Jewishness,
But kept her blue eyes; an Episcopalian
Prelate proclaimed them matched chameleon.
Choosing the right addresses, here, abroad,
They shunned those places where they might be barred;
Even less anxious to be asked to dine
Where hosts catered to kosher accent or exotic skin.

And so he climbed, unclogged by ethnic weights,
An airborne plant, flourishing without roots.
Not one false note was struck—until he died:
His subtly grieving widow could have flayed
The obit writers, ringing crude changes on a clumsy phrase:
"One of the most distinguished members of his race."

M. Carl Holman (1919–1988)

QUESTIONS

1. Vocabulary: *profane* (10), *kosher* (20), *exotic* (20), *ethnic* (21), *obit* (25).
2. Explain Mr. Z's motivation and the strategies he used to achieve his goal.
3. What is the author's attitude toward Mr. Z? Is he satirizing him or the society that produced him? Why does he not give Mr. Z a name?
4. What judgments on Mr. Z are implied by the metaphors in lines 16 and 22? Explain them.
5. What kind of irony is operating in the last line? As you reread the poem, where else do you detect ironic overtones?
6. What is Mr. Z's color?

87. Southern Cop

Let us forgive Ty Kendricks.
The place was Darktown. He was young.
His nerves were jittery. The day was hot.
The Negro ran out of the alley.
And so Ty shot.

Let us understand Ty Kendricks.
The Negro must have been dangerous,
Because he ran;
And here was a rookie with a chance
To prove himself a man.

Let us condone Ty Kendricks
If we cannot decorate.
When he found what the Negro was running for,
It was too late;
And all we can say for the Negro is
It was unfortunate.

Let us pity Ty Kendricks.
He has been through enough,
Standing there, his big gun smoking,
Rabbit-scared, alone,
Having to hear the wenches wail
And the dying Negro moan.

Sterling A. Brown (1901–1989)

QUESTIONS

1. Explain the poem in terms of irony and understatement. Is the irony verbal or dramatic? Trace the slight changes in the irony from stanza to stanza.
2. Does the poem create any sympathy for Ty Kendricks?

88. On Treason

Treason doth never prosper: what's the reason?
For if it prosper, none dare call it treason.

Sir John Harington (1561?–1612)

QUESTION

This two-line epigram is divided by its punctuation into four parts. Which of the four displays verbal irony?

89. Earth

"A planet doesn't explode of itself," said drily
The Martian astronomer, gazing off into the air—
"That they were able to do it is proof that highly
Intelligent beings must have been living there."

John Hall Wheelock (1886–1978)

QUESTION

Is the irony in this poem verbal or dramatic? What one word enables you to answer this question with confidence?

90. My Last Duchess

Ferrara

That's my last duchess painted on the wall,
Looking as if she were alive. I call
That piece a wonder, now; Fra Pandolf's hands
Worked busily a day, and there she stands.
Will't please you sit and look at her? I said
"Fra Pandolf" by design, for never read
Strangers like you that pictured countenance,
The depth and passion of its earnest glance,
But to myself they turned (since none puts by
The curtain I have drawn for you, but I)
And seemed as they would ask me, if they durst,
How such a glance came there; so, not the first
Are you to turn and ask thus. Sir, 'twas not
Her husband's presence only, called that spot
Of joy into the Duchess' cheek; perhaps
Fra Pandolf chanced to say, "Her mantle laps
Over my lady's wrist too much," or, "Paint
Must never hope to reproduce the faint
Half-flush that dies along her throat." Such stuff
Was courtesy, she thought, and cause enough
For calling up that spot of joy. She had
A heart—how shall I say?—too soon made glad,
Too easily impressed; she liked whate'er
She looked on, and her looks went everywhere.
Sir, 'twas all one! My favor at her breast,
The dropping of the daylight in the West,
The bough of cherries some officious fool
Broke in the orchard for her, the white mule
She rode with round the terrace—all and each
Would draw from her alike the approving speech,
Or blush, at least. She thanked men—good! but thanked
Somehow—I know not how—as if she ranked
My gift of a nine-hundred-years-old name
With anybody's gift. Who'd stoop to blame
This sort of trifling? Even had you skill
In speech—which I have not—to make your will

Quite clear to such an one, and say, "Just this
Or that in you disgusts me; here you miss,
Or there exceed the mark"—and if she let
Herself be lessoned so, nor plainly set
Her wits to yours, forsooth, and made excuse—
E'en then would be some stooping; and I choose
Never to stoop. Oh, sir, she smiled, no doubt,
Whene'er I passed her; but who passed without
Much the same smile? This grew; I gave commands;
Then all smiles stopped together. There she stands
As if alive. Will 't please you rise? We'll meet
The company below, then. I repeat,
The Count your master's known munificence
Is ample warrant that no just pretense
Of mine for dowry will be disallowed;
Though his fair daughter's self, as I avowed
At starting, is my object. Nay, we'll go
Together down, sir. Notice Neptune, though,
Taming a sea-horse, thought a rarity,
Which Claus of Innsbruck cast in bronze for me!

Robert Browning (1812–1889)

QUESTIONS

1. Vocabulary: *officious* (27), *munificence* (49).
2. Ferrara is in Italy. The time is during the Renaissance, probably the sixteenth century. To whom is the Duke speaking? What is the occasion? Are the Duke's remarks about his last Duchess a digression, or do they have some relation to the business at hand?
3. Characterize the Duke as fully as you can. How does your characterization differ from the Duke's opinion of himself? What kind of irony is this?
4. Why was the Duke dissatisfied with his last Duchess? Was it sexual jealousy? What opinion do you get of the Duchess's personality, and how does it differ from the Duke's opinion?
5. What characteristics of the Italian Renaissance appear in the poem (marriage customs, social classes, art)? What is the Duke's attitude toward art? Is it insincere?
6. What happened to the Duchess? Should Browning have told us?

CHAPTER EIGHT

Allusion

The famous English diplomat and letter writer Lord Chesterfield once was invited to a great dinner given by the Spanish ambassador. At the conclusion of the meal the host rose and proposed a toast to his master, the king of Spain, whom he compared to the sun. The French ambassador followed with a health to the king of France, whom he likened to the moon. It was then Lord Chesterfield's turn. "Your excellencies have taken from me," he said, "all the greatest luminaries of heaven, and the stars are too small for me to make a comparison of my royal master; I therefore beg leave to give your excellencies—Joshua!"*

For a reader familiar with the Bible—that is, for one who recognizes the biblical allusion—Lord Chesterfield's story will come as a stunning revelation of his wit. For an **allusion**—a reference to something in history or previous literature—is, like a richly connotative word or a symbol, a means of suggesting far more than it says. The one word "Joshua," in the context of Chesterfield's toast, calls up in the reader's mind the whole biblical story of how the Israelite captain stopped the sun and the moon in order that the Israelites might finish a battle and conquer their enemies before nightfall.† The force of the toast lies in its extreme economy; it says so much in so little, and it exercises the mind of the reader to make the connection for himself.

The effect of Chesterfield's allusion is chiefly humorous or witty, but allusions also may have a powerful emotional effect. The essayist William Hazlitt writes of addressing a fashionable audience about the lexicographer Samuel Johnson. Speaking of Johnson's great heart and of his charity to the unfortunate, Hazlitt recounted how, finding a drunken prostitute lying in Fleet Street late at night, Johnson carried her on his

*Samuel Shellabarger, *Lord Chesterfield and His World* (Boston: Little, Brown, 1951) 132.
†Joshua 10:12–14.

broad back to the address she managed to give him. The audience, unable to face the picture of the famous dictionary-maker doing such a thing, broke out in titters and expostulations, whereupon Hazlitt simply said: "I remind you, ladies and gentlemen, of the parable of the Good Samaritan." The audience was promptly silenced.*

Allusions are a means of reinforcing the emotion or the ideas of one's own work with the emotion or ideas of another work or occasion. Because they may compact so much meaning in so small a space, they are extremely useful to the poet.

91. "Out, Out—"

The buzz-saw snarled and rattled in the yard
And made dust and dropped stove-length sticks of wood,
Sweet-scented stuff when the breeze drew across it.
And from there those that lifted eyes could count
Five mountain ranges one behind the other
Under the sunset far into Vermont.
And the saw snarled and rattled, snarled and rattled,
As it ran light, or had to bear a load.
And nothing happened: day was all but done.
Call it a day, I wish they might have said
To please the boy by giving him the half hour
That a boy counts so much when saved from work.
His sister stood beside them in her apron
To tell them "Supper." At the word, the saw,
As if to prove saws knew what supper meant,
Leaped out at the boy's hand, or seemed to leap—
He must have given the hand. However it was,
Neither refused the meeting. But the hand!
The boy's first outcry was a rueful laugh,
As he swung toward them holding up the hand
Half in appeal, but half as if to keep
The life from spilling. Then the boy saw all—
Since he was old enough to know, big boy
Doing a man's work, though a child at heart—
He saw all spoiled. "Don't let him cut my hand off—
The doctor, when he comes. Don't let him, sister!"
So. But the hand was gone already.

*Jacques Barzun, *Teacher in America* (Boston: Little, Brown, 1945) 160.

The doctor put him in the dark of ether.
He lay and puffed his lips out with his breath.
And then — the watcher at his pulse took fright.
No one believed. They listened at his heart.
Little — less — nothing! — and that ended it.
No more to build on there. And they, since they
Were not the one dead, turned to their affairs.

Robert Frost (1874–1963)

QUESTIONS

1. How does this poem differ from a newspaper account that might have dealt with the same incident?
2. To whom does "they" (33) refer? The boy's family? The doctor and medical attendants? Casual onlookers? Need we assume that all these people — whoever they are — turned immediately "to their affairs"? Does the ending of this poem seem to you callous or merely realistic? Would a more tearful and sentimental ending have made the poem better or worse?
3. What figure of speech is used in lines 21–22?

Allusions vary widely in the burden put on them by the poet to convey meaning. Lord Chesterfield risked his whole meaning on his hearers' recognizing his allusion. Robert Frost in "'Out, Out—'" makes his meaning entirely clear even for the reader who does not recognize the allusion contained in the poem's title. His theme is the uncertainty and unpredictability of life, which may be ended accidentally at any moment, and the tragic waste of human potentiality that takes place when such premature deaths occur. A boy who is already "doing a man's work" and gives every promise of having a useful life ahead of him is suddenly wiped out. There seems no rational explanation for either the accident or the death. The only comment to be made is, "No more to build on there."

Frost's title, however, is an allusion to one of the most famous passages in all English literature, and it offers a good illustration of how a poet may use allusion not only to reinforce emotion but also to help define his theme. The passage is that in *Macbeth* in which Macbeth has just been informed of his wife's death. A good many readers will recall the key phrase, "Out, out, brief candle!" with its underscoring of the tragic brevity and uncertainty of life. For some readers, however, the allusion will summon up the whole passage in Act 5, scene 5, in which this phrase occurs. Macbeth's words are:

92. She should have died hereafter;
There would have been a time for such a word.
To-morrow, and to-morrow, and to-morrow
Creeps in this petty pace from day to day
To the last syllable of recorded time;
And all our yesterdays have lighted fools
The way to dusty death. Out, out, brief candle!
Life's but a walking shadow, a poor player,
That struts and frets his hour upon the stage
And then is heard no more. It is a tale
Told by an idiot, full of sound and fury,
Signifying nothing.

Macbeth's first words underscore the theme of premature death. The boy also "should have died hereafter." The rest of the passage, with its marvelous evocation of the vanity and meaninglessness of life, expresses neither Shakespeare's philosophy nor, ultimately, Frost's, but it is Macbeth's philosophy at the time of his bereavement, and it is likely to express the feelings of us all when such tragic accidents occur. Life does indeed seem cruel and meaningless, a tale told by an idiot, signifying nothing, when human life and potentiality are thus without explanation so suddenly ended.

QUESTION

Examine Macbeth's speech for examples of personification, apostrophe, and metonymy. How many metaphors for an individual human life does it present?

Allusions also vary widely in the number of readers to whom they will be familiar. Poets, in using an allusion, as in using a figure of speech, are always in danger of being misunderstood. What appeals powerfully to one reader may lose another reader altogether. But poets must assume a certain fund of common experience in readers. They could not even write about the ocean unless they could assume that readers have seen the ocean or pictures of it. In the same way poets assume a certain common fund of literary experience, most frequently of classical mythology, Shakespeare, or the Bible—particularly the King James Version. Poets are often justified in expecting a rather wide range of literary experience in readers, for the people who read poetry for pleasure are generally intelligent and well-read. But, obviously, beginning readers will not have this range, just as they will not know the meanings of as many words as will more mature readers. Students should therefore be prepared to look up certain allusions, just as they should be eager to look up in their dictionaries the meanings of unfamiliar words. They will find that every increase in knowledge broadens their base for understanding both literature and life.

* * *

93. in Just-

in Just-
spring   when the world is mud-
luscious the little
lame balloonman

whistles   far   and wee

and eddieandbill come
running from marbles and
piracies and it's
spring

when the world is puddle-wonderful

the queer
old balloonman whistles
far   and   wee
and bettyandisbel come dancing

from hop-scotch and jump-rope and

it's
spring
and
   the

      goat-footed

balloonMan   whistles
far
and
wee

e. e. cummings (1894–1962)

QUESTION

Why is the balloonman called "goat-footed"? How does the identification made by this mythological allusion enrich the meaning of the poem?

94. On His Blindness

When I consider how my light is spent
  Ere half my days in this dark world and wide,
  And that one talent which is death to hide
  Lodged with me useless, though my soul more bent
To serve therewith my Maker, and present
  My true account, lest he returning chide,
  "Doth God exact day-labor, light denied?"
  I fondly ask. But Patience, to prevent
That murmur, soon replies, "God doth not need
  Either man's work or his own gifts. Who best
  Bear his mild yoke, they serve him best. His state
Is kingly: thousands at his bidding speed,
  And post o'er land and ocean without rest;
  They also serve who only stand and wait."

John Milton (1608–1674)

QUESTIONS

1. Vocabulary: *spent* (1), *fondly* (8), *prevent* (8), *post* (13).
2. What two meanings has "talent" (3)? What is Milton's "one talent"?
3. The poem is unified and expanded in its dimensions by a biblical allusion that Milton's original readers would have recognized immediately. What is it? If you do not know, look up Matthew 25:14–30. In what ways is the situation in the poem similar to that in the parable? In what ways is it different?
4. What is the point of the poem?

95. Hero and Leander

Both robbed of air, we both lie in one ground,
Both whom one fire had burnt, one water drowned.

John Donne (1572–1631)

QUESTIONS

1. After looking up the story of Hero and Leander (if necessary), explain each of the four parts into which this epigram is divided by its punctuation. Which parts are literal? Which are metaphorical?
2. The subject of the poem is taken from Greek legend; its structure is based on Greek science. Explain.

96. Miniver Cheevy

Miniver Cheevy, child of scorn,
  Grew lean while he assailed the seasons;
He wept that he was ever born,
  And he had reasons.

Miniver loved the days of old
  When swords were bright and steeds were prancing;
The vision of a warrior bold
  Would set him dancing.

Miniver sighed for what was not,
  And dreamed, and rested from his labors;
He dreamed of Thebes and Camelot,
  And Priam's neighbors.

Miniver mourned the ripe renown
  That made so many a name so fragrant;
He mourned Romance, now on the town,
  And Art, a vagrant.

Miniver loved the Medici,
  Albeit he had never seen one;
He would have sinned incessantly
  Could he have been one.

Miniver cursed the commonplace
  And eyed a khaki suit with loathing;
He missed the medieval grace
  Of iron clothing.

Miniver scorned the gold he sought,
  But sore annoyed was he without it;
Miniver thought, and thought, and thought,
  And thought about it.

Miniver Cheevy, born too late,
  Scratched his head and kept on thinking;
Miniver coughed, and called it fate,
  And kept on drinking.

Edwin Arlington Robinson (1869–1935)

QUESTIONS

1. Vocabulary: *khaki* (22). The phrase "on the town" (15) means "on charity" or "down and out."
2. Identify Thebes, Camelot (11), Priam (12), and the Medici (17). What names

and what sort of life does each call up? What does Miniver's love of these names tell about him?
3. Discuss the phrase "child of scorn" (1). What does it mean? In how many ways is it applicable to Miniver?
4. What is Miniver's attitude toward material wealth?
5. The phrase "rested from his labors" (10) alludes to the Bible *and* to Greek mythology. Explore the ironic effect of comparing Miniver to the Creator (Genesis 2:2) and to Hercules. Point out other examples of irony in the poem and discuss their importance.
6. Can we call this a poem about a man whose "fate" was to be "born too late"? Explain your answer.

97. Leda and the Swan

A sudden blow: the great wings beating still
Above the staggering girl, her thighs caressed
By the dark webs, her nape caught in his bill,
He holds her helpless breast upon his breast.

How can those terrified vague fingers push
The feathered glory from her loosening thighs?
And how can body, laid in that white rush,
But feel the strange heart beating where it lies?

A shudder in the loins engenders there
The broken wall, the burning roof and tower
And Agamemnon dead.
Being so caught up,
So mastered by the brute blood of the air,
Did she put on his knowledge with his power
Before the indifferent beak could let her drop?

William Butler Yeats (1865–1939)

QUESTIONS

1. What is the connection between Leda and "The broken wall, the burning roof and tower / And Agamemnon dead"? If you do not know, look up the myth of Leda, and, if necessary, the story of Agamemnon.
2. What is the significance of the question asked in the last two lines?

98. Snow White and the Seven Deadly Sins

Good Catholic girl, she didn't mind the cleaning.
All of her household chores, at first, were small
And hardly labors one could find demeaning.
One's duty was one's refuge, after all.

And if she had her doubts at certain moments
And once confessed them to the Father, she
Was instantly referred to texts in Romans
And Peter's First Epistle, chapter III.

Years passed. More sinful every day, the *Seven*
Breakfasted, grabbed their pitchforks, donned their horns,
And sped to contravene the hopes of heaven,
Sowing the neighbors' lawns with tares and thorns.

She set to work. *Pride*'s wall of looking glasses
Ogled her dimly, smeared with prints of lips;
Lust's magazines lay strewn, bare tits and asses
Weighted by his "devices"—chains, cuffs, whips.

Gluttony's empties covered half the table,
Mingling with *Avarice*'s cards and chips,
And she'd been told to sew a Bill Blass label
Inside the blazer *Envy*'d bought at Gyp's.

She knelt to the cold master bathroom floor as
If a petitioner before the Pope,
Retrieving several pairs of *Sloth*'s soiled drawers,
A sweat-sock and a cake of hairy soap.

Then, as she wiped the Windex from the mirror
She noticed, and the vision made her cry,
How much she'd grayed and paled, and how much clearer
Festered the bruise of *Wrath* beneath her eye.

"No poisoned apple needed for this Princess,"
She murmured, making X's with her thumb.
A car door slammed, bringing her to her senses:
Ho-hum. Ho-hum. It's home from work we come.

And she was out the window in a second,
In time to see a *Handsome Prince*, of course,
Who, spying her distressed condition, beckoned
For her to mount (What else?) his snow-white horse.

Impeccably he spoke. His smile was glowing.
So debonair! So charming! And so *Male*.
She took a step, reversed and without slowing
Beat it to St. Anne's where she took the veil.

R. S. Gwynn (b. 1948)

QUESTIONS

1. Vocabulary: *tares* (12), *impeccably* (37), *took the veil* (40). *Bill Blass* (19) is a fashion designer; *Gyp's* (20) refers to any low-cost clothing store; *making X's* is presumably a charm to ward off evil.
2. Lines 7–8 allude to passages in the Bible. Paul's Epistle to the Romans exhorts the faithful to obedience and due regard to their masters (see, for example, 2.5–9, 12.10–14, 13.1–7). Relevant verses in the third chapter of Peter's First Epistle General include 1, 9, 13–15, 17. How do these lines with their allusions advance this story?
3. How do the details of this poem compare to events in the fairy tale (or the Walt Disney animated film based on it)? What is the meaning of the substitution of "sins" for "dwarfs"? What satirical purpose is served by the allusion?

99. An altered look about the hills

An altered look about the hills—
A Tyrian light the village fills—
A wider sunrise in the morn—
A deeper twilight on the lawn—
A print of a vermilion foot—
A purple finger on the slope—
A flippant fly upon the pane—
A spider at his trade again—
An added strut in chanticleer—
A flower expected everywhere—
An axe shrill singing in the woods—
Fern odors on untraveled roads—
All this and more I cannot tell—
A furtive look you know as well—
And Nicodemus's mystery
Receives its annual reply!

Emily Dickinson (1830–1886)

QUESTIONS

1. Vocabulary: *Tyrian* (2), *chanticleer* (9).
2. What does the list of natural changes indicate? How is that an answer to Nicodemus's questions to Jesus? (If you are not familiar with the allusion, see John 3.4.) Does the meaning of this poem concur or contrast with the meaning of the biblical passage?

100. Abraham to kill him

Abraham to kill him
Was distinctly told.
Isaac was an urchin,
Abraham was old.

Not a hesitation—
Abraham complied.
Flattered by obeisance,
Tyranny demurred.

Isaac, to his children
Lived to tell the tale.
Moral: with a mastiff
Manners may prevail.

Emily Dickinson (1830–1886)

QUESTIONS

1. Vocabulary: *obeisance* (7), *demurred* (8).
2. To whom or to what do "Tyranny" (8) and "mastiff" (11) refer? What figure of speech is each?
3. Who are Abraham and Isaac? What, in the context of the original story, does "demurred" mean? If you cannot answer these questions, read Genesis 22:1–18.
4. What is the reaction of the poet to this Bible story?

101. In the Garden

In the garden there strayed
A beautiful maid
As fair as the flowers of the morn;
The first hour of her life
She was made a man's wife,
And was buried before she was born.

Anonymous

QUESTION

Resolve the paradox by identifying the allusion.

CHAPTER NINE

Meaning and Idea

102. Little Jack Horner

Little Jack Horner
Sat in a corner
Eating a Christmas pie.
He stuck in his thumb
And pulled out a plum
And said, "What a good boy am I!"

Anonymous

The meaning of a poem is the experience it expresses—nothing less. But readers who, baffled by a particular poem, ask perplexedly, "What does it *mean*?" are usually after something more specific than this. They want something they can grasp entirely with their minds. We may therefore find it useful to distinguish the **total meaning** of a poem—the experience it communicates (and which can be communicated in no other way)—from its **prose meaning**—the ingredient that can be separated out in the form of a prose paraphrase (see Chapter 2). If we make this distinction, however, we must be careful not to confuse the two kinds of meaning. The prose meaning is no more the poem than a plum is a pie or than a prune is a plum.

The prose meaning will not necessarily or perhaps even usually be an idea. It may be a story, a description, a statement of emotion, a presentation of human character, or some combination of these. "The Mill" (No. 18) tells a story; "The Eagle" (No. 1) is primarily descriptive; "Western Wind" (No. 47) is an expression of emotion; "My Last Duchess" (No. 90) is an account of human character. None of these poems is directly concerned with ideas. Message hunters will be baffled and disappointed by poetry of this kind, for they will not find what they are looking for, and they may attempt to read some idea into the poem that is really not there. Yet ideas are also part of human experience, and therefore many poems are concerned, at least partially, with presenting ideas. But with these poems message-hunting is an even more dangerous activity, for the message hunters are likely to think that the whole object of reading the poem is to find the message—that the idea is really the only important thing in it. Like Little Jack Horner, they will reach in and pluck out the idea and say, "What a good boy am I!" as if the pie existed for the plum.

The idea in a poem is only part of the total experience that it communicates. The value and worth of the poem are determined by the value of the total experience, not by the truth or the nobility of the idea itself. This is not to say that the truth of the idea is unimportant, or that its validity should not be examined and appraised. But a good idea alone will not make a good poem, nor need an idea with which the reader does not agree ruin one. Good readers of poetry are receptive to all kinds of experience. They are able to make that "willing suspension of disbelief" that Coleridge characterized as constituting poetic faith. When one attends a performance of *Hamlet*, one is willing to forget for the time being that such a person as Hamlet never existed and that the events on the stage are fictions. Likewise, poetry readers should be willing to entertain imaginatively, for the time being, ideas they objectively regard as untrue. It is one way of understanding these ideas better and of enlarging the reader's own experience. The person who believes in God should be able to enjoy a good poem expressing atheistic ideas, just as the atheist should be able to appreciate a good poem in praise of God. The optimist should be able to find pleasure in pessimistic poetry, and the pessimist in optimistic poetry. The teetotaler should be able to enjoy *The Rubáiyát of Omar Khayyám*, and the winebibber a good poem in praise of austerity. The primary value of a poem depends not so much on the truth of the idea presented as on the power with which it is communicated and on its being made a convincing part of a meaningful total experience. We must feel that the idea has been truly and deeply *felt* by the poet, and that the poet is doing something more than merely moralizing. The plum must be made part of a pie. If the plum is properly combined with other ingredients and if the pie is well baked, it should be enjoyable even for persons who do not care for the type of plums from which it is made. Consider, for instance, the following two poems.

103. Barter

Life has loveliness to sell,
    All beautiful and splendid things,
Blue waves whitened on a cliff,
    Soaring fire that sways and sings,
And children's faces looking up,
Holding wonder like a cup.

Life has loveliness to sell,
  Music like a curve of gold,
Scent of pine trees in the rain,
  Eyes that love you, arms that hold,
And for your spirit's still delight,
Holy thoughts that star the night.

Spend all you have for loveliness,
  Buy it and never count the cost;
For one white singing hour of peace
  Count many a year of strife well lost,
And for a breath of ecstasy
Give all you have been, or could be.

Sara Teasdale (1884–1933)

104. Stopping by Woods on a Snowy Evening

Whose woods these are I think I know.
His house is in the village though;
He will not see me stopping here
To watch his woods fill up with snow.

My little horse must think it queer
To stop without a farmhouse near
Between the woods and frozen lake
The darkest evening of the year.

He gives his harness bells a shake
To ask if there is some mistake.
The only other sound's the sweep
Of easy wind and downy flake.

The woods are lovely, dark and deep,
But I have promises to keep,
And miles to go before I sleep,
And miles to go before I sleep.

Robert Frost (1874–1963)

QUESTIONS

1. How do these two poems differ in idea?
2. What contrasts are suggested between the speaker in the second poem and (a) his horse and (b) the owner of the woods?

Both of these poems present ideas, the first more or less explicitly, the second symbolically. Perhaps the best way to get at the idea of the second poem is to ask two questions. First, why does the speaker stop? Second, why does he go on? He stops, we answer, to watch the woods fill up with snow—to observe a scene of natural beauty. He goes on, we answer, because he has "promises to keep"—that is, he has obligations to fulfill. He is momentarily torn between his love of beauty and these other various and complex claims that life has upon him. The small conflict in the poem is symbolic of a larger conflict in life. One part of the sensitive, thinking person would like to give up his life to the enjoyment of beauty and art. But another part is aware of larger duties and responsibilities—responsibilities owed, at least in part, to other human beings. The speaker in the poem would like to satisfy both impulses. But when the two conflict, he seems to suggest, the "promises" must take precedence.

The first poem also presents a philosophy but an opposing one. For this poet, beauty is of such supreme value that any conflicting demand should be sacrificed to it: "Spend all you have for loveliness, / Buy it and never count the cost . . . And for a breath of ecstasy / Give all you have been, or could be." Thoughtful readers will have to choose between these two philosophies—to commit themselves to one or the other—but this commitment should not destroy for them their enjoyment of either poem. If it does, they are reading for plums and not for pies.

Nothing we have said so far in this chapter should be construed as meaning that the truth or falsity of the idea in a poem is a matter of no importance. *Other things being equal*, good readers naturally will, and properly should, value more highly the poem whose idea they feel to be more mature and nearer to the heart of human experience. Some ideas, moreover, may seem so vicious or so foolish or so beyond the pale of normal human decency as to discredit *by themselves* the poems in which they are found. A rotten plum may spoil a pie. But good readers strive for intellectual flexibility and tolerance, and are able to entertain sympathetically ideas other than their own. They often will like a poem whose idea they disagree with better than one with an idea they accept. And, above all, they will not confuse the prose meaning of any poem with its total meaning. They will not mistake plums for pies.

* * *

105. To a Waterfowl

Whither, midst falling dew,
While glow the heavens with the last steps of day,
Far, through their rosy depths, dost thou pursue
Thy solitary way?

Vainly the fowler's eye
Might mark thy distant flight to do thee wrong,
As, darkly seen against the crimson sky,
Thy figure floats along.

Seek'st thou the plashy brink
Of weedy lake, or marge of river wide,
Or where the rocking billows rise and sink
On the chafed ocean side?

There is a Power whose care
Teaches thy way along that pathless coast—
The desert and illimitable air—
Lone wandering, but not lost.

All day thy wings have fanned,
At that far height, the cold, thin atmosphere,
Yet stoop not, weary, to the welcome land,
Though the dark night is near.

And soon that toil shall end;
Soon shalt thou find a summer home, and rest,
And scream among thy fellows; reeds shall bend,
Soon, o'er thy sheltered nest.

Thou'rt gone, the abyss of heaven
Hath swallowed up thy form; yet, on my heart
Deeply has sunk the lesson thou hast given,
And shall not soon depart.

He who, from zone to zone,
Guides through the boundless sky thy certain flight,
In the long way that I must tread alone,
Will lead my steps aright.

William Cullen Bryant (1794–1878)

QUESTIONS

1. Vocabulary: *fowler* (5), *desert* (15), *stoop* (19).
2. What figure of speech unifies the poem?
3. Where is the waterfowl flying? Why? What is "that pathless coast" (14)?
4. What "Power" (13) "guides" (30) the waterfowl to its destination? How does it do so?
5. What lesson does the poet derive from his observations?

106. Design

I found a dimpled spider, fat and white,
On a white heal-all, holding up a moth
Like a white piece of rigid satin cloth—
Assorted characters of death and blight
Mixed ready to begin the morning right,
Like the ingredients of a witches' broth—
A snow-drop spider, a flower like a froth,
And dead wings carried like a paper kite.

What had that flower to do with being white,
The wayside blue and innocent heal-all?
What brought the kindred spider to that height,
Then steered the white moth thither in the night?
What but design of darkness to appall?—
If design govern in a thing so small.

Robert Frost (1874–1963)

QUESTIONS

1. Vocabulary: *characters* (4).
2. The heal-all is a wildflower, usually blue or violet but occasionally white, found blooming along roadsides in the summer. It was once supposed to have healing qualities, hence its name. Of what significance, scientific and poetic, is the fact that the spider, the heal-all, and the moth are all white? Of what poetic significance is the fact that the spider is "dimpled" and "fat" and like a "snow-drop," and that the flower is "innocent" and named "heal-all"?
3. The "argument from design"—that the manifest existence of design in the universe implies the existence of a Great Designer—was a favorite eighteenth-century argument for the existence of God. What twist does Frost give the argument? What answer does he suggest to the question in lines 11–12? How comforting is the apparent concession in line 14?
4. Contrast Frost's poem in content and emotional effect with "To a Waterfowl." Is it possible to like both?

107. The Indifferent

I can love both fair and brown,
Her whom abundance melts, and her whom want betrays,
Her who loves loneness best, and her who masks and plays,
Her whom the country formed, and whom the town,
Her who believes, and her who tries,° — tests
Her who still weeps with spongy eyes,

And her who is dry cork and never cries;
I can love her, and her, and you, and you;
I can love any, so she be not true.° — faithful

Will no other vice content you?
Will it not serve your turn to do as did your mothers?
Or have you all old vices spent, and now would find out others?
Or doth a fear that men are true torment you?
Oh, we are not; be not you so.
Let me, and do you, twenty know.
Rob me, but bind me not, and let me go.
Must I, who came to travail thorough° you, — through
Grow your fixed subject because you are true?

Venus heard me sing this song,
And by love's sweetest part, variety, she swore
She heard not this till now, and that it should be so no more.
She went, examined, and returned ere long,
And said, "Alas, some two or three
Poor heretics in love there be,
Which think to 'stablish dangerous constancy,
But I have told them, 'Since you will be true,
You shall be true to them who are false to you.'"

John Donne (1572–1631)

QUESTIONS

1. Vocabulary: *indifferent* (title), *know* (15), *travail* (17).
2. Who is the speaker? To whom is he speaking? About what is he "indifferent"? What one qualification does he insist on in a lover? Why?
3. Of what vice does he accuse the women of his generation in line 10? How, in his opinion, do they differ from their mothers? Why?
4. Why does Venus investigate the speaker's complaint? Does her investigation confirm or refute his accusation? Who are the "heretics in love" (24) whom she discovers? What punishment does she decree for them?

108. Love's Deity

I long to talk with some old lover's ghost
Who died before the god of love was born.
I cannot think that he who then loved most
Sunk so low as to love one which did scorn.
But since this god produced a destiny,
And that vice-nature, custom, lets it be,
I must love her that loves not me.

Sure, they which made him god meant not so much,
  Nor he in his young godhead practiced it.
But when an even flame two hearts did touch,
  His office was indulgently to fit
Actives to passives. Correspondency
Only his subject was. It cannot be
        Love till I love her that loves me.

But every modern god will° now extend   wants to
  His vast prerogative as far as Jove.
To rage, to lust, to write to, to commend,
  All is the purlieu of the god of love.
Oh, were we wakened by this tyranny
To ungod this child again, it could not be
        I should love her who loves not me.

Rebel and atheist too, why murmur I
  As though I felt the worst that Love could do?
Love might make me leave loving, or might try
  A deeper plague, to make her love me too,
Which, since she loves before, I am loath to see.
Falsehood is worse than hate, and that must be
        If she whom I love should love me.

John Donne (1572–1631)

QUESTIONS

1. Vocabulary: *vice-* (6), *even* (10), *purlieu* (18).
2. Who is the modern "god of love" (2)? Why is he called a "child" (20)? What did "they which made him god" (8) intend to be his duties? How has he gone beyond these duties? Why does the speaker long to talk with some lover's ghost who died before this god was born (1–2)?
3. What is the speaker's situation? Whom does the speaker call "Rebel and atheist" (22)? Why?
4. Why does the speaker rebuke himself for "murmuring" in the final stanza? What two things could Love do to him that have not been done already? Why are they worse? Explain the words "before" (26) and "Falsehood" (27). To what word in the first stanza does "hate" (27) correspond?
5. How does the speaker define "love" in this poem? Is he consistent in his use of the term? How does he differ from the speaker in "The Indifferent" in his conception of love?
6. How do you explain the fact that "Love's Deity" and "The Indifferent," though both by the same poet, express opposite opinions about the value of fidelity in love?

QUESTIONS

1. George Annandale is the central character in two longish poems by Robinson. In one of these, after a visit to his closest friend (who is also his doctor), Annandale is maimed and almost killed in an automobile accident. The doctor hears "a sick crash in the street" and finds his friend in a condition for which there can be no healing and which will only entail intense suffering while he lives. This information, though not essential to understanding Robinson's sonnet, may make it easier. Who is the speaker? Whom is he addressing? Why?
2. Discuss the role of overstatement and understatement in the poem. Why does the speaker call himself a liar and hypocrite? What does he mean by lines 4–5? What does he mean by line 9? What nouns and pronouns does he use in referring to Annandale?
3. Why does he repeat "and I was there" (1, 8)? What meanings has "on the spot" (12)?
4. What is the "slight kind of engine" (13)? What gesture does he make with his hands in explaining it? What has he done—something legal or illegal? Moral or immoral? What is his motivation in revealing what he has done?
5. Does his auditor approve of his action? Does Robinson?
6. Compare or contrast the attitudes expressed in this poem and in "To the Mercy Killers."

111. Alter! When the hills do

Alter! When the hills do.
Falter! When the sun
Question if his glory
Be the perfect one.

Surfeit! When the daffodil
Doth of the dew.
Even as herself, Sir,
I will of you.

Emily Dickinson (1830–1886

ION

peaking to whom? What assertion does the speaker make?

9. To the Mercy Killers

If ever mercy move you murder me,
I pray you, kindly killers, let me live.
Never conspire with death to set me free,
but let me know such life as pain can give.
Even though I be a clot, an aching clench,
a stub, a stump, a butt, a scab, a knob,
a screaming pain, a putrefying stench,
still let me live, so long as life shall throb.
Even though I turn such traitor to myself
as beg to die, do not accomplice me.
Even though I seem not human, a mute shelf
of glucose, bottled blood, machinery
to swell the lung and pump the heart—even so,
do not put out my life. Let me still glow.

Dudley Randall (b. 1914)

QUESTIONS

1. In form this is a Shakespearean sonnet (see page 219), consisting c quatrains and a concluding couplet (units of 4, 4, 4, and 2 lines each structure (organization of thought) it follows the Italian model of and sestet (8- and 6-line units) in which the first eight lines ir thought and the sestet produces some kind of counter-thought. V of thought occurs at the end of line 8 in this sonnet?
2. Identify the paradox in line 2 that introduces the central topic o is also stated in the title, but line 2 states it more effectivel alliteration.)
3. Is the speaker advocating a universal standard of conduct ing his personal desire?

110. How Annandale Went Out

"They called it Annandale—and I was
To flourish, to find words, and to atte
Liar, physician, hypocrite, and frien
I watched him; and the sight was n
As one or two that I have seen els
An apparatus not for me to men
A wreck, with hell between hir
Remained of Annandale; and

112. We outgrow love

We outgrow love like other things
And put it in the drawer,
Till it an antique fashion shows
Like costumes grandsires wore.

Emily Dickinson (1830–1886)

QUESTIONS

1. To what is love metaphorically compared?
2. How does the assertion made in this poem differ from that in the preceding poem? Can you account for the difference?

113. The Caged Skylark

As a dare-gale skylark scanted in a dull cage
  Man's mounting spirit in his bone-house, mean house, dwells—
  That bird beyond the remembering his free fells;
This in drudgery, day-laboring-out life's age.

Though aloft on turf or perch or poor low stage,
  Both sing sometimes the sweetest, sweetest spells,
  Yet both droop deadly sometimes in their cells
Or wring their barriers in bursts of fear or rage.

Not that the sweet-fowl, song-fowl, needs no rest—
Why, hear him, hear him babble and drop down to his nest,
  But his own nest, wild nest, no prison.

Man's spirit will be flesh-bound when found at best,
But uncumbered: meadow-down is not distressed
  For a rainbow footing it nor he for his bones risen.

Gerard Manley Hopkins (1844–1889)

QUESTIONS

1. Vocabulary: *scanted* (1), *fells* (3). What meanings of "mean" (2) are appropriate here? "Turf" (5) is a piece of sod placed in a cage.
2. The speaker expresses a belief in the Christian doctrine of the resurrection of the body. According to this belief, the immortal soul, after death, will be ultimately reunited with the body; this body, however, will be a weightless, perfected, glorified body, not the gross imperfect body of mortal life. Express the analogy in the poem as a pair of mathematical statements of proportion (in the form $a{:}b = c{:}d$ and $e{:}f = g{:}h = i{:}j$), using the following terms: caged

skylark, mortal body, meadow-down, cage, rainbow, spirit-in-life, nest, immortal spirit, wild skylark, resurrected body.

3. Discuss the image of the last two lines as a figure for weightlessness. Why would not a shadow have been as apt as a rainbow for this comparison?

114. The Immortal Part

When I meet the morning beam
Or lay me down at night to dream,
I hear my bones within me say,
"Another night, another day.

"When shall this slough of sense be cast,
This dust of thoughts be laid at last,
The man of flesh and soul be slain
And the man of bone remain?

"This tongue that talks, these lungs that shout,
These thews that hustle us about,
This brain that fills the skull with schemes,
And its humming hive of dreams,—

"These to-day are proud in power
And lord it in their little hour:
The immortal bones obey control
Of dying flesh and dying soul.

"'Tis long till eve and morn are gone:
Slow the endless night comes on,
And late to fulness grows the birth
That shall last as long as earth.

"Wanderers eastward, wanderers west,
Know you why you cannot rest?
'Tis that every mother's son
Travails with a skeleton.

"Lie down in the bed of dust;
Bear the fruit that bear you must;
Bring the eternal seed to light,
And morn is all the same as night.

"Rest you so from trouble sore,
Fear the heat o' the sun no more,
Nor the snowing winter wild,
Now you labor not with child.

"Empty vessel, garment cast,
We that wore you long shall last.
—Another night, another day."
So my bones within me say.

Therefore they shall do my will
To-day while I am master still,
And flesh and soul, now both are strong,
Shall hale the sullen slaves along,

Before this fire of sense decay,
This smoke of thought blown clean away,
And leave with ancient night alone
The stedfast and enduring bone.

A. E. Housman (1859–1936)

QUESTIONS

1. Vocabulary: *slough* (5), *thews* (10), *travails* (24), *hale* (40).
2. Discuss the figures of speech in lines 3–16, 12, 19–27, 41–42, 43.
3. Do you recognize the allusion in stanza 8 (29–32)? If not, refer to poem No. 273. How is the allusion appropriate here?
4. Contrast the meaning of the word *soul* in this poem with its meaning in "The Caged Skylark." How do the two poems differ in idea? Is there any pronounced difference between them in poetic merit?

115. A Dialogue between the Soul and Body

SOUL: Oh, who shall from this dungeon raise
A soul enslaved so many ways?
With bolts of bones, that fettered stands
In feet, and manacled in hands;
Here blinded with an eye, and there
Deaf with the drumming of an ear;
A soul hung up, as 'twere, in chains
Of nerves, and arteries, and veins;
Tortured, besides each other part,
In a vain head, and double heart.

BODY: Oh, who shall me deliver whole
From bonds of this tyrannic soul?
Which, stretched upright, impales me so,
That mine own precipice I go;
And warms and moves this needless frame
(A fever could but do the same)
And, wanting where its spite to try,

Has made me live to let me die;
A body that could never rest,
Since this ill spirit it possessed.

SOUL: What magic could me thus confine
Within another's grief to pine?
Where, whatsoever it complain,
I feel, that cannot feel, the pain,
And all my care itself employs,
That to preserve, which me destroys;
Constrained not only to endure
Diseases, but, what's worse, the cure;
And ready oft the port to gain,
Am shipwrecked into health again.

BODY: But physic° yet could never reach — medicine
The maladies thou me dost teach;
Whom first the cramp of hope does tear,
And then the palsy shakes of fear;
The pestilence of love does heat,
Or hatred's hidden ulcer eat;
Joy's cheerful madness does perplex,
Or sorrow's other madness vex,
Which madness forces me to know,
And memory will not forgo.
What but a soul could have the wit
To build me up for sin so fit?
So architects do square and hew
Green trees that in the forest grew.

Andrew Marvell (1621–1678)

QUESTIONS

1. This debate between two intrinsically joined aspects of human life consists of complaint and counter-complaint, chiefly presented in metaphors. How do the two "characters" extend the metaphor of line 1? How is the presence of a soul in a body like imprisonment in a dungeon? In stanza 2, how is the control of a soul over a body's actions like a tyrant's bondage?
2. What metaphor predominates in stanzas 3–4?
3. Resolve the many paradoxes in the poem (for example, lines 26, 27–28, 29–30).
4. What end is served by this allegorical debate? Does either side win?

CHAPTER TEN

Tone

Tone, in literature, may be defined as the writer's or speaker's attitude toward his subject, his audience, or himself. It is the emotional coloring, or the emotional meaning, of the work and is an extremely important part of the full meaning. In spoken language it is indicated by the inflections of the speaker's voice. If, for instance, a friend tells you, "I'm going to get married today," the facts of the statement are entirely clear. But the emotional meaning of the statement may vary widely according to the tone of voice with which it is uttered. The tone may be ecstatic ("Hooray! I'm going to get married today!"); it may be incredulous ("I can't believe it! I'm going to get married today"); it may be despairing ("Horrors! I'm going to get married today"); it may be resigned ("Might as well face it. I'm going to get married today"). Obviously, a correct interpretation of the tone will be an important part of understanding the full meaning. It may even have rather important consequences. If someone calls you a fool, your interpretation of the tone may determine whether you roll up your sleeves for a fight or walk off with your arm around his shoulder. If a woman says "No" to a proposal of marriage, the man's interpretation of her tone may determine whether he asks her again and wins her or starts going with someone else.

In poetry tone is likewise important. We have not really understood a poem unless we have accurately sensed whether the attitude it manifests is playful or solemn, mocking or reverent, calm or excited. But the correct determination of tone in literature is a much more delicate matter than it is with spoken language, for we do not have the speaker's voice to guide us. We must learn to recognize tone by other means. Almost all the elements of poetry help to indicate its tone: connotation, imagery, and metaphor; irony and understatement; rhythm, sentence construction, and formal pattern. There is therefore no simple formula for recognizing tone. It is an end product of all the elements in a poem. The best we can do is illustrate.

Robert Frost's "Stopping by Woods on a Snowy Evening" (No. 104) seems a simple poem, but it has always afforded trouble to beginning readers. A very good student, asked to interpret it, once wrote this: "The poem means that we are forever passing up pleasures to go onward to what we wrongly consider our obligations. We would like to watch the snow fall on the peaceful countryside, but we always have to rush home to supper and other engagements. Frost feels that the average person considers life too short to stop and take time to appreciate true pleasures." This student did a good job in recognizing the central conflict of the poem but went astray in recognizing its tone. Let's examine why.

In the first place, the fact that the speaker in the poem *does* stop to watch the snow fall in the woods immediately establishes him as a human being with more sensitivity and feeling for beauty than most. He is not one of the people of Wordsworth's sonnet (No. 29) who, "getting and spending," have laid waste their powers and lost the capacity to be stirred by nature. Frost's speaker is contrasted with his horse, who, as a creature of habit and an animal without esthetic perception, cannot understand the speaker's reason for stopping. There is also a suggestion of contrast with the "owner" of the woods, who, if he saw the speaker stopping, might be as puzzled as the horse. (Who most truly "profits" from the woods—its absentee owner or the person who can enjoy its beauty?) The speaker goes on because he has "promises to keep." But the word "promises," though it may here have a wry ironic undertone of regret, has a favorable connotation: people almost universally agree that promises ought to be kept. If the poet had used a different term, say, "things to do," or "business to attend to," or "financial affairs to take care of," or "money to make," the connotations would have been quite different. As it is, the tone of the poem tells us that the poet is sympathetic to the speaker; Frost is endorsing rather than censuring the speaker's action. Perhaps we may go even further. In the concluding two lines, because of their climactic position, because they are repeated, and because "sleep" in poetry is often used figuratively to refer to death, there is a suggestion of symbolic interpretation: "and many years to live before I die." If we accept this interpretation, it poses a parallel between giving oneself up to contemplation of the woods and dying. The poet's total implication would seem to be that beauty is a distinctively human value that deserves its place in a full life but that to devote one's life to its pursuit, at the expense of other obligations and duties, is tantamount to one's death as a responsible being. The poet therefore accepts the choice the speaker makes, though not without a touch of regret.

Differences in tone, and their importance, can perhaps be studied best in poems with similar content. Consider, for instance, the following pair.

116. For a Lamb

I saw on the slant hill a putrid lamb,
Propped with daisies. The sleep looked deep.
The face nudged in the green pillow
But the guts were out for crows to eat.

Where's the lamb? whose tender plaint
Said all for the mute breezes.
Say he's in the wind somewhere,
Say, there's a lamb in the daisies.

Richard Eberhart (b. 1904)

QUESTION

What connotative force do these words possess: "putrid" (1), "guts" (4), "mute" (6); "lamb" (1), "daisies" (2), "pillow" (3), "tender" (5)? Give two relevant denotations of "a lamb in the daisies" (8).

117. Apparently with no surprise

Apparently with no surprise
To any happy flower,
The frost beheads it at its play
In accidental power.

The blond assassin passes on,
The sun proceeds unmoved
To measure off another day
For an approving God.

Emily Dickinson (1830–1886)

QUESTIONS

1. What is the "blond assassin"?
2. What ironies are involved in this poem?

Both of these poems are concerned with natural process; both use contrast as their basic organizing principle—a contrast between life and death, innocence and destruction, joy and tragedy. But in tone the two poems are sharply different. The first is realistic and resigned; its tone is wistful but not pessimistic. The second, though superficially fanciful, is basically grim, almost savage; its tone is horrified. Let's examine the difference.

The title, "For a Lamb," invites associations of innocent, frolicsome youthfulness, with the additional force of traditional Christian usage. These expectations are shockingly halted by the word "putrid." Though the speaker tries to overcome the shock with the more comforting personification implied in "face" and "pillow," the truth is undeniable: the putrefying animal is food for scavengers. The second stanza comes to grips with this truth, and also with the speaker's desire that the lamb might still represent innocence and purity in nature. It mingles fact and desire by hoping that what the lamb represented is still "somewhere" in the wind, that the lamb is both lying in the daisy field and will, in nature's processes, be transformed into the daisies. The reader shares the speaker's sad acceptance of reality.

The second poem makes the same contrast between joyful innocence ("happy flower . . . at its play") and fearful destruction ("beheads it"). The chief difference would seem to be that the cause of destruction—"the blond assassin"—is specifically identified, while the lamb seems to have died in its sleep, pillowed as it is in grass and surrounded by flowers. But the metaphorical sleep is no less a death than that delivered by an assassin—lambs *do* die, and frost actually *does* destroy flowers. In the second poem, what makes the horror of the killing worse is that nothing else in nature is disturbed by it or seems even to notice it. The sun "proceeds unmoved / To measure off another day." Nothing in nature stops or pauses. The flower itself is not surprised. And even God—the God who we have all been told is benevolent and concerned over the least sparrow's fall—seems to approve of what has happened, for He shows no displeasure, and He supposedly created the frost as well as the flower. Further irony lies in the fact that the "assassin" (the word's connotations are of terror and violence) is not dark but "blond," or white (the connotations here are of innocence and beauty). The destructive agent, in other words, is among the most exquisite creations of God's handiwork. The poet, then, is shocked at what has happened, and is even more shocked that nothing else in nature is shocked. What has happened seems inconsistent with a rule of benevolence in the universe. In her ironic reference to an "approving God," therefore, the poet is raising a dreadful question: are the forces that created and govern the universe actually benevolent? And if we think that the poet is unduly disturbed over the death of a flower, we may consider that what is true for the flower is true throughout nature. Death — even early or accidental death, in terrible juxtaposition with beauty — is its constant condition; the fate that befalls the flower befalls us all. In Dickinson's poem, that is the end of the process. In Eberhart's, the potentially terrible irony is directed into a bittersweet acceptance of both death and beauty as natural.

These two poems, then, though superficially similar, are basically as different as night and day. And the difference is primarily one of tone.

Accurately determining tone, whether it be the tone of a rejected marriage proposal or of an insulting remark, is extremely important, both when reading poetry and in real life. For the experienced reader it will be instinctive and automatic. For the beginning reader it will require study. But beyond the general suggestions for reading that we already have made, there are no specific instructions we can give. Recognition of tone requires an increasing familiarity with the meanings and connotations of words, alertness to the presence of irony and other figures, and, above all, careful reading. Poetry cannot be read as one would skim a newspaper or a mystery novel looking merely for facts.

* * *

118. The Coming of Wisdom with Time

Though leaves are many, the root is one;
Through all the lying days of my youth
I swayed my leaves and flowers in the sun;
Now I may wither into the truth.

William Butler Yeats (1865–1939)

QUESTION

Is the poet exulting over a gain or lamenting over a loss?

119. Since there's no help

Since there's no help, come let us kiss and part;
Nay, I have done, you get no more of me,
And I am glad, yea, glad with all my heart
That thus so cleanly I myself can free;
Shake hands forever, cancel all our vows,

And when we meet at any time again,
Be it not seen in either of our brows
That we one jot of former love retain.
Now, at the last gasp of Love's latest breath,
When, his pulse failing, Passion speechless lies,
When Faith is kneeling by his bed of death,
And Innocence is closing up his eyes,
Now, if thou wouldst, when all have given him over,
From death to life thou mightst him yet recover.

Michael Drayton (1563–1631)

QUESTIONS

1. What difference in tone do you find between the first eight lines and the last six? In which part is the speaker more sincere? What differences in rhythm and language help to establish the difference in tone?
2. How many figures are there in the allegorical scene in lines 9–12? What do the pronouns "his" and "him" in lines 10–14 refer to? What is dying? Why? How might the person addressed still restore it from death to life?
3. Define the dramatic situation as precisely as possible, taking into consideration both the man's attitude and the woman's.

120. One dignity delays for all

One dignity delays for all,
One mitred afternoon.
None can avoid this purple,
None evade this crown.

Coach, it insures, and footmen,
Chamber, and state, and throng—
Bells, also, in the village,
As we ride grand along!

What dignified attendants!
What service when we pause!
How loyally at parting
Their hundred hats they raise!

How pomp surpassing ermine
When simple you and I
Present our meek escutcheon
And claim the rank to die!

Emily Dickinson (1830–1886)

QUESTIONS

1. Vocabulary: *mitred* (2), *state* (6), *escutcheon* (15).
2. What is the "dignity" that delays for all? What is its nature? What is being described in stanzas 2 and 3?
3. What figures of speech are combined in "our meek escutcheon" (15)? What metaphorically does it represent?

121. 'Twas warm at first like us

'Twas warm at first like us,
Until there crept upon
A chill, like frost upon a glass,
Till all the scene be gone.

The forehead copied stone,
The fingers grew too cold
To ache, and like a skater's brook
The busy eyes congealed.

It straightened—that was all.
It crowded cold to cold.
It multiplied indifference
As pride were all it could.

And even when with cords
'Twas lowered like a weight,
It made no signal, nor demurred,
But dropped like adamant.

Emily Dickinson (1830–1886)

QUESTIONS

1. Vocabulary: *adamant* (16).
2. What is "It" in the opening line? What is being described in the poem, and between what points in time?
3. How would you describe the tone of this poem? How does it contrast with that of the preceding poem?

122. Crossing the Bar

Sunset and evening star,
　And one clear call for me!
And may there be no moaning of the bar
　When I put out to sea,

But such a tide as moving seems asleep,
  Too full for sound and foam,
When that which drew from out the boundless deep
  Turns again home.

Twilight and evening bell,
  And after that the dark!
And may there be no sadness of farewell
  When I embark;

For though from out our bourne of Time and Place
  The flood may bear me far,
I hope to see my Pilot face to face
  When I have crossed the bar.

Alfred, Lord Tennyson (1809–1892)

QUESTIONS

1. Vocabulary: *bourne* (13).
2. What two sets of figures does Tennyson use for approaching death? What is the precise moment of death in each set?
3. In troubled weather the wind and waves above the sandbar across a harbor's mouth make a moaning sound. What metaphorical meaning has the "moaning of the bar" here (3)? For what kind of death is the speaker wishing? Why does he want "no sadness of farewell" (11)?
4. What is "that which drew from out the boundless deep" (7)? What is "the boundless deep"? To what is it opposed in the poem? Why is "Pilot" (15) capitalized?

123. The Oxen

Christmas Eve, and twelve of the clock.
  "Now they are all on their knees,"
An elder said as we sat in a flock
  By the embers in hearthside ease.

We pictured the meek mild creatures where
  They dwelt in their strawy pen,
Nor did it occur to one of us there
  To doubt they were kneeling then.

So fair a fancy few would weave
  In these years! Yet, I feel,
If someone said on Christmas Eve,
  "Come; see the oxen kneel

"In the lonely barton° by yonder coomb° *farm; valley*
Our childhood used to know,"
I should go with him in the gloom,
Hoping it might be so.

Thomas Hardy (1840–1928)

QUESTIONS

1. Is the simple superstition referred to in this poem opposed to, or identified with, religious faith? With what implications for the meaning of the poem?
2. What are "these years" (10) and how do they contrast with the years of the poet's boyhood? What event in intellectual history between 1840 and 1915 (the date Hardy composed this poem) was most responsible for the change?
3. Both "Crossing the Bar" and "The Oxen" in their last lines use a form of the verb *hope*. By fully discussing tone, establish the precise meaning of hope in each poem. What degree of expectation does it imply? How should the word be handled in reading Tennyson's poem aloud?

124. The Apparition

When by thy scorn, O murderess, I am dead,
And that thou thinkst thee free
From all solicitatiön from me,
Then shall my ghost come to thy bed,
And thee, feigned vestal, in worse arms shall see;
Then thy sick taper° will begin to wink, *candle*
And he, whose thou art then, being tired before,
Will, if thou stir, or pinch to wake him, think
Thou call'st for more,
And in false sleep will from thee shrink.
And then, poor aspen wretch, neglected, thou,
Bathed in a cold quicksilver sweat, wilt lie
A verier° ghost than I. *truer*
What I will say, I will not tell thee now,
Lest that preserve thee; and since my love is spent,
I had rather thou shouldst painfully repent,
Than by my threatenings rest still innocent.

John Donne (1572–1631)

QUESTIONS

1. Vocabulary: *feigned* (5), *aspen* (11), *quicksilver* (12). Are the latter two words used literally or figuratively? Explain.
2. What has been the past relationship between the speaker and the woman addressed? How does a "solicitatiön" differ from a proposal? Why does he call her a "murderess"? What threat does he make against her?

3. In line 15 the speaker proclaims that his love for the woman "is spent." Does the tone of the poem support this contention? Discuss.
4. In line 5 why does the speaker use the word "vestal" instead of "virgin"? Does he believe her not to be a virgin? Of what is he accusing her? (In ancient Rome the vestal virgins tended the perpetual fire in the temple of Vesta. They entered this service between the ages of six and ten, and served for a term of thirty years, during which they were bound to virginity.)
5. The implied metaphor in line 1—that a woman who will not satisfy her lover's desires is "killing" him—was a cliché of Renaissance poetry. What original twist does Donne give it to make it fresh and new?
6. In the scene imagined by the speaker of his ghost's visit to the woman's bed, he finds her "in worse arms"—worse than whose? In what respect? By what will this other man have been "tired before"? Of what will he think she is calling for "more"? What is the speaker implying about himself and the woman in these lines?
7. Why (according to the speaker) will the woman *really* be trying to wake up her bedmate? Why, when she fails, will she be a "verier" ghost than the speaker?
8. What will the ghost say to her that he will not now reveal lest his telling it "preserve" her? Can we know? Does *he* know? Why does he make this undefined threat?
9. For what does the speaker say he wants the woman to "painfully repent"? Of what crime or sin would she remain "innocent" if he revealed now what his ghost would say? What is the speaker's real objective?

125. The Flea

Mark but this flea, and mark in this
How little that which thou deny'st me is;
It sucked me first, and now sucks thee,
And in this flea our two bloods mingled be;
Thou know'st that this cannot be said
A sin, nor shame, nor loss of maidenhead;
   Yet this enjoys before it woo,
   And pampered swells with one blood made of two,
   And this, alas, is more than we would do.

Oh stay, three lives in one flea spare,
Where we almost, yea more than married are,
This flea is you and I, and this
Our marriage bed and marriage temple is;
Though parents grudge, and you, we are met
And cloistered in these living walls of jet.
   Though use° make you apt to kill me, habit
   Let not to that, self-murder added be,
   And sacrilege, three sins in killing three.

Cruel and sudden, hast thou since
Purpled° thy nail in blood of innocence? — crimsoned
Wherein could this flea guilty be,
Except in that drop which it sucked from thee?
Yet thou triumph'st and say'st that thou
Find'st not thyself, nor me, the weaker now.
'Tis true. Then learn how false fears be:
Just so much honor, when thou yield'st to me,
Will waste, as this flea's death took life from thee.

John Donne (1572–1631)

QUESTIONS

1. In many respects this poem is like a miniature play: it has two characters, dramatic conflict, dialogue (though we hear only one speaker), and stage action. The action is indicated by stage directions embodied in the dialogue. What has happened just *preceding* the first line of the poem? What happens *between* the first and second stanzas? What happens *between* the second and third? How does the female character behave and what does she say *during* the third stanza?
2. What has been the past relationship of the speaker and the woman? What has she denied him (2)? How has she habitually "killed" him (16)? Why has she done so? How does it happen that he is still alive? What is his objective in the poem?
3. According to a traditional Renaissance belief, the bloods of lovers "mingled" during sexual intercourse. What is the speaker's argument in stanza 1? Reduce it to paraphrase. How logical is it?
4. What do "parents grudge, and you" in stanza 2? What are the "living walls of jet" (15)? What three things will the woman kill by crushing the flea? What three sins will she commit (18)?
5. Why and how does the woman "triumph" in stanza 3? What is the speaker's response? How logical is his concluding argument?
6. What action, if any, would you infer, follows the conclusion of the poem?
7. "The Apparition" and "The Flea" may both be classified as "seduction poems." How do they differ in tone?

126. Dover Beach

The sea is calm tonight,
The tide is full, the moon lies fair
Upon the straits; — on the French coast the light
Gleams and is gone; the cliffs of England stand,
Glimmering and vast, out in the tranquil bay.
Come to the window, sweet is the night-air!
Only, from the long line of spray
Where the sea meets the moon-blanched land,

Listen! you hear the grating roar
Of pebbles which the waves draw back, and fling,
At their return, up the high strand,
Begin, and cease, and then again begin,
With tremulous cadence slow, and bring
The eternal note of sadness in.

Sophocles long ago
Heard it on the Aegean, and it brought
Into his mind the turbid ebb and flow
Of human misery; we
Find also in the sound a thought,
Hearing it by this distant northern sea.

The Sea of Faith
Was once, too, at the full, and round earth's shore
Lay like the folds of a bright girdle furled.
But now I only hear
Its melancholy, long, withdrawing roar,
Retreating, to the breath
Of the night-wind, down the vast edges drear
And naked shingles° of the world. pebbled beaches

Ah, love, let us be true
To one another! for the world, which seems
To lie before us like a land of dreams,
So various, so beautiful, so new,
Hath really neither joy, nor love, nor light,
Nor certitude, nor peace, nor help for pain;
And we are here as on a darkling plain
Swept with confused alarms of struggle and flight,
Where ignorant armies clash by night.

Matthew Arnold (1822–1888)

QUESTIONS

1. Vocabulary: *strand* (11), *girdle* (23), *darkling* (35). Identify the physical locale of the cliffs of Dover and their relation to the French coast; identify the Aegean and Sophocles.
2. As precisely as possible, define the implied scene: What is the speaker's physical location? Whom is he addressing? What is the time of day and the state of the weather?
3. Discuss the visual and auditory images of the poem and their relation to illusion and reality.
4. The speaker is lamenting the decline of religious faith in his time. Is he himself a believer? Does he see any medicine for the world's maladies?

5. Discuss in detail the imagery in the last three lines. Are the "armies" figurative or literal? What makes these lines so effective?
6. What term or terms would you choose to describe the overall tone of the poem?

127. Church Going

Once I am sure there's nothing going on
I step inside, letting the door thud shut.
Another church: matting, seats, and stone,
And little books; sprawlings of flowers, cut
For Sunday, brownish now; some brass and stuff
Up at the holy end; the small neat organ;
And a tense, musty, unignorable silence,
Brewed God knows how long. Hatless, I take off
My cycle-clips in awkward reverence,

Move forward, run my hand around the font.
From where I stand, the roof looks almost new—
Cleaned, or restored? Someone would know: I don't.
Mounting the lectern, I peruse a few
Hectoring large-scale verses, and pronounce
"Here endeth" much more loudly than I'd meant.
The echoes snigger briefly. Back at the door
I sign the book, donate an Irish sixpence,
Reflect the place was not worth stopping for.

Yet stop I did: in fact I often do,
And always end much at a loss like this,
Wondering what to look for, wondering, too,
When churches fall completely out of use
What we shall turn them into, if we shall keep
A few cathedrals chronically on show,
Their parchment, plate and pyx in locked cases,
And let the rest rent-free to rain and sheep.
Shall we avoid them as unlucky places?

Or, after dark, will dubious women come
To make their children touch a particular stone;
Pick simples for a cancer; or on some
Advised night see walking a dead one?
Power of some sort or other will go on
In games, in riddles, seemingly at random;
But superstition, like belief, must die,
And what remains when disbelief has gone?
Grass, weedy pavement, brambles, buttress, sky,

A shape less recognizable each week,
A purpose more obscure. I wonder who
Will be the last, the very last, to seek
This place for what it was; one of the crew
That tap and jot and know what rood-lofts were?
Some ruin-bibber, randy for antique,
Or Christmas-addict, counting on a whiff
Of gown-and-bands and organ-pipes and myrrh?
Or will he be my representative,

Bored, uninformed, knowing the ghostly silt
Dispersed, yet tending to this cross of ground
Through suburb scrub because it held unspilt
So long and equably what since is found
Only in separation—marriage, and birth,
And death, and thoughts of these—for whom was built
This special shell? For though I've no idea
What this accoutered frowsty barn is worth,
It pleases me to stand in silence here;

A serious house on serious earth it is,
In whose blent air all our compulsions meet,
Are recognized, and robed as destinies.
And that much never can be obsolete,
Since someone will forever be surprising
A hunger in himself to be more serious,
And gravitating with it to this ground,
Which, he once heard, was proper to grow wise in,
If only that so many dead lie round.

Philip Larkin (1922–1985)

QUESTIONS

1. Vocabulary: *hectoring* (14), *pyx* (25), *dubious* (28), *simples* (30), *accoutered* (53), *frowsty* (53), *blent* (56). *Large-scale* (14) indicates a print size suited to oral reading; an *Irish sixpence* (17) was a small coin not legal tender in England, the scene of the poem; *rood-lofts* (41) are architectural features found in many early Christian churches; *bibber* (42) and *randy* (42) are figurative, literally meaning "drunkard" and "lustful"; *gown-and-bands* (44) are ornate robes worn by church officials in religious ceremonies.
2. Like "Dover Beach" (first published in 1867), "Church Going" (1954) is concerned with belief and disbelief. In modern England the landscape is dotted with small churches, often charming in their combination of stone (outside) and intricately carved wood (inside). Some are in ruins, some are badly in need of repair, and some are well kept-up by parishioners who keep them dusted and provide fresh flowers for the diminishing attendance at Sunday

services. These churches invariably have by the entrance a book that visitors can sign as a record of their having been there and a collection box with a sign urging them to drop in a few coins for upkeep, repair, or restoration. In small towns and villages the church is often the chief or only building of architectural or historical interest, and tourist visitors may outnumber parishioners. To which of the three categories of churches mentioned here does Larkin's poem refer?
3. What different denotations does the title contain?
4. In what activity has the speaker been engaging when he stops to see the church? How is it revealed? Why does he stop? Is he a believer? How involved is he in inspecting this church building?
5. Compare the language used by the speakers in "Dover Beach" and "Church Going." Which speaker is more eloquent? Which is more informal and conversational? Without looking back at the texts, try to assign the following words to one poem or the other: *moon-blanched, cycle-clips, darkling, hath, snigger, whiff, drear, brownish, tremulous, glimmering, frowsty, stuff.* Then go back and check your success.
6. Define the tone (the attitude of the speaker or author toward the subject) of "Church Going" as precisely as possible. Compare this tone to that of "Dover Beach."

128. The Dead

These hearts were woven of human joys and cares,
  Washed marvelously with sorrow, swift to mirth.
The years had given them kindness. Dawn was theirs,
  And sunset, and the colors of the earth.
These had seen movement, and heard music; known
  Slumber and waking; loved; gone proudly friended;
Felt the quick stir of wonder; sat alone;
  Touched flowers and furs and cheeks. All this is ended.

There are waters blown by changing winds to laughter
And lit by the rich skies, all day. And after,
  Frost, with a gesture, stays the winds that dance
And wandering loveliness. He leaves a white
  Unbroken glory, a gathered radiance,
A width, a shining peace, under the night.

Rupert Brooke (1887–1915)

QUESTIONS

1. This poem, the fourth in a group of five sonnets collectively entitled *1914*, was written a few months after the outbreak of World War I and the voluntary enlistment of its author in the British navy. To whom do the pronouns "These" (1, 5), "them" (3), and "theirs" (3) refer? What, according to the poet, was the quality of their lives?

2. What is the literal term in the metaphor of which "laughter" (9) is the figurative term? With what word in the first eight lines is it kin?
3. What *happens* in the last six lines? What is the literal term for which the "white / Unbroken glory," "gathered radiance," "width," and "shining peace" are metonymies? How are the last six lines related to the first eight? Why does the poet substitute these metonymies for the literal term? Of what is "night" (14) a symbol?

129. The Death of a Soldier

Life contracts and death is expected,
As in a season of autumn.
The soldier falls.

He does not become a three-days personage,
Imposing his separation,
Calling for pomp.

Death is absolute and without memorial,
As in a season of autumn,
When the wind stops,

When the wind stops and, over the heavens,
The clouds go, nevertheless,
In their direction.

Wallace Stevens (1879–1955)

QUESTIONS

1. What is the effect of the understatement in the first stanza? How does the second stanza call to mind the traditional expectations that the title evokes?
2. To what ordinary meteorological effect does the simile in lines 8–12 refer? What does this comparison say about the meaning of the death of *a* soldier?
3. Which line sums up the thesis of this poem? Is "the death of a soldier" the literal subject?
4. What contrasts of tone do you find between this poem and the preceding one? Compare the tones of these two with those of other poems dealing with their ostensible subject: Owen's "Dulce et Decorum Est" (No. 3) and "Anthem for Doomed Youth" (No. 163), Hardy's "The Man He Killed" (No. 12), and Sassoon's "Base Details" (No. 31).

130. Engraved on the Collar of a Dog Which I Gave to His Royal Highness

I am his Highness' dog at Kew;
Pray tell me, sir, whose dog are you?

Alexander Pope (1688–1744)

QUESTIONS

1. What adjective—or noun—best fits the attitude expressed on the dog's collar?
2. Is the dog in any way symbolic? Explain.

131. Love

There's the wonderful love of a beautiful maid,
  And the love of a staunch true man,
And the love of a baby that's unafraid—
  All have existed since time began.
But the most wonderful love, the Love of all loves,
  Even greater than the love for Mother,
Is the infinite, tenderest, passionate love
  Of one dead drunk for another.

Anonymous

QUESTION

The radical shift in tone makes "Love" come off. If such a shift were unintentional in a poem, what would our view be?

EXERCISES

1. Marvell's "To His Coy Mistress" (No. 53), Housman's "Loveliest of Trees" (No. 56), and Herrick's "To the Virgins, to Make Much of Time" (No. 63) all treat a traditional poetic theme known as the *carpe diem* ("seize the day") theme. They differ sharply, however, in tone. Characterize the tone of each, and point out the differences in poetic management that account for the differences in tone.
2. Describe and account for the differences in tone between the poems in the following pairs:
   a. "The Lamb" (No. 208) and "The Tiger" (No. 209).
   b. "The Unknown Citizen" (No. 83) and "Departmental" (No. 84).
   c. "It sifts from leaden sieves" (No. 45) and "The Snow Man" (No. 286).
   d. "Leda and the Swan" (No. 97) and "Leda's Sister and the Geese" (No. 251).
   e. "Nothing Gold Can Stay" (No. 143) and "Never Again Would Birds' Song Be the Same" (No. 230).
   f. "Fire and Ice" (No. 65) and "Earth" (No. 89).
   g. "The Sheaves" (No. 25) and "An altered look about the hills" (No. 99).
   h. "Ballad of Birmingham" (No. 8) and "Southern Cop" (No. 87).
   i. "The Whipping" (No. 5) and "The Beating" (No. 281).

CHAPTER ELEVEN

Musical Devices

Poetry obviously makes a greater use of the "music" of language than does language that is not poetry. The poet, unlike the person who uses language to convey only information, chooses words for sound as well as for meaning, and uses the sound as a means of reinforcing meaning. So prominent is this musical quality of poetry that some writers have made it the distinguishing term in their definitions of poetry. Edgar Allan Poe, for instance, describes poetry as "music . . . combined with a pleasurable idea." Whether or not it deserves this much importance, verbal music, like connotation, imagery, and figurative language, is one of the important resources that enable the poet to do more than communicate mere information. The poet may indeed sometimes pursue verbal music for its own sake; more often, at least in first-rate poetry, it is an adjunct to the total meaning or communication of the poem.

The poet achieves musical quality in two broad ways: by the choice and arrangement of sounds and by the arrangement of accents. In this chapter we will consider the first of these.

An essential element in all music is repetition. In fact, we might say that all art consists of giving structure to two elements: repetition and variation. All things we enjoy greatly and lastingly have these two elements. We enjoy the sea endlessly because it is always the same yet always different. We enjoy a baseball game because it contains the same complex combination of pattern and variation. Our love of art, then, is rooted in human psychology. We like the familiar, we like variety, but we like them combined. If we get too much sameness, the result is monotony and tedium; if we get too much variety, the result is bewilderment and confusion. The composer of music, therefore, repeats certain musical tones; repeats them in certain combinations, or chords; and repeats them in certain patterns, or melodies. The poet likewise repeats certain sounds in certain combinations and arrangements, and thus adds musical meaning to verse. Consider the following short example.

132. The Turtle

The turtle lives 'twixt plated decks
Which practically conceal its sex.
I think it clever of the turtle
In such a fix to be so fertile.

Ogden Nash (1902–1971)

Here is a little joke, a paradox of animal life to which the author has cleverly drawn our attention. An experiment will show us, however, that much of its appeal lies not so much in what it says as in the manner in which it says it. If, for instance, we recast the verse as prose: "The turtle lives in a shell which almost conceals its sex. It is ingenious of the turtle, in such a situation, to be so prolific," the joke falls flat. Some of its appeal must lie in its metrical form. So now we cast it in unrimed verse:

Because he lives between two decks,
It's hard to tell a turtle's gender.
The turtle is a clever beast
In such a plight to be so fertile.

Here, perhaps, is *some* improvement over the prose version, but still the piquancy of the original is missing. Much of that appeal must have consisted in the use of rime—the repetition of sound in "decks" and "sex," "turtle" and "fertile." So we try once more.

The turtle lives 'twixt plated decks
Which practically conceal its sex.
I think it clever of the turtle
In such a plight to be so fertile.

But for perceptive readers there is still something missing—they may not at first see what—but some little touch that makes the difference between a good piece of verse and a little masterpiece of its kind. And then they see it: "plight" has been substituted for "fix."

But why should "fix" make such a difference? Its meaning is little different from that of "plight"; its only important difference is in sound. But there we are. The final *x* in "fix" catches up the concluding consonant sound in "sex," and its initial *f* is repeated in the initial consonant sound of "fertile." Not only do these sound recurrences provide a subtle gratification to the ear, but they also give the verse structure; they emphasize and draw together the key words of the piece: "sex," "fix," and "fertile."

Poets may repeat any unit of sound from the smallest to the largest. They may repeat individual vowel and consonant sounds, whole syllables, words, phrases, lines, or groups of lines. In each instance, in a good poem, the repetition will serve several purposes: it will please the ear, it will emphasize the words in which the repetition occurs, and it will give structure to the poem. The popularity and initial impressiveness of such repetitions are evidenced by their becoming in many instances embedded in the language as clichés like "wild and woolly," "first and foremost," "footloose and fancy-free," "penny-wise, pound-foolish," "dead as a doornail," "might and main," "sink or swim," "do or die," "pell-mell," "helter-skelter," "harum-scarum," "hocus-pocus." Some of these kinds of repetition have names, as we will see.

A syllable consists of a vowel sound that may be preceded or followed by consonant sounds. Any of these sounds may be repeated. The repetition of initial consonant sounds, as in "tried and true," "safe and sound," "fish or fowl," "rime or reason," is **alliteration**. The repetition of vowel sounds, as in "mad as a hatter," "time out of mind," "free and easy," "slapdash," is **assonance**. The repetition of final consonant sounds, as in "first and last," "odds and ends," "short and sweet," "a stroke of luck," or Shakespeare's "struts and frets" (No. 92) is **consonance**.*

Repetitions may be used alone or in combination. Alliteration and assonance are combined in such phrases as "time and tide," "thick and thin," "kith and kin," "alas and alack," "fit as a fiddle," and Edgar Allan Poe's famous line, "The viol, the violet, and the vine." Alliteration and consonance are combined in such phrases as "crisscross," "last but not least," "lone and lorn," "good as gold," Housman's "Malt does more than Milton can" (No. 10), and Kay's "meanings lost in manners" (No. 27). The combination of assonance and consonance is rime.

Rime is the repetition of the accented vowel sound and all succeeding sounds. It is called **masculine** when the rime sounds involve only one syllable, as in *decks* and *sex* or *support* and *retort*. It is **feminine** when the rime sounds involve two or more syllables, as in *turtle* and *fertile* or *spitefully* and *delightfully*. It is referred to as **internal rime** when one or more

*There is no established terminology for these various repetitions. *Alliteration* is used by some writers to mean any repetition of consonant sounds. *Assonance* has been used to mean the similarity as well as the identity of vowel sounds, or even the similarity of any sounds whatever. *Consonance* has often been reserved for words in which both the initial *and* final consonant sounds correspond, as in *green* and *groan*, *moon* and *mine*. *Rime* (or rhyme) has been used to mean any sound repetition, including alliteration, assonance, and consonance. In the absence of clear agreement on the meanings of these terms, the terminology chosen here has appeared most useful, with support in usage. Labels are useful in analysis. However, the student should learn to recognize the devices and, more importantly, should learn to see their function, without worrying too much over nomenclature.

riming words are *within* the line and as **end rime** when the riming words are at the *ends* of lines. End rime is probably the most frequently used and most consciously sought sound repetition in English poetry. Because it comes at the end of the line, it receives emphasis as a musical effect and perhaps contributes more than any other musical resource except rhythm and meter to give poetry its musical effect as well as its structure. There exists, however, a large body of poetry that does not employ rime and for which rime would not be appropriate. Also, there has always been a tendency, especially noticeable in modern poetry, to substitute approximate rimes for perfect rimes at the ends of lines. **Approximate rimes** (also called slant rimes) include words with any kind of sound similarity, from close to fairly remote. Under approximate rime we include alliteration, assonance, and consonance or their combinations when used at the end of the line; half-rime (feminine rimes in which only half of the word rimes — the accented half, as in *lightly* and *frightful*, or the unaccented half, as in *yellow* and *willow*); and other similarities too elusive to name. "A narrow fellow in the grass" (No. 36), "'Twas warm at first like us" (No. 121), "Toads" (No. 51), and "Mr. Z" (No. 86), to different degrees, all employ various kinds of approximate end rime.

133. That night when joy began

That night when joy began
Our narrowest veins to flush,
We waited for the flash
Of morning's leveled gun.

But morning let us pass,
And day by day relief
Outgrows his nervous laugh,
Grown credulous of peace,

As mile by mile is seen
No trespasser's reproach,
And love's best glasses reach
No fields but are his own.

W. H. Auden (1907–1973)

QUESTIONS

1. What has been the past experience with love of the two people in the poem? What is their present experience? What precisely is the tone of the poem?
2. What basic metaphor underlies the poem? Work it out stanza by stanza. What is "the flash of morning's leveled gun" (3–4)? Does line 10 mean that no

trespasser reproaches the lovers or that no one reproaches the lovers for being trespassers? Does "glasses" (11) refer to spectacles, tumblers, mirrors, or field glasses? Point out three personifications.
3. The rime pattern in the poem is intricate and exact. Work it out, considering alliteration, assonance, and consonance.

In addition to the repetition of individual sounds and syllables, the poet may repeat whole words, phrases, lines, or groups of lines. When such repetition is done according to some fixed pattern, it is called a **refrain**. The refrain is especially common in songlike poetry. Shakespeare's "Winter" (No. 2) and "Spring" (No. 4), and the ballad "Edward" (No. 182) furnish examples of refrains.

We have not nearly exhausted the possibilities of sound repetition by giving names to a few of the more prominent kinds. The complete study of possible kinds of sound repetition in poetry would be so complex, however, that it would break down under its own machinery. Some of the subtlest and loveliest effects escape our net of names. In as short a phrase as this from the prose of John Ruskin—"ivy as light and lovely as the vine"—we notice alliteration in *light* and *lovely*, assonance in *ivy, light*, and *vine*, and consonance in *ivy* and *lovely*, but we have no name to connect the *v* in *vine* with the *v*'s in *ivy* and *lovely*, or the second *l* in *lovely* with the first *l*, or the final syllables of *ivy* and *lovely* with each other; yet these are all an effective part of the music of the line. Also contributing to the music of poetry is the linking of related rather than identical sounds, such as *m* and *n*, or *p* and *b*, or the vowel sounds in *boat, boot*, and *book*.

These various musical repetitions, for trained readers, will ordinarily make an almost subconscious contribution to their reading of the poem: readers will feel their effect without necessarily being aware of what has caused it. There is value, however, in occasionally analyzing a poem for these devices in order to increase awareness of them. A few words of caution are necessary. First, the repetitions are entirely a matter of sound; spelling is irrelevant. *Bear* and *pair* are rimes, but *through* and *rough* are not. *Cell* and *sin, folly* and *philosophy* alliterate, but *sin* and *sugar, gun* and *gem* do not. Second, alliteration, assonance, consonance, and masculine rime are matters that ordinarily involve only stressed or accented syllables; for only such syllables ordinarily make enough impression on the ear to be significant in the sound pattern of the poem. For instance, we should hardly consider *which* and *its* in the second line of "The Turtle" an example of assonance, for neither word is stressed enough in the reading to make it significant as a sound. Third, the words involved in these repetitions must be close enough together that the ear retains the sound, consciously or subconsciously, from its first occurrence to its second. This distance varies according to circumstances, but for alliteration, assonance, and consonance the words ordinarily have to be in the same line or adjacent lines. End rime bridges a longer gap.

134. God's Grandeur

The world is charged with the grandeur of God.
  It will flame out, like shining from shook foil;
  It gathers to a greatness, like the ooze of oil
Crushed. Why do men then now not reck his rod?
Generations have trod, have trod, have trod;
  And all is seared with trade; bleared, smeared with toil;
  And wears man's smudge and shares man's smell: the soil
Is bare now, nor can foot feel, being shod.

And for all this, nature is never spent;
  There lives the dearest freshness deep down things;
And though the last lights off the black West went
  Oh, morning, at the brown brink eastward, springs—
Because the Holy Ghost over the bent
  World broods with warm breast and with ah! bright wings.

Gerard Manley Hopkins (1844–1889)

QUESTIONS

1. What is the theme of this sonnet?
2. The image in lines 3–4 possibly refers to olive oil being collected in great vats from crushed olives, but the image is much disputed. Explain the simile in line 2 and the symbols in lines 7–8 and 11–12.
3. Explain "reck his rod" (4), "spent" (9), "bent" (13).
4. Using different-colored pencils, encircle and connect examples of alliteration, assonance, consonance, and internal rime. Do these help to carry the meaning?

We should not leave the impression that the use of these musical devices is necessarily or always valuable. Like the other resources of poetry, they can be judged only in the light of the poem's total intention. Many of the greatest works of English poetry—for instance, *Hamlet* and *King Lear* and *Paradise Lost*—do not employ end rime. Both alliteration and rime, especially feminine rime, become humorous or silly if used excessively or unskillfully. If the intention is humorous, the result is delightful; if not, fatal. Shakespeare, who knew how to use all these devices to the utmost advantage, parodied their unskillful use in lines like "The preyful princess pierced and pricked a pretty pleasing prickett" in *Love's Labor's Lost* and

> Whereat with blade, with bloody, blameful blade,
> He bravely broached his boiling bloody breast

in *A Midsummer Night's Dream*. Swinburne parodied his own highly alliterative style in "Nephelidia" with lines like "Life is the lust of a lamp for the light that is dark till the dawn of the day when we die." Used skillfully and judiciously, however, musical devices provide a palpable and delicate pleasure to the ear and, even more important, add dimension to meaning.

* * *

135. We Real Cool

The Pool Players.
Seven At The Golden Shovel.

We real cool. We
Left school. We

Lurk late. We
Strike straight. We

Sing sin. We
Thin gin. We

Jazz June. We
Die soon.

Gwendolyn Brooks (b. 1917)

QUESTIONS

1. In addition to end rime, what other musical devices does this poem employ?
2. Try reading this poem with the pronouns at the beginning of the lines instead of at the end. What is lost?
3. English teachers in a certain urban school were once criticized for having their students read this poem: it was said to be immoral. Was the criticism justified? Why or why not?

136. Blackberry Sweet

Black girl black girl
lips as curved as cherries
full as grape bunches
sweet as blackberries

Black girl black girl
when you walk you are
magic as a rising bird
or a falling star

Black girl black girl
what's your spell to make
the heart in my breast
jump stop shake

Dudley Randall (b. 1914)

QUESTIONS

1. Refrains traditionally are placed at the ends of stanzas. How does this poem differ? With what effect?
2. Discuss the relation of form and content in the poem. How are the separate stanzas unified in themselves and yet linked to the others? How does each stanza achieve climax? How does the poem as a whole achieve climax?

137. Counting-Out Rhyme

Silver bark of beech, and sallow
Bark of yellow birch and yellow
  Twig of willow.

Stripe of green in moosewood maple,
Color seen in leaf of apple,
  Bark of popple.

Wood of popple pale as moonbeam,
Wood of oak for yoke and barn-beam,
  Wood of hornbeam.

Silver bark of beech, and hollow
Stem of elder, tall and yellow
  Twig of willow.

Edna St. Vincent Millay (1892–1950)

QUESTIONS

1. List all instances of alliteration, assonance, consonance, half-rime, internal rime, and word repetition.
2. How serious is the purpose of this poem?
3. What is a "counting-out rhyme"? Can you remember any from your childhood? What is being counted here?

138. As imperceptibly as grief

As imperceptibly as grief
The summer lapsed away,
Too imperceptible at last
To seem like perfidy.

A quietness distilled
As twilight long begun,
Or nature spending with herself
Sequestered afternoon.

The dusk drew earlier in,
The morning foreign shone—
A courteous, yet harrowing grace,
As guest who would be gone.

And thus, without a wing
Or service of a keel,
Our summer made her light escape
Into the beautiful.

Emily Dickinson (1830–1886)

QUESTIONS

1. What are the subject and tone of the poem? Explain its opening simile.
2. Discuss the ways in which approximate rimes, alliteration, and the consonant sounds in the last stanza contribute to the meaning and tone.
3. What possible meanings have the last two lines?

139. Parting, without a Sequel

She has finished and sealed the letter
At last, which he so richly has deserved,
With characters venomous and hatefully curved,
And nothing could be better.

But even as she gave it
Saying to the blue-capped functioner of doom,
"Into his hands," she hoped the leering groom
Might somewhere lose and leave it.

Then all the blood
Forsook the face. She was too pale for tears,
Observing the ruin of her younger years.
She went and stood

Under her father's vaunting oak
Who kept his peace in wind and sun, and glistened
Stoical in the rain; to whom she listened
If he spoke.

And now the agitation of the rain
Rasped his sere leaves, and he talked low and gentle
Reproaching the wan daughter by the lintel;
Ceasing and beginning again.

Away went the messenger's bicycle,
His serpent's track went up the hill forever,
And all the time she stood there hot as fever
And cold as any icicle.

John Crowe Ransom (1888–1974)

QUESTIONS

1. Identify the figures of speech in lines 3 and 22 and discuss their effectiveness. Are there traces of dramatic irony in the poem? Where?
2. Is the oak literal or figurative? Neither? Both? Discuss the meanings of "vaunting" (13), "stoical" (15), "sere" (18), and "lintel" (19).
3. Do you find any trite language in the poem? Where? What does it tell us about the girl's action?
4. W. H. Auden has defined poetry as "the clear expression of mixed feelings." Discuss the applicability of the definition to this poem. Try it out on other poems.
5. A feminine rime that involves two syllables is known also as a **double rime**. Find examples in the poem of both perfect and approximate double rimes. A feminine rime that involves three syllables is a **triple rime**. Find one example of a triple rime. Which lines employ masculine or **single rimes**, either perfect or approximate?

140. Thistles

Against the rubber tongues of cows and the hoeing hands of men
Thistles spike the summer air
Or crackle open under a blue-black pressure.

Every one a revengeful burst
Of resurrection, a grasped fistful
Of splintered weapons and Icelandic frost thrust up

From the underground stain of a decayed Viking.
They are like pale hair and the gutturals of dialects.
Every one manages a plume of blood.

Then they grow grey, like men.
Mown down, it is a feud. Their sons appear,
Stiff with weapons, fighting back over the same ground.

Ted Hughes (b. 1930)

QUESTIONS

1. What natural characteristics of thistles are included in the poem? What identity do the similes and metaphors create for these plants?
2. What do the allusions to the violence of the marauding Vikings add to the poem? How are modern-day thistles like a resurrection of those warlike voyagers? Is this poem about thistles, about Vikings, or about some more universal subject?
3. What musical devices does the poem display? How do they suit the topic?

141. Shoe Shop

I shut the door on the racket
Of rush hour traffic,
Inhale the earthy, thick
Perfume of leather and pipe tobacco.

The place might be a barbershop
Where the air gets lathered with gossip.
You can almost hear the whippersnap
Of the straightedge on the razor strop.

It might be a front for agitators,
But there's no back room. A rabble
Of boots and shoes lies tumbled
In heaps like a hoard of potatoes.

The cobbler, broad as a blacksmith,
Turns a shoe over his pommel,
Pummels the sole, takes the nail
He's bit between his teeth,

And drives it into the heel. Hunched
At his workbench, he pays the old shoe
More attention than me. "Help you?"
He grunts, as if the man held a grudge

Against business. He gives my run-over
Loafer a look. "Plastic," he spits.
"And foreign-made. Doubt I can fix it."
I could be holding a dead gopher.

"The Europeans might make good shoes,
But I never see them. Cut the price.
Advertise! Never mind the merchandise.
You buy yourself a pair, brand new,

"The welt will be cardboard
Where it ought to be leather.
There's nothing to hold the shoe together."
He stows my pair in a cupboard.

"And all of them tan with acid.
The Mexicans make fancy boots, but they cure
Their leather in cow manure. Wear
Them out in the rain once. Rancid?

"I had a guy bring me a pair.
Wanted me to get rid of the stink.
Honest to God. I hate to think
My customers are crazy, but I swear."

He curses factories, inflation,
And I welcome the glow of conspiracy.
Together we plot, half seriously,
A counter industrial revolution.

His pride's been steeped in bitterness,
His politics tanned with elbow-grease.
To hear him fume and bitch, you'd guess
His guerrilla warfare's hopeless.

But talk about job satisfaction!
To take a tack from a tight-lipped smile,
Stick it like a thorn in an unworn sole,
To heft the hammer, and whack it!

When I step back out in the street
The city looks flimsy as a movie set.

Barton Sutter (b. 1949)

QUESTIONS

1. Identify the rime scheme of the poem. What kinds of rimes does it use? What lines contain perfect rimes?
2. Contrast the language (diction and syntax) of this poem with that of "To Autumn" (No. 41) or "Ulysses" (No. 67). Is it less poetic?
3. What kinds of imagery does the poem employ? Is it less rich in imagery than the poems just named?

4. Identify and discuss the appropriateness of the metaphors and similes in lines 6, 10–12, 22, 24, 45, 46, 48. What links stanzas 3, 11, 12? What is a "counter industrial revolution" (44)?
5. Explain the apparent contradiction between the cobbler's "bitterness" (45) and his "job satisfaction" (49). Why does the city look "flimsy as a movie set" (54) to the narrator when he leaves the shop?

142. Traveling through the dark

Traveling through the dark I found a deer
dead on the edge of the Wilson River road.
It is usually best to roll them into the canyon:
that road is narrow; to swerve might make more dead.

By glow of the tail-light I stumbled back of the car
and stood by the heap, a doe, a recent killing;
she had stiffened already, almost cold.
I dragged her off; she was large in the belly.

My fingers touching her side brought me the reason—
her side was warm; her fawn lay there waiting,
alive, still, never to be born.
Beside that mountain road I hesitated.

The car aimed ahead its lowered parking lights;
under the hood purred the steady engine.
I stood in the glare of the warm exhaust turning red;
around our group I could hear the wilderness listen.

I thought hard for us all—my only swerving—,
then pushed her over the edge into the river.

William Stafford (b. 1914)

QUESTIONS

1. State precisely the speaker's dilemma. What kind of person is he? Does he make the right decision? Why does he call his hesitation "my only swerving" (17), and how does this connect with the word "swerve" in line 4?
2. What different kinds of imagery and of image contrasts give life to the poem? Do any of the images have symbolic overtones?
3. At first glance this poem may appear to be without end rime. Looking closer, do you find any correspondences between lines 2 and 4 in each stanza? Between the final words of the concluding couplet? Can you find any line-end in the poem without some connection in sound to another line-end in its stanza?

143. Nothing Gold Can Stay

Nature's first green is gold,
Her hardest hue to hold.
Her early leaf's a flower;
But only so an hour.
Then leaf subsides to leaf.
So Eden sank to grief,
So dawn goes down to day.
Nothing gold can stay.

Robert Frost (1874–1963)

QUESTIONS

1. Explain the paradoxes in lines 1 and 3.
2. Discuss the poem as a series of symbols. What are the symbolic meanings of "gold" in the final line of the poem?
3. Discuss the contributions of alliteration, assonance, consonance, rime, and other repetitions to the effectiveness of the poem.

EXERCISE

Discuss the various ways in which the following poems make use of refrain:

1. "Winter" (No. 2)
2. "Spring" (No. 4)
3. "Southern Cop" (No. 87)
4. "in Just-" (No. 93)
5. "Edward" (No. 182)
6. "The Lamb" (No. 208)
7. "Riddle" (No. 236)
8. "Fear no more" (No. 273)
9. "Ettrick" (No. 280)
10. "Do Not Go Gentle into That Good Night" (No. 291)

CHAPTER TWELVE

Rhythm and Meter

Our love of rhythm and meter is rooted even deeper in us than our love of musical repetition. It is related to the beat of our hearts, the pulse of our blood, the intake and outflow of air from our lungs. Everything that we do naturally and gracefully we do rhythmically. There is rhythm in the way we walk, the way we swim, the way we ride a horse, the way we swing a golf club or a baseball bat. So native is rhythm to us that we read it, when we can, into the mechanical world around us. Our clocks go tick-tick-tick-tick, but we hear them go tick-tock, tick-tock in an endless trochaic. The click of the railway wheels beneath us patterns itself into a tune in our heads. Unquestionably, language that is rhythmical holds a strong appeal for us.

The term **rhythm** refers to any wavelike recurrence of motion or sound. In speech it is the natural rise and fall of language. All language is to some degree rhythmical, for all language involves some kind of alternation between accented and unaccented syllables. Language varies considerably, however, in the degree to which it exhibits rhythm. In some forms of speech the rhythm is so unobtrusive or so unpatterned that we are scarcely, if at all, aware of it. In other forms of speech the rhythm is so pronounced that we may be tempted to tap our foot to it.

Meter is the kind of rhythm we can tap our foot to. In metrical language the accents are arranged to occur at apparently equal intervals of time, and it is this interval we mark off with the tap of our foot. Metrical language is called **verse**. Nonmetrical language is **prose**. Not all poetry is metrical, nor is all metrical language poetry. *Verse* and *poetry* are not synonymous terms, nor is a *versifier* necessarily a *poet*.

The study of meter is a fascinating but highly complex subject. It is by no means an absolute prerequisite to an enjoyment, even a rich enjoyment, of poetry. But a knowledge of its fundamentals does have certain values. It can make the beginning reader more aware of the rhythmical effects of poetry and of how poetry should be read. It can enable the more advanced reader to analyze how certain effects are achieved, to see how rhythm is adapted to thought, and to explain what makes one poem (in this respect) better than another. The beginning student ought to have at least an elementary knowledge of the subject. It is not so difficult as its terminology might suggest.

In every word of more than one syllable, one syllable is *accented* or *stressed*, that is, given more prominence in pronunciation than the rest.* We say in*ter,* *en*ter, inter*vene,* *en*terprise, in*ter*pret. These accents are indicated in the dictionary, and only rarely are words in good poems accented differently: *on*ly cannot be pronounced on*ly*. If words of even one syllable are arranged into a sentence, we give certain words or syllables more prominence than the rest. We say: "He *went* to the *store*" or "*Ann* is *driv*ing her *car*." There is nothing mysterious about this; it is the normal process of language. The only difference between prose and verse is that in prose these accents occur more or less haphazardly; in verse the poet has arranged them to occur at regular intervals.

The word *meter* comes from a word meaning "measure." To measure something we must have a unit of measurement. For measuring length we use the inch, the foot, and the yard; for measuring time we use the second, the minute, and the hour. For measuring verse we use the foot, the line, and (sometimes) the stanza.

The basic metrical unit, the **foot**, consists normally of one accented syllable plus one or two unaccented syllables, though occasionally there may be no unaccented syllables, and very rarely there may be three. For diagramming verse, various systems of visual symbols have been invented. In this book we shall use a short curved line to indicate an unaccented syllable and a short horizontal line to indicate an accented syllable. We generally do not attempt through longer or shorter horizontal lines to distinguish between heavier or lighter accents (but see the exception on page 192). A vertical bar will indicate the division between feet. The basic kinds of feet are shown in the first table on the next page.

*Though the words *accent* and *stress* generally are used interchangeably, as here, a distinction is sometimes made between them in technical discussions. **Accent**, the relative prominence given a syllable in relation to its neighbors, is then said to result from one or more of four causes: *stress*, or force of utterance, producing loudness; *duration*; *pitch*; and *juncture*, the manner of transition between successive sounds. Of these, *stress*, in English verse, is the most important.

Examples		Name of foot	Name of meter*	
in-*ter*,	the *sun*	Iamb	Iambic	Duple meters
en-ter,	*went* to	Trochee	Trochaic	
in-ter-*vene*,	in a *hut*	Anapest	Anapestic	Triple meters
en-ter-prise,	*col*-or of	Dactyl	Dactylic	
true-blue		Spondee	(Spondaic)	
truth		Monosyllabic foot		

The secondary unit of measurement, the **line**, is measured by naming the number of feet in it. The following names are used:

Monometer	one foot	Pentameter	five feet
Dimeter	two feet	Hexameter	six feet
Trimeter	three feet	Heptameter	seven feet
Tetrameter	four feet	Octameter	eight feet

The third unit, the **stanza**, consists of a group of lines whose metrical pattern is repeated throughout the poem. Since not all verse is written in stanzas, we shall save our discussion of this unit till a later chapter.

The process of measuring verse is referred to as **scansion**. To *scan* any specimen of verse, we do three things: (1) we identify the prevailing foot, (2) we name the number of feet in a line—if this length follows any regular pattern, and (3) we describe the stanza pattern—if there is one. We may try out our skill on the following poem.

144. Virtue

Sweet day, so cool, so calm, so bright,
The bridal of the earth and sky;
The dew shall weep thy fall to night,
For thou must die.

*In the spondee the accent is thought of as being distributed equally or almost equally over the two syllables and is sometimes referred to as a hovering accent. No whole poems are written in spondees or monosyllabic feet; hence there are only four basic meters: iambic, trochaic, anapestic, and dactylic. Iambic and trochaic are **duple meters** because they employ two-syllable feet; anapestic and dactylic are **triple meters** because they employ three-syllable feet.

Sweet rose, whose hue, angry and brave,
Bids the rash gazer wipe his eye;
Thy root is ever in its grave,
And thou must die.

Sweet spring, full of sweet days and roses,
A box where sweets compacted lie;
My music shows ye have your closes,
And all must die.

Only a sweet and virtuous soul,
Like seasoned timber, never gives;
But though the whole world turn to coal,
Then chiefly lives.

George Herbert (1593–1633)

QUESTIONS

1. Vocabulary: *bridal* (2), *brave* (5), *closes* (11).
2. How are the four stanzas interconnected? How do they build to a climax? How does the fourth contrast with the first three?

The first step in scanning a poem is to read it normally according to its prose meaning, listening to where the accents fall, and perhaps beating time with the hand. If we have any doubt about how a line should be marked, we should skip it temporarily and go on to lines where we feel greater confidence—that is, to those lines which seem most regular, with accents that fall unmistakably at regular intervals. In "Virtue" lines 3, 10, and 14 clearly fall into this category, as do also the short lines 4, 8, and 12. Lines 3, 10, and 14 may be marked as follows:

The dew | shall weep | thy fall | to night, | 3
A box | where sweets | com- pact- | ed lie; | 10
Like sea- | soned tim- | ber, nev- | er gives. | 14

Lines 4, 8, and 12 are so nearly identical that we may let line 4 represent all three:

For thou | must die. | 4

Surveying what we have done so far, we may with some confidence say that the prevailing metrical foot of the poem is iambic; we also reasonably may hypothesize that the second and third lines of each stanza are tetrameter (four-foot) lines and that the fourth line is dimeter. What about the first line? Line 1 contains eight syllables, and the last six are clearly iambic:

> Sweet day, | so cool, | so calm, | so bright. | 1

This too, then, is a tetrameter line, and the only question is whether to mark the first foot as another iamb or as a spondee. Many metrists, emphasizing the priority of pattern, would mark it as an iamb. Clearly, however, the word "Sweet" is more important and receives more emphasis in a sensitive reading than the three "so's" in the line. Other metrists, therefore, would give it equal emphasis with "day" and mark the first foot as a spondee. Neither marking can be called incorrect. It is a matter of the reader's personal judgment or of his metrical philosophy. Following my own preference, I mark it as a spondee, and mark the first foot in lines 5 and 9 correspondingly. Similar choices occur at several points in the poem (lines 11, 15, and 16). Many readers will quite legitimately perceive line 16 as parallel to lines 4, 8, and 12. Others, however, may argue that the word "Then"—emphasizing what happens to the virtuous soul when everything else has perished—has an importance that should be reflected in both the reading and the scansion, and they will therefore mark the first foot of this line as a spondee:

> Then chief- | ly lives. | 16

These readers also will see the third foot in line 15 as a spondee:

> But though | the whole | world turn | to coal. | 15

Lines 2 and 7 introduce a different problem. Most readers, encountering these lines in a paragraph of prose, would read them thus:

> The bri- dal of the earth and sky; 2
> Thy root is ev- er in its grave. 7

But this reading leaves us with an anomalous situation. First, we have only three accents where our hypothetical pattern calls for four. Second, we have three unaccented syllables occurring together, a situation almost never encountered in verse of duple meter. From this situation we learn an important principle: though normal reading of the sentences in a poem establishes its metrical pattern, the metrical pattern so established in turn influences the reading. A circular process is at work. In this poem the pressure of the pattern will cause most sensitive readers to stress the second of the three unaccented syllables slightly more than those on either side of it. In scansion we recognize this slight increase of stress by promoting the syllable to the status of an accented syllable. Thus we mark lines 2 and 7 respectively thus:

The bri- | dal of | the earth | and sky; | 2
Thy root | is ev- | er in | its grave. | 7

Line 5 presents a situation about which there can be no dispute. The word "angry," though it occurs in a position where we would expect an iamb, *must* be accented on the first syllable, and thus must be marked as a trochee:

Sweet rose, | whose hue, | an- gry | and brave. | 5

There is little question also that the following line begins with a trochee in the first foot, followed by a spondee:

Bids the | rash gaz- | er wipe | his eye. | 6

Similarly, the word "Only," beginning line 13, is accented on the first syllable, thus introducing a trochaic substitution in the first foot of that line. Line 13 also presents another problem. A modern reader perceives the word "virtuous" as a three-syllable word, but the poet (writing in the seventeenth century, when metrical requirements were stricter than they are today) would probably have meant the word to be pronounced as two syllables (*ver-tyus*). Following the tastes of my century, I mark it as three, thus introducing an anapest instead of the expected iamb in the last foot:

On- ly | a sweet | and vir- | tu- ous soul. | 13

In doing this, however, I am consciously "modernizing"—altering the intention of the poet for the sake of a contemporary audience.

One problem remains. In the third stanza, lines 9 and 11 differ from the other lines of the poem in two respects: (a) they contain nine rather than eight syllables; (b) they end on unaccented syllables.

Sweet spring, | full of | sweet days | and ros- | es, 9
My mu- | sic shows | ye have | your clos- | es. 11

Such left-over unaccented syllables are not counted in identifying and naming the meter. These lines are both tetrameter, and if we tap our foot while reading them, we shall tap it four times. Metrical verse will often have one and sometimes two left-over unaccented syllables. In iambic and anapestic verse they will come at the end of lines; in trochaic and dactylic verse they will come at the beginning.

Our metrical analysis of "Virtue" is complete. Though (mainly for ease of discussion) we have skipped about eccentrically, we have indicated a scansion for all its lines. "Virtue" is written in iambic meter (meaning that most of its feet are iambs) and is composed of four-line stanzas, the first three lines tetrameter, and the final line dimeter. We are now ready to make a few generalizations about scansion.

1. Good readers ordinarily will not stop to scan a poem they are reading, and they certainly will not read a poem with the exaggerated emphasis on accented syllables that we sometimes give them in order to make the scansion more apparent. However, occasional scansion of a poem has value, as will become more apparent in the next chapter, which discusses the relation of sound and meter to sense. We shall give just one example here. The structure of meaning in "Virtue" is unmistakable. It consists of three parallel stanzas concerning things that die, followed by a contrasting fourth stanza concerning the one thing that does not die. The first three stanzas all begin with the word "Sweet" preceding a noun, and the first metrical foot in these stanzas—whether we consider it iamb or spondee—is the same. The contrasting fourth stanza, however, begins with a trochee, thus departing from both the previous pattern and from the basic meter of the poem. This departure is significant, for the word "Only" is the hinge upon which the structure of the poem turns, and the metrical reversal gives it emphasis. Thus meter serves meaning.

2. Scansion is at best a gross way of describing the rhythmical quality of a poem. It depends on classifying all syllables into either accented or unaccented categories and on ignoring the sometimes considerable difference between degrees of accent. Whether we call a syllable accented or unaccented depends, moreover, on its degree of accent relative to the syllables on either side of it. In lines 2 and 7 of "Virtue," the accents on "of" and "in" are obviously much lighter than on the other accented syllables in the line. Unaccented syllables also vary in weight. In line 5 "whose" is clearly heavier than "-gry" and "and," and is arguably heavier even than the accented "of" and "in" of lines 2 and 7. The most ardent champion of spondees, moreover, would concede that the accentual weight is not really equivalent in "Sweet rose": the noun shoulders more of the burden. Scansion is thus incapable of dealing with the subtlest rhythmical effects in poetry. It is nevertheless a useful and serviceable tool. Any measurement device more refined or sensitive would be too complicated to be widely serviceable.

3. Scansion is not an altogether exact science. Within certain limits we may say that a certain scansion is right or wrong, but beyond these limits qualified readers might legitimately disagree. Line 11 of "Virtue" provides the best example. Many metrists—those wanting scansion to reflect as closely as possible the underlying pattern—would mark it as perfectly regular: a succession of four iambs. Others—those wishing the scansion to reveal more nearly the nuances of a sensitive reading—would find that three sensitive readers might read this line in three different ways. One might stress "ye"; a second, "your"; and a third, both. The result is four possible scansions for this line:

> My mu- | sic shows | ye have | your close- | es, 11
> My mu- | sic shows | ye have | your close- | es, 11
> My mu- | sic shows | ye have | your close- | es, 11
> My mu- | sic shows | ye have | your close- | es. 11

Notice that the divisions between feet have no meaning except to help us identify the meter. They do not correspond to real divisions in the line; indeed, they fall often in the middle of a word. We place them where we do only to display the metrical pattern most clearly—in other words, to reveal regularity. If line 14 is marked

> Like sea- | soned tim- | ber, nev- | er gives, | 14

it yields four regular iambs. If it were marked

> Like | sea- soned | tim- ber, | nev- er | gives, 14

it would consist of an unaccented "left-over" syllable, three trochees, and a monosyllabic foot. The basic pattern of the poem would be obscured.

4. Finally—and this is the most important generalization of all—perfect regularity of meter is no criterion of merit. Beginning students sometimes get the notion that it is. If the meter is smooth and perfectly regular, they feel that the poet has handled the meter successfully and deserves all credit for it. Actually, a moderately talented versifier can easily make language go ta-*dum* ta-*dum* ta-*dum*. But there are two reasons why this is not generally desirable. The first is that, as we have said, all art consists essentially of repetition and variation. If a meter alternates too regularly between light and heavy beats, the result is to banish variation; the meter becomes mechanical and, for any sensitive reader, monotonous. The second is that, once a basic meter has been established, any deviations from it become highly significant and provide a means by

which the poet can use meter to reinforce meaning. If a meter is too perfectly regular, the probability is that the poet, instead of adapting rhythm to meaning, has simply forced the meaning into a metrical straitjacket.

Actually, what gives the skillful use of meter its greatest effectiveness is that it consists, not of one rhythm, but of two. One of these is the *expected* rhythm. The other is the *heard* rhythm. Once we have determined the basic meter of a poem, say, iambic tetrameter, we expect that this rhythm will continue. Thus a silent drumbeat is set up in our minds, and this drumbeat constitutes the expected rhythm. But the actual rhythm of the words — the heard rhythm — will sometimes confirm this expected rhythm and sometimes not. Thus the two rhythms are counterpointed, and the appeal of the verse is magnified, just as when two melodies are counterpointed in music, or as when two swallows, flying together and following the same general course but with individual variations, make a much more eye-catching pattern than one swallow flying alone. If the heard rhythm conforms too closely to the expected rhythm, the meter becomes dull and uninteresting. If it departs too far from the expected rhythm, there ceases to be an expected rhythm. If the irregularity is too great, meter disappears and the result is prose rhythm or free verse (see page 186).

There are several ways in which the poet can introduce variation into the meter. The most obvious way is by the substitution of other kinds of feet for regular feet. In our scansion of line 9 of "Virtue," for instance, we found a spondee, a trochee, and another spondee substituted for the expected iambs in the first three feet (plus an unexpected unaccented syllable left over at the end of the line). A less obvious but equally important means of variation is through simple phrasing and variation of degrees of accent. Though we began our scansion of "Virtue" by marking lines 3, 10, and 14 as perfectly regular, there is actually a considerable difference among them. Line 3 is quite regular, for the phrasing corresponds with the metrical pattern, and the line can be read ta-*dum* ta-*dum* ta-*dum* ta-*dum*. Line 10 is less regular, for the three-syllable word "compacted" cuts across the division between two feet. We should read it ta-*dum* ta-*dum* ta-*dump*-ty *dum*. Line 14 is the least regular of the three, for it shows no correspondence between phrasing and metrical division. We should read this line ta-*dump*-ty *dump*-ty, *dump*-ty *dum*. Finally, variation can be introduced by grammatical and rhetorical pauses. The comma in line 14, by introducing a grammatical pause, provides an additional variation from its perfect regularity. Probably the most violently irregular line in the poem is line 5,

Sweet rose, | whose hue, | an- gry | and brave, |

for here the spondaic substitution in the first foot, and the unusual trochaic substitution in the middle of a line in the third foot, are set off and emphasized by grammatical pauses, and also (as we have noted) the unaccented "whose" is considerably heavier than the other two unaccented syllables in the line. Significantly, the violent irregularity of this line (only slightly diminished in the next) corresponds with, and reinforces, the most violent image in the poem. Again, meter serves meaning.

The uses of rhythm and meter are several. Like the musical repetitions of sound, the musical repetitions of accent can be pleasing for their own sake. In addition, rhythm works as an emotional stimulus and serves, when used well, to heighten our attention to and awareness of what is going on in a poem. Finally, by choice of meter, and by skillful use of variation within the metrical framework, the poet can adapt the sound of verse to its content and thus make meter a powerful reinforcement of meaning. Nevertheless, we should avoid the notion that there is any mystical correspondence between certain meters and certain emotions. There are no "happy" meters and no "melancholy" ones. The choice of meter is probably less important for poets than how they handle it after they have chosen it. However, some meters are swifter than others, some slower; some are more lilting than others, some more dignified. Poets can choose meters that are appropriate or inappropriate to the content of the poem, and by their handling of them can increase or decrease the appropriateness. A swift, lilting meter used for a serious and grave subject will probably keep the reader from feeling any really deep emotion, while a more dignified meter will intensify the emotion. In all great poetry, meter works intimately with the other elements of the poem to produce the appropriate total effect.

We must not forget, of course, that poetry need not be metrical at all. Like alliteration and rime, like metaphor and irony, like even imagery, meter is simply one resource poets may use. Their job is to employ resources to the best advantage for the object they have in mind—the kind of experience they wish to express. And on no other basis can we judge them.

SUPPLEMENTAL NOTE

Of the four standard meters, iambic is by far the most common. Perhaps eighty percent of metered poetry in English is iambic. Anapestic meter (examples: "The Chimney Sweeper," No. 78, and "In the Garden," No. 101) is next most common. Trochaic meter (example:

"Counting-Out Rhyme," No. 137) is relatively infrequent. Dactylic meter is so rare as to be almost a museum specimen ("Bedtime Story," No. 250, in stanzas of three tetrameter lines followed by a dimeter line, is the sole example in this book).

Because of the predominance of iambic and anapestic meters in English verse, and because most anapestic poems have a high percentage of iambic substitutions, Robert Frost has written that in our language there are virtually but two meters: "strict iambic and loose iambic."* This is, of course, an overstatement; but, like many overstatements, it contains a good deal of truth. "Strict iambic" is strictly duple meter: it admits no trisyllabic substitutions. Trochees, spondees, and occasionally, monosyllabic feet may be substituted for the expected iambs, but not anapests or dactyls. The presence of a triple foot has such a conspicuous effect in speeding up or loosening up a line that the introduction of a few of them quite alters the nature of the meter. Herbert's "Virtue" is written in "strict iambic" (most of its feet are iambic; and, with the dubious exception of "virtuous," it contains no trisyllabic feet). "In the Garden" and "The Chimney Sweeper" (after its difficult first stanza) are anapestic (most of their feet are anapests). But e. e. cummings's "if everything happens that can't be done" (No. 148), though by actual count it has more iambic feet than anapestic, *sounds* more like "The Chimney Sweeper" than it does like "Virtue." It would be impossible to define what percentage of anapestic feet a poem must have before it ceases seeming iambic and begins seeming anapestic, but it would be considerably less than fifty percent and might be more like twenty-five percent. At any rate, a large number of poems fall into an area between "strict iambic" and "prevailingly anapestic," and they might be fittingly described as iambic-anapestic (what Frost called "loose iambic").

Finally, the importance of the final paragraph preceding this note must be underscored: *poetry need not be metrical at all*. Following the prodigious example of Walt Whitman in the nineteenth century, more and more twentieth-century poets have turned to the writing of *free verse*. **Free verse**, by our definition, is not verse at all; that is, it is not metrical. It may be rimed or unrimed but is more often the latter. The only difference between free verse and rhythmical prose is that free verse introduces one additional rhythmical unit, the line. The arrangement into lines divides the material into rhythmical units, or cadences. Beyond its line arrangement there are no necessary differences between it

*"The Figure a Poem Makes," *Selected Prose of Robert Frost* (New York: Holt, 1966) 17–18.

and rhythmical prose. Probably more than fifty percent of published contemporary poetry is written in free verse.

To add one further variation, a number of contemporary poets have begun writing "prose poems," or poems in prose (example: Carolyn Forché's "The Colonel," No. 226). It is too early to determine whether this is a passing fashion or will be a lasting development.

EXERCISES

1 An important term that every student of poetry should know (and should be careful not to confuse with *free verse*) is *blank verse*. **Blank verse** has a very specific meter: it is *iambic pentameter, unrimed*. It has a special name because it is the principal English meter, that is, the meter that has been used for a large proportion of the greatest English poetry, including the tragedies of Shakespeare and the epics of Milton. Iambic pentameter in English seems especially suitable for the serious treatment of serious themes. The natural movement of the English language tends to be iambic. Lines shorter than pentameter tend to be songlike, not suited to sustained treatment of serious material. Lines longer than pentameter tend to break up into shorter units, the hexameter line being read as two three-foot units, the heptameter line as a four-foot and a three-foot unit, and so on. Rime, while highly appropriate to most short poems, often proves a handicap for a long and lofty work. (The word *blank* implies that the end of the line is "blank," that is, bare of rime.)

Of the following poems, four are in blank verse, four are in free verse, and two are in other meters. Determine in which category each belongs.

a. "Birches" (No. 227)
b. "Grace to Be Said at the Supermarket" (No. 259)
c. "Ulysses" (No. 67)
d. "Base Details" (No. 31)
e. Excerpt from *Macbeth* (No. 92)
f. "'Out, Out—'" (No. 91)
g. "Musée des Beaux Arts" (No. 204)
h. "Dover Beach" (No. 126)
i. "Mirror" (No. 19)
j. "Riddle" (No. 236)

2. Another useful distinction is that between end-stopped lines and run-on lines. An **end-stopped line** is one in which the end of the line corresponds with a natural speech pause; a **run-on line** is one in which the sense of the line hurries on into the next line. (There are, of course, all degrees of end-stop and run-on. A line ending with a period or semicolon is heavily end-stopped. A line without punctuation at the end is normally considered a run-on line, but it is less forcibly run-on if it ends at a natural speech pause—as between subject and predicate—than if it ends, say, between an article and its noun, between an auxiliary and its verb, or between a preposition and its object.) The use of run-on lines is one way the poet can make use of grammatical or rhetorical pauses to vary a basic meter.

a. Examine "Sound and Sense" (No. 160) and "My Last Duchess" (No. 90). Both are written in the same meter: iambic pentameter, rimed in couplets.

Is their general rhythmical effect quite similar or markedly different? What accounts for the difference? Does the contrast support our statement that the way poets handle meter is more important than their choice of a meter?

b. Examine "The Hound" (No. 43) and "The Dance" (No. 169). Which is the more forcibly run-on in the majority of its lines? Describe the difference in effect.

* * *

145. "Introduction" to *Songs of Innocence*

Piping down the valleys wild,
Piping songs of pleasant glee,
On a cloud I saw a child,
And he laughing said to me:

"Pipe a song about a Lamb."
So I piped with merry cheer.
"Piper, pipe that song again."
So I piped; he wept to hear.

"Drop thy pipe, thy happy pipe;
Sing thy songs of happy cheer."
So I sung the same again
While he wept with joy to hear.

"Piper, sit thee down and write
In a book that all may read."
So he vanished from my sight,
And I plucked a hollow reed,

And I made a rural pen,
And I stained the water clear,
And I wrote my happy songs
Every child may joy to hear.

William Blake (1757–1827)

QUESTIONS

1. Poets have traditionally been thought of as inspired by one of the Muses (Greek female divinities whose duties were to nurture the arts). Blake's *Songs of Innocence*, a book of poems about childhood and the state of innocence, includes "The Chimney Sweeper" (No. 78) and "The Lamb" (No. 208). In this introductory poem to the book, what function is performed by the child upon a cloud?
2. What is symbolized by "a Lamb" (5)?

3. What three stages of poetic composition are suggested in stanzas 1–2, 3, and 4–5 respectively?
4. What features of the poems in his book does Blake hint at in this "Introduction"? Name at least four.
5. Mark the stressed and unstressed syllables in lines 1–2 and 9–10. Do they establish the basic meter of the poem? If so, is that meter iambic or trochaic? Or could it be either? Some metrists have discarded the distinction between iambic and trochaic, and between anapestic and dactylic, as being artificial. The important distinction, they feel, is between duple and triple meters. Does this poem support their claim?

146. It takes all sorts

It takes all sorts of in- and outdoor schooling
To get adapted to my kind of fooling.

Robert Frost (1874–1963)

QUESTIONS

1. What is the poet saying about the nature of his poetry?
2. Scan the poem. Is it iambic or trochaic? Or could it be either? How does this poem differ from Blake's "Introduction" in illustrating the ambiguity of the distinction between the two meters?

147. Epitaph on an Army of Mercenaries

These, in the day when heaven was falling,
  The hour when earth's foundations fled,
Followed their mercenary calling
  And took their wages and are dead.

Their shoulders held the sky suspended;
  They stood, and earth's foundations stay;
What God abandoned, these defended,
  And saved the sum of things for pay.

A. E. Housman (1859–1936)

QUESTIONS

1. The Battle of Ypres (October 31, 1914), early in World War I, pitted a small army of British "regulars" against a much larger force of German volunteers. German newspapers described the conflict as one between young German volunteers and British "mercenaries." Housman first published this poem in the London *Times* on October 31, 1917, the third anniversary of the battle. Who are "These" (1)? Is the tone of the poem one of tribute or one of cynical scorn for "These"? How does the poet use the word "mercenary"?

2. In scanning Herbert's "Virtue," we discovered two lines that had an unaccented syllable left over at the end that we did not count in determining the meter. How does this poem differ from "Virtue" in its use of such lines? The meter of this poem is iambic tetrameter. Does this sufficiently describe its metrical form?

148. if everything happens that can't be done

if everything happens that can't be done
(and anything's righter
than books
could plan)
the stupidest teacher will almost guess
(with a run
skip
around we go yes)
there's nothing as something as one

one hasn't a why or because or although
(and buds know better
than books
don't grow)
one's anything old being everything new
(with a what
which
around we come who)
one's everyanything so

so world is a leaf so tree is a bough
(and birds sing sweeter
than books
tell how)
so here is away and so your is a my
(with a down
up
around again fly)
forever was never till now

now i love you and you love me
(and books are shuter
than books
can be)
and deep in the high that does nothing but fall
(with a shout
each
around we go all)
there's somebody calling who's we

we're anything brighter than even the sun
(we're everything greater
than books
might mean)
we're everyanything more than believe
(with a spin
leap
alive we're alive)
we're wonderful one times one

e. e. cummings (1894–1962)

QUESTIONS

1. Explain the last line. Of what very familiar idea is this poem a fresh treatment?
2. The poem is based on a contrast between heart and mind (or love and learning). Which does the speaker prefer? What symbols express the dichotomy?
3. What is the tone of the poem?
4. Which lines of each stanza regularly rime with each other (either perfect or approximate rime)? How does the poet link the stanzas?
5. What is the basic metrical scheme of the poem? What does the meter contribute to the tone? What line (in the fourth stanza) most clearly states the subject and occasion of the poem? How does meter underline its significance?
6. Can you suggest any reason why the poet did not write lines 2–4 and 6–8 of each stanza as one line each? What metrical variations does the poet use in lines 6–8 of each stanza and with what effect?
7. In scanning "Virtue" (No. 144) we spoke of a circular process in which normal reading establishes the metrical pattern that then partially determines how the poem should be read. Whether, for instance, we read a word like *fire* as one syllable (riming with *hire*) or two syllables (riming with *liar*) may depend on the meter. The word *every* can be pronounced as having two syllables (*ev'ry*) or three (*ev-er-y*). How should it be pronounced in lines 14 and 38? In lines 18 and 41?

149. Oh who is that young sinner

Oh who is that young sinner with the handcuffs on his wrists?
And what has he been after that they groan and shake their fists?
And wherefore is he wearing such a conscience-stricken air?
Oh they're taking him to prison for the color of his hair.

'Tis a shame to human nature, such a head of hair as his;
In the good old time 'twas hanging for the color that it is;
Though hanging isn't bad enough and flaying would be fair
For the nameless and abominable color of his hair.

Oh a deal of pains he's taken and a pretty price he's paid
To hide his poll or dye it of a mentionable shade;

But they've pulled the beggar's hat off for the world to see and stare,
And they're taking him to justice for the color of his hair.

Now 'tis oakum for his fingers and the treadmill for his feet,
And the quarry-gang on Portland in the cold and in the heat,
And between his spells of labor in the time he has to spare
He can curse the God that made him for the color of his hair.

A. E. Housman (1859–1936)

QUESTIONS

1. Vocabulary: *poll* (10), *oakum* (13). *Portland* (14), an English peninsula, is the site of a famous criminal prison.
2. What kind of irony does the poem exhibit? Explain.
3. What symbolic meanings are suggested by "the color of his hair"?
4. This poem represents a kind of meter that we have not yet discussed. It *may* be scanned as iambic heptameter:

   Oh who | is that | young sin- | ner with | the hand- | cuffs on | his wrists? |

   But you will probably find yourself reading it as a four-beat line:

   Oh who | is that young sin- | ner with the hand- | cuffs on his wrists? |

   Although the meter is duple insofar as there is an alternation between unaccented and accented syllables, there is also an alternation in the degree of stress on the accented syllables: the first, third, fifth, and seventh stresses being heavier than the second, fourth, and sixth; the result is that the two-syllable feet tend to group themselves into larger units. We may scan it as follows, using a short line for a light accent, a longer one for a heavy accent:

   Oh who | is that young sin- | ner with the hand- | cuffs on his wrists? |
   And what | has he been af- | ter that they groan | and shake their fists? |
   And where- | fore is he wear- | ing such a con- | science strick-en air? |
   Oh they're tak- | ing him to pris- | on for the col- | or of his hair. |

   This kind of meter, in which there is an alternation between heavy and light stresses, is known as **dipodic** (two-footed) **verse**. The alternation may not be perfect throughout, but it will be frequent enough to establish a pattern in the reader's mind. Now scan the last three stanzas.

150. Down by the Salley Gardens

Down by the salley° gardens my love and I did meet;   °willow
She passed the salley gardens with little snow-white feet.
She bid me take love easy, as the leaves grow on the tree;

But I, being young and foolish, with her would not agree.
In a field by the river my love and I did stand,
And on my leaning shoulder she laid her snow-white hand.
She bid me take life easy, as the grass grows on the weirs;
But I was young and foolish, and now am full of tears.

William Butler Yeats (1865–1939)

QUESTIONS

1. Vocabulary: *weirs* (7).
2. This poem introduces an additional kind of metrical variation—the metrical pause or rest. Unlike grammatical and rhetorical pauses, the metrical pause affects scansion. If you beat out the rhythm of this poem with your hand, you will find that the fourth beat of each line regularly falls *between* syllables (except possibly in lines 3 and 7). A **metrical pause**, then, is a pause that replaces an accented syllable. It is usually found in verse that has a pronounced lilt or swing. The first line of Yeats's poem may be scanned as follows (the metrical pause is represented with an *x*):

   Down by | the sal- | ley gar- | dens^x | my love | and I | did meet. |

   The third line might be scanned in several ways, as the following alternatives suggest:

   She bid | me take | love eas- | y, as | the leaves | grow on | the tree, |
   She bid | me take | love eas- | y,^{x} | as the leaves | grow on | the tree. |

   Scan the rest of the poem.

151. Had I the Choice

Had I the choice to tally greatest bards,
To limn their portraits, stately, beautiful, and emulate at will,
Homer with all his wars and warriors—Hector, Achilles, Ajax,
Or Shakespeare's woe-entangled Hamlet, Lear, Othello—Tennyson's
  fair ladies,
Meter or wit the best, or choice conceit to wield in perfect rhyme,
  delight of singers;
These, these, O sea, all these I'd gladly barter,
Would you the undulation of one wave, its trick to me transfer,
Or breathe one breath of yours upon my verse,
And leave its odor there.

Walt Whitman (1819–1892)

QUESTIONS

1. Vocabulary: *tally* (1), *limn* (2), *conceit* (5).
2. What poetic qualities does Whitman propose to barter in exchange for what? What qualities do the sea and its waves symbolize?
3. What kind of "verse" is this? Why does Whitman prefer it to "meter" and "perfect rhyme"?

152. The Aim Was Song

Before man came to blow it right
   The wind once blew itself untaught,
And did its loudest day and night
   In any rough place where it caught.

Man came to tell it what was wrong:
   It hadn't found the place to blow;
It blew too hard—the aim was song.
   And listen—how it ought to go!

He took a little in his mouth,
   And held it long enough for north
To be converted into south,
   And then by measure blew it forth.

By measure. It was word and note,
   The wind the wind had meant to be—
A little through the lips and throat.
   The aim was song—the wind could see.

Robert Frost (1874–1963)

QUESTIONS

1. Frost invents a myth about the origin of poetry. What implications does it suggest about the relation of man to nature and of poetry to nature?
2. Contrast the thought and form of this poem with Whitman's.
3. Scan the poem and identify its meter. How does the poet give variety to a regular metrical pattern?

153. Nevertheless

you've seen a strawberry
      that's had a struggle; yet
      was, where the fragments met,

a hedgehog or a star-
    fish for the multitude
    of seeds. What better food

than apple seeds — the fruit
    within the fruit — locked in
    like counter-curved twin

hazelnuts? Frost that kills
    the little rubber-plant-
    leaves of *kok-saghyz*-stalks, can't

harm the roots; they still grow
    in frozen ground. Once where
    there was a prickly-pear-

leaf clinging to barbed wire,
    a root shot down to grow
    in the earth two feet below;

as carrots form mandrakes
    or a ram's-horn root some-
    times. Victory won't come

to me unless I go
    to it; a grape tendril
    ties a knot in knots till

knotted thirty times — so
    the bound twig that's under-
    gone and over-gone, can't stir.

The weak overcomes its
    menace, the strong over-
    comes itself. What is there

like fortitude! What sap
    went through that little thread
    to make the cherry red!

Marianne Moore (1887–1972)

QUESTIONS

1. Vocabulary: *kok-saghyz* (12), *prickly-pear* (15), *mandrakes* (19).
2. This apparently random collection of examples from botanical nature actually proceeds through a sequence that begins with two types of seed-bearing fruit. Where does it go from there, and what does it end up with?

3. What human meaning does the speaker draw from these botanical examples? How do the examples support that meaning?
4. This poem is an example of **syllabic verse**, which counts only the number of syllables per line regardless of accents. (Sylvia Plath's "Metaphors" [No. 50] is another example.) Describe its formal pattern, including its rime scheme. Although the form appears arbitrary in its line-breaks and stanza-breaks, it is in fact tightly formalized. How is such a form appropriate to the meaning of the poem?

154. Break, break, break

Break, break, break,
    On thy cold gray stones, O sea!
And I would that my tongue could utter
    The thoughts that arise in me.

O, well for the fisherman's boy,
    That he shouts with his sister at play!
O, well for the sailor lad,
    That he sings in his boat on the bay!

And the stately ships go on
    To their haven under the hill;
But O for the touch of a vanished hand,
    And the sound of a voice that is still!

Break, break, break,
    At the foot of thy crags, O sea!
But the tender grace of a day that is dead
    Will never come back to me.

Alfred, Lord Tennyson (1809–1892)

QUESTIONS

1. In lines 3–4 the speaker wishes he could put his thoughts into words. Does he make those thoughts explicit in the course of the poem?
2. What aspects of life are symbolized by the two images in stanza 2? By the image in lines 9–10? How do lines 11–12 contrast with those images?
3. The basic meter of this poem is anapestic, and all but two lines are trimeter. Which two? What other variations from a strict anapestic trimeter do you find? How many lines (and which ones) display a strict anapestic pattern? With this much variation, would you be justified in calling the poem free verse? Do the departures from a strict metrical norm contribute to the meaning?

CHAPTER THIRTEEN

Sound and Meaning

Rhythm and sound cooperate to produce what we call the music of poetry. This music, as we have pointed out, may serve two general functions: it may be enjoyable in itself, or it may be used to reinforce meaning and intensify the communication.

Pure pleasure in sound and rhythm exists from a very early age in the human being—probably from the age the baby first starts cooing in its cradle, certainly from the age that children begin chanting nursery rimes and skipping rope. The appeal of the following verse, for instance, depends almost entirely on its "music":

155.

Pease | por-ridge | hot, |
Pease | por-ridge | cold, |
Pease | por-ridge | in the | pot |
Nine | days | old. |

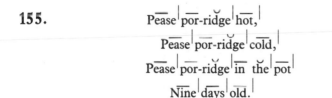

There is very little sense here; the attraction comes from the emphatic rhythm, the emphatic rimes (with a strong contrast between the short vowel and short final consonant of *hot-pot* and the long vowel and long final consonant combination of *cold-old*), and the heavy alliteration (exactly half the words begin with *p*). From nonsense rimes such as this, many of us graduate to a love of more meaningful poems whose appeal resides largely in the sound they make. Much of the pleasure that we find in poems like Vachel Lindsay's "The Congo" and Edgar Allan Poe's "The Bells" lies in their musical qualities.

The peculiar function of poetry as distinguished from music, however, is to convey not sounds but meaning or experience *through* sounds. In third- and fourth-rate poetry, sound and rhythm sometimes distract attention from sense. In first-rate poetry the sound exists not for its own sake nor for mere decoration, but as a medium of meaning. Its function is to support the leading player, not to steal the scene.

The poet may reinforce meaning through sound in numerous ways. Without claiming to exhaust them, perhaps we can include most of the chief means under four general headings.

First, the poet can choose words whose sound in some degree suggests their meaning. In its narrowest sense this is called onomatopoeia. **Onomatopoeia**, strictly defined, means the use of words which, at least supposedly, sound like what they mean, such as *hiss*, *snap*, and *bang*.

156. Song: Come unto these yellow sands

Come unto these yellow sands,
    And then take hands.
Curtsied when you have and kissed,
    The wild waves whist,° — being hushed
Foot it featly° here and there, — nimbly
And, sweet sprites, the burden° bear. — refrain
    Hark, hark!
      Bow-wow.
    The watch-dogs bark!
      Bow-wow.
Hark, hark! I hear
The strain of strutting chanticleer
Cry, "Cock-a-doodle-doo!"

William Shakespeare (1564–1616)

In these lines, "bark," "bow-wow," and "cock-a-doodle-doo" are onomatopoetic words. In addition, Shakespeare has reinforced the onomatopoetic effect with the repeated use of "hark," which sounds like "bark." The usefulness of onomatopoeia, of course, is strictly limited, because it can be used only where the poet is describing sound, and most poems do not describe sound. And the use of pure onomatopoeia, as in the preceding example, is likely to be fairly trivial except as it forms an incidental part of a more complex poem. But by combining onomatopoeia with other devices that help convey meaning, the poet can achieve subtle and beautiful effects whose recognition is one of the keenest pleasures in reading poetry.

In addition to onomatopoetic words there is another group of words, sometimes called **phonetic intensives**, whose sound, by a process as yet obscure, to some degree connects with their meaning. An initial *fl-* sound, for instance, is often associated with the idea of moving light, as in *flame, flare, flash, flicker, flimmer*. An initial *gl-* also frequently accompanies the idea of light, usually unmoving, as in *glare, gleam, glint, glow, glisten*. An initial *sl-* often introduces words meaning "smoothly wet," as in *slippery, slick, slide, slime, slop, slosh, slobber, slushy*. An initial *st-* often suggests strength, as in *staunch, stalwart, stout, sturdy, stable, steady, stocky, stern, strong, stubborn, steel*. Short *-i-* often goes with the idea of smallness, as in *inch, imp, thin, slim, little, bit, chip, sliver, chink, slit, sip, whit, tittle, snip, wink, glint, glimmer, flicker, pigmy, midge, chick, kid, kitten, minikin, miniature*. Long *-o-* or *-oo-* may suggest melancholy or sorrow, as in *moan, groan, woe, mourn, forlorn, toll, doom, gloom, moody*. Final *-are* sometimes goes with the idea of a big light or noise, as *flare, glare, stare, blare*. Medial *-att-* suggests some kind of particled movement, as in *spatter, scatter, shatter, chatter, rattle, prattle, clatter, batter*. Final *-er* and *-le* indicate repetition, as in *glitter, flutter, shimmer, whisper, jabber, chatter, clatter, sputter, flicker, twitter, mutter*, and *ripple, bubble, twinkle, sparkle, rattle, rumble, jingle*. None of these various sounds is invariably associated with the idea that it seems to suggest, and, in fact, a short *-i-* is found in *thick* as well as *thin*, in *big* as well as *little*. Language is a complex phenomenon. But there is enough association between these sounds and ideas to suggest some sort of intrinsic if obscure relationship. A word like *flicker*, though not onomatopoetic (for it does not refer to sound) would seem somehow to suggest its sense, with the *fl-* suggesting moving light, the *-i-* suggesting smallness, the *-ck-* suggesting sudden cessation of movement (as in *crack, peck, pick, hack*, and *flick*), and the *-er* suggesting repetition. The above list of sound-idea correspondences is only a very partial one. A complete list, though it would involve only a small proportion of words in the language, would probably be a longer list than that of the more strictly onomatopoetic words, to which they are related.

157. Splinter

The voice of the last cricket
across the first frost
is one kind of good-by.
It is so thin a splinter of singing.

Carl Sandburg (1878–1967)

QUESTIONS

1. Why is "so thin a splinter" a better choice of metaphor than *so small an atom* or *so meager a morsel*?
2. How does the poet intensify the effect of the two phonetic intensives in line 4?

A second way that the poet can reinforce meaning through sound is to choose sounds and group them so that the effect is smooth and pleasant sounding (*euphonious*) or rough and harsh sounding (*cacophonous*). The vowels are in general more pleasing than the consonants, for the vowels are musical tones, whereas the consonants are merely noises. A line with a high percentage of vowel sounds in proportion to consonant sounds will therefore tend to be more melodious than one in which the proportion is low. The vowels and consonants themselves differ considerably in quality. The "long" vowels, such as those in *fate, reed, rime, coat, food*, and *dune* are fuller and more resonant than the "short" vowels, as in *fat, red, rim, cot, foot*, and *dun*. Of the consonants, some are fairly mellifluous, such as the "liquids," *l, m, n*, and *r*; the soft *v* and *f* sounds; the semivowels *w* and *y*; and such combinations as *th* and *wh*. Others, such as the "plosives," *b, d, g, k, p*, and *t*, are harsher and sharper in their effect. These differences in sound are the poet's materials. Good poets, however, will not necessarily seek out the sounds that are pleasing and attempt to combine them in melodious combinations. Rather, they will use **euphony** and **cacophony** as they are appropriate to content. Consider, for instance, the following poem.

158. Upon Julia's Voice

So smooth, so sweet, so silvery is thy voice,
As, could they hear, the Damned would make no noise,
But listen to thee (walking in thy chamber)
Melting melodious words to Lutes of Amber.

Robert Herrick (1591–1674)

QUESTION

Literally, an amber lute is as nonsensical as a silver voice. What connotations do "Amber" and "silvery" have that contribute to the meaning of this poem?

There are no strictly onomatopoetic words in this poem, and yet the sound seems marvelously adapted to the sense. Especially remarkable are the first and last lines, those most directly concerned with Julia's voice. In the first line the sounds that most strike the ear are the unvoiced *s*'s and the soft *v*'s, supported by voiced *th*: "*S*o *s*moo*th*, *s*o *s*weet, *s*o *s*il*v*ery is *th*y *v*oi*ce*." (A voiced consonant sound is accompanied by vibration of the vocal cords—*th*en is voiced, *th*in is not. Notice that the terminal *-ce* in "voice" is an example of the unvoiced *s* sound: as with alliteration, spelling is irrelevant.) In the fourth line the predominating sounds are the liquid consonants *m*, *l*, and *r*, supported by a *w*: "*M*e*l*ting *m*e*l*o-dious *w*o*r*ds to *L*utes of A*m*be*r*." The least euphonious line in the poem, on the other hand, is the second, where the subject is the tormented in hell, not Julia's voice. Here the prominent sounds are the *d*'s, supported by a voiced *s* (a voiced *s* buzzes, unlike the sibilant unvoiced *s*'s in line 1), and two *k* sounds: "A*s*, *c*oul*d* they hear, the *D*amne*d* would ma*k*e no noi*s*e." Throughout the poem there is a remarkable correspondence between the pleasant-sounding and the pleasant in idea, the unpleasant-sounding and the unpleasant in idea.

A third way in which a poet can reinforce meaning through sound is by controlling the speed and movement of the lines by the choice and use of meter, by the choice and arrangement of vowel and consonant sounds, and by the disposition of pauses. In meter the unaccented syllables usually go faster than the accented syllables; hence the triple meters are swifter than the duple. But the poet can vary the tempo of any meter by the use of substitute feet. Generally, whenever two or more unaccented syllables come together, the effect will be to speed up the pace of the line; when two or more accented syllables come together, the effect will be to slow it down. This pace will also be affected by the vowel lengths and by whether the sounds are easily run together. The long vowels take longer to pronounce than the short ones. Some words are easily run together, while others demand that the position of the mouth be re-formed before the next word is uttered. It takes much longer, for instance, to say, "Watch dogs catch much meat" than to say, "My aunt is away," though the number of syllables is the same. And finally the poet can slow down the speed of a line through the introduction of grammatical and rhetorical pauses. Consider lines 54–56 from Tennyson's "Ulysses" (No. 67):

> The lights / be-gin / to twin- / kle from / the rocks; /
> The long / day wanes; / the slow / moon climbs; / the deep /
> Moans round / with man- / y voi- / ces . . .

In these lines Tennyson wished the movement to be slow, in accordance with the slow waning of the long day and the slow climbing of the moon. His meter is iambic pentameter. This is not a swift meter, but in lines 55–56 he slows it down further, (1) by introducing three spondaic feet, thus bringing three accented syllables together in three separate places; (2) by choosing for his accented syllables words that have long vowel sounds or dipthongs that the voice hangs on to: "long," "day," "wanes," "slow," "moon," "climbs," "deep," "moans," "round"; (3) by choosing words that are not easily run together (except for "day" and "slow," each of these words begins and ends with consonant sounds that require varying degrees of readjustment of the mouth before pronunciation can continue); and (4) by introducing two grammatical pauses, after "wanes" and "climbs," and a rhetorical pause after "deep." The result is an extremely effective use of the movement of the verse to accord with the movement suggested by the words.*

A fourth way for a poet to fit sound to sense is to control both sound and meter in such a way as to emphasize words that are important in meaning. This can be done by highlighting such words through alliteration, assonance, consonance, or rime; by placing them before a pause; or by skillfully placing or displacing them in the metrical scheme. We already have seen how Ogden Nash uses alliteration and consonance to emphasize and link the three major words ("sex," "fix," and "fertile") in his little verse "The Turtle" (No. 132), and how George Herbert pivots the structure of meaning in "Virtue" (No. 144) on a trochaic substitution in the initial foot of his final stanza. For an additional example, let us look again at "Since there's no help" (No. 119). This poem is a sonnet—fourteen lines of iambic pentameter—in which a lover threatens to leave his sweetheart forever if she will not go to bed with him. In the first eight lines he pretends to be *glad* that they are breaking off their relationship so cleanly. In the last six lines, however, he paints a vivid picture of the death of his personified Love/Passion for her but intimates that even at this last moment ("Now") she could restore it to life again—by satisfying his sexual desires.

> Now, at | the last | gasp of | Love's la | -test breath, |
> When, his pulse failing, Passion speechless lies,
> When Faith is kneeling by his bed of death,
> And In | -no-cence | is clos | -ing up | his eyes, |
> Now, if | thou wouldst, | when all | have given | him o | -ver,†
> From death | to life | thou mightst | him yet | re-cov | -er.

The emphasis is on *Now*. In a matter of seconds, the speaker indicates, it will be too late: his Love/Passion will be dead, and he himself will be gone. The word "Now" begins line 9. It also begins a new sentence and a

*In addition, Tennyson uses one onomatopoetic word ("moans") and one phonetic intensive ("twinkle").

†Drayton probably intended "given" to be pronounced as one syllable (*giv'n*), and most sixteenth-century readers would have pronounced it thus in this poem.

QUESTIONS

1. Is the dog a dog only or also a symbol?
2. The first line presents a visual and auditory image; the second line makes a comment. But does the second line *call up images*? Does it suggest more than it says? Would the poem have been more or less effective if the second line had been, "He was frisky and lively when he was a pup"?

We may well conclude our discussion of the adaptation of sound to sense by analyzing this very brief poem. It consists of one riming anapes-tic tetrameter couplet. Its content is a contrast between the decrepitude of an old dog and his friskiness as a pup. The scansion is as follows:

The old | dog barks back- | ward with-out | get-ting up. |
I | can re-mem- | ber when he | was a pup. |

How is sound fitted to sense? In the first place, the triple meter chosen
by the poet is a swift meter, but in the first line he has jammed it up in a
emarkable way by substituting a kind of foot so rare that English pros-
dy has no name for it (the Greeks, who "measured" their verse by
ration of syllables rather than accent, called it a *molussus*); at any rate,
a foot in which the accent is distributed over three syllables. This
following the accented syllable in the first foot, creates a situation
four accented syllables are pushed up together. In addition, each
se accented syllables begins and ends with a strong consonant
or cluster of consonant sounds, so that they cannot be run to-
n pronunciation—the mouth must be re-formed between sylla-
he *old dog barks back-*." The result is to slow down the line dras-
damage its rhythmical quality severely, and to make it difficult
dced, the line is as decrepit as the old dog who turns his head
master but does not get up. When we get to the second line,
e contrast is startling. The rhythm is swift and regular, the
in vowels or liquid consonants that are easily run together,
ripples fluently off the tongue. In addition, where the first
proportion of explosive and cacophonous consonants—
rks backward without *getting up*"—the consonants in the
predominantly smoother and more graceful—"I *can re-*
was a pup." Thus the motion and the sound of the lines
accord with the visual images they suggest. In addi-
ine the poet has supported the onomatopoetic word
cho *back*, so that the sound reinforces the auditory

new direction in the poem. It is separated from what has gone before by a period at the end of the preceding line. Metrically it initiates a trochee, thus breaking away from the poem's basic iambic meter (line 8 is perfectly regular). In all these ways—its initial position in line, sentence, and thought, and its metrical irregularity—the word "Now" is given extraordinary emphasis appropriate to its importance in the context. Its repetition in line 13 reaffirms this importance, and there again it is given emphasis by its positional and metrical situation. It begins both a line and the final riming couplet, is separated by punctuation from the line before, and participates in a metrical inversion. (The lines before ar after are metrically regular.)

While Herbert and Drayton use metrical deviation to give em to important words, Tennyson, in the concluding line of "Ulysse marked regularity, plus skillful use of grammatical pauses, to a same effect:

> We are | not now | that strength | which in old | days |
> Moved earth | and heav-en, | that | which we are. |
> One e-qual tem-per of | he-ro-ic hearts, |
> Made weak | by time | and fate, | but stron
> To strive, | to seek, | to find, | and not | t

The blank verse rhythm throughout "Ulyss varied, but the last line is not only regu regular, for a number of reasons. First, no words cross over the divisions betw syllables are all very small and unim "and," whereas the accented sylla and a very important "not." Th grammatical pause pointed off cause a pronounced alternat brings the accent down on t mer blows. The line ring

159. The Spar

The
I can

image. If the poem does a great deal in just two lines, this skillful adaptation of sound to sense is one very important reason.

In analyzing verse for correspondence between sound and sense, we need to be very cautious not to make exaggerated claims. A great deal of nonsense has been written about the moods of certain meters and the effects of certain sounds, and it is easy to suggest correspondences that exist really only in our imaginations. Nevertheless, the first-rate poet has nearly always an instinctive tact about handling sound so that it in some degree supports meaning; the inferior poet is usually obtuse to these correspondences. One of the few absolute rules that can be applied to the judgment of poetry is that the form should be adequate to the content. This rule does not mean that there must always be a close and easily demonstrable correspondence. It does mean that there will be no glaring discrepancies. Poor poets, and even good poets in their third-rate work, sometimes go horribly wrong.

The two selections that introduce this chapter illustrate, first, the use of sound in verse almost purely for its own sake ("Pease porridge hot"), and, second, the use of sound in verse almost purely to *imitate* meaning ("Hark, hark! Bow-wow"), and they are, as significant poetry, perhaps the most trivial passages in the whole book. But in between these extremes there is an abundant range of poetic possibilities where sound is pleasurable for itself without violating meaning and where sound to varying degrees corresponds with and corroborates meaning; and in this rich middle range lie many of the greatest pleasures of reading poetry.

EXERCISE

In each of the following paired quotations, the named poet wrote the version that more successfully adapts sound to sense. As specifically as possible, account for the superiority of the better version.

1. a. Go forth—and Virtue, ever in your sight,
   Shall be your guide by day, your guard by night.
   b. Go forth—and Virtue, ever in your sight,
   Shall point your way by day, and keep you safe at night.

Charles Churchill

2. a. How charming is divine philosophy!
   Not harsh and rough as foolish men suppose
   But musical as is the lute of Phoebus.
   b. How charming is divine philosophy!
   Not harsh and crabbed as dull fools suppose
   But musical as is Apollo's lute.

John Milton

3. a. All day the fleeing crows croak hoarsely over the snow.
   b. All day the out-cast crows croak hoarsely across the whiteness.

Elizabeth Coatsworth

4. a. Your talk attests how bells of singing gold
Would sound at evening over silent water.
b. Your low voice tells how bells of singing gold
Would sound at twilight over silent water. *Edwin Arlington Robinson*

5. a. A thousand streamlets flowing through the lawn,
The moan of doves in gnarled ancient oaks,
And quiet murmuring of countless bees.
b. Myriads of rivulets hurrying through the lawn,
The moan of doves in immemorial elms,
And murmuring of innumerable bees. *Alfred, Lord Tennyson*

6. a. It is the lark that sings so out of tune,
Straining harsh discords and unpleasing sharps.
b. It is the lark that warbles out of tune
In harsh discordant tones with doleful flats. *William Shakespeare*

7. a. "Artillery" and "armaments" and "implements of war"
Are phrases too severe to please the gentle Muse.
b. Bombs, drums, guns, bastions, batteries, bayonets, bullets,—
Hard words, which stick in the soft Muses' gullets. *Lord Byron*

8. a. The hands of the sisters Death and Night incessantly softly wash
again, and ever again, this soiled world.
b. The hands of the soft twins Death and Night repeatedly wash
again, and ever again, this dirty world. *Walt Whitman*

9. a. The curfew sounds the knell of parting day,
The lowing cattle slowly cross the lea,
The plowman goes wearily plodding his homeward way,
Leaving the world to the darkening night and me.
b. The curfew tolls the knell of parting day,
The lowing herd wind slowly o'er the lea,
The plowman homeward plods his weary way,
And leaves the world to darkness and to me. *Thomas Gray*

10. a. Let me chastise this odious, gilded bug,
This painted son of dirt, that smells and bites.
b. Yet let me flap this bug with gilded wings,
This painted child of dirt, that stinks and stings. *Alexander Pope*

* * *

160. Sound and Sense

True ease in writing comes from art, not chance,
As those move easiest who have learned to dance.
'Tis not enough no harshness gives offense,
The sound must seem an echo to the sense:
Soft is the strain when Zephyr gently blows,
And the smooth stream in smoother numbers flows;
But when loud surges lash the sounding shore,
The hoarse, rough verse should like the torrent roar;
When Ajax strives some rock's vast weight to throw,

The line too labors, and the words move slow;
Not so, when swift Camilla scours the plain,
Flies o'er the unbending corn, and skims along the main.
Hear how Timotheus' varied lays surprise,
And bid alternate passions fall and rise!

Alexander Pope (1688–1744)

QUESTIONS

1. Vocabulary: *numbers* (6), *lays* (13).
2. This excerpt is from a long poem (called *An Essay on Criticism*) on the arts of writing and judging poetry. Which line states the thesis of the passage?
3. There are four classical allusions: Zephyr (5) was god of the west wind; Ajax (9), a Greek warrior noted for his strength; Camilla (11), a legendary queen reputedly so fleet of foot that she could run over a field of grain without bending the blades or over the sea without wetting her feet; Timotheus (13), a famous Greek rhapsodic poet. Does the use of these allusions enable Pope to achieve greater economy?
4. Copy the passage and scan it. Then, considering both meter and sounds, show how Pope practices what he preaches. (Incidentally, on which syllable should "alternate" in line 14 be accented? Does the meter help you to know the pronunciation of "Timotheus'" in line 13?)

161. I like to see it lap the miles

I like to see it lap the miles,
And lick the valleys up,
And stop to feed itself at tanks,
And then, prodigious, step

Around a pile of mountains,
And, supercilious, peer
In shanties by the sides of roads,
And then a quarry pare

To fit its ribs,
And crawl between,
Complaining all the while
In horrid, hooting stanza,
Then chase itself down hill

And neigh like Boanerges;
Then, punctual as a star,
Stop—docile and omnipotent—
At its own stable door.

Emily Dickinson (1830–1886)

QUESTIONS

1. Vocabulary: *prodigious* (4), *supercilious* (6), *Boanerges* (14).
2. What basic metaphor underlies the poem? Identify the literal and the metaphorical terms and explain how you were able to make both identifications.
3. What additional figures of speech do you find in lines 8, 12, 15, 16, and 17? Explain their appropriateness.
4. Point out examples of alliteration, assonance, and consonance. Does this poem have a rime scheme?
5. Considering such things as sounds and sound repetitions, grammatical pauses, run-on lines, monosyllabic and polysyllabic words, onomatopoeia, and meter, explain in detail how sound is fitted to sense in this poem.

162. Heaven-Haven

A Nun Takes the Veil

I have desired to go
  Where springs not fail,
To fields where flies no sharp and sided hail
  And a few lilies blow.

And I have asked to be
  Where no storms come,
Where the green swell is in the havens dumb,
  And out of the swing of the sea.

Gerard Manley Hopkins (1844–1889)

QUESTIONS

1. Vocabulary: *blow* (4).
2. Who is the speaker and what is the situation? Explain the metaphors that form the substance of the poem. What things are being compared?
3. Comment on the meaning of "springs" (2) and on the effectiveness of the poet's choice of "lilies" (4).
4. How do the sound repetitions of the title reinforce the meaning? Are there other instances in the poem where sound reinforces meaning?
5. Scan the poem. (The meter is basically iambic, but there is a great deal of variation.) How does the meter reinforce meaning, especially in the last line? What purpose is served by the displacement of "not" (2) from its normal order?

163. Anthem for Doomed Youth

What passing-bells for these who die as cattle?
Only the monstrous anger of the guns.
Only the stuttering rifles' rapid rattle
Can patter out their hasty orisons.
No mockeries now for them; no prayers nor bells,

Nor any voice of mourning save the choirs—
The shrill, demented choirs of wailing shells;
And bugles calling for them from sad shires.

What candles may be held to speed them all?
Not in the hands of boys, but in their eyes
Shall shine the holy glimmers of good-byes.
The pallor of girls' brows shall be their pall;
Their flowers the tenderness of patient minds,
And each slow dusk a drawing-down of blinds.

Wilfred Owen (1893–1918)

QUESTIONS

1. Vocabulary: *passing-bells* (1), *orisons* (4), *shires* (8), *pall* (12).
2. How do the octave and the sestet of this sonnet differ in (a) geographical setting, (b) subject matter, (c) kind of imagery used, and (d) tone? Who are the "boys" (10) and "girls" (12) referred to in the sestet? It was the custom during World War I to draw down the blinds in homes where a son had been lost (14).
3. What central metaphorical image runs throughout the poem? What secondary metaphors build up the central one?
4. Why are the "doomed youth" said to die "as cattle" (1)? Why would prayers, bells, and so on, be "mockeries" for them (5)?
5. Show how sound is adapted to sense throughout the poem.

164. Eight O'Clock

He stood, and heard the steeple
  Sprinkle the quarters on the morning town.
One, two, three, four, to market-place and people
  It tossed them down.

Strapped, noosed, nighing his hour,
  He stood and counted them and cursed his luck;
And then the clock collected in the tower
  Its strength, and struck.

A. E. Housman (1859–1936)

QUESTIONS

1. Vocabulary: *quarters* (2).
2. Eight A.M. was the traditional hour in England for putting condemned men to death. Discuss the force of "morning" (2) and "struck" (8). Discuss the appropriateness of the image of the clock collecting its strength. Can you suggest any reason for the use of "nighing" (5) rather than *nearing*?
3. Scan the poem and note its musical devices. Comment on the adaptation of sound to sense.

165. Remembered Morning

The axe rings in the wood,
And the children come,
Laughing and wet from the river;
And all goes on as it should.
I hear the murmur and hum
Of their morning forever.

The water ripples and slaps
The white boat at the dock;
The fire crackles and snaps.
The little noise of the clock
Goes on and on in my heart,
Of my heart parcel and part.

O happy early stir!
A girl comes out on the porch
And the door slams after her.
She sees the wind in the birch,
And then the running day
Catches her into its way.

Janet Lewis (b. 1899)

QUESTIONS

1. What is the effect of the poem's being written in the present tense? What is the tone of the poem?
2. Examine the poem for its visual and auditory imagery. Some words are onomatopoetic, and some suggest an imitation of sound without actually possessing onomatopoeia: distinguish between these two sets of words.

166. The Sound of Night

And now the dark comes on, all full of chitter noise.
Birds huggermugger crowd the trees,
the air thick with their vesper cries,
and bats, snub seven-pointed kites,
skitter across the lake, swing out,
squeak, chirp, dip, and skim on skates
of air, and the fat frogs wake and prink
wide-lipped, noisy as ducks, drunk
on the boozy black, gloating chink-chunk.

And now on the narrow beach we defend ourselves from dark.
The cooking done, we build our firework

bright and hot and less for outlook
than for magic, and lie in our blankets
while night nickers around us. Crickets
chorus hallelujahs; paws, quiet
and quick as raindrops, play on the stones
expertly soft, run past and are gone;
fish pulse in the lake; the frogs hoarsen.

Now every voice of the hour—the known, the supposed, the strange,
the mindless, the witted, the never seen—
sing, thrum, impinge, and rearrange
endlessly; and debarred from sleep we wait
for the birds, importantly silent,
for the crease of first eye-licking light,
for the sun, lost long ago and sweet.
By the lake, locked black away and tight,
we lie, day creatures, overhearing night.

Maxine Kumin (b. 1925)

QUESTIONS

1. Vocabulary: the poem contains a wealth of words that seem chosen for their sounds rather than their denotations—but, from *chitter* (1) through *thrum* (21), the "sound effect" words do in fact have meanings. Be sure to look up any whose precise meanings are not clear to you.
2. Describe the rime scheme of the poem, taking into account both approximate and exact rimes.
3. The title identifies the general subject. In addition to presenting and imitating the sounds, what does the poem say about them—and about the speaker?

167. I heard a fly buzz when I died

I heard a fly buzz when I died.
The stillness in the room
Was like the stillness in the air
Between the heaves of storm.

The eyes around had wrung them dry,
And breaths were gathering firm
For that last onset when the king
Be witnessed in the room.

I willed my keepsakes, signed away
What portion of me be
Assignable; and then it was
There interposed a fly

With blue, uncertain, stumbling buzz
Between the light and me;
And then the windows failed, and then
I could not see to see.

Emily Dickinson (1830–1886)

QUESTIONS

1. It is important to understand the sequence of events in this death-bed scene. Arrange the following events in correct chronological order: (a) the willing of keepsakes, (b) the weeping of mourners, (c) the appearance of the fly, (d) the preternatural stillness in the room.
2. What or who are the "eyes" and the "breaths" in lines 5–6? What figures of speech are involved in these lines? Is the speaker making out her will in lines 9–11? What *is* she doing?
3. What sort of expectation is set up by phrases like "last onset," "the king," and "be witnessed"?
4. Explain "the windows failed" (15) and "I could not see to see" (16).
5. What is the rime scheme? What kinds of rime are employed? Explain the marvelous effectiveness of line 13, in terms of both imagery and sound.
6. Explain the point of the poem. How do you interpret the fly?

168. The Bench of Boors

In bed I muse on Teniers' boors,
Embrowned and beery losels all:
        A wakeful brain
        Elaborates pain:
Within low doors the slugs of boors
Laze and yawn and doze again.

In dreams they doze, the drowsy boors,
Their hazy hovel warm and small:
        Thought's ampler bound
        But chill is found:
Within low doors the basking boors
Snugly hug the ember-mound.

Sleepless, I see the slumberous boors
Their blurred eyes blink, their eyelids fall:
        Thought's eager sight
        Aches—overbright!
Within low doors the boozy boors
Cat-naps take in pipe-bowl light.

Herman Melville (1819–1891)

QUESTIONS

1. Vocabulary: *boors* (title), *losels* (2), *slugs* (5).
2. David Teniers the Younger, a seventeenth-century Flemish painter, was famous for his genre paintings of peasant life. What was the essential characteristic of this life according to the poem? What symbolism do you find in the fifth line of each stanza?
3. What is the relation of the third and fourth lines of each stanza to the speaker? To the boors? How does the form of the stanza emphasize the contrast in thought?
4. Comment on other correspondences between sound and meaning.

169. The Dance

In Breughel's great picture, The Kermess,
the dancers go round, they go round and
around, the squeal and the blare and the
tweedle of bagpipes, a bugle and fiddles
tipping their bellies (round as the thick-
sided glasses whose wash they impound)
their hips and their bellies off balance
to turn them. Kicking and rolling about
the Fair Grounds, swinging their butts, those
shanks must be sound to bear up under such
rollicking measures, prance as they dance
in Breughel's great picture, The Kermess.

William Carlos Williams (1883–1963)

QUESTIONS

1. Peter Breughel the Elder was a sixteenth-century Flemish painter of peasant life. A *kermess* is an annual outdoor festival or fair. How do the form, the meter, and the sounds of this poem reinforce its content?
2. Explore the similarities and differences between this poem and the preceding one, both as to form and content.

CHAPTER FOURTEEN

Pattern

Art, ultimately, is organization. It is a searching after order, after form. Many consider the primal artistic act to have been God's creation of the universe out of chaos, shaping the formless into form; and every artist since, on a lesser scale, has sought to imitate that act—to reduce the chaotic in experience to a meaningful and pleasing order by means of selection and arrangement. For this reason we evaluate a poem partially by the same criteria that an English instructor uses to evaluate a theme—by its unity, its coherence, and its proper placing of emphasis. A well-constructed poem contains neither too little nor too much; every part of the poem belongs where it is and could be placed nowhere else; any interchanging of two stanzas, two lines, or even two words, would to some extent damage the poem and make it less effective. We come to feel, with a truly first-rate poem, that the choice and placement of every word is inevitable, that it could not be otherwise.

In addition to the internal ordering of materials—the arrangement of ideas, images, and thoughts, which we may refer to as the poem's **structure**—the poet may impose some external pattern on a poem, may give it not only an inside logical order but an outside symmetry, or form. Such formality appeals to the human instinct for design, the instinct that has prompted people, at various times, to tattoo and paint their bodies, to decorate their swords and armor with beautiful and complex tracery, and to choose patterned fabrics for their clothing, carpets, curtains, and wallpapers. The poet appeals to our love of the shapely.

In general, a poem may be cast in one of three broad kinds of form: continuous form, stanzaic form, and fixed form. In **continuous form**, as illustrated by "The Widow's Lament in Springtime" (No. 39), "After Apple-Picking" (No. 35), "Ulysses" (No. 67), and "My Last Duchess" (No. 90), the element of design is slight. The lines follow each other without formal grouping, the only breaks being dictated by units of meaning, as paragraphs are in prose. But even here there are degrees of pattern. "The Widow's Lament in Springtime" has neither regular meter nor rime. "After Apple-Picking," on the other hand, is metrical; it has no regularity in length of line, but the meter is prevailingly iambic;

also every line rimes with another, though not according to any fixed pattern. "Ulysses" is regular in both meter and length of line: it is unrimed iambic pentameter, or blank verse. And to these regularities "My Last Duchess" adds regularity of rime, for it is written in riming pentameter couplets. Thus, in increasing degrees, the authors of "After Apple-Picking," "Ulysses," and "My Last Duchess" have chosen a predetermined pattern in which to cast their work.

In **stanzaic form** the poet writes in a series of **stanzas**, that is, repeated units having the same number of lines, usually the same metrical pattern, and often an identical rime scheme. The poet may choose some traditional stanza pattern (poetry, like colleges, is rich in tradition) or invent an original one. The traditional stanza patterns (for example, terza rima, ballad meter, rime royal, Spenserian stanza) are many, and the student specializing in literature will wish to become familiar with some of them; the general student should know that they exist. Often the use of one of these traditional stanza forms constitutes a kind of literary allusion. The reader who is conscious of its traditional use or of its use by a previous great poet will be aware of subtleties in the communication that a less well-read reader may miss.

Stanzaic form, like continuous form, exhibits degrees of formal pattern. The poem "in Just-" (No. 93) is divided into alternating stanzas of four lines and one line, but neither the four-line stanzas nor the one-line stanzas have any resemblance to each other. In "Poem in October" (No. 176) the stanzas are alike in length of line but are without a regular pattern of rime. In "The Aim Was Song" (No. 152) a rime pattern is added to a metrical pattern. In Shakespeare's "Winter" (No. 2) a refrain is employed in addition to the patterns of meter and rime. The following poem illustrates additional elements of design:

170. the greedy the people

the greedy the people
(as if as can yes)
they sell and they buy
and they die for because
though the bell in the steeple
says Why

the chary the wary
(as all as can each)
they don't and they do
and they turn to a which
though the moon in her glory
says Who

the busy the millions
(as you're as can i'm)
they flock and they flee
through a thunder of seem
though the stars in their silence
say Be

the cunning the craven
(as think as can feel)
they when and they how
and they live for until
though the sun in his heaven
says Now

the timid the tender
(as doubt as can trust)
they work and they pray
and they bow to a must
though the earth in her splendor
says May

e. e. cummings (1894–1962)

QUESTIONS

1. This poem is a constellation of interlocking patterns. To appreciate them fully, read it first in the normal fashion, one line after another, then read all the first lines of the stanzas, followed by all the second lines, all the third lines, and so on. Having done this, describe (a) the rime scheme; (b) the metrical design; (c) the pattern of musical devices in the first lines; (d) the syntactical pattern. Prepare a model of the poem, writing out the recurring words, leaving blanks for varying words, and indicating recurring parts of speech in parentheses. The model for the third lines would be: *they (verb) and they (verb)*. Describe the pattern of meaning. How do the last two lines of each stanza relate to the first four? What blanks in your model are to be filled in by words related in meaning?
2. A trademark of e. e. cummings as a poet is his imaginative freedom with parts of speech. For instance, in line 21 he uses conjunctions as verbs. What different parts of speech does he use as nouns in the fourth line of each stanza? Can you see meanings for these unusual nouns? Explain the contrast between the last words in the fourth and sixth lines of each stanza. What two meanings has the final word of the poem?
3. Sum up briefly the meaning of the poem.

A stanza form may be described by designating four things: the rime scheme (if there is one), the position of the refrain (if there is one), the prevailing metrical foot, and the number of feet in each line. Rime scheme is traditionally designated by using letters of the alphabet to indicate the riming lines, and x for unrimed lines. Refrain lines may be indicated by a capital letter, and the number of feet in the line by a numerical exponent after the letter. Thus the stanza pattern of Browning's "Meeting at Night" (No. 32) is iambic tetrameter *abccba* (or iambic $abccba^4$); that of cummings's "if everything happens that can't be done" (No. 148) is anapestic $a^4x^2x^1a^1b^4x^1x^1b^2a^3$; that of Donne's "A Hymn to God the Father" (No. 30) is iambic $abab^5A^4B^2$. Stanzaic poetry not written in traditional metrical feet can be described similarly: Moore's "Nevertheless" (No. 153) is syllabic xaa^6.

A **fixed form** is a traditional pattern that applies to a whole poem. In French poetry many fixed forms have been widely used: rondeaus, rondels, villanelles, triolets, sestinas, ballades, double ballades, and others. In English poetry, though most of the fixed forms have been experimented with, perhaps only two—the limerick and the sonnet—have really taken hold.

The **limerick**, though really a subliterary form, will serve to illustrate the fixed form in general. Its pattern is anapestic $aa^3bb^2a^3$:

171.

I sat | next the Duch- | ess at tea. |
It was just | as I feared | it would be: |
Her rum- | blings ab-dom- | i-nal
Were sim- | ply a-bom- | i-na-ble
And eve- | ry-one thought | it was me! |

Anonymous

QUESTION

The limerick form freely allows the use of a substitute foot in the first foot of any line but insists as a rule upon strict adherence to anapestic meter thereafter. The preceding limerick, by these standards, is defective, for one too many unaccented syllables has been squeezed in at the end of line 4; moreover, *abdominal* and *abominable* are imperfect rimes (because of the second *b* in *abominable*). Both of these flaws disappear if *abominable* is replaced by *phenomenal*, or if *internal* and *infernal* are chosen as the rimes in lines 3–4. In the face of such appropriate substitutions, can you make a case for preferring the defective version?

The limerick form is used exclusively for humorous and nonsense verse, for which, with its short lines, swift catchy meter, and emphatic rimes, it is particularly suitable. By trying to recast these little jokes and bits of nonsense in a different meter and pattern or into prose, we may discover how much of their effect they owe particularly to the limerick form. There is, of course, no magical or mysterious identity between certain forms and certain types of content, but there may be more or less correspondence. A form may be appropriate or inappropriate. The limerick form is inappropriate for the serious treatment of serious material.

The **sonnet** is less rigidly prescribed than the limerick. It must be fourteen lines in length, and it almost always is iambic pentameter, but in structure and rime scheme there may be considerable leeway. Most sonnets, however, conform more or less closely to one of two general models or types, the Italian and the English.

The **Italian** or *Petrarchan* **sonnet** (so called because the Italian poet Petrarch practiced it so extensively) is divided usually between eight lines called the **octave**, using two rimes arranged *abbaabba*, and six lines called the **sestet**, using any arrangement of either two or three rimes: *cdcdcd* and *cdecde* are common patterns. The division between octave and sestet in the Italian sonnet (indicated by the rime scheme and sometimes marked off in printing by a space) usually corresponds to a division of thought. The octave presents a situation and the sestet a comment, or the octave an idea and the sestet an example, or the octave a question and the sestet an answer. Thus the form reflects the structure.

172. On First Looking into Chapman's Homer

Much have I traveled in the realms of gold,
  And many goodly states and kingdoms seen;
  Round many western islands have I been
Which bards in fealty to Apollo hold.
Oft of one wide expanse had I been told
  That deep-browed Homer ruled as his demesne;
  Yet did I never breathe its pure serene
Till I heard Chapman speak out loud and bold:
Then felt I like some watcher of the skies
  When a new planet swims into his ken;
Or like stout Cortez when with eagle eyes
  He stared at the Pacific—and all his men
Looked at each other with a wild surmise—
  Silent, upon a peak in Darien.

John Keats (1795–1821)

QUESTIONS

1. Vocabulary: *fealty* (4), *Apollo* (4), *demesne* (6), *ken* (10). *Darien* (14) is an ancient name for the Isthmus of Panama.
2. John Keats, at twenty-one, could not read Greek and was probably acquainted with Homer's *Iliad* and *Odyssey* only through the translations of

Alexander Pope, which to him very likely seemed prosy and stilted. Then one day he and a friend found a vigorous poetic translation by the Elizabethan poet George Chapman. Keats and his friend, enthralled, sat up late at night excitedly reading aloud to each other from Chapman's book. Toward morning Keats walked home and, before going to bed, wrote the above sonnet and sent it to his friend. What common ideas underlie the three major figures of speech in the poem?
3. What is the rime scheme? What division of thought corresponds to the division between octave and sestet?
4. Balboa, not Cortez, discovered the Pacific. How seriously does this mistake detract from the value of the poem?

The **English** or *Shakespearean* **sonnet** (invented by the English poet Surrey and made famous by Shakespeare) is composed of three quatrains and a concluding couplet, riming *abab cdcd efef gg*. Again, the units marked off by the rimes and the development of the thought often correspond. The three quatrains, for instance, may present three examples and the couplet a conclusion or (as in the following example) the quatrains three metaphorical statements of one idea and the couplet an application.

173. That time of year

That time of year thou mayst in me behold
When yellow leaves, or none, or few, do hang
Upon those boughs which shake against the cold,
Bare ruined choirs where late the sweet birds sang.
In me thou see'st the twilight of such day
As after sunset fadeth in the west,
Which by and by black night doth take away,
Death's second self, that seals up all in rest.
In me thou see'st the glowing of such fire,
That on the ashes of his youth doth lie
As the deathbed whereon it must expire,
Consumed with that which it was nourished by.
This thou perceivest, which makes thy love more strong,
To love that well which thou must leave ere long.

William Shakespeare (1564–1616)

QUESTIONS

1. What are the three major images introduced by the three quatrains? What do they have in common? Can you see any reason for presenting them in this particular order, or might they be rearranged without loss?
2. Each of the images is to some degree complicated rather than simple. For instance, what additional image is introduced by "Bare ruined choirs" (4)? Explain its appropriateness.

3. What additional comparisons are introduced in the second and third quatrains? Explain line 12.
4. Whom does the speaker address? What assertion does he make in the concluding couplet, and with what degree of confidence? Paraphrase these lines so as to state their meaning as clearly as possible.

Initially, it may seem absurd that poets should choose to confine themselves in an arbitrary fourteen-line mold with prescribed meter and rime scheme. They do so partly from the desire to carry on a tradition, as all of us carry out certain traditions for their own sake, else why should we bring a tree indoors at Christmas time? But, in addition, the tradition of the sonnet has proved useful because, like the limerick, it seems effective for certain types of subject matter and treatment. Though these cannot be as narrowly limited or as rigidly described as for the limerick, the sonnet is usually most effective when used for the serious treatment of love but has also been used for the discussion of death, religion, political situations, and related subjects. Again, there is no magical affinity between form and subject, or treatment, and excellent sonnets have been written outside these traditional areas. The sonnet tradition has also proved useful because it has provided a challenge to the poet. Inferior poets, of course, are often defeated by that challenge: they will use unnecessary words to fill out the meter or inappropriate words for the sake of rime. Good poets are inspired by the challenge: it will call forth ideas and images that might not otherwise have come. They will subdue the form rather than be subdued by it; they will make it do what they require. There is no doubt that the presence of a net makes good tennis players more precise in their shots than they otherwise would be. And finally, there is in all form the pleasure of form itself.

EXERCISES

1. Examine the following sonnets; classify each (when possible) as primarily Italian or primarily English; then specify how closely in form and structure each adheres to or how far it departs from the polarities represented by "On First Looking into Chapman's Homer" and "That time of year":
   a. "The world is too much with us" (No. 29)
   b. "The Caged Skylark" (No. 113)
   c. "Design" (No. 106)
   d. From *Romeo and Juliet* (No. 177)
   e. "Since there's no help" (No. 119)
   f. "The Dead" (No. 128)
   g. "Batter my heart, three-personed God" (No. 80)
   h. "Ozymandias" (No. 79)
   i. "Leda and the Swan" (No. 97)

j. "How Annandale Went Out" (No. 110)
k. "Anthem for Doomed Youth" (No. 163)
l. "Ending" (No. 224)

2. "The Story We Know" (No. 181), "One Art" (No. 206), "The Freaks at Spurgin Road Field" (No. 239), and "Do Not Go Gentle into That Good Night" (No. 291) are all examples of a French fixed form known as the **villanelle**. After studying their formal features, formulate a definition for the villanelle. *Hint:* Start with No. 291, the "purest" example of the form; then examine the extent to which the others conform to or depart from that norm.

* * *

174. A Handful of Limericks

There was a young lady from Niger
Who smiled as she rode on a tiger;
  They returned from the ride
  With the lady inside
And the smile on the face of the tiger.

Anonymous

There was a young lady of Lynn
Who was so uncommonly thin
  That when she essayed
  To drink lemonade
She slipped through the straw and fell in.

Anonymous

A tutor who tooted the flute
Tried to teach two young tooters to toot.
  Said the two to the tutor,
  "Is it harder to toot, or
To tutor two tooters to toot?"

Carolyn Wells (1862–1942)

There was a young maid who said, "Why
Can't I look in my ear with my eye?
  If I put my mind to it,
  I'm sure I can do it.
You never can tell till you try."

Anonymous

A goat on a stroll near a brook
Found an old movie film and partook.
  "Was it good?" asked his mate.
  Said the goat, "Second-rate!
Not nearly as good as the book!"

Martin Bristow Smith (b. 1916)

An epicure dining at Crewe
Found a rather large mouse in his stew.
  Said the waiter, "Don't shout
  And wave it about
Or the rest will be wanting one too."

Anonymous

There was a young lady named Bright
Whose speed was much faster than light.
  She set out one day
  In a relative way
And returned on the previous night.

Anonymous

A cannibal said to her mate
Who was in a deplorable state
  Of discomfort, "My dear,
  Do you think it's the beer
Or is it just someone you ate?"

A. N. Wilkins (b. 1925)

175. Two Japanese Haiku

  The lightning flashes!
And slashing through the darkness,
  A night-heron's screech.

A lightning gleam:
  into darkness travels
    a night heron's scream.

Matsuo Bashō (1644–1694)

  The falling flower
I saw drift back to the branch
  Was a butterfly.

Fallen flowers rise
  back to the branch—I watch:
    oh . . . butterflies!

Moritake (1452–1540)

QUESTION

The **haiku**, a Japanese form, consists of three lines of five, seven, and five syllables each. The translators of the versions on the left (Earl Miner and Babette Deutsch respectively) preserve this syllable count; the translator of the right-hand versions (Harold G. Henderson) seeks to preserve the sense of formal structure by making the first and last lines rime. Moritake's haiku, as Miss Deutsch points out, "refers to the Buddhist proverb that the fallen flower never returns to the branch; the broken mirror never again reflects." From these two examples, what would you say are the characteristics of effective haiku?

176. Poem in October

It was my thirtieth year to heaven
Woke to my hearing from harbor and neighbor wood
And the mussel pooled and the heron
Priested shore
The morning beckon
With water praying and call of seagull and rook
And the knock of sailing boats on the net webbed wall
Myself to set foot
That second
In the still sleeping town and set forth.

My birthday began with the water-
Birds and the birds of the winged trees flying my name
Above the farms and the white horses
And I rose
In rainy autumn
And walked abroad in a shower of all my days.
High tide and the heron dived when I took the road
Over the border
And the gates
Of the town closed as the town awoke.

A springful of larks in a rolling
Cloud and the roadside bushes brimming with whistling
Blackbirds and the sun of October
Summery
On the hill's shoulder,
Here were fond climates and sweet singers suddenly
Come in the morning where I wandered and listened
To the rain wringing
Wind blow cold
In the woods faraway under me.

Pale rain over the dwindling harbor
And over the sea wet church the size of a snail
With its horns through mist and the castle
Brown as owls
But all the gardens
Of spring and summer were blooming in the tall tales
Beyond the border and under the lark full cloud.
There could I marvel
My birthday
Away but the weather turned around.

It turned away from the blithe country
And down the other air and the blue altered sky
Streamed again a wonder of summer
With apples
Pears and red currants
And I saw in the turning so clearly a child's
Forgotten mornings when he walked with his mother
Through the parables
Of sun light
And the legends of the green chapels

And the twice told fields of infancy
That his tears burned my cheeks and his heart moved in mine.
These were the woods the river and sea
Where a boy
In the listening
Summertime of the dead whispered the truth of his joy
To the trees and the stones and the fish in the tide.
And the mystery
Sang alive
Still in the water and singingbirds.

And there could I marvel my birthday
Away but the weather turned around. And the true
Joy of the long dead child sang burning
In the sun.
It was my thirtieth
Year to heaven stood there then in the summer noon
Though the town below lay leaved with October blood.
O may my heart's truth
Still be sung
On this high hill in a year's turning.

Dylan Thomas (1914–1953)

QUESTIONS

1. The setting is a small fishing village on the coast of Wales. The poet's first name in Welsh means "water" (12). Trace the poet's walk in relation to the village, the weather, and the time of day.
2. "The weather turned around" (40, 62) is an expression indicating a change in the weather or the direction of the wind. In what psychological sense does the weather turn around during the poet's walk? Who is "the long dead child" (63), and what kind of child was he? With what wish does the poem close?
3. Explain "thirtieth year to heaven" (1), "horns" (33), "tall tales" (36), "green chapels" (50), "October blood" (67).
4. The elaborate stanza pattern in this poem is based not on the meter (which is very free) but on a syllable count. How many syllables are there in each line of the stanza? (In line 1 "thirtieth" may be counted as only two syllables.) Notice that stanzas 1 and 3 consist of exactly one sentence each.
5. The poem makes considerable use of approximate rime, though not according to a regular pattern. Point out examples.

177. From *Romeo and Juliet*

ROMEO If I profane with my unworthiest hand
This holy shrine, the gentle sin is this;
My lips, two blushing pilgrims, ready stand
To smooth that rough touch with a tender kiss.
JULIET Good pilgrim, you do wrong your hand too much,
Which mannerly devotion shows in this;
For saints have hands that pilgrims' hands do touch,
And palm to palm is holy palmers' kiss.
ROMEO Have not saints lips, and holy palmers too?
JULIET Ay, pilgrim, lips that they must use in prayer.
ROMEO O! then, dear saint, let lips do what hands do;
They pray, grant thou, lest faith turn to despair.
JULIET Saints do not move,° though grant for prayers' sake.
ROMEO Then move not, while my prayers' effect I take.

° move: propose, instigate

William Shakespeare (1564–1616)

QUESTIONS

1. These fourteen lines have been lifted out of Act 1, scene 5, of Shakespeare's play. They are the first words exchanged between Romeo and Juliet, who are meeting, for the first time, at a masquerade ball given by her father. Struck by Juliet's beauty, Romeo has come up to greet her. What stage action accompanies this passage?

2. What is the basic metaphor created by such religious terms as "profane" (1), "shrine" (2), "pilgrims" (3), "holy palmers" (8)? How does this metaphor affect the tone of the relationship between Romeo and Juliet?
3. What play on words do you find in lines 8 and 13–14? What two meanings has line 11?
4. By meter and rime scheme, these lines form a sonnet. Do you think this was coincidental or intentional on Shakespeare's part? Discuss.

178. Death, be not proud

Death, be not proud, though some have callèd thee
Mighty and dreadful, for thou art not so;
For those whom thou think'st thou dost overthrow
Die not, poor death, nor yet canst thou kill me.
From rest and sleep, which but thy pictures be,
Much pleasure — then, from thee much more must flow;
And soonest° our best men with thee do go, readiest
Rest of their bones and soul's delivery.
Thou art slave to fate, chance, kings, and desperate men,
And dost with poison, war, and sickness dwell;
And poppy or charms can make us sleep as well,
And better than thy stroke. Why swell'st thou then?
One short sleep passed, we wake eternally,
And death shall be no more; death, thou shalt die.

John Donne (1572–1631)

QUESTIONS

1. What two figures of speech dominate the poem?
2. Why should death not be proud? List the speaker's major reasons. Are they consistent? Logical? Persuasive?
3. Discuss the tone of the poem. Is the speaker (a) a man of assured faith with a firm conviction that death is not to be feared or (b) a man desperately trying to convince himself that there is nothing to fear in death?
4. In form this sonnet blends the English and Italian models. Explain. Is its organization of thought closer to the Italian or the English sonnet?

179. The Imperfect Paradise

If God had stopped work after the fifth day
With Eden full of vegetables and fruits,
If oak and lilac held exclusive sway
Over a kingdom made of stems and roots,
If landscape were the genius of creation
And neither man nor serpent played a role
And God must look to wind for lamentation
And not to picture postcards of the soul,

Would he have rested on his bank of cloud
With nothing in the universe to lose,
Or would he hunger for a human crowd?
Which would a wise and just creator choose:
The green hosannas of a budding leaf
Or the strict contract between love and grief?

Linda Pastan (b. 1932)

QUESTIONS

1. The poem alludes to Genesis 1 (the creation of the world) but also looks forward to the fall of Adam, and to universal human predicaments. Does the speaker imply an answer to the question in lines 12–14?
2. In form this is an English sonnet. How does its structure match the formal expectations?

180. Acquainted with the Night

I have been one acquainted with the night.
I have walked out in rain—and back in rain.
I have outwalked the furthest city light.

I have looked down the saddest city lane.
I have passed by the watchman on his beat
And dropped my eyes, unwilling to explain.

I have stood still and stopped the sound of feet
When far away an interrupted cry
Came over houses from another street,

But not to call me back or say good-by;
And further still at an unearthly height
One luminary clock against the sky

Proclaimed the time was neither wrong nor right.
I have been one acquainted with the night.

Robert Frost (1874–1963)

QUESTIONS

1. How does the speaker reveal the strength of his purpose in his night-walking? Can you specify what that purpose is? What symbolic meanings does the night hold?
2. How is the poem structured into sentences? What is the effect of repeating the phrase "I have"? Of repeating line 1 at the conclusion? How do these repetitions affect the tone of the poem?
3. Some critics have interpreted the "luminary clock" (12) literally—as the illuminated dial of a tower clock; others have interpreted it figuratively as the full

moon. Of what, in either case, is it a symbol? Does the clock tell accurate chronometric time? What kind of "time" is it proclaiming in line 13? Is knowing *that* kind of time the speaker's quest?

4. The poem contains 14 lines—like a sonnet. But its rime scheme is **terza rima**, an interlocking scheme with the pattern *aba bcb cdc*, etc., a formal arrangement that implies continual progression. How does Frost bring the progression to an end? Terza rima was the form memorably employed by Dante for his *Divine Comedy*, of which the *Inferno* is the best-known section. In what ways does Frost's poem allude to the subject and framework of that poem?

181. The Story We Know

The way to begin is always the same. Hello,
Hello. Your hand, your name. So glad, Just fine,
and Good-bye at the end. That's every story we know,

and why pretend? But lunch tomorrow? No?
Yes? An omelette, salad, chilled white wine?
The way to begin is simple, sane, Hello,

and then it's Sunday, coffee, the *Times*, a slow
day by the fire, dinner at eight or nine
and Good-bye. In the end, this is a story we know

so well we don't turn the page, or look below
the picture, or follow the words to the next line:
The way to begin is always the same Hello.

But one night, through the latticed window, snow
begins to whiten the air, and the tall white pine.
Good-bye is the end of every story we know

that night, and when we close the curtains, oh,
we hold each other against that cold white sign
of the way we all begin and end. *Hello,*
Good-bye is the only story. We know, we know.

Martha Collins (b. 1940)

QUESTIONS

1. What have lines 1, 6, 12, and 18 in common? What have lines 3, 9, 15, and 19 in common?
2. What is the rime scheme?
3. Show how the words "Hello" and "Good-bye" acquire deeper meanings as the poem progresses. What do they refer to or symbolize in the last two lines? Why is the phrase "we know" repeated in the last line?
4. This poem is a villanelle. How closely does it conform to the definition of a villanelle that you formulated on page 221?

182. Edward

"Why docs your sword so drip with blood,
Edward, Edward,
Why does your sword so drip with blood,
And why so sad go ye, O?"
"O I have killed my hawk so good,
Mother, Mother,
O I have killed my hawk so good,
And I had no more but he, O."

"Your hawk's blood was never so red,
Edward, Edward,
Your hawk's blood was never so red,
My dear son, I tell thee, O."
"O I have killed my red-roan steed,
Mother, Mother,
O I have killed my red-roan steed,
That once was so fair and free, O."

"Your steed was old, and ye have got more,
Edward, Edward,
Your steed was old, and ye have got more,
Some other grief ye feel, O."
"O I have killed my father dear,
Mother, Mother,
O I have killed my father dear,
Alas, and woe is me, O!"

"And what penance will ye do for that,
Edward, Edward,
And what penance will ye do for that,
My dear son, now tell me, O."
"I'll set my feet in yonder boat,
Mother, Mother,
I'll set my feet in yonder boat,
And I'll fare over the sea, O."

"And what will ye do with your towers and your hall,
Edward, Edward,
And what will ye do with your towers and your hall,
That were so fair to see, O?"
"I'll let them stand till they down fall,
Mother, Mother,
I'll let them stand till they down fall,
For here nevermore must I be, O."

"And what will ye leave to your children and wife,
Edward, Edward,
And what will ye leave to your children and wife,
When ye go over the sea, O?"
"The world is large, let them beg through life,
Mother, Mother,
The world is large, let them beg through life,
For them nevermore will I see, O."

"And what will ye leave to your own mother dear,
Edward, Edward,
And what will ye leave to your own mother dear?
My dear son, now tell me, O."
"The curse of hell from me shall ye bear,
Mother, Mother,
The curse of hell from me shall ye bear,
Such counsels you gave to me, O."

Anonymous

QUESTIONS

1. What has Edward done and why? Where do the two climaxes of the poem come?
2. Tell as much as you can about Edward and his feelings toward what he has done. From what class of society is he? Why does he at first give false answers to his mother's questions? What reversal of feelings and loyalties has he undergone? Do his answers about his hawk and steed perhaps indicate his present feelings toward his father? How do you explain his behavior to his wife and children? What are his present feelings toward his mother?
3. Tell as much as you can about Edward's mother. Why does she ask what Edward has done—doesn't she already know? Is there any clue as to the motivation of her counsel? How skillful is she in her questioning? What do we learn about her from her dismissal of Edward's steed as "old" and only one of many (17)? From her asking Edward what penance *he* will do for his act (25)? From her reference to herself as Edward's "own mother dear" (49)?
4. Structure and form are both important in this poem. Could any of the stanzas be interchanged without loss, or do they build up steadily to the two climaxes? What effect has the constant repetition of the two short refrains, "Edward, Edward" and "Mother, Mother"? What is the effect of the final "O" at the end of each speech? Does the repetition of each question and answer simply waste words or does it add to the suspense and emotional intensity? (Try reading the poem omitting the third and seventh lines of each stanza. Is it improved or weakened?)
5. Much of what happened is implied; much is omitted. Does the poem gain anything in power from what is *not* told?

183. A Christmas Tree

Star,
If you are
A love compassionate,
You will walk with us this year.
We face a glacial distance, who are here
Huddld
At your feet.

William Burford (b. 1927)

QUESTION

Why do you think the author misspelled "huddled" in line 6?

EXERCISE

The typographical shape of a poem on the page (whether, for example, it is printed with a straight left-hand margin or with a system of indentations) is determined sometimes by the poet, sometimes by the printer, sometimes by an editor. Examine each of the following poems and try to deduce what *principle* (if any) determined its typographical design:

1. "The Mill" (No. 18)
2. "To a Waterfowl" (No. 105)
3. "Constantly risking absurdity" (No. 225)
4. "To His Coy Mistress" (No. 53)
5. "Poem in October" (No. 176)
6. "The Lamb" (No. 208)
7. "Offspring" (No. 252)
8. "Dream Deferred" (No. 58)

CHAPTER FIFTEEN

Bad Poetry and Good

The attempt to evaluate a poem should never be made before the poem is understood; and, unless one has developed the capacity to feel some poetry deeply, any judgments one makes will be worthless. A person who likes no wines can hardly be a judge of them. But the ability to make judgments, to discriminate between good and bad, great and good, good and half-good, is surely a primary object of all liberal education, and one's appreciation of poetry is incomplete unless it includes discrimination. Of the mass of verse that appears in print each year, most is "stale, flat, and unprofitable"; a very, very little is of any enduring value.

In judging a poem, as in judging any work of art, we need to ask three basic questions: (1) *What is its central purpose?* (2) *How fully has this purpose been accomplished?* (3) *How important is this purpose?* We need to answer the first question in order to understand the poem. Questions 2 and 3 are those by which we evaluate it. Question 2 measures the poem on a scale of perfection. Question 3 measures it on a scale of significance. And, just as the area of a rectangle is determined by multiplying its measurements on two scales, breadth and height, so the greatness of a poem is determined by multiplying its measurements on two scales, perfection and significance. If the poem measures well on the first of these scales, we call it a good poem, at least of its kind. If it measures well on both scales, we call it a great poem.*

The measurement of a poem is a much more complex process, of course, than is the measurement of a rectangle. It cannot be done as

*As indicated in the footnote on page 26, some objection has been made to the use of the term "purpose" in literary criticism. For the two evaluative criteria suggested above may be substituted these two: (1) *How thoroughly are the materials of the poem integrated or unified?* (2) *How many and how diverse are the materials that it integrates?* Thus a poem becomes successful in proportion to the tightness of its organization—that is, according to the degree to which all its elements work together and require each other to produce the total effect—and it becomes great in proportion to its scope—that is, according to the amount and diversity of the material it amalgamates into unity.

exactly. Agreement on the measurements will never be complete. Yet over a period of time the judgments of qualified readers* tend to coalesce: there comes to be more agreement than disagreement. There is almost universal agreement, for instance, that Shakespeare is the greatest of English poets. Although qualified readers might disagree sharply as to whether Donne or Keats is the superior poet—or Wordsworth or Chaucer, or Shelley or Pope—they nearly all agree that each of these is superior to Kipling or Longfellow. And there is almost universal agreement that Kipling and Longfellow are superior to James Whitcomb Riley or Rod McKuen.

But your problem is to be able to discriminate, not between already established reputations, but between poems—poems you have not seen before and of which, perhaps, you do not even know the author. Here, of course, you will not always be right—even the most qualified readers occasionally go badly astray—but you should, we hope, be able to make broad distinctions with a higher average of success than you could when you began this book. And, unless you allow yourself to petrify, your ability to do this should improve throughout your college years and beyond.

For answering the first of our evaluative questions, *How fully has the poem's purpose been accomplished?* there are no easy yardsticks that we can apply. We cannot ask, Is the poem melodious? Does it have smooth meter? Does it use good grammar? Does it contain figures of speech? Are the rimes perfect? Excellent poems exist without any of these attributes. We can judge any element in a poem only as it contributes or fails to contribute to the achievement of the central purpose; and we can judge the total poem only as these elements work together to form an integrated whole. But we can at least attempt a few generalizations. A perfect poem contains no excess words, no words that do not bear their full weight in contributing to the total meaning, and no words that are used just to fill out the meter. Each word is the best word for expressing the total meaning: there are no inexact words forced by the rime scheme or the metrical pattern. The word order is the best order for expressing the author's total meaning; distortions or departures from normal order are for emphasis or some other meaningful purpose. The diction, the images, and the figures of speech are fresh, not trite (except, of course, when the poet uses trite language deliberately for purposes of irony). The sound of the poem does not clash with its sense, nor the form with

*Throughout this discussion the term "qualified reader" is of utmost importance. By a qualified reader we mean briefly a person with considerable experience of literature and considerable experience of life: a person of intelligence, sensitivity, and knowledge.

its content; and in general both sound and pattern are used to support meaning. The organization of the poem is the best possible organization: images and ideas are so effectively arranged that any rearrangement would be harmful to the poem. Always remember, however, that a good poem may have flaws. We should never damn a poem for its flaws if these flaws are amply compensated for by positive excellence.

If a poem is to have true excellence, it must be in some sense a "new" poem; it must exact a fresh response from the qualified reader. It will not be merely imitative of previous literature nor appeal to stock, pre-established ways of thinking and feeling that in some readers are automatically stimulated by words like *mother, baby, home, country, faith*, or *God*, much as a vending machine dispenses a product when the right amount is inserted in the slot.

And here, perhaps, we should discuss the kinds of poems that most frequently "fool" inexperienced readers (and occasionally a few experienced ones) and sometimes achieve tremendous popularity without winning the respect of most good readers. These poems are frequently published on greeting cards or in anthologies entitled *Poems of Inspiration, Poems of Courage*, or *Heart-Throbs*. The people who write such poems and the people who like them are often the best of people, but they are not poets or lovers of poetry in any genuine sense. They are lovers of conventional ideas or sentiments or feelings, which they like to see expressed with the adornment of rime and meter, and which, when so expressed, they respond to in predictable ways.

Of the several varieties of inferior poetry, we shall concern ourselves with three: the sentimental, the rhetorical, and the purely didactic. All three are perhaps unduly dignified by the name of poetry. They might more aptly be described as verse.

Sentimentality is indulgence in emotion for its own sake, or expression of more emotion than an occasion warrants. Sentimentalists are gushy, stirred to tears by trivial or inappropriate causes; they weep at all weddings and all funerals; they are made ecstatic by manifestations of young love; they clip locks of hair, gild baby shoes, and talk baby talk; they grow compassionate over hardened criminals when they are punished. Their opposites are callous or unfeeling people. The ideal is the person who responds sensitively on appropriate occasions and feels deeply on occasions that deserve deep feeling, but who has nevertheless a certain amount of emotional reserve, a certain command over feelings. Sentimental *literature* is "tear-jerking" literature. It aims primarily at stimulating the emotions directly rather than at communicating experience truly and freshly; it depends on trite and well-tried formulas for exciting emotion; it revels in old oaken buckets, rocking chairs, mother love, and the pitter-patter of little feet; it oversimplifies; it is unfaithful to the full complexity of human experience. In this book the best example of sentimental verse is the first seven lines of the anonymous "Love" (No. 131). If this verse had ended as it began, it would have been pure sentimentalism. The eighth line redeems it by making us realize that the writer is not serious and thus transfers the piece from the classification of sentimental verse to that of humorous verse. In fact, the writer is poking fun at sentimentality by showing that in its most maudlin form it is characteristic of drunks.

Rhetorical poetry uses a language more glittering and high flown than its substance warrants. It offers a spurious vehemence of language—language without a corresponding reality of emotion or thought underneath. It is oratorical, overelegant, artificially eloquent. It is superficial and, again, often basically trite. It loves rolling phrases like "from the rocky coast of Maine to the sun-washed shores of California" and "our heroic dead" and "Old Glory." It deals in generalities. At its worst it is bombast. In this book an example is offered by the two lines quoted from the play-within-a-play in Shakespeare's *A Midsummer Night's Dream*:

> Whereat with blade, with bloody, blameful blade,
> He bravely broached his boiling bloody breast.

Another example may be found in the player's recitation in *Hamlet* (in Act 2, scene 2):

> Out, out, thou strumpet Fortune! All you gods,
> In general synod take away her power,
> Break all the spokes and fellies from her wheel,
> And bowl the round nave down the hill of heaven
> As low as to the fiends!

Didactic poetry has as a primary purpose to teach or preach. It is probable that all the very greatest poetry teaches in subtle ways, without being expressly didactic; and much expressly didactic poetry ranks high in poetic excellence: that is, it accomplishes its teaching without ceasing to be poetry. But when the didactic purpose supersedes the poetic purpose, when the poem communicates information or moral instruction only, then it ceases to be didactic poetry and becomes didactic verse. Such verse appeals to people who read poetry primarily for noble thoughts or inspiring lessons and like them prettily expressed. It is recognizable often by its lack of any specific situation, the flatness of its diction, the poverty of its imagery and figurative language, its emphasis on moral platitudes, its lack of poetic freshness. It is either very trite or has little to distinguish it from informational prose except rime or meter. Bryant's "To a Waterfowl" (No. 105) is an example of didactic *poetry*. The familiar couplet

Early to bed and early to rise,
Makes a man healthy, wealthy, and wise

is more aptly characterized as didactic *verse*.

Undoubtedly, so far in this chapter, we have spoken too categorically, have made our distinctions too sharp and definite. All poetic excellence is a matter of degree. There are no absolute lines between sentimentality and true emotion, artificial and genuine eloquence, didactic verse and didactic poetry. Though the difference between extreme examples is easy to recognize, subtler discriminations are harder to make. But a primary distinction between the educated person and the ignorant one is the ability to make informed judgments.

A final caution to students: in making judgments on literature, always be honest. Do not pretend to like what you really do not like. Do not be afraid to admit a liking for what you do like. A genuine enthusiasm for the second-rate is much better than false enthusiasm or no enthusiasm at all. Be neither hasty nor timorous in making your judgments. When you have attentively read a poem and thoroughly considered it, decide what you think. Do not hedge, equivocate, or try to find out others' opinions before forming your own. But, having formed an opinion and expressed it, do not allow it to petrify. Compare your opinion *then* with the opinions of others; allow yourself to change it when convinced of its error: in this way you learn. Honesty, courage, and humility are the necessary moral foundations for all genuine literary judgment.

In the poems for comparison that follow in this chapter, the distinction to be made is not always between bad and good; it may be between varying degrees of poetic merit.

* * *

184. God's Will for You and Me

Just to be tender, just to be true,
Just to be glad the whole day through,
Just to be merciful, just to be mild,
Just to be trustful as a child,
Just to be gentle and kind and sweet,
Just to be helpful with willing feet,

Just to be cheery when things go wrong,
Just to drive sadness away with a song,
Whether the hour is dark or bright,
Just to be loyal to God and right,
Just to believe that God knows best,
Just in his promises ever to rest—
Just to let love be our daily key,
That is God's will for you and me.

185. Pied Beauty

Glory be to God for dappled things—
  For skies of couple-color as a brinded cow;
    For rose-moles all in stipple upon trout that swim;
Fresh-firecoal chestnut-falls; finches' wings;
  Landscape plotted and pieced—fold, fallow and plow;
    And all trades, their gear and tackle and trim.

All things counter, original, spare, strange;
  Whatever is fickle, freckled (who knows how?)
    With swift, slow; sweet, sour; adazzle, dim;
He fathers-forth whose beauty is past change:
                Praise him.

QUESTION

Which is the superior poem? Explain in full.

186. If you were coming in the fall

If you were coming in the fall,
I'd brush the summer by
With half a smile, and half a spurn,
As housewives do a fly.

If I could see you in a year,
I'd wind the months in balls,
And put them each in separate drawers
For fear the numbers fuse.

If only centuries delayed,
I'd count them on my hand,
Subtracting till my fingers dropped
Into Van Dieman's land.

If certain, when this life was out,
That yours and mine should be,
I'd toss it yonder like a rind,
And take eternity.

But now, uncertain of the length
Of this that is between,
It goads me, like the goblin bee,
That will not state its sting.

187. The Want of You

The want of you is like no other thing;
It smites my soul with sudden sickening;
It binds my being with a wreath of rue—
  This want of you.

It flashes on me with the waking sun;
It creeps upon me when the day is done;
It hammers at my heart the long night through—
  This want of you.

It sighs within me with the misting skies;
Oh, all the day within my heart it cries,
Old as your absence, yet each moment new—
  This want of you.

Mad with demand and aching with despair,
It leaps within my heart and you are—where?
God has forgotten, or he never knew—
  This want of you.

QUESTION

Which of these poems is more specific in its language and imagery?

188. A Poison Tree

I was angry with my friend:
I told my wrath, my wrath did end.
I was angry with my foe:
I told it not, my wrath did grow.

And I watered it in fears,
Night and morning with my tears;

And I sunnèd it with smiles,
And with soft deceitful wiles.

And it grew both day and night
Till it bore an apple bright;
And my foe beheld it shine,
And he knew that it was mine,

And into my garden stole
When the night had veiled the pole:° sky
In the morning glad I see
My foe outstretched beneath the tree.

189. The Most Vital Thing in Life

When you feel like saying something
  That you know you will regret,
Or keenly feel an insult
  Not quite easy to forget,
That's the time to curb resentment
  And maintain a mental peace,
For when your mind is tranquil
  All your ill-thoughts simply cease.

It is easy to be angry
  When defrauded or defied,
To be peeved and disappointed
  If your wishes are denied;
But to win a worthwhile battle
  Over selfishness and spite,
You must learn to keep strict silence
  Though you know you're in the right.

So keep your mental balance
  When confronted by a foe,
Be it enemy in ambush
  Or some danger that you know.
If you are poised and tranquil
  When all around is strife,
Be assured that you have mastered
  The most vital thing in life.

QUESTION

Which poem has more poetic merit? Explain.

190. Longing

Come to me in my dreams, and then
By day I shall be well again!
For then the night will more than pay
The hopeless longing of the day.

Come, as thou cam'st a thousand times,
A messenger from radiant climes,
And smile on thy new world, and be
As kind to others as to me!

Or, as thou never cam'st in sooth,
Come now, and let me dream it truth;
And part my hair, and kiss my brow,
And say: *My love! why sufferest thou?*

Come to me in my dreams, and then
By day I shall be well again!
For then the night will more than pay
The hopeless longing of the day.

191. To Marguerite

Yes! in the sea of life enisled,
With echoing straits between us thrown,
Dotting the shoreless watery wild,
We mortal millions live *alone*.
The islands feel the enclasping flow
And then their endless bounds they know.

But when the moon their hollows lights,
And they are swept by balms of spring,
And in their glens, on starry nights,
The nightingales divinely sing;
And lovely notes, from shore to shore,
Across the sounds and channels pour—

Oh! then a longing like despair
Is to their farthest caverns sent;
For surely once, they feel, we were
Parts of a single continent!
Now round us spreads the watery plain—
Oh might our marges meet again!

Who ordered that their longing's fire
Should be, as soon as kindled, cooled?
Who renders vain their deep desire?—
A God, a God their severance ruled!
And bade betwixt their shores to be
The unplumbed, salt, estranging sea.

QUESTION

Both poems are by Matthew Arnold (1822–1888). Which of the two could have been written only by a great poet? Explain.

192. The Long Voyage

Not that the pines were darker there,
nor mid-May dogwood brighter there,
nor swifts more swift in summer air;
    it was my own country,

having its thunderclap of spring,
its long midsummer ripening,
its corn hoar-stiff at harvesting,
    almost like any country,

yet being mine; its face, its speech,
its hills bent low within my reach,
its river birch and upland beech
    were mine, of my own country.

Now the dark waters at the bow
fold back, like earth against the plow;
foam brightens like the dogwood now
    at home, in my own country.

193. Breathes there the man

Breathes there the man, with soul so dead,
Who never to himself hath said,
  This is my own, my native land!
Whose heart hath ne'er within him burned,
As home his footsteps he hath turned,
  From wandering on a foreign strand?

If such there breathe, go, mark him well;
For him no minstrel raptures swell;
High though his titles, proud his name,
Boundless his wealth as wish can claim—
Despite those titles, power, and pelf,
The wretch, concentered all in self,
Living, shall forfeit fair renown,
And, doubly dying, shall go down
To the vile dust from whence he sprung,
Unwept, unhonored, and unsung.

QUESTION

Which poem communicates the more genuine poetic emotion? Which is more rhetorical? Justify your answer.

194. Happiness Makes Up in Height for What It Lacks in Length

Oh, stormy stormy world,
The days you were not swirled
Around with mist and cloud,
Or wrapped as in a shroud,
And the sun's brilliant ball
Was not in part or all
Obscured from mortal view—
Were days so very few
I can but wonder whence
I get the lasting sense
Of so much warmth and light.
If my mistrust is right
It may be altogether
From one day's perfect weather,
When starting clear at dawn,
The day swept clearly on
To finish clear at eve.
I verily believe
My fair impression may
Be all from that one day
No shadow crossed but ours
As through its blazing flowers
We went from house to wood
For change of solitude.

195. A Day

What does it take to make a day?
A lot of love along the way:
It takes a morning and a noon,
A father's voice, a mother's croon;
It takes some task to challenge all
The powers that a man may call
His own: the powers of mind and limb;
A whispered word of love; a hymn
Of hope — a comrade's cheer —
A baby's laughter and a tear;
It takes a dream, a hope, a cry
Of need from some soul passing by;
A sense of brotherhood and love;
A purpose sent from God above;
It takes a sunset in the sky,
The stars of night, the winds that sigh;
It takes a breath of scented air,
A mother's kiss, a baby's prayer.
That is what it takes to make a day:
A lot of love along the way.

QUESTION

Which poem presents a sentimental view of human experience?

196. Little Boy Blue

The little toy dog is covered with dust,
  But sturdy and staunch he stands;
And the little toy soldier is red with rust,
  And his musket moulds in his hands.
Time was when the little toy dog was new,
  And the soldier was passing fair;
And that was the time when our Little Boy Blue
  Kissed them and put them there.

"Now, don't you go till I come," he said,
  "And don't you make any noise!"
So, toddling off to his trundle-bed,
  He dreamt of the pretty toys;
And, as he was dreaming, an angel song
  Awakened our Little Boy Blue —
Oh! the years are many, the years are long,
  But the little toy friends are True!

Ay, faithful to Little Boy Blue they stand
 Each in the same old place—
Awaiting the touch of a little hand,
 The smile of a little face;
And they wonder, as waiting the long years through
 In the dust of that little chair,
What has become of our Little Boy Blue,
 Since he kissed them and put them there.

197. The Toys

My little Son, who looked from thoughtful eyes
And moved and spoke in quiet grown-up wise,
Having my law the seventh time disobeyed,
I struck him, and dismissed
With hard words and unkissed,
His Mother, who was patient, being dead.
Then, fearing lest his grief should hinder sleep,
I visited his bed,
But found him slumbering deep,
With darkened eyelids, and their lashes yet
From his late sobbing wet.
And I, with moan,
Kissing away his tears, left others of my own;
For, on a table drawn beside his head,
He had put, within his reach,
A box of counters and a red-veined stone,
A piece of glass abraded by the beach,
And six or seven shells,
A bottle with bluebells,
And two French copper coins, ranged there with careful art,
To comfort his sad heart.
So when that night I prayed
To God, I wept, and said:
Ah, when at last we lie with trancèd breath,
Not vexing Thee in death,
And thou rememberest of what toys
We made our joys,
How weakly understood
Thy great commanded good,
Then, fatherly not less
Than I whom Thou hast moulded from the clay,
Thou'lt leave Thy wrath, and say,
"I will be sorry for their childishness."

QUESTION

One of these poems has an obvious appeal for the beginning reader. The other is likely to have more meaning for the mature reader. Try to explain in terms of sentimentality and honesty.

198. Loitering with a vacant eye

Loitering with a vacant eye
Along the Grecian gallery,
And brooding on my heavy ill,
I met a statue standing still.
Still in marble stone stood he,
And steadfastly he looked at me.
"Well met," I thought the look would say,
"We both were fashioned far away;
We neither knew, when we were young,
These Londoners we live among."

Still he stood and eyed me hard,
An earnest and a grave regard:
"What, lad, drooping with your lot?
I too would be where I am not.
I too survey that endless line
Of men whose thoughts are not as mine.
Years, ere you stood up from rest,
On my neck the collar prest;
Years, when you lay down your ill,
I shall stand and bear it still.
Courage, lad, 'tis not for long:
Stand, quit you like stone, be strong."
So I thought his look would say;
And light on me my trouble lay,
And I stept out in flesh and bone
Manful like the man of stone.

199. Be Strong

Be strong!
We are not here to play,—to dream, to drift.
We have hard work to do and loads to lift.
Shun not the struggle,—face it: 'tis God's gift.

Be strong!
Say not the days are evil. Who's to blame?
And fold the hands and acquiesce, — O shame!
Stand up, speak out, and bravely, in God's name.

Be strong!
It matters not how deep intrenched the wrong,
How hard the battle goes, the day how long;
Faint not, — fight on! Tomorrow comes the song.

QUESTIONS

1. The "Grecian gallery" (2), in the first poem of this pair, is a room in the British Museum in London. Who is the speaker? Who is the speaker in the second poem?
2. Which is the superior poem? Discuss.

CHAPTER SIXTEEN

Good Poetry and Great

If a poem has successfully met the test in the question, *How fully has it accomplished its purpose?* we are ready to subject it to our second evaluative question, *How important is its purpose?*

Great poetry must, of course, be good poetry. Noble intent alone cannot redeem a work that does not measure high on the scale of accomplishment; otherwise the sentimental and purely didactic verse of much of the last chapter would stand with the world's masterpieces. But once a work has been judged as successful on the scale of execution, its final standing will depend on its significance of purpose.

Suppose, for instance, we consider three poems in our text: the limerick "A tutor who tooted the flute" by Carolyn Wells (No. 174); the poem "It sifts from leaden sieves" by Emily Dickinson (No. 45), and Shakespeare's sonnet "That time of year" (No. 173). Each of these would probably be judged by competent critics as highly successful in what it sets out to do. Wells has attempted a tongue-twister in strict limerick form, and she succeeds magnificently. Her poem is filled with a tooting of *oo*'s, a clatter of *t*'s, and a swarming of *-or*'s and *-er*'s. Every foot of the poem contains at least one of these sounds; most contain several. Moreover, this astounding feat is accomplished in verse that contains no unnecessary or inappropriate words, no infelicities of grammar or syntax. We are delighted by its sheer technical virtuosity. But what is this limerick *about*? Nothing of the slightest interest. It makes no attempt to communicate significant human experience. Its true subject is the ingenuity of its wordplay. Like an ornately decorated Easter egg, its value lies in its shell rather than in its content. Indeed, we should hardly call it poetry at all; it is highly accomplished, brilliantly clever *verse*. Emily Dickinson's poem, in contrast, *is* poetry, and very good poetry. It appeals richly to our senses and to our imaginations, and it succeeds excellently in its purpose: to convey the appearance and the quality of falling and newly fallen snow as well as a sense of the magic and the mystery of nature. Yet, when we compare this excellent poem with Shakespeare's, we again see important differences. Although the first poem engages the senses and the imagination and may affect us with wonder and cause us to meditate on nature, it does not deeply engage the emotions or the intellect. It does not come as close to the core of human living and suffering as does Shakespeare's sonnet. In fact, it is concerned primarily with that staple of small talk, the weather. On the other hand, Shakespeare's sonnet evokes the universal human concerns of growing old, approaching death, and love. Of these three selections, then, Shakespeare's is the greatest. It "says" more than Emily Dickinson's poem or the limerick; it communicates a richer experience; it successfully accomplishes a more significant purpose. The discriminating reader will get from it a deeper enjoyment, because it is nourishing as well as delightful.

Great poetry engages the whole person—senses, imagination, emotion, intellect; it does not touch us merely on one or two sides of our nature. Great poetry seeks not merely to entertain us but to bring us—along with pure pleasure—fresh insights, or renewed insights, and important insights, into the nature of human experience. Great poetry, we might say, gives us a broader and deeper understanding of life, of our fellows, and of ourselves, always with the qualification, of course, that the kind of insight literature gives is not necessarily the kind that can be summed up in a simple "lesson" or "moral." It is *knowledge—felt* knowledge, *new* knowledge—of the complexities of human nature and of the tragedies and sufferings, the excitements and joys, that characterize human experience.

Is Shakespeare's sonnet a *great* poem? It is, at least, a great *sonnet*. Greatness, like goodness, is relative. If we compare any of Shakespeare's sonnets with his greatest plays—*Macbeth, Othello, Hamlet, King Lear, The Tempest*—another big difference appears. What is undertaken and accomplished in these plays is enormously greater, more difficult, and more complex than could ever be undertaken or accomplished in a single sonnet. Greatness in literature, in fact, cannot be entirely dissociated from size. In literature, as in basketball and football, a good big player is better than a good little player. The greatness of a poem is in proportion to the range and depth and intensity of experience that it brings to us: its amount of life. Shakespeare's plays offer us a multiplicity of life and a depth of living that could never be compressed into the fourteen lines of a sonnet. They organize a greater complexity of life and experience into unity.

Yet, after all, we have provided no easy yardsticks or rule-of-thumb measures for literary judgment. There are no mechanical tests. The final measuring rod can be only the responsiveness, the maturity, the taste and discernment of the cultivated reader. Such taste and discernment are partly a native endowment, partly the product of experience, partly the achievement of conscious study, training, and intellectual effort. They cannot be achieved suddenly or quickly; they can never be achieved in perfection. The pull is a long and a hard one. But success, even relative success, brings enormous rewards in enrichment and command of life.

*   *   *

200. The Canonization

For God's sake, hold your tongue, and let me love!
    Or chide my palsy or my gout,
My five gray hairs or ruined fortune flout;
With wealth your state, your mind with arts improve,
   Take you a course,° get you a place,   career
    Observe his honor° or his grace,°   judge; bishop
Or the king's real or his stamped face°   on a coin
   Contemplate; what you will, approve,°   try out
      So you will let me love.

Alas, alas, who's injured by my love?
  What merchant ships have my sighs drowned?
Who says my tears have overflowed his ground?
When did my colds a forward° spring remove?   early
    When did the heats which my veins fill
    Add one more to the plaguy bill?
Soldiers find wars, and lawyers find out still
    Litigious men which quarrels move,
      Though she and I do love.

Call us what you will, we are made such by love.
    Call her one, me another fly;°   moth
We are tapers too, and at our own cost die;
And we in us find the eagle and the dove;
    The phoenix riddle hath more wit°   meaning
    By us; we two, being one, are it.
So to one neutral thing both sexes fit.
   We die and rise the same, and prove
      Mysterious by this love.

We can die by it, if not live by love,
    And if unfit for tombs and hearse
Our legend be, it will be fit for verse;
And if no piece of chronicle° we prove, history
    We'll build in sonnets pretty rooms:
    As well a well-wrought urn becomes
The greatest ashes as half-acre tombs,
    And by these hymns all shall approve° confirm
        Us canonized for love,

And thus invoke us: "You whom reverend love
    Made one another's hermitage,
You to whom love was peace, that now is rage,
Who did the whole world's soul contract, and drove
    Into the glasses of your eyes
    (So made such mirrors and such spies
That they did all to you epitomize)
    Countries, towns, courts: beg from above
        A pattern of your love!"

John Donne (1572–1631)

QUESTIONS

1. Vocabulary: *canonization* (title), *tapers* (21), *phoenix* (23), *invoke* (37), *epitomize* (43). "Real" (7), pronounced as two syllables, puns on *royal*. The "plaguy bill" (15) is a list of plague victims. The word "die" (21, 26, 28) in seventeenth-century slang meant to experience the sexual climax. To understand lines 21 and 28, one also needs to be familiar with the Renaissance superstition that every act of sexual intercourse shortened one's life by one day. The "eagle" and the "dove" (22) are symbols for strength and mildness. "Pattern" (45) is a model that one can copy.
2. Who is the speaker and what is his condition? How old is he? To whom is he speaking? What has his auditor been saying to him before the opening of the poem? What sort of values can we ascribe to the auditor by inference from the first stanza? What value does the speaker oppose to these? How does the stanzaic pattern of the poem emphasize this value?
3. The sighs and tears, the fevers and chills, in the second stanza, were commonplace in the love poetry of Donne's time. How does Donne make them fresh? What is the speaker's argument in this stanza? How does it begin to turn from pure defense to offense in the last three lines of the stanza?
4. How are the things to which the lovers are compared in the third stanza *arranged*? Does their arrangement reflect in any way the arrangement of the whole poem? Elucidate line 21. Interpret or paraphrase lines 23–27.
5. Explain the first line of the fourth stanza. What status does the speaker claim for himself and his beloved in the last line of this stanza?

6. In what sense is the last stanza an invocation? Who speaks in it? To whom? What powers are ascribed to the lovers in it?
7. What do the following words from the poem have in common: "Mysterious" (27), "hymns" (35), "canonized" (36), "reverend" (37), "hermitage" (38)? What judgment about love does the speaker make by the use of these words?

201. Home Burial

He saw her from the bottom of the stairs
Before she saw him. She was starting down,
Looking back over her shoulder at some fear.
She took a doubtful step and then undid it
To raise herself and look again. He spoke
Advancing toward her: "What is it you see
From up there always?—for I want to know."
She turned and sank upon her skirts at that,
And her face changed from terrified to dull.
He said to gain time: "What is it you see?"
Mounting until she cowered under him.
"I will find out now—you must tell me, dear."
She, in her place, refused him any help,
With the least stiffening of her neck and silence.
She let him look, sure that he wouldn't see,
Blind creature; and awhile he didn't see.
But at last he murmured, "Oh," and again, "Oh."

"What is it—what?" she said.

"Just that I see."

"You don't," she challenged. "Tell me what it is."

"The wonder is I didn't see at once.
I never noticed it from here before.
I must be wonted to it—that's the reason.
The little graveyard where my people are!
So small the window frames the whole of it.
Not so much larger than a bedroom, is it?
There are three stones of slate and one of marble,
Broad-shouldered little slabs there in the sunlight
On the sidehill. We haven't to mind *those*.
But I understand: it is not the stones,
But the child's mound—"

"Don't, don't, don't,
don't," she cried.

She withdrew, shrinking from beneath his arm
That rested on the banister, and slid downstairs;
And turned on him with such a daunting look,
He said twice over before he knew himself:
"Can't a man speak of his own child he's lost?"

"Not you!—Oh, where's my hat? Oh, I don't need it!
I must get out of here. I must get air.—
I don't know rightly whether any man can."

"Amy! Don't go to someone else this time.
Listen to me. I won't come down the stairs."
He sat and fixed his chin between his fists.
"There's something I should like to ask you, dear."

"You don't know how to ask it."

"Help me, then."

Her fingers moved the latch for all reply.

"My words are nearly always an offense.
I don't know how to speak of anything
So as to please you. But I might be taught,
I should suppose. I can't say I see how.
A man must partly give up being a man
With womenfolk. We could have some arrangement
By which I'd bind myself to keep hands off
Anything special you're a-mind to name.
Though I don't like such things 'twixt those that love.
Two that don't love can't live together without them.
But two that do can't live together with them."
She moved the latch a little. "Don't—don't go.
Don't carry it to someone else this time.
Tell me about it if it's something human.
Let me into your grief. I'm not so much
Unlike other folks as your standing there
Apart would make me out. Give me my chance.
I do think, though, you overdo it a little.
What was it brought you up to think it the thing
To take your mother-loss of a first child
So inconsolably—in the face of love.
You'd think his memory might be satisfied—"

"There you go sneering now!"

"I'm not, I'm not!

You make me angry. I'll come down to you.
God, what a woman! And it's come to this,
A man can't speak of his own child that's dead."

"You can't because you don't know how to speak.
If you had any feelings, you that dug
With your own hand—how could you?—his little grave;
I saw you from that very window there,
Making the gravel leap and leap in air,
Leap up, like that, like that, and land so lightly
And roll back down the mound beside the hole.
I thought, Who is that man? I didn't know you.
And I crept down the stairs and up the stairs
To look again, and still your spade kept lifting.
Then you came in. I heard your rumbling voice
Out in the kitchen, and I don't know why,
But I went near to see with my own eyes.
You could sit there with the stains on your shoes
Of the fresh earth from your own baby's grave
And talk about your everyday concerns.
You had stood the spade up against the wall
Outside there in the entry, for I saw it."

"I shall laugh the worst laugh I ever laughed.
I'm cursed. God, if I don't believe I'm cursed."

"I can repeat the very words you were saying:
'Three foggy mornings and one rainy day
Will rot the best birch fence a man can build.'
Think of it, talk like that at such a time!
What had how long it takes a birch to rot
To do with what was in the darkened parlor?
You *couldn't* care! The nearest friends can go
With anyone to death, comes so far short
They might as well not try to go at all.
No, from the time when one is sick to death,
One is alone, and he dies more alone.
Friends make pretense of following to the grave,
But before one is in it, their minds are turned
And making the best of their way back to life
And living people, and things they understand.
But the world's evil. I won't have grief so
If I can change it. Oh, I won't, I won't!"

"There, you have said it all and you feel better.
You won't go now. You're crying. Close the door.
The heart's gone out of it: why keep it up?
Amy! There's someone coming down the road!"

"*You*—oh, you think the talk is all. I must go—
Somewhere out of this house. How can I make you—"

"If—you—do!" She was opening the door wider.
"Where do you mean to go? First tell me that.
I'll follow and bring you back by force. I *will!*—"

Robert Frost (1874–1963)

QUESTIONS

1. Vocabulary: *wonted* (22).
2. The poem centers on a conflict between husband and wife. What causes the conflict? Why does Amy resent her husband? What is *his* dissatisfaction with Amy?
3. Characterize the husband and wife respectively. What is the chief difference between them? Does the poem take sides? Is either presented more sympathetically than the other?
4. The poem does not say how long the couple have been married or how long the child has been buried. Does it contain suggestions from which we may make rough inferences?
5. The husband and wife both generalize on the other's faults during the course of the poem, attributing them to all men or to all women or to people in general. Point out these generalizations. Are they valid?
6. Finish the unfinished sentences in lines 30, 66, 113, 114.
7. Comment on the function of lines 25, 39, 92–93.
8. Following are three paraphrased and abbreviated versions of statements made in published discussions of the poem. Which would you support? Why?
   a. The young wife is gradually persuaded by her husband's kind yet firm reasonableness to express her feelings in words and to recognize that human nature is limited and cannot sacrifice everything to sorrow. Though she still suffers from excess grief, the crisis is past, and she will eventually be brought back to life.
   b. At the end, the whole poem is epitomized by the door that is neither open nor shut. The wife cannot really leave; the husband cannot really make her stay. Neither husband nor wife is capable of decisive action, of either self-liberation or liberation of the other.
   c. Her husband's attempt to talk, since it is the wrong kind of talk, only leads to her departure at the poem's end.

202. The Love Song of J. Alfred Prufrock

S'io credesse che mia risposta fosse
A persona che mai tornasse al mondo,
Questa fiamma staria senza piu scosse.
Ma perciocche giammai di questo fondo
Non torno vivo alcun, s'i'odo il vero,
Senza tema d'infamia ti rispondo.

Let us go then, you and I,
When the evening is spread out against the sky
Like a patient etherized upon a table;
Let us go, through certain half-deserted streets,
The muttering retreats
Of restless nights in one-night cheap hotels
And sawdust restaurants with oyster-shells:
Streets that follow like a tedious argument
Of insidious intent
To lead you to an overwhelming question . . .
Oh, do not ask, "What is it?"
Let us go and make our visit.

In the room the women come and go
Talking of Michelangelo.

The yellow fog that rubs its back upon the window-panes,
The yellow smoke that rubs its muzzle on the window-panes
Licked its tongue into the corners of the evening,
Lingered upon the pools that stand in drains,
Let fall upon its back the soot that falls from chimneys,
Slipped by the terrace, made a sudden leap,
And seeing that it was a soft October night,
Curled once about the house, and fell asleep.

And indeed there will be time
For the yellow smoke that slides along the street,
Rubbing its back upon the window-panes;
There will be time, there will be time
To prepare a face to meet the faces that you meet;
There will be time to murder and create,
And time for all the works and days of hands
That lift and drop a question on your plate;
Time for you and time for me,

And time yet for a hundred indecisions,
And for a hundred visions and revisions,
Before the taking of a toast and tea.

In the room the women come and go
Talking of Michelangelo.

And indeed there will be time
To wonder, "Do I dare?" and "Do I dare?"
Time to turn back and descend the stair,
With a bald spot in the middle of my hair—
(They will say: "How his hair is growing thin!")
My morning coat, my collar mounting firmly to the chin,
My necktie rich and modest, but asserted by a simple pin—
(They will say: "But how his arms and legs are thin!")
Do I dare
Disturb the universe?
In a minute there is time
For decisions and revisions which a minute will reverse.

For I have known them all already, known them all:—
Have known the evenings, mornings, afternoons,
I have measured out my life with coffee spoons;
I know the voices dying with a dying fall
Beneath the music from a farther room.
So how should I presume?

And I have known the eyes already, known them all—
The eyes that fix you in a formulated phrase,
And when I am formulated, sprawling on a pin,
When I am pinned and wriggling on the wall,
Then how should I begin
To spit out all the butt-ends of my days and ways?
And how should I presume?

And I have known the arms already, known them all—
Arms that are braceleted and white and bare
(But in the lamplight, downed with light brown hair!)
Is it perfume from a dress
That makes me so digress?
Arms that lie along a table, or wrap about a shawl.
And should I then presume?
And how should I begin?

* * *

Shall I say, I have gone at dusk through narrow streets
And watched the smoke that rises from the pipes
Of lonely men in shirt-sleeves, leaning out of windows? . . .

I should have been a pair of ragged claws
Scuttling across the floors of silent seas.

* * *

And the afternoon, the evening, sleeps so peacefully!
Smoothed by long fingers,
Asleep . . . tired . . . or it malingers,
Stretched on the floor, here beside you and me.
Should I, after tea and cakes and ices,
Have the strength to force the moment to its crisis?
But though I have wept and fasted, wept and prayed,
Though I have seen my head (grown slightly bald) brought in
upon a platter,
I am no prophet—and here's no great matter;
I have seen the moment of my greatness flicker,
And I have seen the eternal Footman hold my coat, and snicker,
And in short, I was afraid.

And would it have been worth it, after all,
After the cups, the marmalade, the tea,
Among the porcelain, among some talk of you and me,
Would it have been worth while,
To have bitten off the matter with a smile,
To have squeezed the universe into a ball
To roll it toward some overwhelming question,
To say: "I am Lazarus, come from the dead,
Come back to tell you all, I shall tell you all"—
If one, settling a pillow by her head,
Should say: "That is not what I meant at all.
That is not it, at all."

And would it have been worth it, after all,
Would it have been worth while,
After the sunsets and the dooryards and the sprinkled streets,
After the novels, after the teacups, after the skirts that trail
along the floor—
And this, and so much more?—
It is impossible to say just what I mean!
But as if a magic lantern threw the nerves in patterns on a
screen:

Would it have been worth while
If one, settling a pillow or throwing off a shawl,
And turning toward the window, should say:
"That is not it at all,
That is not what I meant, at all."

* * *

No! I am not Prince Hamlet, nor was meant to be;
Am an attendant lord, one that will do
To swell a progress, start a scene or two,
Advise the prince; no doubt, an easy tool,
Deferential, glad to be of use,
Politic, cautious, and meticulous:
Full of high sentence, but a bit obtuse;
At times, indeed, almost ridiculous—
Almost, at times, the Fool.

I grow old . . . I grow old . . .
I shall wear the bottoms of my trousers rolled.° cuffed

Shall I part my hair behind? Do I dare to eat a peach?
I shall wear white flannel trousers, and walk upon the beach.
I have heard the mermaids singing, each to each.

I do not think that they will sing to me.

I have seen them riding seaward on the waves
Combing the white hair of the waves blown back
When the wind blows the water white and black.

We have lingered in the chambers of the sea
By sea-girls wreathed with seaweed red and brown
Till human voices wake us, and we drown.

T. S. Eliot (1888–1965)

QUESTIONS

1. Vocabulary: *insidious* (9), *Michelangelo* (14), *muzzle* (16), *malingers* (77), *progress* (113), *deferential* (115), *politic* (116), *meticulous* (116), *sentence* (117).
2. This poem may be for some readers the most difficult in the book, because it uses a "stream of consciousness" technique (that is, it presents the apparently random thoughts going through a person's head within a certain time interval), in which the transitional links are psychological rather than logical, and also because it uses allusions you may be unfamiliar with. Even if you do not at first understand the poem in detail, you should be able to get from it a quite

accurate picture of Prufrock's character and personality. What kind of person is he? (Answer this as fully as possible.) From what class of society does he come? What one line especially well sums up the nature of his past life? A brief initial orientation may be helpful: Prufrock is apparently on his way, at the beginning of the poem, to a late afternoon tea, at which he wishes (or does he?) to make a declaration of love to some lady who will be present. The "you and I" of the first line are divided parts of Prufrock's own nature, for he is experiencing internal conflict. Does he or does he not make the declaration? Where does the climax of the poem come? If the portion leading up to the climax is devoted to Prufrock's effort to prepare himself psychologically to make the declaration (or to postpone such effort), what is the portion after the climax devoted to?

3. The poem contains a number of striking or unusual figures of speech. Most of them in some way reflect Prufrock's own nature or his desires or fears. From this point of view discuss lines 2–3; 15–22 and 75–78; 57–58; 73–74; and 124–31. What figure of speech is lines 73–74? In what respect is the title ironic?
4. The poem makes extensive use of literary allusion. The Italian epigraph is a passage from Dante's *Inferno* in which a man in Hell tells a visitor that he would never tell his story if there were a chance that it would get back to living ears. In line 29 the phrase "works and days" is the title of a long poem—a description of agricultural life and a call to toil—by the early Greek poet Hesiod. Line 52 echoes the opening speech of Shakespeare's *Twelfth Night.* The prophet of lines 81–83 is John the Baptist, whose head was delivered to Salome by Herod as a reward for her dancing (Matthew 14:1–11, and Oscar Wilde's play *Salome*). Line 92 echoes the closing six lines of Marvell's "To His Coy Mistress" (No. 53). Lazarus (94–95) may be either the beggar Lazarus (of Luke 16) who was not permitted to return from the dead to warn a rich man's brothers about Hell, the Lazarus (of John 11) whom Christ raised from death, or both. Lines 111–19 allude to a number of characters from Shakespeare's *Hamlet*: Hamlet himself, the chamberlain Polonius, and various minor characters including probably Rosencrantz, Guildenstern, and Osric. "Full of high sentence" (117) echoes Chaucer's description of the Clerk of Oxford in the Prologue to *The Canterbury Tales*. Relate as many of these allusions as you can to the character of Prufrock. How is Prufrock particularly like Hamlet, and how is he unlike him? Contrast Prufrock with the speaker in "To His Coy Mistress."

203. Sunday Morning

1

Complacencies of the peignoir, and late
Coffee and oranges in a sunny chair,
And the green freedom of a cockatoo
Upon a rug mingle to dissipate
The holy hush of ancient sacrifice.
She dreams a little, and she feels the dark

Encroachment of that old catastrophe,
As a calm darkens among water-lights.
The pungent oranges and bright, green wings
Seem things in some procession of the dead,
Winding across wide water, without sound.
The day is like wide water, without sound,
Stilled for the passing of her dreaming feet
Over the seas, to silent Palestine,
Dominion of the blood and sepulchre.

2

Why should she give her bounty to the dead?
What is divinity if it can come
Only in silent shadows and in dreams?
Shall she not find in comforts of the sun,
In pungent fruit and bright, green wings, or else
In any balm or beauty of the earth,
Things to be cherished like the thought of heaven?
Divinity must live within herself:
Passions of rain, or moods in falling snow;
Grievings in loneliness, or unsubdued
Elations when the forest blooms; gusty
Emotions on wet roads on autumn nights;
All pleasures and all pains, remembering
The bough of summer and the winter branch.
These are the measures destined for her soul.

3

Jove in the clouds had his inhuman birth.
No mother suckled him, no sweet land gave
Large-mannered motions to his mythy mind.
He moved among us, as a muttering king,
Magnificent, would move among his hinds,
Until our blood, commingling, virginal,
With heaven, brought such requital to desire
The very hinds discerned it, in a star.
Shall our blood fail? Or shall it come to be
The blood of paradise? And shall the earth
Seem all of paradise that we shall know?
The sky will be much friendlier then than now,
A part of labor and a part of pain,
And next in glory to enduring love,
Not this dividing and indifferent blue.

4

She says, "I am content when wakened birds,
Before they fly, test the reality
Of misty fields, by their sweet questionings;
But when the birds are gone, and their warm fields
Return no more, where, then, is paradise?"
There is not any haunt of prophecy,
Nor any old chimera of the grave,
Neither the golden underground, nor isle
Melodious, where spirits gat them home,
Nor visionary south, nor cloudy palm
Remote on heaven's hill, that has endured
As April's green endures; or will endure
Like her remembrance of awakened birds,
Or her desire for June and evening, tipped
By the consummation of the swallow's wings.

5

She says, "But in contentment I still feel
The need of some imperishable bliss."
Death is the mother of beauty; hence from her,
Alone, shall come fulfillment to our dreams
And our desires. Although she strews the leaves
Of sure obliteration on our paths,
The path sick sorrow took, the many paths
Where triumph rang its brassy phrase, or love
Whispered a little out of tenderness,
She makes the willow shiver in the sun
For maidens who were wont to sit and gaze
Upon the grass, relinquished to their feet.
She causes boys to pile new plums and pears
On disregarded plate. The maidens taste
And stray impassioned in the littering leaves.

6

Is there no change of death in paradise?
Does ripe fruit never fall? Or do the boughs
Hang always heavy in that perfect sky,
Unchanging, yet so like our perishing earth,
With rivers like our own that seek for seas
They never find, the same receding shores
That never touch with inarticulate pang?

Why set the pear upon those river-banks
Or spice the shores with odors of the plum?
Alas, that they should wear our colors there,
The silken weavings of our afternoons,
And pick the strings of our insipid lutes!
Death is the mother of beauty, mystical,
Within whose burning bosom we devise
Our earthly mothers waiting, sleeplessly.

7

Supple and turbulent, a ring of men
Shall chant in orgy on a summer morn
Their boisterous devotion to the sun,
Not as a god, but as a god might be,
Naked among them, like a savage source.
Their chant shall be a chant of paradise,
Out of their blood, returning to the sky;
And in their chant shall enter, voice by voice,
The windy lake wherein their lord delights,
The trees, like serafin, and echoing hills,
That choir among themselves long afterward.
They shall know well the heavenly fellowship
Of men that perish and of summer morn.
And whence they came and whither they shall go
The dew upon their feet shall manifest.

8

She hears, upon that water without sound,
A voice that cries, "The tomb in Palestine
Is not the porch of spirits lingering.
It is the grave of Jesus, where he lay."
We live in an old chaos of the sun,
Or old dependency of day and night,
Or island solitude, unsponsored, free,
Of that wide water, inescapable.
Deer walk upon our mountains, and the quail
Whistle about us their spontaneous cries;
Sweet berries ripen in the wilderness;
And, in the isolation of the sky,
At evening, casual flocks of pigeons make
Ambiguous undulations as they sink,
Downward to darkness, on extended wings.

Wallace Stevens (1879–1955)

QUESTIONS

1. Vocabulary: *peignoir* (1), *hinds* (35), *requital* (37), *chimera* (52), *consummation* (60), *obliteration* (66), *serafin* (seraphim) (100). "Gat" (54) is an obsolete past tense of "get."
2. The poem presents a woman meditating on questions of death, mutability, and permanence, beginning with a stanza that sets the stage and shows her being drawn to these questions beyond her conscious will. The meditation proper is structured as a series of questions and answers stated in direct or indirect quotations, with the answer to a preceding question suggesting a further question, and so forth. In reading through the poem, paraphrase the sequence of implied or stated questions, and the answers to them.
3. The opening scene (stanza 1), in a collection of images and details, indicates the means the woman has chosen to avoid thinking of the typical "Sunday morning" topic, the Christian religion. Define the means she employs. Trace the further references to fruits and birds throughout the poem, and explain the ordering principle that ties them together (for example, what development of idea or attitude is implied in the sequence oranges/plums and pears/wild berries?).
4. What symbolic meanings are implied by the images of (a) water, (b) the sun, and (c) birds and other animals?
5. Why does the woman give up her desire for unchanging permanence? With what does she replace it? What is her final attitude toward a world that includes change and death? What is meant by "Death is the mother of beauty" (63, 88)?
6. The poet wrote, "This is not essentially a woman's meditation on religion and the meaning of life. It is anybody's meditation" (*Letters of Wallace Stevens*, ed. Holly Stevens [New York: Knopf, 1966] 250). Can you justify that claim?
7. "The Canonization," "Home Burial," "The Love Song of J. Alfred Prufrock," and "Sunday Morning" are all dramatic poems. "The Canonization" is a dramatic monologue (one person is speaking to another, whose replies we do not hear). Frost's poem (though it has a slight narrative element) is largely a dialogue between two speakers who speak in their own voices. Eliot's poem is a highly allusive soliloquy, or interior monologue. "Sunday Morning" combines descriptive scene-setting with an interior debate of question and answer. In what ways do the dramatic structures of these poems facilitate what they have to say?

PART 2

Poems for Further Reading

204. Musée des Beaux Arts

About suffering they were never wrong,
The Old Masters: how well they understood
Its human position; how it takes place
While someone else is eating or opening a window or just
   walking dully along;
How, when the aged are reverently, passionately waiting
For the miraculous birth, there always must be
Children who did not specially want it to happen, skating
On a pond at the edge of the wood:
They never forgot
That even the dreadful martyrdom must run its course
Anyhow in a corner, some untidy spot
Where the dogs go on with their doggy life and the
   torturer's horse
Scratches its innocent behind on a tree.

In Brueghel's *Icarus*, for instance: how everything turns away
Quite leisurely from the disaster; the plowman may
Have heard the splash, the forsaken cry,
But for him it was not an important failure; the sun shone
As it had to on the white legs disappearing into the green
Water; and the expensive delicate ship that must have seen
Something amazing, a boy falling out of the sky,
Had somewhere to get to and sailed calmly on.

W. H. Auden (1907–1973)

205. On Reading Poems to a Senior Class at South High

Before
I opened my mouth
I noticed them sitting there
as orderly as frozen fish
in a package.

Slowly water began to fill the room
though I did not notice it
till it reached
my ears

and then I heard the sounds
of fish in an aquarium
and I knew that though I had
tried to drown them

with my words
that they had only opened up
like gills for them
and let me in.

Together we swam around the room
like thirty tails whacking words
till the bell rang
puncturing
a hole in the door

where we all leaked out

They went to another class
I suppose and I home

where Queen Elizabeth
my cat met me
and licked my fins
till they were hands again.

D. C. Berry (b. 1942)

206. One Art

The art of losing isn't hard to master;
so many things seem filled with the intent
to be lost that their loss is no disaster.

Lose something every day. Accept the fluster
of lost door keys, the hour badly spent.
The art of losing isn't hard to master.

Then practice losing farther, losing faster:
places, and names, and where it was you meant
to travel. None of these will bring disaster.

I lost my mother's watch. And look! my last, or
next-to-last, of three loved houses went.
The art of losing isn't hard to master.

I lost two cities, lovely ones. And, vaster,
some realms I owned, two rivers, a continent.
I miss them, but it wasn't a disaster.

—Even losing you (the joking voice, a gesture
I love) I shan't have lied. It's evident
the art of losing's not too hard to master
though it may look like (*Write* it!) like disaster.

Elizabeth Bishop (1911–1979)

207. Eternity

He who binds to himself a joy
Does the wingèd life destroy;
But he who kisses the joy as it flies
Lives in eternity's sunrise.

William Blake (1757–1827)

208. The Lamb

Little Lamb, who made thee?
Dost thou know who made thee?
Gave thee life and bid thee feed
By the stream and o'er the mead;
Gave thee clothing of delight,
Softest clothing wooly bright;
Gave thee such a tender voice,
Making all the vales rejoice!
Little Lamb, who made thee?
Dost thou know who made thee?

Little Lamb, I'll tell thee,
Little Lamb, I'll tell thee!
He is callèd by thy name,
For he calls himself a Lamb;
He is meek and he is mild,
He became a little child;
I a child and thou a lamb,
We are callèd by his name.
Little Lamb, God bless thee.
Little Lamb, God bless thee.

William Blake (1757–1827)

209. The Tiger

Tiger! Tiger! burning bright
In the forests of the night,
What immortal hand or eye
Could frame thy fearful symmetry?

In what distant deeps or skies
Burnt the fire of thine eyes?
On what wings dare he aspire?
What the hand dare seize the fire?

And what shoulder, and what art,
Could twist the sinews of thy heart?
And when thy heart began to beat,
What dread hand forged thy dread feet?

What the hammer? what the chain?
In what furnace was thy brain?
What the anvil? what dread grasp
Dare its deadly terrors clasp?

When the stars threw down their spears,
And watered heaven with their tears,
Did he smile his work to see?
Did he who made the Lamb make thee?

Tiger! Tiger! burning bright
In the forests of the night,
What immortal hand or eye
Dare frame thy fearful symmetry?

William Blake (1757–1827)

210. Stefansson Island

105° W – 74° N

Stefansson: a walrus of a man
whose walk is paced to sled dogs
on the offshore ice. Time drags
behind him now, but tundra sun
still lights the winter island of his mind.

Alaska blizzards drift his hair;
there is seal meat in him, the warmth
of blubber, a white bear's strength.
His eyelids tighten in the glare
of memory, the ranges of the Yukon map his skin.

As on the Beaufort Sea, where man
walks small across the frozen tides,
he in his glacial knowledge plods
to tame not barren lands to man,
but man to what is barren. Across the moving ice

he walked three months, Martin Point
to a far island, six hundred miles

STEFANSSON ISLAND Vilhjalmur Stefansson (1879–1962) was a Canadian-born Arctic explorer.

by stars: three men, six dogs, seals
to kill between the floes; and plant-
life on whatever shore, to prove how prayer may starve

a man where science can find food.
He is a hunter still, exiled
from the arctic night, yet reconciled
to shape a snowblind course. Outward
on mush ice he moves, with no fear of magnetic error.

No South can thaw this polar man.
But close to compass North, an island
maps his name, where dovekies ride downwind
to breed. And there the solstice sun
fires lichen into arctic bloom, as if in praise of him.

Philip Booth (b. 1925)

211. If thou must love me

If thou must love me, let it be for naught
Except for love's sake only. Do not say
"I love her for her smile—her look—her way
Of speaking gently—for a trick of thought
That falls in well with mine, and certes brought
A sense of pleasant ease on such a day"—
For these things in themselves, Beloved, may
Be changed, or change for thee—and love, so wrought,
May be unwrought so. Neither love me for
Thine own dear pity's wiping my cheeks dry—
A creature might forget to weep, who bore
Thy comfort long, and lose thy love thereby!
But love me for love's sake, that evermore
Thou mayst love on, through love's eternity.

Elizabeth Barrett Browning (1806–1861)

212. Good Times

My Daddy has paid the rent
and the insurance man is gone
and the lights is back on
and my uncle Brud has hit
for one dollar straight
and they is good times
good times
good times

My Mama has made bread
and Grampaw has come
and everybody is drunk
and dancing in the kitchen
and singing in the kitchen
oh these is good times
good times
good times

oh children think about the
good times

Lucille Clifton (b. 1936)

213. Song of the Rabbits outside the Tavern

We who play under the pines,
We who dance in the snow
That shines blue in the light of the moon
Sometimes halt as we go,
Stand with our ears erect,
Our noses testing the air,
To gaze at the golden world
Behind the windows there.

Suns they have in a cave
And stars each on a tall white stem,
And the thought of fox or night owl
Seems never to trouble them,
They laugh and eat and are warm,
Their food seems ready at hand,
While hungry out in the cold
We little rabbits stand.

But they never dance as we dance,
They have not the speed nor the grace.
We scorn both the cat and the dog
Who lie by their fireplace.
We scorn them licking their paws,
Their eyes on an upraised spoon,
We who dance hungry and wild
Under a winter's moon.

Elizabeth Coatsworth (1893–1986)

214. Kubla Khan

In Xanadu did Kubla Khan
A stately pleasure-dome decree:
Where Alph, the sacred river, ran
Through caverns measureless to man
   Down to a sunless sea.
So twice five miles of fertile ground
With walls and towers were girdled round:
And here were gardens bright with sinuous rills,
Where blossomed many an incense-bearing tree;
And here were forests ancient as the hills,
Enfolding sunny spots of greenery.

But oh! that deep romantic chasm which slanted
Down the green hill athwart a cedarn cover!
A savage place! as holy and enchanted
As e'er beneath a waning moon was haunted
By woman wailing for her demon-lover!
And from this chasm, with ceaseless turmoil seething,
As if this earth in fast thick pants were breathing,
A mighty fountain momently was forced:
Amid whose swift half-intermitted burst
Huge fragments vaulted like rebounding hail,
Or chaffy grain beneath the thresher's flail:
And 'mid these dancing rocks at once and ever
It flung up momently the sacred river.
Five miles meandering with a mazy motion
Through wood and dale the sacred river ran,
Then reached the caverns measureless to man,
And sank in tumult to a lifeless ocean:
And 'mid this tumult Kubla heard from far
Ancestral voices prophesying war!

   The shadow of the dome of pleasure
   Floated midway on the waves;
   Where was heard the mingled measure
   From the fountain and the caves.
It was a miracle of rare device,
A sunny pleasure-dome with caves of ice!

   A damsel with a dulcimer
   In a vision once I saw:
   It was an Abyssinian maid,
   And on her dulcimer she played,

Singing of Mount Abora.
Could I revive within me
Her symphony and song,
To such a deep delight, 'twould win me,
That with music loud and long,
I would build that dome in air,
That sunny dome! those caves of ice!
And all who heard should see them there,
And all should cry, Beware! Beware!
His flashing eyes, his floating hair!
Weave a circle round him thrice,
And close your eyes with holy dread,
For he on honey-dew hath fed,
And drunk the milk of Paradise.

Samuel Taylor Coleridge (1772–1834)

215. The Listeners

"Is there anybody there?" said the Traveler,
Knocking on the moonlit door;
And his horse in the silence champed the grasses
Of the forest's ferny floor:
And a bird flew up out of the turret,
Above the Traveler's head:
And he smote upon the door again a second time;
"Is there anybody there?" he said.
But no one descended to the Traveler;
No head from the leaf-fringed sill
Leaned over and looked into his grey eyes,
Where he stood perplexed and still.
But only a host of phantom listeners
That dwelt in the lone house then
Stood listening in the quiet of the moonlight
To that voice from the world of men:
Stood thronging the faint moonbeams on the dark stair,
That goes down to the empty hall,
Hearkening in an air stirred and shaken
By the lonely Traveler's call.
And he felt in his heart their strangeness,
Their stillness answering his cry,
While his horse moved, cropping the dark turf,
'Neath the starred and leafy sky;

For he suddenly smote on the door, even
  Louder, and lifted his head: —
"Tell them I came, and no one answered,
  That I kept my word," he said.
Never the least stir made the listeners,
  Though every word he spake
Fell echoing through the shadowiness of the still house
  From the one man left awake:
Ay, they heard his foot upon the stirrup,
  And the sound of iron on stone,
And how the silence surged softly backward,
  When the plunging hoofs were gone.

Walter de la Mare (1873–1956)

216. The Lifeguard

In a stable of boats I lie still,
From all sleeping children hidden.
The leap of a fish from its shadow
Makes the whole lake instantly tremble.
With my foot on the water, I feel
The moon outside

Take on the utmost of its power.
I rise and go out through the boats.
I set my broad sole upon silver,
On the skin of the sky, on the moonlight,
Stepping outward from earth onto water
In quest of the miracle

This village of children believed
That I could perform as I dived
For one who had sunk from my sight.
I saw his cropped haircut go under.
I leapt, and my steep body flashed
Once, in the sun.

Dark drew all the light from my eyes.
Like a man who explores his death
By the pull of his slow-moving shoulders,
I hung head down in the cold,
Wide-eyed, contained, and alone
Among the weeds,

And my fingertips turned into stone
From clutching immovable blackness.
Time after time I leapt upward
Exploding in breath, and fell back
From the change in the children's faces
At my defeat.

Beneath them, I swam to the boathouse
With only my life in my arms
To wait for the lake to shine back
At the risen moon with such power
That my steps on the light of the ripples
Might be sustained.

Beneath me is nothing but brightness
Like the ghost of a snow field in summer.
As I move toward the center of the lake,
Which is also the center of the moon,
I am thinking of how I may be
The savior of one

Who has already died in my care.
The dark trees fade from around me.
The moon's dust hovers together.
I call softly out, and the child's
Voice answers through blinding water.
Patiently, slowly,

He rises, dilating to break
The surface of stone with his forehead.
He is one I do not remember
Having ever seen in his life.
The ground that I stand on is trembling
Upon his smile.

I wash the black mud from my hands.
On a light given off by the grave,
I kneel in the quick of the moon
At the heart of a distant forest
And hold in my arms a child
Of water, water, water.

James Dickey (b. 1923)

217. Because I could not stop for Death

Because I could not stop for Death,
He kindly stopped for me;
The carriage held but just ourselves
And Immortality.

We slowly drove; he knew no haste,
And I had put away
My labor and my leisure too,
For his civility.

We passed the school, where children strove,
At recess, in the ring,
We passed the fields of gazing grain,
We passed the setting sun,

Or rather, he passed us;
The dews drew quivering and chill;
For only gossamer, my gown;
My tippet, only tulle.

We paused before a house that seemed
A swelling of the ground;
The roof was scarcely visible.
The cornice, in the ground.

Since then, 'tis centuries, and yet
Feels shorter than the day
I first surmised the horses' heads
Were toward eternity.

Emily Dickinson (1830–1886)

218. I taste a liquor never brewed

I taste a liquor never brewed,
From tankards scooped in pearl;
Not all the vats upon the Rhine
Yield such an alcohol!

Inebriate of air am I,
And debauchee of dew,
Reeling, through endless summer days,
From inns of molten blue.

When landlords turn the drunken bee
Out of the foxglove's door,
When butterflies renounce their drams,
I shall but drink the more!

Till seraphs swing their snowy hats,
And saints to windows run,
To see the little tippler
Leaning against the sun!

Emily Dickinson (1830–1886)

219. There's a certain slant of light

There's a certain slant of light,
Winter afternoons,
That oppresses like the heft
Of cathedral tunes.

Heavenly hurt it gives us.
We can find no scar
But internal difference
Where the meanings are.

None may teach it any—
'Tis the seal despair,
An imperial affliction
Sent us of the air.

When it comes the landscape listens,
Shadows hold their breath.
When it goes 'tis like the distance
On the look of death.

Emily Dickinson (1830–1886)

220. The Good-Morrow

I wonder, by my troth, what thou and I
Did till we loved? were we not weaned till then,
But sucked on country pleasures childishly?
Or snorted we in the seven sleepers' den?
'Twas so; but this, all pleasures fancies be.
If ever any beauty I did see,
Which I desired, and got, 'twas but a dream of thee.

THE GOOD-MORROW 4. *seven sleepers' den:* a cave where, according to Christian legend, seven youths escaped persecution and slept for two centuries.

And now good-morrow to our waking souls,
Which watch not one another out of fear;
For love all love of other sights controls,
And makes one little room an everywhere.
Let sea-discoverers to new worlds have gone;
Let maps to other,° worlds on worlds have shown; others
Let us possess one world; each hath one, and is one.

My face in thine eye, thine in mine appears,
And true plain hearts do in the faces rest;
Where can we find two better hemispheres
Without sharp north, without declining west?
Whatever dies was not mixed equally;
If our two loves be one, or thou and I
Love so alike that none can slacken, none can die.

John Donne (1572–1631)

221. The Triple Fool

I am two fools, I know,
For loving, and for saying so
In whining poetry.
But where's the wiseman that would not be I
If she did not deny?
Then, as the earth's inward, narrow, crooked lanes
Do purge sea water's fretful salt away,
I thought if I could draw my pains
Through rhyme's vexations, I should them allay.
Grief brought to numbers° cannot be so fierce, verse
For he tames it that fetters it in verse.

But when I have done so,
Some man, his art and voice to show,
Doth set and sing my pain,
And by delighting many, frees again
Grief, which verse did restrain.
To love and grief tribute of verse belongs,
But not of such which pleases when 'tis read;° read aloud
Both are increasèd by such songs,
For both their triumphs so are publishèd,
And I, which was two fools, do so grow three.
Who are a little wise, the best fools be.

John Donne (1572–1631)

222. Song: Go and catch a falling star

Go and catch a falling star,
  Get with child a mandrake root,
Tell me where all past years are,
  Or who cleft the devil's foot,
Teach me to hear mermaids singing,
  Or to keep off envy's stinging,
      And find
      What wind
Serves to advance an honest mind.

If thou be'st born to strange sights,
  Things invisible to see,
Ride ten thousand days and nights,
  Till age snow white hairs on thee,
Thou, when thou return'st, wilt tell me
  All strange wonders that befell thee,
      And swear
      No where
Lives a woman true and fair.

If thou find'st one, let me know;
  Such a pilgrimage were sweet.
Yet do not; I would not go,
  Though at next door we might meet.
Though she were true when you met her,
  And last till you write your letter,
      Yet she
      Will be
False, ere I come, to two or three.

John Donne (1572–1631)

223. Vergissmeinnicht

Three weeks gone and the combatants gone,
returning over the nightmare ground
we found the place again, and found
the soldier sprawling in the sun.

SONG 2. *mandrake:* supposed to resemble a human being because of its forked root.

VERGISSMEINNICHT The German title means "Forget me not." The author, an English poet, fought with a tank battalion in World War II.

The frowning barrel of his gun
overshadowing. As we came on
that day, he hit my tank with one
like the entry of a demon.

Look. Here in the gunpit spoil
the dishonored picture of his girl
who has put: *Steffi.*° *Vergissmeinnicht* — a girl's name
in a copybook gothic script.

We see him almost with content
abased, and seeming to have paid
and mocked at by his own equipment
that's hard and good when he's decayed.

But she would weep to see to-day
how on his skin the swart flies move;
the dust upon the paper eye
and the burst stomach like a cave.

For here the lover and killer are mingled
who had one body and one heart.
And death who had the soldier singled
has done the lover mortal hurt.

Keith Douglas (1920–1944)

224. Ending

The love we thought would never stop
now cools like a congealing chop.
The kisses that were hot as curry
are bird-pecks taken in a hurry.
The hands that held electric charges
now lie inert as four moored barges.
The feet that ran to meet a date
are running slow and running late.
The eyes that shone and seldom shut
are victims of a power cut.
The parts that then transmitted joy
are now reserved and cold and coy.
Romance, expected once to stay,
has left a note saying GONE AWAY.

Gavin Ewart (b. 1916)

225. Constantly risking absurdity

Constantly risking absurdity
and death
whenever he performs
above the heads
of his audience
the poet like an acrobat
climbs on rime
to a high wire of his own making
and balancing on eyebeams
above a sea of faces
paces his way
to the other side of day
performing entrechats
and sleight-of-foot tricks
and other high theatrics
and all without mistaking
any thing
for what it may not be

For he's the super realist
who must perforce perceive
taut truth
before the taking of each stance or step
in his supposed advance
toward that still higher perch
where Beauty stands and waits
with gravity
to start her death-defying leap

And he
a little charleychaplin man
who may or may not catch
her fair eternal form
spreadeagled in the empty air
of existence

Lawrence Ferlinghetti (b. 1919)

226. The Colonel

What you have heard is true. I was in his house. His wife carried a tray of coffee and sugar. His daughter filed her nails, his son went out for the night. There were daily papers, pet dogs, a pistol on the cushion beside him. The moon swung bare on its black cord over the house. On the television was a cop show. It was in English. Broken bottles were embedded in the walls around the house to scoop the kneecaps from a man's legs or cut his hands to lace. On the windows there were gratings like those in liquor stores. We had dinner, rack of lamb, good wine, a gold bell was on the table for calling the maid. The maid brought green mangoes, salt, a type of bread. I was asked how I enjoyed the country. There was a brief commercial in Spanish. His wife took everything away. There was some talk then of how difficult it had become to govern. The parrot said hello on the terrace. The colonel told it to shut up, and pushed himself from the table. My friend said to me with his eyes: say nothing. The colonel returned with a sack used to bring groceries home. He spilled many human ears on the table. They were like dried peach halves. There is no other way to say this. He took one of them in his hands, shook it in our faces, dropped it into a water glass. It came alive there. I am tired of fooling around he said. As for the rights of anyone, tell your people they can go fuck themselves. He swept the ears to the floor with his arm and held the last of his wine in the air. Something for your poetry, no? he said. Some of the ears on the floor caught this scrap of his voice. Some of the ears on the floor were pressed to the ground.

May 1978

Carolyn Forché (b. 1950)

227. Birches

When I see birches bend to left and right
Across the lines of straighter darker trees,
I like to think some boy's been swinging them.
But swinging doesn't bend them down to stay
As ice-storms do. Often you must have seen them
Loaded with ice a sunny winter morning
After a rain. They click upon themselves
As the breeze rises, and turn many-colored
As the stir cracks and crazes their enamel.
Soon the sun's warmth makes them shed crystal shells
Shattering and avalanching on the snow-crust—
Such heaps of broken glass to sweep away
You'd think the inner dome of heaven had fallen.
They are dragged to the withered bracken by the load,
And they seem not to break; though once they are bowed
So low for long, they never right themselves:
You may see their trunks arching in the woods
Years afterwards, trailing their leaves on the ground
Like girls on hands and knees that throw their hair
Before them over their heads to dry in the sun.
But I was going to say when Truth broke in
With all her matter-of-fact about the ice-storm

I should prefer to have some boy bend them
As he went out and in to fetch the cows—
Some boy too far from town to learn baseball,
Whose only play was what he found himself,
Summer or winter, and could play alone.
One by one he subdued his father's trees
By riding them down over and over again
Until he took the stiffness out of them,
And not one but hung limp, not one was left
For him to conquer. He learned all there was
To learn about not launching out too soon
And so not carrying the tree away
Clear to the ground. He always kept his poise
To the top branches, climbing carefully
With the same pains you use to fill a cup
Up to the brim, and even above the brim.
Then he flung outward, feet first, with a swish,
Kicking his way down through the air to the ground.
So was I once myself a swinger of birches.
And so I dream of going back to be.
It's when I'm weary of considerations,
And life is too much like a pathless wood
Where your face burns and tickles with the cobwebs
Broken across it, and one eye is weeping
From a twig's having lashed across it open.
I'd like to get away from earth awhile
And then come back to it and begin over.
May no fate willfully misunderstand me
And half grant what I wish and snatch me away
Not to return. Earth's the right place for love:
I don't know where it's likely to go better.
I'd like to go by climbing a birch tree,
And climb black branches up a snow-white trunk
Toward heaven, till the tree could bear no more,
But dipped its top and set me down again.
That would be good both going and coming back.
One could do worse than be a swinger of birches.

Robert Frost (1874–1963)

228. Desert Places

Snow falling and night falling fast, oh, fast
In a field I looked into going past,
And the ground almost covered smooth in snow,
But a few weeds and stubble showing last.

The woods around it have it—it is theirs.
All animals are smothered in their lairs.
I am too absent-spirited to count;
The loneliness includes me unawares.

And lonely as it is that loneliness
Will be more lonely ere it will be less—
A blanker whiteness of benighted snow
With no expression, nothing to express.

They cannot scare me with their empty spaces
Between stars—on stars where no human race is.
I have it in me so much nearer home
To scare myself with my own desert places.

Robert Frost (1874–1963)

229. Mending Wall

Something there is that doesn't love a wall,
That sends the frozen-ground-swell under it
And spills the upper boulders in the sun,
And makes gaps even two can pass abreast.
The work of hunters is another thing:
I have come after them and made repair
Where they have left not one stone on a stone,
But they would have the rabbit out of hiding,
To please the yelping dogs. The gaps I mean,
No one has seen them made or heard them made,
But at spring mending-time we find them there.
I let my neighbor know beyond the hill;
And on a day we meet to walk the line
And set the wall between us once again.
We keep the wall between us as we go.
To each the boulders that have fallen to each.
And some are loaves and some so nearly balls
We have to use a spell to make them balance:
"Stay where you are until our backs are turned!"
We wear our fingers rough with handling them.
Oh, just another kind of outdoor game,
One on a side. It comes to little more:
There where it is we do not need the wall:
He is all pine and I am apple orchard.
My apple trees will never get across
And eat the cones under his pines, I tell him.
He only says, "Good fences make good neighbors."
Spring is the mischief in me, and I wonder

If I could put a notion in his head:
"*Why* do they make good neighbors? Isn't it
Where there are cows? But here there are no cows.
Before I built a wall I'd ask to know
What I was walling in or walling out,
And to whom I was like to give offense.
Something there is that doesn't love a wall,
That wants it down." I could say "Elves" to him,
But it's not elves exactly, and I'd rather
He said it for himself. I see him there,
Bringing a stone grasped firmly by the top
In each hand, like an old-stone savage armed.
He moves in darkness as it seems to me,
Not of woods only and the shade of trees.
He will not go behind his father's saying,
And he likes having thought of it so well
He says again, "Good fences make good neighbors."

Robert Frost (1874–1963)

230. Never Again Would Birds' Song Be the Same

He would declare and could himself believe
That the birds there in all the garden round
From having heard the daylong voice of Eve
Had added to their own an oversound,
Her tone of meaning but without the words.
Admittedly an eloquence so soft
Could only have had an influence on birds
When call or laughter carried it aloft.
Be that as may be, she was in their song.
Moreover her voice upon their voices crossed
Had now persisted in the woods so long
That probably it never would be lost.
Never again would birds' song be the same.
And to do that to birds was why she came.

Robert Frost (1874–1963)

231. Pushing

Me and my brother would jump off the porch
mornings for a better view of the cars
that raced around the corner up Olds Ave.,
naming the make and year; this was '58

and his voice still young enough to wait for
how I'd say the names right to the air.
Cold mornings in Lansing we'd stop the mile
to school in the high-priced grocery nearly there
and the owner, maybe a decent White man
whose heavy dark hair and far Lebanese look
had caught too many kids at his candy,
would follow us down the aisles and say,
"I know what you boys is up to, big-eyed
and such, so you better be going your way—
buy something or else you got to leave."
We'd rattle the pennies we had and go
but coming home buy some nutchews to stay
and try his nerve again, because we didn't steal
but warmed ourselves till Ray would ask me why—
till, like big brothers will, one day I guessed,
"Some things you do because you want to.
Some things you do because you can't."
In what midwest warmth there was we'd laugh,
throw some snowballs high where the sun was
breaking up the clouds.

Christopher Gilbert (b. 1945)

232. Of Money

Give money me, take friendship whoso list,° — wishes
For friends are gone come once adversity,
When money yet remaineth safe in chest,
That quickly can thee bring from misery.
Fair face show friends when riches do abound;
Come time of proof, farewell, they must away.
Believe me well, they are not to be found,
If God but send thee once a lowering day.
Gold never starts aside, but in distress
Finds ways enough to ease thine heaviness.

Barnabe Googe (1540–1594)

233. Channel Firing

That night your great guns, unawares,
Shook all our coffins as we lay,
And broke the chancel window-squares,
We thought it was the Judgment-day

And sat upright. While drearisome
Arose the howl of wakened hounds:
The mouse let fall the altar-crumb,
The worms drew back into the mounds,

The glebe cow drooled. Till God called, "No;
It's gunnery practice out at sea
Just as before you went below;
The world is as it used to be:

"All nations striving strong to make
Red war yet redder. Mad as hatters
They do no more for Christès sake
Than you who are helpless in such matters.

"That this is not the judgment-hour
For some of them's a blessed thing,
For if it were they'd have to scour
Hell's floor for so much threatening. . . .

"Ha, ha. It will be warmer when
I blow the trumpet (if indeed
I ever do; for you are men,
and rest eternal sorely need)."

So down we lay again. "I wonder,
Will the world ever saner be,"
Said one, "than when He sent us under
In our indifferent century!"

And many a skeleton shook his head.
"Instead of preaching forty year,"
My neighbor Parson Thirdly said,
"I wish I had stuck to pipes and beer."

Again the guns disturbed the hour,
Roaring their readiness to avenge,
As far inland as Stourton Tower,
And Camelot, and starlit Stonehenge.

April 1914

Thomas Hardy (1840–1928)

CHANNEL FIRING 35–36. *Stourton Tower:* memorial at the spot where Alfred the Great resisted the invading Danes in 879; *Camelot:* legendary capital of Arthur's kingdom; *Stonehenge:* mysterious circle of huge stones erected in Wiltshire by very early inhabitants of Britain. The three references move backward in time through the historic, the legendary, and the prehistoric.

234. The Darkling Thrush

I leant upon a coppice gate
  When Frost was specter-gray,
And Winter's dregs made desolate
  The weakening eye of day.
The tangled bine-stems scored the sky
  Like strings of broken lyres,
And all mankind that haunted nigh
  Had sought their household fires.

The land's sharp features seemed to be
  The Century's corpse outleant,
His crypt the cloudy canopy,
  The wind his death-lament.
The ancient pulse of germ and birth
  Was shrunken hard and dry,
And every spirit upon earth
  Seemed fervorless as I.

At once a voice arose among
  The bleak twigs overhead
In a full-hearted evensong
  Of joy illimited;
An aged thrush, frail, gaunt, and small,
  In blast-beruffled plume,
Had chosen thus to fling his soul
  Upon the growing gloom.

So little cause for carolings
  Of such ecstatic sound
Was written on terrestrial things
  Afar or nigh around,
That I could think there trembled through
  His happy good-night air
Some blessed Hope, whereof he knew
  And I was unaware.

31 December 1900

Thomas Hardy (1840–1928)

235. Redemption

Having been tenant long to a rich Lord,
  Not thriving, I resolvèd to be bold,
  And make a suit unto him, to afford
A new small-rented lease and cancel the old.

In heaven at his manor I him sought:
They told me there that he was lately gone
About some land which he had dearly bought
Long since on earth, to take possessiön.
I straight returned, and knowing his great birth,
Sought him accordingly in great resorts;
In cities, theaters, gardens, parks, and courts:
At length I heard a ragged noise and mirth
Of thieves and murderers; there I him espied,
Who straight, "Your suit is granted," said, and died.

George Herbert (1593–1633)

236. Riddle

From Belsen a crate of gold teeth,
from Dachau a mountain of shoes,
from Auschwitz a skin lampshade.
Who killed the Jews?

Not I, cries the typist,
not I, cries the engineer,
not I, cries Adolf Eichmann,
not I, cries Albert Speer.

My friend Fritz Nova lost his father—
a petty official had to choose.
My friend Lou Abrahms lost his brother.
Who killed the Jews?

David Nova swallowed gas,
Hyman Abrahms was beaten and starved.
Some men signed their papers,
and some stood guard,

and some herded them in,
and some dropped the pellets,
and some spread the ashes,
and some hosed the walls,

RIDDLE 1–3. *Belsen, Dachau, Auschwitz:* sites of Nazi concentration camps. 7. *Adolf Eichmann* (1906–1962), Nazi official who organized anti-Jewish activities, especially the shipping of Jews to the concentration camps. 8. *Albert Speer* (1905–1981), Hitler's chief architect and later minister of armaments whose efficient methods greatly improved the production of war materials.

and some planted the wheat,
and some poured the steel,
and some cleared the rails,
and some raised the cattle.

Some smelled the smoke,
some just heard the news.
Were they Germans? Were they Nazis?
Were they human? Who killed the Jews?

The stars will remember the gold,
the sun will remember the shoes,
the moon will remember the skin.
But who killed the Jews?

William Heyen (b. 1940)

237. Bredon Hill

In summertime on Bredon
  The bells they sound so clear;
Round both the shires they ring them
  In steeples far and near,
  A happy noise to hear.

Here of a Sunday morning
  My love and I would lie,
And see the colored counties,
  And hear the larks so high
  About us in the sky.

The bells would ring to call her
  In valleys miles away:
"Come all to church, good people;
  Good people, come and pray."
  But here my love would stay.

And I would turn and answer
  Among the springing thyme,
"Oh, peal upon our wedding,
  And we will hear the chime,
  And come to church in time."

But when the snows at Christmas
  On Bredon top were strown,
My love rose up so early
  And stole out unbeknown
  And went to church alone.

They tolled the one bell only,
  Groom there was none to see,
The mourners followed after,
  And so to church went she,
  And would not wait for me.

The bells they sound on Bredon,
  And still the steeples hum.
"Come all to church, good people,"—
  Oh, noisy bells, be dumb;
  I hear you, I will come.

A. E. Housman (1859–1936)

238. To an Athlete Dying Young

The time you won your town the race
We chaired you through the market-place;
Man and boy stood cheering by,
And home we brought you shoulder-high.

To-day, the road all runners come,
Shoulder-high, we bring you home,
And set you at your threshold down,
Townsman of a stiller town.

Smart lad, to slip betimes away
From fields where glory does not stay
And early though the laurel grows
It withers quicker than the rose.

Eyes the shady night has shut
Cannot see the record cut,
And silence sounds no worse than cheers
After earth has stopped the ears:

Now you will not swell the rout
Of lads that wore their honors out,
Runners whom renown outran
And the name died before the man.

So set, before its echoes fade,
The fleet foot on the sill of shade,
And hold to the low lintel up
The still-defended challenge-cup.

And round that early-laureled head
Will flock to gaze the strengthless dead,
And find unwithered on its curls
The garland briefer than a girl's.

A. E. Housman (1859–1936)

239. The Freaks at Spurgin Road Field

The dim boy claps because the others clap.
The polite word, handicapped, is muttered in the stands.
Isn't it wrong, the way the mind moves back.

One whole day I sit, contrite, dirt, L.A.
Union Station, '46, sweating through last night.
The dim boy claps because the others clap.

Score, 5 to 3. Pitcher fading badly in the heat.
Isn't it wrong to be or not be spastic?
Isn't it wrong, the way the mind moves back.

I'm laughing at a neighbor girl beaten to scream
by a savage father and I'm ashamed to look.
The dim boy claps because the others clap.

The score is always close, the rally always short.
I've left more wreckage than a quake.
Isn't it wrong, the way the mind moves back.

The afflicted never cheer in unison.
Isn't it wrong, the way the mind moves back
to stammering pastures where the picnic should have worked.
The dim boy claps because the others clap.

Richard Hugo (1923–1982)

240. The Death of the Ball Turret Gunner

From my mother's sleep I fell into the State,
And I hunched in its belly till my wet fur froze.
Six miles from earth, loosed from its dream of life,
I woke to black flak and the nightmare fighters.
When I died they washed me out of the turret with a hose.

Randall Jarrell (1914–1965)

241. Song: To Celia

Drink to me only with thine eyes,
And I will pledge with mine;
Or leave a kiss but in the cup,
And I'll not look for wine.
The thirst that from the soul doth rise
Doth ask a drink divine,
But might I of Jove's nectar sup,
I would not change for thine.

I sent thee late° a rosy wreath, lately
Not so much honoring thee
As giving it a hope that there
It could not withered be.
But thou thereon didst only breathe,
And sent'st it back to me;
Since when, it grows, and smells, I swear,
Not of itself, but thee.

Ben Jonson (1573?–1637)

242. La Belle Dame sans Merci

A Ballad

O, what can ail thee, knight-at-arms,
Alone and palely loitering?
The sedge has withered from the lake,
And no birds sing.

O, what can ail thee, knight-at-arms,
So haggard and so woe-begone?
The squirrel's granary is full,
And the harvest's done.

I see a lily on thy brow,
With anguish moist and fever dew;
And on thy cheeks a fading rose
Fast withereth too.

I met a lady in the meads,
Full beautiful—a faery's child,
Her hair was long, her foot was light,
And her eyes were wild.

LA BELLE DAME SANS MERCI The title means "The beautiful lady without pity."

I made a garland for her head,
And bracelets too, and fragrant zone;
She looked at me as she did love,
And made sweet moan.

I set her on my pacing steed,
And nothing else saw all day long;
For sidelong would she bend, and sing
A faery's song.

She found me roots of relish sweet,
And honey wild, and manna dew,
And sure in language strange she said—
"I love thee true."

She took me to her elfin grot,
And there she wept and sighed full sore,
And there I shut her wild wild eyes
With kisses four.

And there she lullèd me asleep
And there I dreamed—Ah! woe betide!
The latest dream I ever dreamed
On the cold hill side.

I saw pale kings and princes too,
Pale warriors, death-pale were they all;
They cried—"La Belle Dame sans Merci
Hath thee in thrall!"

I saw their starved lips in the gloam
With horrid warning gapèd wide,
And I awoke and found me here
On the cold hill's side.

And this is why I sojourn here
Alone and palely loitering,
Though the sedge has withered from the lake,
And no birds sing.

John Keats (1795–1821)

243. Ode on a Grecian Urn

Thou still unravished bride of quietness,
Thou foster-child of silence and slow time,
Sylvan historian, who canst thus express
A flowery tale more sweetly than our rhyme:

What leaf-fringed legend haunts about thy shape
  Of deities or mortals, or of both,
    In Tempe or the dales of Arcady?
  What men or gods are these? What maidens loth?
What mad pursuit? What struggle to escape?
    What pipes and timbrels? What wild ecstasy?

Heard melodies are sweet, but those unheard
  Are sweeter; therefore, ye soft pipes, play on;
Not to the sensual ear, but, more endeared,
  Pipe to the spirit ditties of no tone:
Fair youth, beneath the trees, thou canst not leave
  Thy song, nor ever can those trees be bare;
    Bold lover, never, never canst thou kiss,
Though winning near the goal—yet, do not grieve;
    She cannot fade, though thou hast not thy bliss,
  For ever wilt thou love, and she be fair!

Ah, happy, happy boughs! that cannot shed
  Your leaves, nor ever bid the spring adieu;
And, happy melodist, unwearièd,
  For ever piping songs for ever new;
More happy love! more happy, happy love!
  For ever warm and still to be enjoyed,
    For ever panting and for ever young;
All breathing human passion far above,
  That leaves a heart high-sorrowful and cloyed,
    A burning forehead, and a parching tongue.

Who are these coming to the sacrifice?
  To what green altar, O mysterious priest,
Lead'st thou that heifer lowing at the skies,
  And all her silken flanks with garlands drest?
What little town by river or sea shore,
  Or mountain-built with peaceful citadel,
    Is emptied of its folk, this pious morn?
And, little town, thy streets for evermore
  Will silent be; and not a soul to tell
    Why thou art desolate, can e'er return.

O Attic shape! Fair attitude! with brede
  Of marble men and maidens overwrought,
With forest branches and the trodden weed;
  Thou, silent form, dost tease us out of thought
As doth eternity: Cold Pastoral!
  When old age shall this generation waste,
    Thou shalt remain, in midst of other woe

Than ours, a friend to man, to whom thou say'st,
Beauty is truth, truth beauty,—that is all
Ye know on earth, and all ye need to know.

John Keats (1795–1821)

244. Ode to a Nightingale

My heart aches, and a drowsy numbness pains
My sense, as though of hemlock° I had drunk, — a poison
Or emptied some dull opiate to the drains
One minute past, and Lethe-wards had sunk:
'Tis not through envy of thy happy lot,
But being too happy in thine happiness,—
That thou, light-wingèd Dryad° of the trees, — wood nymph
In some melodious plot
Of beechen green, and shadows numberless,
Singest of summer in full-throated ease.

O for a draught of vintage! that hath been
Cooled a long age in the deep-delvèd earth,
Tasting of Flora° and the country green, — goddess of flowers
Dance, and Provençal song, and sunburnt mirth!
O for a beaker full of the warm South,
Full of the true, the blushful Hippocrene,
With beaded bubbles winking at the brim,
And purple-stainèd mouth;
That I might drink, and leave the world unseen,
And with thee fade away into the forest dim:

Fade far away, dissolve, and quite forget
What thou among the leaves hast never known,
The weariness, the fever, and the fret
Here, where men sit and hear each other groan;
Where palsy shakes a few, sad, last gray hairs,
Where youth grows pale, and specter-thin, and dies;
Where but to think is to be full of sorrow
And leaden-eyed despairs,
Where Beauty cannot keep her lustrous eyes,
Or new Love pine at them beyond to-morrow.

ODE ON A GRECIAN URN 49–50. In the 1820 edition of Keats's poems the words "Beauty is truth, truth beauty" were enclosed in quotation marks, and the poem is often reprinted that way. It is now generally agreed, however, on the basis of contemporary transcripts of Keats's poem, that Keats intended the entire last two lines to be spoken by the urn.

ODE TO A NIGHTINGALE 4. *Lethe:* river of forgetfulness in the Greek underworld. 14. *Provençal:* Provence, a wine-growing region in southern France famous, in the Middle Ages, for troubadours. 16. *Hippocrene:* fountain of the Muses on Mt. Helicon in Greece.

Away! away! for I will fly to thee,
Not charioted by Bacchus and his pards,
But on the viewless° wings of Poesy, invisible
Though the dull brain perplexes and retards:
Already with thee! tender is the night,
And haply the Queen-Moon is on her throne,
Clustered around by all her starry Fays;
But here there is no light,
Save what from heaven is with the breezes blown
Through verdurous glooms and winding mossy ways.

I cannot see what flowers are at my feet,
Nor what soft incense hangs upon the boughs,
But, in embalmèd° darkness, guess each sweet perfumed
Wherewith the seasonable month endows
The grass, the thicket, and the fruit-tree wild;
White hawthorn, and the pastoral eglantine;
Fast fading violets covered up in leaves;
And mid-May's eldest child,
The coming musk-rose, full of dewy wine,
The murmurous haunt of flies on summer eves.

Darkling° I listen; and, for many a time in darkness
I have been half in love with easeful Death,
Called him soft names in many a musèd rhyme,
To take into the air my quiet breath;
Now more than ever seems it rich to die,
To cease upon the midnight with no pain,
While thou art pouring forth thy soul abroad
In such an ecstasy!
Still wouldst thou sing, and I have ears in vain—
To thy high requiem become a sod.

Thou wast not born for death, immortal Bird!
No hungry generations tread thee down;
The voice I hear this passing night was heard
In ancient days by emperor and clown:
Perhaps the self-same song that found a path
Through the sad heart of Ruth, when, sick for home,
She stood in tears amid the alien corn;
The same that oft-times hath
Charmed magic casements, opening on the foam
Of perilous seas, in faery lands forlorn.

32. *Bacchus . . . pards:* Bacchus, god of wine, had a chariot drawn by leopards. 66. *Ruth:* see Bible, Ruth 2.

ell
ıy sole self!
› well
ng elf.
ıem fades
the still stream,
'tis buried deep
es:
; dream?
› I wake or sleep?

John Keats (1795–1821)

September
:y, black blackberries
breakfast,
y, a penalty
g the black art
g; and as I stand among them
my mouth, the ripest berries
n to my tongue,
s do, certain peculiar words
unched,
e-syllabled lumps,
squinch open, and splurge well
rtled, icy, black language
ting in late September.

Galway Kinnell (b. 1927)

;aid to me

den said to me the other day
ıtly, I think), "Say, etheridge,
ne the black boys don't run off
: white boys do?"
ed my jaw and scratched my head
id (innocently, I think), "Well, suh,
: for sure, but I reckon it's cause
n't got no wheres to run to."

Etheridge Knight (1933–1991)

247. Aubade

I work all day, and get half drunk at night.
Waking at four to soundless dark, I stare.
In time the curtain-edges will grow light.
Till then I see what's really always there:
Unresting death, a whole day nearer now,
Making all thought impossible but how
And where and when I shall myself die.
Arid interrogation: yet the dread
Of dying, and being dead,
Flashes afresh to hold and horrify.

The mind blanks at the glare. Not in remorse
—The good not done, the love not given, time
Torn off unused—nor wretchedly because
An only life can take so long to climb
Clear of its wrong beginnings, and may never;
But at the total emptiness for ever,
The sure extinction that we travel to
And shall be lost in always. Not to be here,
Not to be anywhere,
And soon; nothing more terrible, nothing more true

This is a special way of being afraid
No trick dispels. Religion used to try,
That vast moth-eaten musical brocade
Created to pretend we never die,
And specious stuff that says *No rational being*
Can fear a thing it will not feel, not seeing
That this is what we fear—no sight, no sound,
No touch or taste or smell, nothing to think with,
Nothing to love or link with,
The anaesthetic from which none come round.

And so it stays just on the edge of vision,
A small unfocused blur, a standing chill
That slows each impulse down to indecision.
Most things may never happen: this one will,
And realization of it rages out
In furnace-fear when we are caught without
People or drink. Courage is no good:
It means not scaring others. Being brave
Lets no one off the grave.
Death is no different whined at than withstood.

Slowly light strengthens, and the room takes shape.
It stands plain as a wardrobe, what we know,
Have always known, know that we can't escape,
Yet can't accept. One side will have to go.
Meanwhile telephones crouch, getting ready to ring
In locked-up offices, and all the uncaring
Intricate rented world begins to rouse.
The sky is white as clay, with no sun.
Work has to be done.
Postmen like doctors go from house to house.

Philip Larkin (1922–1985)

248. The Fox

I think I must have lived
once before, not as a man or woman
but as a small, quick fox pursued
through fields of grass and grain
by ladies and gentlemen on horseback.
This would explain my nose
and the small dark tufts of hair
that rise from the base of my spine.
It would explain why I am
so seldom invited out to dinner
and when I am I am never
invited back. It would explain
my loathing for those on horseback
in Central Park and how I can
so easily curse them and challenge
the men to fight and why no matter
how big they are or how young
they refuse to dismount,
for at such times, rock in hand,
I must seem demented.
My anger is sudden and total,
for I am a man to whom anger
usually comes slowly, spreading
like a fever along my shoulders
and back and turning my stomach
to a stone, but this fox anger
is lyrical and complete, as I stand
in the pathway shouting and refusing

to budge, feeling the dignity
of the small creature menaced
by the many and larger. Yes,
I must have been that unseen fox
whose breath sears the thick bushes
and whose eyes burn like opals
in the darkness, who humps
and shits gleefully in the horsepath
softened by moonlight and goes on
feeling the steady measured beat
of his fox heart like a wordless
delicate song, and the quick forepaws
choosing the way unerringly
and the thick furred body following
while the tail flows upward,
too beautiful a plume for anyone
except a creature who must proclaim
not ever ever ever
to mounted ladies and their gentlemen.

Philip Levine (b. 1928)

249. Watchmaker God

Say life is the one-way trip, the one-way flight,
say this without hysterical undertones—
then you could say you stood in the cold light of science,
seeing as you are seen, espoused to fact.
Strange, life is both the fire and fuel; and we,
the animals and objects, must be here
without striking a spark of evidence
that anything that ever stopped living
ever falls back to living when life stops.
There's a pale romance to the watchmaker God
of Descartes and Paley; He drafted and installed

WATCHMAKER GOD 10–11. The French philosopher René Descartes (1596–1650), widely regarded as the founder of modern philosophy, devised a system of philosophical truth based on mathematical principles and devoted to strict rationalism. The English philosopher William Paley (1743–1805) found proof of the existence of God in the design evident in nature, particularly in the mechanisms of the human body. He also devised the famous analogy of God to a watchmaker, arguing that if one discovers a watch, one must assume a maker of the watch, and that the existence of the natural world therefore proves the existence of its creator.

us in the Apparatus. He loved to tinker;
but having perfected what He had to do,
stood off shrouded in his loneliness.

Robert Lowell (1917–1977)

250. Bedtime Story

Long long ago when the world was a wild place
Planted with bushes and peopled by apes, our
Mission Brigade was at work in the jungle.
  Hard by the Congo

Once, when a foraging detail was active
Scouting for green-fly, it came on a gray man, the
Last living man, in the branch of a baobab
  Stalking a monkey.

Earlier men had disposed of, for pleasure,
Creatures whose names we scarcely remember—
Zebra, rhinoceros, elephants, wart-hog,
  Lion, rats, deer. But

After the wars had extinguished the cities
Only the wild ones were left, half-naked
Near the Equator: and here was the last one,
  Starved for a monkey.

By then the Mission Brigade had encountered
Hundreds of such men: and their procedure,
History tells us, was only to feed them:
  Find them and feed them;

Those were the orders. And this was the last one.
Nobody knew that he was, but he was. Mud
Caked on his flat gray flanks. He was crouched, half-
  Armed with a shaved spear

Glinting beneath broad leaves. When their jaws cut
Swathes through the bark and he saw fine teeth shine,
Round eyes roll round and forked arms waver
  Huge as the rough trunks

Over his head, he was frightened. Our workers
Marched through the Congo before he was born, but
This was the first time perhaps that he'd seen one.
  Staring in hot still

Silence, he crouched there: then jumped. With a long swing
Down from his branch, he had angled his spear too
Quickly, before they could hold him, and hurled it
   Hard at the soldier

Leading the detail. How could he know Queen's
Orders were only to help him? The soldier
Winced when the tipped spear pricked him. Unsheathing his
   Sting was a reflex.

Later the Queen was informed. There were no more
Men. An impetuous soldier had killed off,
Purely by chance, the penultimate primate.
   When she was certain,

Squadrons of workers were fanned through the Congo
Detailed to bring back the man's picked bones to be
Sealed in the archives in amber. I'm quite sure
   Nobody found them

After the most industrious search, though.
Where had the bones gone? Over the earth, dear,
Ground by the teeth of the termites, blown by the
   Wind, like the dodo's.

George MacBeth (b. 1932)

251. Leda's Sister and the Geese

All the boys always wanted her, so
it was no surprise about the swan-
man, god, whatever he was. That day

I was stuck at home, as usual, while
she got to moon around the lake
supposedly picking lilies for dye. Think *I*

would have let some pair of wings catch me,
bury me under the weight of the sky?
She came home whimpering, whined out

the whole story, said she was "sore afraid"
she'd got pregnant. Hunh. "Sore"
I'll bet, the size she described, and

pregnant figures: no guess who'll get
to help her with the kid or, Hera forbid,
more than one (twins run in our damned

family). "Never you mind, dear," Mother said.
"Your sister will take on your chores."
Sure. As though I wasn't already doing

twice as many of my own. So now
I clean, I spin, I weave, I bake,
fling crusts to feed these birds I wish

to Hades every day; while she sits smug
in a wicker chair, and eats sweetmeats,
and combs and combs that ratty golden hair.

Katharyn Howd Machan (b. 1952)

252. Offspring

I tried to tell her:
        This way the twig is bent.
        Born of my trunk and strengthened by my roots,
        you must stretch newgrown branches
        closer to the sun
        than I can reach.

I wanted to say:
        Extend my self to that far atmosphere
        only my dreams allow.

But the twig broke,
and yesterday I saw her
walking down an unfamiliar street,
        feet confident
        face slanted upward toward a threatening sky,
and
        she was smiling
        and she was
        her very free,
        her very individual,
        unpliable
        own.

Naomi Long Madgett (b. 1923)

253. Getting Out

That year we hardly slept, waking like inmates
who beat the walls. Every night
another refusal, the silent work
of tightening the heart.
Exhausted, we gave up; escaped
to the apartment pool, swimming those laps
until the first light relieved us.

Days were different: FM and full-blast
blues, hours of guitar "you gonna miss me
when I'm gone." Think how you tried
to pack up and go, for weeks stumbling
over piles of clothing, the unstrung tennis rackets.
Finally locked into blame, we paced
that short hall, heaving words like furniture.

I have the last unshredded pictures
of our matching eyes and hair. We've kept
to separate sides of the map,
still I'm startled by men who look like you.
And in the yearly letter, you're sure to say
you're happy now. Yet I think of the lawyer's bewilderment
when we cried, the last day. Taking hands
we walked apart, until our arms stretched
between us. We held on tight, and let go.

Cleopatra Mathis (b. 1947)

254. Trinity Place

The pigeons that peck at the grass in Trinity Churchyard
Are pompous as bankers. They walk with an air, they preen
Their prosperous feathers. They smugly regard their beauty.
They are plump, they are sleek. It is only the men who are lean.

The pigeons scan with disfavor the men who sit there,
Listless in sun or shade. The pigeons sidle
Between the gravestones with shrewd, industrious motions.
The pigeons are busy. It is only the men who are idle.

The pigeons sharpen their beaks on the stones, and they waddle
In dignified search of their proper, their daily bread.
Their eyes are small with contempt for the men on the benches.
It is only the men who are hungry. The pigeons are fed.

Phyllis McGinley (1905–1978)

255. Summer in England, 1914

On London fell a clearer light;
Caressing pencils of the sun
Defined the distances, the white
Houses transfigured one by one,
The "long, unlovely street" impearled.
Oh, what a sky has walked the world!

Most happy year! And out of town
The hay was prosperous, and the wheat;
The silken harvest climbed the down:
Moon after moon was heavenly-sweet,
Stroking the bread within the sheaves,
Looking 'twixt apples and their leaves.

And while this rose made round her cup,
The armies died convulsed. And when
This chaste young silver sun went up
Softly, a thousand shattered men,
One wet corruption, heaped the plain,
After a league-long throb of pain.

Flower following tender flower; and birds
And berries; and benignant skies
Made thrive the serried flocks and herds.—
Yonder are men shot through the eyes.
Love, hide thy face
From man's unpardonable race.

Alice Meynell (1847–1922)

256. Oedipus

The gang wanted to give Oedipus Rex a going away present.
He had been a good hard-working father and king.
And besides it is the custom in this country
To give gifts on departure.

But we didn't know what to give Oedipus; he had everything.
Even in his loss, he had more than average.
So we gave him a traveling case, fitted, which we personally
Should have liked to receive.

Josephine Miles (1911–1985)

SUMMER IN ENGLAND, 1914 5. The quoted phrase is from Tennyson's *In Memoriam A. H. H.*, included in this volume as poem No. 289.

257. What Are Years?

What is our innocence,
what is our guilt? All are
naked, none is safe. And whence
is courage: the unanswered question,
the resolute doubt,—
dumbly calling, deafly listening—that
in misfortune, even death,
encourages others
and in its defeat, stirs

the soul to be strong? He
sees deep and is glad, who
accedes to mortality
and in his imprisonment rises
upon himself as
the sea in a chasm, struggling to be
free and unable to be,
in its surrendering
finds its continuing.

So he who strongly feels,
behaves. The very bird,
grown taller as he sings, steels
his form straight up. Though he is captive,
his mighty singing
says, satisfaction is a lowly
thing, how pure a thing is joy.
This is mortality,
this is eternity.

Marianne Moore (1887–1972)

258. The Amateurs of Heaven

Two lovers to a midnight meadow came
High in the hills, to lie there hand in hand
Like effigies and look up at the stars,
The never-setting ones set in the North
To circle the Pole in idiot majesty,
And wonder what was given them to wonder.

Being amateurs, they knew some of the names
By rote, and could attach the names to stars
And draw the lines invisible between

That humbled all the heavenly things to farm
And forest things and even kitchen things,
A bear, a wagon, a long-handled ladle;

Could wonder at the shadow of the world
That brought those lights to light, could wonder too
At the ancestral eyes and the dark mind
Behind them that had reached the length of light
To name the stars and draw the animals
And other stuff that dangled in the height,

Or was it in the deep? Did they look in
Or out, the lovers? till they grew bored
As even lovers will, and got up to go,
But drunken now, with staggering and dizziness,
Because the spell of earth had moved them so,
Hallucinating that the heavens moved.

Howard Nemerov (1920–1991)

259. Grace to Be Said at the Supermarket

That God of ours, the Great Geometer,
Does something for us here, where He hath put
(if you want to put it that way) things in shape,
Compressing the little lambs in orderly cubes,
Making the roast a decent cylinder,
Fairing the tin ellipsoid of a ham,
Getting the luncheon meat anonymous
In squares and oblongs with the edges bevelled
Or rounded (streamlined, maybe, for greater speed).

Praise Him, He hath conferred aesthetic distance
Upon our appetites, and on the bloody
Mess of our birthright, our unseemly need,
Imposed significant form. Through Him the brutes
Enter the pure Euclidean kingdom of number,
Free of their bulging and blood-swollen lives
They come to us holy, in cellophane
Transparencies, in the mystical body,

That we may look unflinchingly on death
As the greatest good, like a philosopher should.

Howard Nemerov (1920–1991)

260. The Victims

When Mother divorced you, we were glad. She took it and
took it, in silence, all those years and then
kicked you out, suddenly, and her
kids loved it. Then you were fired, and we
grinned inside, the way people grinned when
Nixon's helicopter lifted off the South
Lawn for the last time. We were tickled
to think of your office taken away,
your secretaries taken away,
your luncheons with three double bourbons,
your pencils, your reams of paper. Would they take your
suits back, too, those dark
carcasses hung in your closet, and the black
noses of your shoes with their large pores?
She had taught us to take it, to hate you and take it
until we pricked with her for your
annihilation, Father. Now I
pass the bums in doorways, the white
slugs of their bodies gleaming through slits in their
suits of compressed silt, the stained
flippers of their hands, the underwater
fire of their eyes, ships gone down with the
lanterns lit, and I wonder who took it and
took it from them in silence until they had
given it all away and had nothing
left but this.

Sharon Olds (b. 1942)

261. Through Ruddy Orchards

Through ruddy orchards now the grip of stems
Gives, — how easily! — and plunging bright,
— How furthering the thing to fall so bright! —
To earth comes back the fruit
With flavors of the light.

Through ruddy orchards, watch, where so much now
Is burnished to a health by the wild sun,
The falling and the falling . . . But these
That lurch in the wind and hold, what shall they be?
Why, they will wilt upon the tree,

The sun will take its golden back;
They will swing there, wry and wrinkled,
Till the white frost turns them black.

Through ruddy orchards, then, streams the deep wind—
The rife and lusty lungs of autumn wind;—
Then, cracked on rocks and bruised to brown,
Or sweet in caverns of the grass,
Or this, or that; but down, but down!

Mary Oliver (b. 1935)

262. Speaking

I take him outside
under the trees,
have him stand on the ground.
We listen to the crickets,
cicadas, million years old sound.
Ants come by us.
I tell them,
"This is he, my son.
This boy is looking at you.
I am speaking for him."

The crickets, cicadas,
the ants, the millions of years
are watching us,
hearing us.
My son murmurs infant words,
speaking, small laughter
bubbles from him.
Tree leaves tremble.
They listen to this boy
speaking for me.

Simon J. Ortiz (b. 1941)

263. The Sad Children's Song

This house is a wreck said the children
when they came home with their children
Your papers are all over the place
The chairs are covered with books
and look   brown leaves are piled on the floor
under the wandering Jews

Your face is a wreck said the children
when they came home with their children
There are lines all over your face
your necks like curious turtles
Why did you let yourself go?
Where are you going without us?

This world is a wreck said the children
When they came home with their children
There are bombs all over the place
There's no water   the fields are all poisoned
Why did you leave things like this
Where can we go said the children
what can we say to our children?

Grace Paley (b. 1922)

264. The Hat Lady

In a childhood of hats—
my uncles in homburgs and derbies,
Fred Astaire in high black silk,
the yarmulke my grandfather wore
like the palm of a hand
cradling the back of his head—
only my father went hatless,
even in winter.

And in the spring,
when a turban of leaves appeared
on every tree, the Hat Lady came
with a fan of pins in her mouth
and pins in her sleeves,
the Hat Lady came—
that Saint Sebastian of pins,
to measure my mother's head.

I remember a hat of dove-grey felt
that settled like a bird
on the nest of my mother's hair.
I remember a pillbox that tilted
over one eye—pure Myrna Loy,
and a navy straw with cherries caught
at the brim that seemed real enough
for a child to want to pick.

THE HAT LADY 3. *Fred Astaire* and 21. *Myrna Loy:* popular film stars of the mid-twentieth century.

Last year when the chemicals
took my mother's hair, she wrapped
a towel around her head. And the Hat Lady came,
a bracelet of needles on each arm,
and led her to a place
where my father and grandfather waited,
head to bare head, and Death
winked at her and tipped his cap.

Linda Pastan (b. 1932)

265. Spinster

Now this particular girl
During a ceremonious April walk
With her latest suitor
Found herself, of a sudden, intolerably struck
By the birds' irregular babel
And the leaves' litter.

By this tumult afflicted, she
Observed her lover's gestures unbalance the air,
His gait stray uneven
Through a rank wilderness of fern and flower.
She judged petals in disarray,
The whole season, sloven.

How she longed for winter then! —
Scrupulously austere in its order
Of white and black
Ice and rock, each sentiment within border,
And heart's frosty discipline
Exact as a snowflake.

But here — a burgeoning
Unruly enough to pitch her five queenly wits
Into vulgar motley —
A treason not to be borne. Let idiots
Reel giddy in bedlam spring:
She withdrew neatly.

And round her house she set
Such a barricade of barb and check
Against mutinous weather
As no mere insurgent man could hope to break
With curse, fist, threat
Or love, either.

Sylvia Plath (1932–1963)

266. What is our life?

What is our life? A play of passion,
Our mirth the music of division;
Our mothers' wombs the tiring-houses be
Where we are dressed for this short comedy;
Heaven the judicious sharp spectator is
That sits and marks still° who doth act amiss; always
Our graves that hide us from the searching sun
Are like drawn curtains when the play is done.
Thus march we playing to our latest rest,
Only we die in earnest, that's no jest.

Sir Walter Ralegh (1552?–1618)

267. Bells for John Whiteside's Daughter

There was such speed in her little body,
And such lightness in her footfall,
It is no wonder her brown study
Astonishes us all.

Her wars were bruited in our high window.
We looked among orchard trees and beyond
Where she took arms against her shadow,
Or harried unto the pond

The lazy geese, like a snow cloud
Dripping their snow on the green grass,
Tricking and stopping, sleepy and proud,
Who cried in goose, Alas,

For the tireless heart within the little
Lady with rod that made them rise
From their noon apple-dreams and scuttle
Goose-fashion under the skies!

But now go the bells, and we are ready,
In one house we are sternly stopped
To say we are vexed at her brown study,
Lying so primly propped.

John Crowe Ransom (1888–1974)

WHAT IS OUR LIFE? 2. *music of division:* music dividing scenes of a play. 3. *tiring-houses:* dressing-rooms in a theater.

268. Turning Pro

There are just so many years
you can play amateur baseball
without turning pro
All of a sudden you realize
you're ten years older than
everybody in the dugout
and that the shortstop could
be your son

The front office complains
about your slowness in making
the line-up
They send down memos about
your faulty bunts and point out
how the runners are always faking
you out
"His ability to steal bases
has faded" they say
They say they can't convince
the accountant that there's such
a thing as "Old Time's Sake"
But just as the scribes were
beginning to write you
off
as a has-been on his last leg
You pulled out that fateful
shut-out
and the whistles went off
and the fireworks scorched a
747
And your name lit up the scoreboard
and the fans carried you on their
shoulders right out of the stadium
and into the majors

Ishmael Reed (b. 1938)

269. Nani

Sitting at her table, she serves
the sopa de arroz° to me — rice soup
instinctively, and I watch her,
the absolute *mamá*, and eat words

I might have had to say more
out of embarrassment. To speak,
now-foreign words I used to speak,
too, dribble down her mouth as she serves
me albóndigas.° No more   spiced meatballs
than a third are easy to me.
By the stove she does something with words
and looks at me only with her
back. I am full. I tell her
I taste the mint, and watch her speak
smiles at the stove. All my words
make her smile. Nani° never serves   granny
herself, she only watches me
with her skin, her hair. I ask for more.

I watch the *mamá* warming more
tortillas for me. I watch her
fingers in the flame for me.
Near her mouth, I see a wrinkle speak
of a man whose body serves
the ants like she serves me, then more words
from more wrinkles about children, words
about this and that, flowing more
easily from these other mouths. Each serves
as a tremendous string around her,
holding her together. They speak
nani was this and that to me
and I wonder just how much of me
will die with her, what were the words
I could have been, was. Her insides speak
through a hundred wrinkles, now, more
than she can bear, steel around her,
shouting, then, What is this thing she serves?

She asks me if I want more.
I own no words to stop her.
Even before I speak, she serves.

Alberto Ríos (b. 1952)

270. Mr. Flood's Party

Old Eben Flood, climbing alone one night
Over the hill between the town below
And the forsaken upland hermitage
That held as much as he should ever know

On earth again of home, paused warily.
The road was his with not a native near;
And Eben, having leisure, said aloud,
For no man else in Tilbury Town to hear:

"Well, Mr. Flood, we have the harvest moon
Again, and we may not have many more;
The bird is on the wing, the poet says,
And you and I have said it here before.
Drink to the bird." He raised up to the light
The jug that he had gone so far to fill,
And answered huskily: "Well, Mr. Flood,
Since you propose it, I believe I will."

Alone, as if enduring to the end
A valiant armor of scarred hopes outworn,
He stood there in the middle of the road
Like Roland's ghost winding a silent horn.
Below him, in the town among the trees,
Where friends of other days had honored him,
A phantom salutation of the dead
Rang thinly till old Eben's eyes were dim.

Then, as a mother lays her sleeping child
Down tenderly, fearing it may awake,
He set the jug down slowly at his feet
With trembling care, knowing that most things break;
And only when assured that on firm earth
It stood, as the uncertain lives of men
Assuredly did not, he paced away,
And with his hand extended paused again:

"Well, Mr. Flood, we have not met like this
In a long time; and many a change has come
To both of us, I fear, since last it was
We had a drop together. Welcome home!"
Convivially returning with himself,
Again he raised the jug up to the light;
And with an acquiescent quaver said:
"Well, Mr. Flood, if you insist, I might.

MR. FLOOD'S PARTY 11. *bird:* Mr. Flood is quoting from *The Rubáiyát of Omar Khayyám*, "The bird of Time . . . is on the wing." 20. *Roland:* hero of the French epic poem *The Song of Roland*. He died fighting a rearguard action for Charlemagne against the Moors in Spain; before his death he sounded a call for help on his famous horn, but the king's army arrived too late.

"Only a very little, Mr. Flood—
For auld lang syne. No more, sir; that will do."
So, for the time, apparently it did,
And Eben evidently thought so too;
For soon amid the silver loneliness
Of night he lifted up his voice and sang,
Secure, with only two moons listening,
Until the whole harmonious landscape rang—

"For auld lang syne." The weary throat gave out,
The last word wavered, and the song was done.
He raised again the jug regretfully
And shook his head, and was again alone.
There was not much that was ahead of him,
And there was nothing in the town below—
Where strangers would have shut the many doors
That many friends had opened long ago.

Edwin Arlington Robinson (1869–1935)

271. Richard Cory

Whenever Richard Cory went down town,
We people on the pavement looked at him:
He was a gentleman from sole to crown,
Clean favored, and imperially slim.

And he was always quietly arrayed,
And he was always human when he talked;
But still he fluttered pulses when he said,
"Good-morning," and he glittered when he walked.

And he was rich—yes, richer than a king—
And admirably schooled in every grace:
In fine, we thought that he was everything
To make us wish that we were in his place.

So on we worked, and waited for the light,
And went without the meat, and cursed the bread;
And Richard Cory, one calm summer night,
Went home and put a bullet through his head.

Edwin Arlington Robinson (1869–1935)

272. I knew a woman

I knew a woman, lovely in her bones,
When small birds sighed, she would sigh back at them;
Ah, when she moved, she moved more ways than one:
The shapes a bright container can contain!
Of her choice virtues only gods should speak,
Or English poets who grew up on Greek
(I'd have them sing in chorus, cheek to cheek).

How well her wishes went! She stroked my chin,
She taught me Turn, and Counter-turn, and Stand;
She taught me Touch, that undulant white skin;
I nibbled meekly from her proffered hand;
She was the sickle; I, poor I, the rake,
Coming behind her for her pretty sake
(But what prodigious mowing we did make).

Love likes a gander, and adores a goose:
Her full lips pursed, the errant note to seize;
She played it quick, she played it light and loose;
My eyes, they dazzled at her flowing knees;
Her several parts could keep a pure repose,
Or one hip quiver with a mobile nose
(She moved in circles, and those circles moved).

Let seed be grass, and grass turn into hay:
I'm martyr to a motion not my own;
What's freedom for? To know eternity.
I swear she cast a shadow white as stone.
But who would count eternity in days?
These old bones live to learn her wanton ways:
(I measure time by how a body sways).

Theodore Roethke (1908–1963)

273. Fear no more

Fear no more the heat o' the sun,
   Nor the furious winter's rages;
Thou thy worldly task hast done,
   Home art gone, and ta'en thy wages.
Golden lads and girls all must,
As chimney-sweepers, come to dust.

Fear no more the frown o' the great;
Thou art past the tyrant's stroke;
Care no more to clothe and eat;
To thee the reed is as the oak.
The scepter, learning, physic,° must — art of healing
All follow this, and come to dust.

Fear no more the lightning-flash,
Nor the all-dreaded thunder-stone;° — thunderbolt
Fear not slander, censure rash;
Thou hast finished joy and moan.
All lovers young, all lovers must
Consign to thee,° and come to dust. — yield to your condition

William Shakespeare (1564–1616)

274. Let me not to the marriage of true minds

Let me not to the marriage of true minds
Admit impediments. Love is not love
Which alters when it alteration finds,
Or bends with the remover to remove.
O no! it is an ever-fixèd mark
That looks on tempests and is never shaken;
It is the star to every wandering bark,
Whose worth's unknown, although his height be taken.
Love's not Time's fool, though rosy lips and cheeks
Within his bending sickle's compass come;
Love alters not with his brief hours and weeks,
But bears it out even to the edge of doom.
If this be error and upon me proved,
I never writ, nor no man ever loved.

William Shakespeare (1564–1616)

275. My mistress' eyes

My mistress' eyes are nothing like the sun;
Coral is far more red than her lips' red:
If snow be white, why then her breasts are dun;
If hairs be wires, black wires grow on her head.
I have seen roses damasked,° red and white, — of different colors
But no such roses see I in her cheeks;
And in some perfumes is there more delight
Than in the breath that from my mistress reeks.° — exhales

I love to hear her speak, yet well I know
That music hath a far more pleasing sound:
I grant I never saw a goddess go,—
My mistress, when she walks, treads on the ground.
And yet, by heaven, I think my love as rare
As any she belied with false compare.

William Shakespeare (1564–1616)

276. The Fly

O hideous little bat, the size of snot,
With polyhedral eye and shabby clothes,
To populate the stinking cat you walk
The promontory of the dead man's nose,
Climb with the fine leg of a Duncan-Phyfe
    The smoking mountains of my food
        And in a comic mood
    In mid-air take to bed a wife.

Riding and riding with your filth of hair
On gluey foot or wing, forever coy,
Hot from the compost and green sweet decay,
Sounding your buzzer like an urchin toy—
You dot all whiteness with diminutive stool,
    In the tight belly of the dead
        Burrow with hungry head
    And inlay maggots like a jewel.

At your approach the great horse stomps and paws
Bringing the hurricane of his heavy tail;
Shod in disease you dare to kiss my hand
Which sweeps against you like an angry flail;
Still you return, return, trusting your wing
    To draw you from the hunter's reach
        That learns to kill to teach
    Disorder to the tinier thing.

My peace is your disaster. For your death
Children like spiders cup their pretty hands
And wives resort to chemistry of war.
In fens of sticky paper and quicksands
You glue yourself to death. Where you are stuck
    You struggle hideously and beg,
        You amputate your leg
    Imbedded in the amber muck.

But I, a man, must swat you with my hate,
Slap you across the air and crush your flight,
Must mangle with my shoe and smear your blood,
Expose your little guts pasty and white,
Knock your head sidewise like a drunkard's hat,
  Pin your wings under like a crow's,
    Tear off your flimsy clothes
  And beat you as one beats a rat.

Then like Gargantua I stride among
The corpses strewn like raisins in the dust,
The broken bodies of the narrow dead
That catch the throat with fingers of disgust.
I sweep. One gyrates like a top and falls
  And stunned, stone blind, and deaf
    Buzzes its frightful F
  And dies between three cannibals.

Karl Shapiro (b. 1913)

277. Shut In

Like many of us, born too late,
(like all of us, fenced in by fate),
    the late October fly
    will fondly live and die

insensible of the allure
of carrion or cow manure.
    Withindoors day and night,
    propelled by appetite,

he circles with approving hums
a morning's manna-fall of crumbs
    hoping to find a smear
    of jelly somewhere near.

In such an easeful habitat
while autumn wanes he waxes fat
    and languorous, but not
    enough to let the swat

of hasty, rolled-up magazine
eliminate him from the scene.
    Outside, the air is chill.
    Inside, he's hard to kill.

Patrolling with adhesive feet
the ceiling under which we eat,
    he captures at a glance
    the slightest threat or chance,

and flaunts the facets of his eyes
that make him prince of household spies.
    And as he watches, we,
    if we look up, will see

a life of limits, like our own,
enclosed within a temperate zone,
    not harsh, not insecure,
    no challenge to endure,

but yet, with every buzz of need,
by trifles running out of speed.
    One day he will be gone.
    Then the real cold comes on.

Robert B. Shaw (b. 1947)

278. Powwow

(Tama Reservation, Iowa, 1949)

They all see the same movies.
        They shuffle on one leg,
                Scuffing the dust up,
        Shuffle on the other.
They are all the same:
        A Sioux dance to the spirits,
        A war dance by four Chippewa,
        A Dakota dance for rain.
                We wonder why we came.
Even tricked out in the various braveries—
        Black buffalo tassels, beadwork, or the brilliant
        Feathers at the head, at the buttocks—
Even in long braids and the gaudy face paints,
                They all dance with their eyes turned
        Inward, like a woman nursing
A sick child she already knows
        Will die. For the time, she nurses it
        All the same. The loudspeakers shriek;
                We leave our bleacher seats to wander
        Among the wickiups and lean-tos

In a search for hot dogs. The Indians
Are already packing; have
Resumed green dungarees and khaki,
Castoff combat issues of World War II.
(Only the Iroquois do not come here;
They work in structural steel; they have a contract
Building the United Nations
And Air Force installations for our future wars.)
These, though, have dismantled their hot-dog stand
And have to drive all night
To jobs in truck stops and all-night filling stations.
We ask directions and
They scuttle away from us like moths.
Past the trailers,
Beyond us, one tepee is still shining
Over all the rest. Inside, circled by a ring
Of children, in the glare
Of one bare bulb, a shrunken fierce-eyed man
Squat at his drum, all bones and parchment,
While his dry hands move
On the drumhead, always drumming, always
Raising his toothless, drawn jaw to the light
Like a young bird drinking, like a chained dog,
Howling his tribe's song for the restless young
Who wander in and out.
Words of such great age,
Not even he remembers what they mean.
We tramp back to our car,
Then nearly miss the highway, squinting
Through red and yellow splatterings on the windshield,
The garish and beautiful remains
Of grasshoppers and dragonflies
That go with us, that do not live again.

W. D. Snodgrass (b. 1926)

279. Small Town with One Road

We could be here. This is the valley
And its black strip of highway, big-eyed
With rabbits that won't get across.
Kids could make it, though.
They leap barefoot to the store—
Sweetness on their tongues, red stain of laughter.
They are the spectators of fun.

Hot dimes fall from their palms,
Chinks of light, and they eat
Candies all the way home
Where there's a dog for each hand,
Cats, chickens in the yard.
A pot bangs and water runs in the kitchen.
Beans, they think, and beans it will be,
Brown soup that's muscle for the field
And crippled steps to a ladder
Okie or Mexican, Jew that got lost,
It's a hard life where the sun looks.
The cotton gin stands tall in the money dream
And the mill is a paycheck for
A wife—and perhaps my wife
Who, when she was a girl,
Boxed peaches and plums, hoed
Papa's field that wavered like a mirage
That wouldn't leave. We could go back.
I could lose my job, this easy one
That's only words, and pick up a shovel,
Hoe, broom that takes it away.
Worry is my daughter's story.
She touches my hand. We suck roadside
Snowcones in the shade
And look about. Behind sunglasses
I see where I stood: a brown kid
Getting across. "He's like me,"
I tell my daughter, and she stops her mouth.
He looks both ways and then leaps
Across the road where riches
Happen on a red tongue.

Gary Soto (b. 1952)

280. Ettrick

When we first rade down Ettrick,
Our bridles were ringing, our hearts were dancing,
The waters were singing, the sun was glancing,
An' blithely our voices rang out thegither,°   together
As we brushed the dew frae° the blooming heather,   from
    When we first rade down Ettrick.

ETTRICK Ettrick is a small village near Selkirk in the "Border" district of southern Scotland, an area famed for its folk ballads.

When we next rade down Ettrick,
The day was dying, the wild birds calling,
The wind was sighing, the leaves were falling,
An' silent an' weary, but closer thegither,
We urged our steeds thro' the faded heather,
When we next rade down Ettrick.

When I last rade down Ettrick,
The winds were shifting, the storm was waking,
The snow was drifting, my heart was breaking,
For we never again were to ride thegither,
In sun or storm on the mountain heather,
When I last rade down Ettrick.

Alicia Ann Spottiswood ("Lady John Scott") (1810–1900)

281. The Beating

The first blow caught me sideways, my jaw
Shifted. The second beat my skull against my
Brain. I raised my arm against the third.
Downward my wrist fell crooked. But the sliding

Flood of sense across the ribs caught in
My lungs. I fell for a long time,
One knee bending. The fourth blow balanced me.
I doubled at the kick against my belly.

The fifth was light. I hardly felt the
Sting. And down, breaking against my side, my
Thighs, my head. My eyes burst closed, my
Mouth the thick blood curds moved through. There

Were no more lights. I was flying. The
Wind, the place I lay, the silence.
My call came to a groan. Hands touched
My wrist. Disappeared. Something fell over me.

Now this white room tortures my eye.
The bed too soft to hold my breath,
Slung in plaster, caged in wood.
Shapes surround me.

No blow! No blow!
They only ask the thing I turn
Inside the black ball of my mind,
The one white thought.

Ann Stanford (1916–1987)

282. Comfort

Somewhere I read that high and low notes
disappear from the human voice on the telephone,
too expensive to send. But I'd pay
for the lost inflection in my mother's call:
She says my father wakes up sweating,
the whole front of his pajamas sopping wet,
and maybe her tone could have told me
don't worry, or isn't this strange?
But she hurries on. I'm afraid to ask why
for it might mean something dark she's avoiding,
the side effects of his new drug,
or the final shape of their marriage.
This far away I forget the ordinary
habits that surround bad news; no doubt
my father, after he swallows his pills for angina,
still reads Marcus Aurelius.
I remember the worn copy
underneath the seat of his armchair,
and the pencil marks below *mildness of temper,*
cheerfulness and *sobriety in all things.*
I think he puts the book down sooner nowadays
which may mean that he knows it by heart
or even that he's learned to hear
the low moan, rising from the Emperor's lips,
which the black letters sternly hide.

Maura Stanton (b. 1946)

283. Dandelions

You won't find them in places where society goes,
Like flower shows.
Their affections
Run more to junk yards and other low-rent sections—
Not flowers to make perfume of or wear.
People see them in their lawns and swear.
Cows eat them and their milk tastes funny.
Bees make them into honey.
The farmer turns them under with his plow,
Or makes them into wine if he knows how.
They hang around street corners on pipestem legs,
And taste good in salad with vinegar and hard-boiled eggs.

COMFORT 16. *Marcus Aurelius:* second-century Roman Emperor and Stoic philosopher.

In broken bricks and cinders they
Do well. Also in clay.
Hills they prefer to valleys.
They like to grow
Where kids go,
In vacant lots and alleys.
Little girls use them for various things,
Such as money. They put them on strings,
Or hold them under their chins to see if they like butter.
Golfers knock their heads off with a putter.
You can split them with your tongue to make long curls,
Which small comedians wear to look like girls.
They hug the earth where lawnmowers mow,
And so survive.
Elsewhere they stretch taller.
In areas where nothing else will grow
They thrive—
More like the sun than sunflowers,
Only smaller.
They can't be stopped although you hoe and spray them;
The best that you can hope is to delay them.
No skirmish ever proves to be the last;
No victory quite manages to stay won.
They seem to propagate about as fast
As a middle-aged gardener can run.
There isn't any more that you can say
About these tawny, undesired plants
(Teeth of the lion is what they're called in France)
Except that certain things are here to stay,
Things that don't pertain to public good,
Such as firecrackers, unplanned parenthood,
Snowballs, or a bedtime story—
Things you'd never dream
Of including in a modern social scheme.
Dandelions fall in this category.

Will D. Stanton (b. 1918)

284. Disillusionment of Ten O'Clock

The houses are haunted
By white night-gowns.
None are green,
Or purple with green rings,

Or green with yellow rings,
Or yellow with blue rings.
None of them are strange,
With socks of lace
And beaded ceintures.° sashes
People are not going
To dream of baboons and periwinkles.
Only, here and there, an old sailor,
Drunk and asleep in his boots,
Catches tigers
In red weather.

Wallace Stevens (1879–1955)

285. The Poems of Our Climate

Clear water in a brilliant bowl,
Pink and white carnations. The light
In the room more like a snowy air,
Reflecting snow. A newly-fallen snow
At the end of winter when afternoons return.
Pink and white carnations—one desires
So much more than that. The day itself
Is simplified: a bowl of white,
Cold, a cold porcelain, low and round,
With nothing more than the carnations there.

Say even that this complete simplicity
Stripped one of all one's torments, concealed
The evilly compounded, vital I
And made it fresh in a world of white,
A world of clear water, brilliant-edged,
Still one would want more, one would need more,
More than a world of white and snowy scents.

There would still remain the never-resting mind,
So that one would want to escape, come back
To what had been so long composed.
The imperfect is our paradise.
Note that, in this bitterness, delight,
Since the imperfect is so hot in us,
Lies in flawed words and stubborn sounds.

Wallace Stevens (1879–1955)

286. The Snow Man

One must have a mind of winter
To regard the frost and the boughs
Of the pine-trees crusted with snow;

And have been cold a long time
To behold the junipers shagged with ice,
The spruces rough in the distant glitter

Of the January sun; and not to think
Of any misery in the sound of the wind,
In the sound of a few leaves,

Which is the sound of the land
Full of the same wind
That is blowing in the same bare place

For the listener, who listens in the snow,
And, nothing himself, beholds
Nothing that is not there and the nothing that is.

Wallace Stevens (1879–1955)

287. On Its Way

Orange on its way
to ash. Anger that a night

will quench. Passion
in its honey swell

pumpkin-plump before the rot.
Bush of fire

everywhere. Fur of hillside
running flame. Rush of heat

to rosehip cheek. Ripeness
on its way to frost.

Glare of blood
before the black. Foxquick

pulse. The sun a den.
Heartkill. And the gold

a gun. It is death
that tints the leaves.

May Swenson (1919–1989)

288. A Description of the Morning

Now hardly here and there a hackney-coach
Appearing, showed the ruddy morn's approach.
Now Betty from her master's bed had flown,
And softly stole to discompose her own.
The slip-shod 'prentice from his master's door
Had pared the dirt, and sprinkled round the floor.
Now Moll had whirled her mop with dextrous airs,
Prepared to scrub the entry and the stairs.
The youth with broomy stumps began to trace
The kennel's edge, where wheels had worn the place.
The small-coal man was heard with cadence deep,
Till drowned in shriller notes of chimney-sweep.
Duns at his lordship's gate began to meet;
And Brickdust Moll had screamed through half the street.
The turnkey now his flock returning sees,
Duly let out a-nights to steal for fees.
The watchful bailiffs take their silent stands;
And schoolboys lag with satchels in their hands.

Jonathan Swift (1667–1745)

289. From *In Memoriam A. H. H.*

Dark house, by which once more I stand
Here in the long unlovely street,
Doors, where my heart was used to beat
So quickly, waiting for a hand,

A hand that can be clasped no more—
Behold me, for I cannot sleep,
And like a guilty thing I creep
At earliest morning to the door.

He is not here; but far away
The noise of life begins again,
And ghastly through the drizzling rain
On the bald street breaks the blank day.

Alfred, Lord Tennyson (1809–1892)

A DESCRIPTION OF THE MORNING 9. *youth:* he is apparently searching for salvage. 10. *kennel:* gutter. 14. *Brickdust:* red-complexioned.

IN MEMORIAM A. H. H. This poem and poem No. 290 are part of a sequence composed after the death at the age of twenty-two of the poet's closest friend, the fiancé of his sister.

290. From *In Memoriam A. H. H.*

The time draws near the birth of Christ:
    The moon is hid; the night is still;
    The Christmas bells from hill to hill
Answer each other in the mist.

Four voices of four hamlets round,
    From far and near, on mead and moor,
    Swell out and fail, as if a door
Were shut between me and the sound.

Each voice four changes on the wind,
    That now dilate, and now decrease,
    Peace and goodwill, goodwill and peace,
Peace and goodwill, to all mankind.

This year I slept and woke with pain,
    I almost wished no more to wake,
    And that my hold on life would break
Before I heard those bells again:

But they my troubled spirit rule,
    For they controlled me when a boy;
    They bring me sorrow touched with joy,
The merry merry bells of Yule.

Alfred, Lord Tennyson (1809–1892)

291. Do Not Go Gentle into That Good Night

Do not go gentle into that good night,
Old age should burn and rave at close of day;
Rage, rage against the dying of the light.

Though wise men at their end know dark is right,
Because their words had forked no lightning they
Do not go gentle into that good night.

Good men, the last wave by, crying how bright
Their frail deeds might have danced in a green bay,
Rage, rage against the dying of the light.

Wild men who caught and sang the sun in flight,
And learn, too late, they grieved it on its way
Do not go gentle into that good night.

Grave men, near death, who see with blinding sight
Blind eyes could blaze like meteors and be gay,
Rage, rage against the dying of the light.

And you, my father, there on the sad height,
Curse, bless, me now with your fierce tears, I pray.
Do not go gentle into that good night.
Rage, rage against the dying of the light.

Dylan Thomas (1914–1953)

292. Fern Hill

Now as I was young and easy under the apple boughs
About the lilting house and happy as the grass was green,
  The night above the dingle starry,
    Time let me hail and climb
  Golden in the heydays of his eyes,
And honored among wagons I was prince of the apple towns
And once below a time I lordly had the trees and leaves
    Trail with daisies and barley
  Down the rivers of the windfall light.

And as I was green and carefree, famous among the barns
About the happy yard and singing as the farm was home,
  In the sun that is young once only,
    Time let me play and be
  Golden in the mercy of his means,
And green and golden I was huntsman and herdsman, the calves
Sang to my horn, the foxes on the hills barked clear and cold,
    And the sabbath rang slowly
  In the pebbles of the holy streams.

All the sun long it was running, it was lovely, the hay
Fields high as the house, the tunes from the chimneys, it was air
  And playing, lovely and watery
    And fire green as grass.
  And nightly under the simple stars
As I rode to sleep the owls were bearing the farm away,

All the moon long I heard, blessed among stables, the nightjars
  Flying with the ricks, and the horses
    Flashing into the dark.

And then to awake, and the farm, like a wanderer white
With the dew, come back, the cock on his shoulder: it was all
  Shining, it was Adam and maiden,
    The sky gathered again
  And the sun grew round that very day.
So it must have been after the birth of the simple light
In the first, spinning place, the spellbound horses walking warm
  Out of the whinnying green stable
    On to the fields of praise.

And honored among foxes and pheasants by the gay house
Under the new made clouds and happy as the heart was long,
  In the sun born over and over,
    I ran my heedless ways,
  My wishes raced through the house high hay
And nothing I cared, at my sky blue trades, that time allows
In all his tuneful turning so few and such morning songs
  Before the children green and golden
    Follow him out of grace,

Nothing I cared, in the lamb white days, that time would take me
Up to the swallow thronged loft by the shadow of my hand,
  In the moon that is always rising,
    Nor that riding to sleep
  I should hear him fly with the high fields
And wake to the farm forever fled from the childless land.
Oh as I was young and easy in the mercy of his means,
    Time held me green and dying
  Though I sang in my chains like the sea.

Dylan Thomas (1914–1953)

293. Reapers

Black reapers with the sound of steel on stones
Are sharpening scythes. I see them place the hones
In their hip-pockets as a thing that's done,
And start their silent swinging, one by one.

Black horses drive a mower through the weeds,
And there, a field rat, startled, squealing bleeds,
His belly close to ground. I see the blade,
Blood-stained, continue cutting weeds and shade.

Jean Toomer (1894–1967)

294. The Virgins

Down the dead streets of sun-stoned Frederiksted,
the first free port to die for tourism,
strolling at funeral pace, I am reminded
of life not lost to the American dream;
but my small-islander's simplicities
can't better our new empire's civilized
exchange of cameras, watches, perfumes, brandies
for the good life, so cheaply underpriced
that only the crime rate is on the rise
in streets blighted with sun, stone arches
and plazas blown dry by the hysteria
of rumor. A condominium drowns
in vacancy; its bargains are dusted,
but only a jeweled housefly drones
over the bargains. The roulettes spin
rustily to the wind—the vigorous trade
that every morning would begin afresh
by revving up green water round the pierhead
heading for where the banks of silver thresh.

Derek Walcott (b. 1930)

295. Divorcée

The sentence—Life without a prison—struck
Her friends as stern and undeserved. Instead,
She merited some tighter bond, the luck
Of finding someone else whose heart and bed

THE VIRGINS 1. *Frederiksted:* chief port of St. Croix, largest of the American Virgin Islands, a free port where goods can be bought without payment of customs duties and therefore at bargain prices. The economy of St. Croix, once based on sugar cane, is now chiefly dependent on tourism. Like the other American Virgin Islands, St. Croix has suffered from uncontrolled growth, building booms, unevenly distributed prosperity, destruction of natural beauty, and pollution. 5. *my . . . simplicities:* The poet is a native of St. Lucia in the West Indies. 16. *trade:* cf. trade wind.

Were still in need, like hers, of rumpling then
Of smoothing down together. Children fled
At their appointed hour and left her men,
And time, but not a man. She grew to dread
The sharp metallic dropping of her lock
On vacant evenings, came to count the ticks
Of leaky faucets or the clanging shock
Of radiators as the ratchet clicks
Of no return inside a wound-down life:
Unneeded mother now, no more a wife.

C. Webster Wheelock (b. 1939)

296. When I Heard the Learn'd Astronomer

When I heard the learn'd astronomer,
When the proofs, the figures, were ranged in columns before me,
When I was shown the charts and diagrams, to add, divide,
  and measure them,
When I sitting heard the astronomer where he lectured with much
  applause in the lecture-room,
How soon unaccountable I became tired and sick,
Till rising and gliding out I wandered off by myself,
In the mystical moist night-air, and from time to time,
Looked up in perfect silence at the stars.

Walt Whitman (1819–1892)

297. The Writer

In her room at the prow of the house
Where light breaks, and the windows are tossed with linden,
My daughter is writing a story.

I pause in the stairwell, hearing
From her shut door a commotion of typewriter-keys
Like a chain hauled over a gunwale.

Young as she is, the stuff
Of her life is a great cargo, and some of it heavy:
I wish her a lucky passage.

But now it is she who pauses,
As if to reject my thought and its easy figure.
A stillness greatens, in which

The whole house seems to be thinking,
And then she is at it again with a bunched clamor
Of strokes, and again is silent.

I remember the dazed starling
Which was trapped in that very room, two years ago;
How we stole in, lifted a sash

And retreated, not to affright it;
And how for a helpless hour, through the crack of the door,
We watched the sleek, wild, dark

And iridescent creature
Batter against the brilliance, drop like a glove
To the hard floor, or the desk-top,

And wait then, humped and bloody,
For the wits to try it again; and how our spirits
Rose when, suddenly sure,

It lifted off from a chair-back,
Beating a smooth course for the right window
And clearing the sill of the world.

It is always a matter, my darling,
Of life or death, as I had forgotten. I wish
What I wished you before, but harder.

Richard Wilbur (b. 1921)

298. Poem

As the cat
climbed over
the top of

the jamcloset
first the right
forefoot

carefully
then the hind
stepped down

into the pit of
the empty
flowerpot

William Carlos Williams (1883–1963)

299. To Waken an Old Lady

Old age is
a flight of small
cheeping birds
skimming
bare trees
above a snow glaze.
Gaining and failing
they are buffeted
by a dark wind—
But what?
On harsh weedstalks
the flock has rested,
the snow
is covered with broken
seedhusks
and the wind tempered
by a shrill
piping of plenty.

William Carlos Williams (1883–1963)

300. Eggs

Morning broke like an egg
on the kitchen floor and I hated
them, too, eggs, how easily they broke
and ran, yellow insides spilling out, oozing

and staining, the flawed
beneath what's beautiful. And I hated
my father, the one cock
in the henhouse, who laid the plate

on the table and made me
eat, who told me not to get up
until I was done, every bite. And I hated
how I gagged and cried, day

after day, until there was no time
left and he'd give in and I'd go off
to school like that, again, hungry.
But why did I hate eggs

so much? Freud, old banty rooster, who knew
a thing or two about such things, might say
I hated myself, hated the egg
growing in secret deep inside my body,

the secret about to be spilled
to the world, and maybe I did.
Or maybe it's the way the egg
repeats itself again and again, a perfect

oval every time, the way I found myself,
furious, standing by my own child's bed
holding a belt, and hit, and saw her face
dissolve in a yolk. But that doesn't say

enough about why we hoard
our hurts like golden eggs and foolishly
wait for them to hatch, why
we faced each other across the table,

my father and I, and fought
our battles over eggs and never fought
with them, never once picked up
those perfect ovals and sent them singing

back and forth across the room, the spell
broken like shells, until we were
covered with them, our faces golden
and laughing, both of us beautiful and flawed.

Susan Wood (b. 1946)

301. Portrait

It was a heartfelt game, when it began—
polish and cook and sew and mend, contrive,
move between sink and stove, keep flower-beds weeded—
all her love needed was that it was needed,
and merely living kept the blood alive.

Now an old habit leads from sink to stove,
mends and keeps clean the house that looks like home,
and waits in hunger dressed to look like love
for the calm return of those who, when they come,
remind her: this was a game, when it began.

Judith Wright (b. 1915)

302. Sailing to Byzantium

That is no country for old men. The young
In one another's arms, birds in the trees
—Those dying generations—at their song,
The salmon-falls, the mackerel-crowded seas,
Fish, flesh, or fowl, commend all summer long
Whatever is begotten, born, and dies.
Caught in that sensual music all neglect
Monuments of unaging intellect.

An aged man is but a paltry thing,
A tattered coat upon a stick, unless
Soul clap its hands and sing, and louder sing
For every tatter in its mortal dress,
Nor is there singing school but studying
Monuments of its own magnificence;
And therefore I have sailed the seas and come
To the holy city of Byzantium.

O sages standing in God's holy fire
As in the gold mosaic of a wall,
Come from the holy fire, perne° in a gyre, spin
And be the singing-masters of my soul.
Consume my heart away; sick with desire
And fastened to a dying animal
It knows not what it is; and gather me
Into the artifice of eternity.

Once out of nature I shall never take
My bodily form from any natural thing,
But such a form as Grecian goldsmiths make
Of hammered gold and gold enameling
To keep a drowsy Emperor awake;
Or set upon a golden bough to sing
To lords and ladies of Byzantium
Of what is past, or passing, or to come.

William Butler Yeats (1865–1939)

SAILING TO BYZANTIUM *Byzantium:* Ancient eastern capital of the Roman Empire; in this poem symbolically a holy city of the imagination. 1. *That:* Ireland, or the ordinary sensual world. 27–31. *such . . . Byzantium:* The Byzantine Emperor Theophilus had made for himself mechanical golden birds which sang upon the branches of a golden tree.

303. The Second Coming

Turning and turning in the widening gyre
The falcon cannot hear the falconer;
Things fall apart; the center cannot hold;
Mere anarchy is loosed upon the world,
The blood-dimmed tide is loosed, and everywhere
The ceremony of innocence is drowned;
The best lack all conviction, while the worst
Are full of passionate intensity.

Surely some revelation is at hand;
Surely the Second Coming is at hand.
The Second Coming! Hardly are those words out
When a vast image out of *Spiritus Mundi*
Troubles my sight: somewhere in sands of the desert
A shape with lion body and the head of a man,
A gaze blank and pitiless as the sun,
Is moving its slow thighs, while all about it
Reel shadows of the indignant desert birds.
The darkness drops again; but now I know
That twenty centuries of stony sleep
Were vexed to nightmare by a rocking cradle,
And what rough beast, its hour come round at last,
Slouches towards Bethlehem to be born?

William Butler Yeats (1865–1939)

304. The Wild Swans at Coole

The trees are in their autumn beauty,
The woodland paths are dry,
Under the October twilight the water
Mirrors a still sky;
Upon the brimming water among the stones
Are nine-and-fifty swans.

THE SECOND COMING In Christian legend the prophesied "Second Coming" may refer either to Christ or to Antichrist. Yeats believed in a cyclical theory of history in which one historical era would be replaced by an opposite kind of era every two thousand years. Here, the anarchy in the world following World War I (the poem was written in 1919) heralds the end of the Christian era. 12. *Spiritus Mundi:* the racial memory or collective unconscious mind of mankind (literally, world spirit).

THE WILD SWANS AT COOLE Coole Park, in County Galway, Ireland, was the estate of Lady Augusta Gregory, Yeats's patroness and friend. Beginning in 1897, Yeats regularly summered there for many years.

The nineteenth autumn has come upon me
Since I first made my count;
I saw, before I had well finished,
All suddenly mount
And scatter wheeling in great broken rings
Upon their clamorous wings.

I have looked upon those brilliant creatures,
And now my heart is sore,
All's changed since I, hearing at twilight,
The first time on this shore,
The bell-beat of their wings above my head,
Trod with a lighter tread.

Unwearied still, lover by lover,
They paddle in the cold
Companionable streams or climb the air;
Their hearts have not grown old;
Passion or conquest, wander where they will,
Attend upon them still.

But now they drift on the still water,
Mysterious, beautiful;
Among what rushes will they build,
By what lake's edge or pool
Delight men's eyes when I awake some day
To find they have flown away?

William Butler Yeats (1865–1939)

APPENDIX

Writing about Poetry

WRITING ABOUT POETRY

I. Why Write about Literature?

Written assignments in a literature class have two purposes: (1) to give you additional practice in writing clearly and persuasively, and (2) to deepen your understanding of literary works by leading you to read and think about a few works more searchingly than you might otherwise do. But these two purposes are private. To be successful, your paper must have a public purpose as well: it should be written to enlighten others besides yourself. Even if no one else ever reads your paper, you should never treat it as a private note to your instructor. You should write every paper as if it were intended for publication.

II. For Whom Do You Write?

The audience for whom you write will govern both the content and expression of your paper. You need to know something about your readers' backgrounds—national, racial, social, religious—and be able to make intelligent guesses about their knowledge, interests, and previous reading. In writing about George Herbert's "Peace" (page 88) for a Hindu audience, you would need to include explanations of Christian belief and biblical stories that would be unnecessary for a western European or American audience. But the most crucial question about an audience is, *Has it read the work you are writing about?* The book reviewer in your Sunday paper generally writes about a newly published book that the audience has not read. A reviewer's purpose is to let readers know something of what the book is about and to give them some notion of whether they will enjoy or profit from reading it. At an opposite extreme, the scholar writing in a specialized scholarly journal can generally assume an audience that *has* read the work, that has a knowledge of previous interpretations of the work, and that is familiar with other works in its period or genre. The scholar's purpose, not infrequently, is to persuade this audience that some new information or some new way of looking at the work appreciably deepens or alters its meaning or significance.

Clearly, essays written for such different audiences and with such different purposes differ considerably in content, organization, and style. Book reviewers reviewing a new novel will include a general idea of its plot while being careful not to reveal the outcome. Scholars will assume that readers already know the plot and will have no compunction about discussing its outcome. Reviewers will try to write interestingly and engagingly about the novel and to persuade readers that they have valid grounds for their opinions of its worth, but their manner will generally be informal. Scholars are more interested in presenting a cogent argument, logically arranged, and solidly based on evidence. They will be more formal, and may use critical terms and refer to related works that would be unfamiliar to nonspecialized readers. In documentation the two types of essays will be quite different. Reviewers' only documentation is normally the identification of the novel's title, author, publisher, and price, at the top of the review. For other information and opinions they hope that a reader will rely on their intelligence, knowledge, and judgment. Scholars, on the other hand, may furnish an elaborate array of citations of other sources of information, allowing the reader to verify the accuracy or basis of any important part of their argument. Scholars expect to be challenged, and they see to it that all parts of their arguments are buttressed.

For whom, then, should *you* write? Unless your instructor stipulates (or you request) a different audience, the best plan is to assume that you are writing for the other members of your class. Pretend that your class publishes a journal of which it also constitutes the readership. Your instructor is the editor and determines editorial policy. If you write on a poem that has been assigned for class reading, you assume that your audience is familiar with it. (This kind of paper is generally of the greatest educational value, for it is most open to challenge and class discussion, and places on you a heavier burden of proof.) If you compare an assigned poem with one that has not been assigned, you must gauge what portion of your audience is familiar with the unassigned poem, and proceed accordingly. If the unassigned poem is a later sonnet in the Shakespearean form, which you are comparing to one by Shakespeare, you will not need to provide a definition of the rime scheme of the form, for you can assume that *this* audience is familiar with the form of a sonnet; but you cannot assume familiarity with all of the sonnets of Shakespeare. You know that, as members of the same class, your readers have certain backgrounds and interests in common and are at comparable levels of education. Anything you know about your audience may be important for how you write your paper and what you put in it.

III. Choosing a Topic

As editor of this imaginary publication, your instructor is responsible for the nature of its contents. Instructors may be very specific in their assignments, or they may be very general, inviting you to submit a paper on any subject within a broadly defined area of interest. They will also have editorial policies concerning length of papers, preparation of manuscripts, and deadlines for submission (all of which should be meticulously heeded). Instructors may further specify whether the paper should be entirely the work of your own critical thinking, or whether it is to be an investigative assignment—that is, one involving research into what other writers have written concerning your subject and the use of their findings, where relevant, to help you support your own conclusions.

Let us consider four kinds of papers you might write: (1) papers that focus on a single poem; (2) papers of comparison and contrast; (3) papers on a number of poems by a single author; and (4) papers on a number of poems having some feature other than authorship in common.

1. Papers that Focus on a Single Poem

If your assignment is a specific one (Who are the speakers in Mari Evans's "When in Rome" [page 31] and what is the relationship between them? What does personification add to Tennyson's "The Eagle" [page 5]? How is structure fitted to form in Shakespeare's "That time of year" [page 219]?), your task is clear-cut. You have only to read the selection carefully (obviously more than once), formulate your answer, and support it with corroborating evidence from within the text as cogently and convincingly as possible. In order to convince your readers that your answer is the best one, you will need to examine and account for apparently contrary evidence as well as clearly supportive evidence; otherwise skeptical readers, reluctant to change their minds, might simply refer to "important points" that you have "overlooked."

Specific questions like these, when they are central to the poem and may be a matter of dispute, make excellent topics for papers. You may discover them for yourself when you disagree with a classmate about the interpretation of a poem. The study questions following many of the selections in this anthology frequently suggest topics of this kind.

If your assignment is more general, and if you are given some choice as to what poem you wish to write on, it is usually best to choose one you enjoyed, whether or not you entirely understood it. (You are more likely to write a good paper on a selection you liked than on one you disliked, and you should arrive at a fuller understanding of it while thinking through your paper.) You must then decide what kind of paper you will write, taking into account the length and kind of selection you have chosen and the amount of space at your disposal. Probably your paper will be either an *explication* or an *analysis*.

An *explication* (literally, an "unfolding") has been defined as "an examination of a work of literature for a knowledge of each part, for the relations of these parts to each other, and for their relations to the whole."* It is a detailed elucidation of a work, sometimes line by line or word by word, which is interested not only in *what* that work means but in *how* it means what it means. It thus considers all relevant aspects of a work—speaker, connotative words and double meanings, images, figurative language, allusions, form, structure, sound, rhythm—and discusses, if not all of these, at least the most important. (There is no such thing as exhausting the meanings and the ways to those meanings in a really rich piece of literature, and the explicator must settle for something less than completeness.) Explication follows from what we sometimes call "close reading"—looking at a piece of writing, as it were, through a magnifying glass.

Clearly, the kinds of literature for which an explication is appropriate are limited. First, the work must be rich enough to repay the kind of close attention demanded. One would not think of explicating "Thirty days hath September" (unless for purposes of parody), for it has no meanings that need elucidation and no "art" worthy of comment. Second, the work must be short enough to be encompassed in a relatively brief discussion. A thorough explication of *Othello* would be longer than the play itself and would tire the patience of the most dogged reader. Explications work best with short poems. (Sonnets like Shakespeare's "That time of year" [page 219] and Frost's "Design" [page 136] almost beg for explication.) Explication sometimes may also be appropriate for passages in long poems, as, for example, the lines spoken by Macbeth after the death of his wife (page 123) or the "sonnet" from *Romeo and Juliet* (page 225). But explication as a critical form should perhaps be separated from explication as a method. Whenever you elucidate even a small part of a literary work by a close examination that relates it to the whole, you are essentially explicating (unfolding). For

*George Arms, "A Note on Explication," *Western Review* 15 (1950): 57.

example, if you elaborate at length on the multiple denotations and connotations of the two words in the title of Siegfried Sassoon's "Base Details" (page 48) as they relate to that poem's central purpose, you are explicating the title.

For a sample of an explication, see "A Study of Reading Habits," page 370. The text of this book uses the explicative method frequently, but has no pure examples of explication. The discussions of "A Noiseless Patient Spider" (page 81) and "You, Andrew Marvell" (pages 84–85) come close to being explications, and might have been so designated had they included discussions of other relevant aspects of the poems (connotative language, imagery, structure and form, and so forth). The General Questions for Analysis and Evaluation of poetry on page 29 should be helpful to you in writing an explication of a poem. Not all the questions will be applicable to every poem, and you need not answer all those that are applicable, but you should start by considering all that apply and then work with those that are central and important for your explication.

An *analysis* (literally a "breaking up" or separation of something into its constituent parts), instead of trying to examine all parts of a work in relation to the whole, selects for examination *one* aspect or element or part that relates to the whole. Clearly, an analysis is a better approach to longer works and to prose works than is an explication. A literary work may be usefully approached through almost any of its elements, so long as you relate this element to the central meaning or the whole. (An analysis of meter is pointless unless it shows how meter serves the meaning.) As always, it is important to choose a topic appropriate to the space available. "Visual and auditory imagery in 'The Love Song of J. Alfred Prufrock'" (page 255) is too large a topic to be usefully treated in one or two pages, but the irony of the refrain about the women talking of Michelangelo could be suited to such a length. Conversely, it might be too great a challenge to write a ten-page essay on so limited a topic, though the Michelangelo refrain could contribute a valuable page or two of discussion in a longer essay about Eliot's irony, or about the various effects of the refrains in the poem.

2. Papers of Comparison and Contrast

The comparison and contrast of two poems having one or more features in common may be an illuminating exercise, because the similarities highlight the differences, or vice versa, and thus lead to a better understanding not only of both pieces but of literary processes in general. The works selected may be similar in subject but different in tone, similar in meaning but different in literary value, similar in means but different in the ends they achieve, or, conversely, similar in tone but different in subject, similar in literary value but different in meaning, and so on. In writing such a paper, it is usually best to decide first whether the similarities or the differences are more significant, begin with a brief summary of the less significant, and then concentrate on the more significant.*

3. Papers on a Number of Poems by a Single Author

Most readers, when they discover a poem they particularly like, look for other works by the same author. The paper that focuses on a single author rather than a single work is the natural corollary of such an interest. The most common concern in a paper of this type is to identify the characteristics that make this author different from other authors and therefore of particular interest to the writer. What are the poet's characteristic subjects, attitudes, or themes? With what kinds of life does the poet characteristically deal? What are the poet's preferred literary forms? What tones does the poet favor? Is the poet ironic, witty, serious, comic, tragic? Is the poet's vision directed principally inward or outward? In short, what configuration of patterns makes the poet's fingerprints unique? Your paper may consider one or more of these questions.†

A more ambitious type of paper on a single poet examines the poems for signs of development. The attitudes that any person, especially a

*A number of selections in this book have been "paired" to encourage just this kind of study: "Ulysses" and "Curiosity," "Dust of Snow" and "Soft Snow" in Chapter 6; "The Unknown Citizen" and "Departmental" in Chapter 7; "Abraham to kill him" and "An altered look about the hills" in Chapter 8; "Barter" and "Stopping by Woods on a Snowy Evening," "To a Waterfowl" and "Design," "The Indifferent" and "Love's Deity," "To the Mercy Killers" and "How Annandale Went Out," "We outgrow love" and "The Immortal Part" in Chapter 9; "For a Lamb" and "Apparently with no surprise," "One dignity delays for all" and "'Twas warm at first like us," "Crossing the Bar" and "The Oxen," "The Apparition" and "The Flea," "Dover Beach" and "Church Going," "The Dead" and "The Death of a Soldier" in Chapter 10; "Had I the Choice" and "The Aim Was Song" in Chapter 12; and eight pairs of poems in Chapter 15.

†John Donne, Emily Dickinson, and Robert Frost are represented in this anthology by a sufficient number of poems to support such a paper without turning to outside sources.

poet, takes toward the world, may change with the passing from adolescence to adulthood to old age. So also may a poet's means of expressing attitudes and judgments. Though some authors are remarkably consistent in outlook and expression throughout their careers, others manifest surprising changes. What are the differences between early Yeats, middle Yeats, and late Yeats? To write such a paper, you must have accurate information about the dates when works were written, and the works must be read in chronological order. When you have mastered the differences, you may be able to illustrate them through close examination of two or three poems — one for each stage.

When readers become especially interested in the works of a particular poet, they may develop a curiosity about that poet's life as well. This is a legitimate interest, and, if there is sufficient space and your editor/instructor permits it, you may want to incorporate biographical information into your paper. If so, however, you should heed three caveats. First, your main interest should be in the literature itself; the biographical material should be subordinated to and used in service of your examination of the work. In general, discuss only those aspects of the poet's life that bear directly on the work: biography should not be used as "filler." Second, you should be extremely cautious about identifying an event in a work with an event in the life of the author. Almost never are poems exact transcriptions of the writers' personal experiences. Authors fictionalize themselves when they put themselves into imaginative works. If you consider that even in autobiographies (where they intend to give accurate accounts of their lives) writers must select incidents from the vast complexity of their experiences, that the memory of past events may be defective, and that at best writers work from their own points of view — in short, when you realize that even autobiography cannot be an absolutely reliable transcription of historical fact — you should be more fully prepared not to expect such an equation in works whose object is imaginative truth. Third, you must document the sources of your information about the author's life (see pages 361–66, 374).

4. Papers on a Number of Poems with Some Feature in Common Other than Authorship

Papers on poems by various poets that have some feature in common — subject, form, poetic devices, and the like — where the purpose is to discover different ways that different works may use or regard that common feature, are often illuminating. Probably the most familiar paper of this type is the one that treats works having a similar thematic concern (love, war, religious belief or doubt, art, adolescence, initiation, maturity, old age, death, parents and children, racial conflict, social injustice). But a paper may also examine particular forms of literature, for example, the Italian sonnet, the dramatic monologue, the descriptive lyric. Topics of this kind may be further limited by time or place or number—Elizabethan love lyrics, poetry of the Vietnam war, four attitudes toward death, satires of bureaucracy.

IV. Proving Your Point

In writing about literature, your object generally is to convince your readers that your understanding of a work is valid and important and to lead them to share that understanding. When writing about other subjects, it may be appropriate to persuade your readers through various rhetorical means—through eloquent diction, devices of suspense, analogies, personal anecdotes, and the like. But readers of essays about literature usually look for "proof." They want you to show them *how* the work, or the element you are discussing, does what you claim it does. Like scientists who require proof of the sort that they can duplicate in their own laboratories, readers of criticism want access to the process of inference, analysis, and deduction that has led to your conclusions, so that they may respond as you have done.

To provide this proof is no easy task, for it depends on your own mastery of reading and of writing. You must understand what a poem means and what its effects are; you must be able to point out precisely how it communicates that meaning and how it achieves those effects; and you must be able to present your experience of it clearly and directly. When you have spent considerable time in coming to understand and respond to a work of literature, it may become so familiar that it seems self-evident to you, and you will need to "back off" sufficiently to be able to put yourself in your readers' position—they may have vague feelings about the poem ("I like it" or "It moves me deeply"), without knowing what it is that produced those feelings. It is your job to refine the feelings and define away the vagueness.

Some forms of "proof" rarely do the job. Precision does not result from explaining a metaphor metaphorically ("When Shakespeare's Juliet calls parting from Romeo a 'sweet sorrow,' the reader is reminded of taking bitter-tasting medicine"). Nor can you prove anything about a work by hypothesizing about what it might have been if it did not contain what it does ("If Dickinson had concluded 'A narrow fellow in the grass' by writing 'Without gasping for breath / And feeling chilled,' the poem would be much less effective" — this is equivalent to saying "If the poem were not what it is, it would not be what it is"). Your own personal experiences will rarely help your readers ("My anxiety, excitement, and awkwardness at my first skiing lesson were like the mixed feelings Prufrock imagines for himself at the tea party" — *your* reader hasn't shared your experience of that lesson). Even your personal history of coming to understand a literary work will seldom help ("At a first reading, Williams's 'The Red Wheelbarrow' seems empty and pointless, until one realizes its meaning" — most literature does not yield up its richness on a first reading, so this approach has nothing to add to your reader's understanding). Just as in formal logic argument by analogy is not regarded as valid, so in critical discourse analogies are usually unconvincing ("The rhythm of this sonnet is like the trot of a three-legged racehorse"). These strategies all have in common the looseness and vagueness of trying to define something by saying what it is not, or what it is like, rather than dealing with what it *is*.

"Proof" in writing about literature is primarily an exercise in strict definition. Juliet's phrase "sweet sorrow" (quoted in the preceding paragraph) derives its feeling from the paradoxical linking of sweetness and grief as a representation of the conflicting emotions of love. To provide an appropriate definition of the effect of the phrase, you would need to identify the figure of speech as oxymoron, and to investigate the way in which love can simultaneously inflict pain and give pleasure, and you might find it useful to point to the alliteration that ties these opposites together. Obviously, comparing this kind of proof to that required by science is inexact, since what you are doing is reminding your readers, or perhaps informing them, of feelings that are associated with language, not of the properties of chemical compounds. Furthermore, a scientific proof is incomplete if it does not present every step in a process. If that requirement were placed on literary analysis, a critical essay would be interminable, since more can always be said about any interpretive point. So, rather than attempting to prove every point that you make, you should aim to demonstrate that your *method* of analysis is valid by providing persuasive proof of your major point or points. If you have shown that your handling of a major point is sound, your readers will tend to trust your judgment on lesser matters.

V. Writing the Paper

The general procedures for writing a good paper on literature are much the same as the procedures for writing a good paper on any subject.

1. As soon as possible after receiving the assignment, read carefully and thoughtfully the literary materials on which it is based, mulling over the problem to be solved or—if the assignment is general—a good choice of subject, jotting down notes, and sidelining or underlining important passages with a pencil if the book is your own.* If possible, read the material more than once.

2. Then, rather than proceeding directly to the writing of the paper, put the materials aside for several days and let them steep in your mind. The advantage of this is that your unconscious mind, if you have truly placed the problem in it, will continue to work on the problem while you are engaged in other activities, indeed even while you are asleep. Repeated investigations into the psychology of creativity have shown that great solutions to scientific and artistic problems frequently occur while the scientist or artist is thinking of something else; the answer pops into consciousness as if out of nowhere but really out of the hidden recesses of the mind where it has been quietly incubating. Whether this apparent "miracle" happens to you or not, it is probable that you will have more ideas when you sit down to write after a period of incubation than you will if you try to write your paper immediately after reading the materials.

3. When you are ready to write (allow yourself as long an incubation period as possible, but also allow ample time for writing, looking things up, revising, copying your revision, and correcting your final copy), jot down a list of the ideas you have, select connecting ideas relevant to your problem or to a single acceptable subject, and formulate a thesis statement that will clearly express in one sentence what you wish to say about that subject. Make a rough outline, rearranging your ideas in the order that will best support your thesis. Do they make a coherent case? Have you left out anything necessary to demonstrate your thesis? If so, add it in the proper place. Then begin to write, using your rough outline as a guide. Write this first draft as swiftly as possible, not bothering about sentence structure, grammar, diction, spelling, or verification

*If you use a library book, make notes of the page or line numbers of such passages so that you can readily find them again.

of sources. Concentrate on putting on paper what is in your head and on your outline without interrupting the flow of thought for any other purpose. If alternative ways of expressing a thought occur to you, put them all down for a later decision. Nothing is more unprofitable than staring at a blank sheet of paper, chewing on a pencil—or staring at a blank monitor, hearing the word processor's hum—wondering, "How shall I begin?" Just begin. Get something down on paper. It may look awful, but you can shape and polish it later.

4. Once you have something on paper, it is much easier to see what should be done with it. The next step is to revise. Does your paper proceed from an introductory paragraph that either defines the problem to be solved or states your thesis, through a series of logically arranged paragraphs that advance toward a solution of the problem or demonstrate your thesis, to a final paragraph that either solves the problem or sums up and restates your thesis but in somewhat different words? If not, analyze the difficulty. Do the paragraphs need reorganization or amplification? Are more examples needed? Does the thesis itself need modification? Make whatever adjustments are necessary for a logical and convincing demonstration. This may require a rewriting of the paper, or it may call only for a few strike-outs, insertions, and circlings with arrows showing that a sentence or paragraph should be shifted from one place to another.

5. In your revision (if not earlier), make sure that the stance expressed in your statements and judgments is firm and forthright, not weak and wishy-washy. Don't allow your paper to become a sump of phrases like "it seems to me that," "I think [or feel] that," "this word might connote," "this line could mean," and "in my opinion." Your readers know that the content of your paper expresses your thoughts; you need to warn them only when it expresses someone else's. And don't be weak-kneed in expressing your opinion. Even though you are not 100 percent sure of your rightness, write as if you are presenting a truth. Realizing beforehand that you will need to state your interpretations and conclusions confidently also should help you to strive for a greater degree of certainty as you read and interpret.

6. Having revised your paper for the logic, coherence, confidence, and completeness of its argument, your next step is to revise it for effectiveness of expression. Do this slowly and carefully. How many words can you cut out without loss of meaning? Are your sentences constructed for maximum force and economy? Are they correctly punctuated? Do the pronouns have clear antecedents? Do the verbs agree with their subjects? Are the tenses consistent? Have you chosen the most exact words and spelled them correctly? Now is the time to use the dictionary, to verify quotations and other references, and to supply whatever documentation is needed. A conscientious writer may put a paper through several revisions.

7. After all is in order, write or type your final copy, being sure to follow the editorial policies of your instructor for the submission of manuscripts.

8. Read over your final copy slowly and carefully, and correct any mistakes (omissions, repetitions, typographical errors) you may have made in copying from your draft. This final step—too often omitted due to haste or fatigue—is extremely important and may make the difference between an *A* or a *C* paper, or between a *C* paper and an *F*. It is easy to make careless mistakes in copying, but your editor should not be counted on to recognize the difference between a copying error and one of ignorance. Moreover, the smallest error may utterly destroy the sense of what you have written: omission of a "not" may make your paper say the exact opposite of what you meant it to say. Few editors require or want you to recopy or retype a whole page of your paper at this stage. It is enough to make neat corrections in ink on the paper itself.

VI. Introducing Quotations

In writing about literature it is often desirable, sometimes imperative, to quote from the work under discussion. Quoted material is needed (a) to provide essential evidence in support of your argument, and (b) to set before your reader any passage that you are going to examine in detail. It will also keep your reader in contact with the text and allow you to use felicitous phrasing from the text to enhance your own presentation. You must, however, be careful not to overquote. If a paper consists of more than 20 percent quotation, it loses the appearance of closely knit argument and seems instead merely a collection of quotations strung together like clothes hung out on a line to dry. Avoid, especially, unnecessary use of long quotations. Readers tend to skip them. Consider carefully whether the quoted material may not be more economically presented by paraphrase or effectively shortened by ellipsis (see Q9 below). Readers faced with a long quotation may reasonably expect you to examine it in some detail; that is, the longer your quotation, the more you should do with it. As with every other aspect of good writing, the amount of quotation one uses is a matter of intelligence and tact and cannot be decreed. Effective use of quotation is an art.

Principles and "Rules"

There is no legislative body that establishes laws governing the formal aspects of quoting, documenting, or any other aspect of writing. The only "rules" are the editorial policies of the publisher to whom you submit your work. There is, however, a national organization—the Modern Language Association of America—that is so influential that its policies for its own publications and its recommendations for others are adopted by most journals of literary criticism and scholarship. The instructions below are in general accord with those stated in the *MLA Handbook for Writers of Research Papers*, 3rd edition, by Joseph Gibaldi and Walter S. Achtert (New York: MLA, 1988). In your course, your instructor will inform you of any editorial policies in effect that differ from those given here or in the *MLA Handbook*. The examples used in this section are all drawn from Housman's "Terence, this is stupid stuff" (pages 16–18).

Q1. If the quotation is short (normally not more than two or three lines of verse), put it in quotation marks and introduce it directly into the text of your essay.

```
  Terence, in a rejoinder to his friend's complaint
  about the melancholy sobriety of his poetry, re-
a minds him, "There's brisker pipes than poetry,"
b and the English gentry "brews / Livelier liquor
  than the Muse" (16, 19-20).
```

Q2. If the quotation is long (normally more than three lines of verse), begin it on a new line (and resume the text of your essay on a new line also); double-space it (like the rest of your paper); and indent it twice as far from the left margin (ten spaces) as you do for a new paragraph (five spaces). If a ten-space indentation is unsuitable because the verse lines are either too long or too short, center the quotation between the margins. *Do not enclose it in quotation marks*. Since the indentation and the line arrangement both signal a quotation, the use of quotation marks would be redundant.

```
In the final verse paragraph, Terence describes
the terror of Mithridates's would-be assassins:
     They poured strychnine in his cup
     And shook to see him drink it up:
     They shook, they stared as white's
          their shirt:
     Them it was their poison hurt. (71–74)
```

The two boxed examples illustrate (Q1) the "run-in" quotation, where the quotation is "run in" with the writer's own text, and (Q2) the "set-off" or "block" quotation, which is separated from the writer's text.

Q3. In quoting verse, it is extremely important to preserve the line arrangement of the original, for the verse line is a rhythmical unit and thus affects meaning. When more than one line of verse is run in, the lines are separated by a virgule (or diagonal slash), and capitalization after the first line follows that of the original (see Q1.b. above).

Q4. In general, sentences containing a quotation are punctuated as they would be if there were no quotation. In Q1.a. above, a comma precedes the quoted sentence as it would if there were no quotation marks. In Q2, a colon precedes the quoted sentence because it is long and complex. In Q1.b., there is no punctuation at all before the quotation. Do not put punctuation before a quotation unless it is otherwise called for.

Q5. Your quotation must combine with its introduction to make a grammatically correct sentence. The normal processes of grammar and syntax, like the normal processes of punctuation, are unaffected by quoting. Subjects must agree with their verbs, verbs must be consistent in tense, pronouns must have their normal relation with antecedents.

WRONG	`Terence says, "And I myself a sterling lad" (34).` (Incomplete sentence)
RIGHT	`Terence calls himself "a sterling lad" (34).`

VI.

WRONG	`Terence's friend complains, "'tis our turn now / To hear such tunes as killed the cow" (9–10).` (The pronoun "our" does not agree in number or person with its antecedent "friend.")
RIGHT	`Terence's friend, on behalf of the others, complains: "We poor lads, 'tis our turn now / To hear such tunes as killed the cow" (9–10).`

WRONG	`Terence says that "the world, it was the old world yet" (39).` (Incorrect mixture of direct and indirect quotation)
RIGHT	`Terence says, "the world, it was the old world yet" (39).`

WRONG	`Terence says that he "have been to Ludlow fair" (29).` (Subject and verb of subordinate clause lack agreement.)
RIGHT	`Terence says that he has "been to Ludlow fair" (29).`

Q6. Your introduction must supply enough context to make the quotation meaningful. Be careful that all pronouns in the quotation have clearly identifiable antecedents.

WRONG	`Terence begins his narration by saying, "Why, if 'tis dancing you would be, / There's brisker pipes than poetry" (15–16).` (Who wants to dance?)

RIGHT

```
Terence begins his reply to his friend by
saying, "Why, if 'tis dancing you would be, /
There's brisker pipes than poetry"(15–16).
```

Q7. The words within your quotation marks must be quoted *exactly* from the original.

WRONG

```
Terence confesses that "in lovely muck he's
lain," where he slept "happily till he woke
again" (35–36).
```

Q8. It is permissible to insert or supply words in a quotation *if* you enclose them within brackets. Brackets (parentheses with square corners) are used to indicate *editorial* changes or additions. If parentheses were used, the reader might interpret the enclosed material as *authorial* (as part of the quotation). Since brackets do not appear on all typewriters, you may have to put them in with pen or pencil. Avoid excessive use of brackets: they have a pedantic air. Find other solutions. Often paraphrase will serve as well as quotation.

CORRECT

```
Terence confesses that "in lovely muck [he's]
lain," where he slept "happ[ily] till [he]
woke again" (35–36).
```

BETTER

```
Terence confesses that when drunk he's slept
in muck -- and happily, until he woke up.
```

Notice that a word or letters within brackets can either replace a word in the original (as in the substitution of "he's" for the original "I've") or be added to explain or complete the original (as with "-ily"). Since a reader understands that brackets signal either substitutions or additions, it is superfluous to include the words for which the substitutions are made.

WRONG

```
Terence confesses that "in lovely muck he's
[I've] lain" (35).
```

Your sentences, including bracketed words, must read as if there were no brackets:

RIGHT Terence summarizes his philosophy when he advises his friend:

> Therefore, since the world has still
> Much good, but much less good than ill,
> And . . . Luck's a chance, but trouble's sure,
> [You should] face it as a wise man would,
> And train for ill and not for good.
> (43–48)

Q9. It is permissible to omit words from quoted material, but *only* if the omission is indicated. Three spaced periods are used to indicate the omission (technically they are called "ellipsis marks"). The third line in the preceding quotation is an example. If there are four periods, one is the normal period at the end of a sentence; the other three indicate the ellipsis.

The statement just concluded, if quoted, might be shortened in the following way: "It is permissible to omit words . . . if the omission is indicated. Three spaced periods are used to indicate the omission. . . . If there are four periods, one is the normal period at the end of a sentence."

Q10. Single quotation marks are used for quotations within quotations. Thus, if double quotes occur *within* a run-in quotation, they should be reduced to single quotes. (In a block quotation, the quotation marks would remain unchanged.)

Terence (who speaks the whole poem) begins by quoting a complaining friend. To the demand for "'a tune to dance to,'" Terence instead offers a defense of sober poetry that will "do good to heart and head" (14, 55).

Q11. At the conclusion of a run-in quotation, commas and periods are conventionally placed *within* quotation marks; semicolons and colons are placed outside. (The convention is based on appearance, not on logic.) Question marks and exclamation points are placed inside if they belong to the quoted sentence, outside if they belong to your sentence. (This is logic.) Special rules apply when the quotation is followed by parenthetical documentation (see PD4, page 365). The following examples are all correct:

```
"Mithridates, he died old," Terence concludes (76).
Terence concludes, "Mithridates, he died old" (76).
"Why was Burton built on Trent?" Terence asks (18).
Does Housman endorse the friend's preference for "a
    tune to dance to" (14)?
```

VII. Documentation

Documentation is the process of identifying the sources of materials used in your paper. The sources are of two kinds: primary and secondary. *Primary* sources are materials written *by* the author being studied, and may be confined to the single work being discussed. *Secondary* sources are materials by other writers *about* the author or work being discussed, or materials having some bearing on that work. Documentation serves two purposes: (1) it enables your readers to check any material they may think you have misinterpreted; (2) it enables you to make proper acknowledgment of information, ideas, opinions, or phraseology that are not your own.

It is difficult to overemphasize the second of these purposes. The use of someone else's ideas or insights in your own words, since it does not require quotation marks, makes an even heavier demand for acknowledgment than quoted material does. Although you need not document matters of common knowledge, your use without acknowledgment of material that is uniquely someone else's is not only dishonest but illegal, and could result in penalties ranging from an *F* on the paper through expulsion from school to a term in jail, depending on the magnitude of the offense.

Documentation may be given in (a) the text of your essay; (b) parentheses placed within the text of your essay; or (c) a list of Works Cited placed at the end of your essay but keyed to parenthetical references within the essay. The three methods are progressively more formal.

Documentation by a list of Works Cited is required when several sources have contributed to an essay—and is necessary in a research paper or term paper for which you have consulted a number of works. If you are assigned such a project in conjunction with studying this book, your instructor will supply you with information about the method to use. The *MLA Handbook for Writers of Research Papers* (mentioned earlier) provides a full account of the appropriate method, in the event that your instructor does not supply you with other information.

In any case, the type of documentation required in your class will be chosen by your instructor, who may wish to have you practice several methods so that you will learn their use.

1. Textual Documentation

Every literary essay contains textual documentation. A title like "Dramatic Irony in 'My Last Duchess'" identifies the poem that will furnish the main materials in a paper. A paragraph beginning "In the second verse paragraph . . ." locates more specifically the source of what follows. An informally documented essay is one that relies on textual documentation exclusively. Perhaps the majority of articles published in newspapers and periodicals with wide circulation are of this kind. Informal documentation works best for essays written on a single short work, without use of secondary sources, for readers without great scholarly expectations. A first-rate paper could be written on Wallace Stevens's "Sunday Morning" using only textual documentation. The poet's name and the title of the poem mentioned somewhere near the beginning of the essay, plus a few phrases like "In the opening stanza" or "In the vision of the orgiastic future" or "The final image of the pigeons" might provide all the documentation needed for this audience. The poem is short enough that the reader can easily locate any detail within it. If the essay is intended for our hypothetical journal published by your literature class (all of whose members are using the same anthology), its readers can readily locate the poem. But the informal method, although less appropriate, can also be used for more complex subjects, and can even accommodate secondary sources with phrases like "As Helen Vendler points out in her study of Stevens's longer poems . . ."

Principles and "Rules"

TD1. Enclose titles of short stories, articles, and poems (unless they are book-length) in quotation marks; underline titles of plays, magazines, newspapers, and books. Do not underline or put the title of your own paper in quotation marks. The general principle is that titles of separate publications are underlined; titles of selections or parts of books are put within quotation marks. Full-length plays, like *Othello* and *Oedipus Rex*, though often reprinted as part of an anthology, are elsewhere published as separate books and should be underlined. Underlining, in manuscripts, is equivalent to italics in printed matter.

TD2. Capitalize the first word and all important words in titles. Do not capitalize articles, prepositions, and conjunctions except when they begin the title ("The Unknown Citizen," "To the Virgins, to Make Much of Time," "A Dialogue between the Soul and Body").

TD3. When the title above a poem is identical with its first line or a major part of its first line, there is a strong presumption that the poet left the poem untitled and the editor or anthologist has used the first line or part of it to serve as a title. In such a case you may *use* the first line as a title, but should not *refer* to it as a title (don't write: "The poet's repetition of his title in his first line emphasizes . . ."). In using it as a title, capitalize only those words that are capitalized in the first line.

TD4. Never use page numbers in the body of your discussion, for a page is not a constituent part of a poem. You may refer in your discussion to verse paragraphs, sections, stanzas, and lines, as appropriate, but use page numbers *only* in parenthetical documentation where a specific edition of the work has been named.

TD5. Spell out numerical references when they precede the unit they refer to; use numbers when they follow the unit (the second paragraph, or paragraph 2; the fourth line, or line 4; the tenth stanza, or stanza 10). Use the first of these alternative forms sparingly, and only with small numbers. Never write "In the thirty-fourth and thirty-fifth lines . . . ," for to do so is to waste good space and irritate your reader; write "In lines 34–35 . . ."

2. Parenthetical Documentation

Parenthetical documentation makes possible fuller and more precise accreditation without a forbidding apparatus of footnotes or an extensive list of Works Cited. It is the method most often required for a paper using only the primary source, or, at most, two or three sources—as, for example, most of the writing assigned in an introductory literature course. The information given in parenthetical documentation should enable your reader to turn easily to the exact source of a quotation or a reference. At the first mention of a work (which may well precede the first quotation from it), full publishing details should be given, but parenthetical documentation should supplement textual documentation; that is, information provided in the text of your essay should not be repeated within the parentheses. For the readers of our hypothetical journal, the first reference to a poem might look like this:

> In "Home Burial" (Robert Frost, reprinted in Laurence Perrine and Thomas R. Arp, Sound and Sense, 8th ed. [San Diego: Harcourt, 1992] 251–54), the poet examines . . .

Notice in this entry that brackets are used for parentheses within parentheses. In subsequent references only inclusive line numbers need be given:

> Amy's silent gesture underscores her sense that her husband cannot understand her feelings: "Her fingers moved the latch for all reply" (44).

If more than one source is used, each must be identified, if referred to a second time, by an abbreviated version of the main entry, normally the author's last name or, if several works by a single author are cited, by the title of the work; in any case, use the shortest identification that will differentiate the source from all others.

Principles and "Rules"

PD1. For the first citation from a book, give the author's name; the title of the selection; the name of the book from which it is taken; the editor (preceded by the abbreviation ed. for "edited by") or the translator (preceded by the abbreviation trans. for "translated by"); the edition (designated by an Arabic number) if there has been more than one; the city of publication (the first one will suffice if there is more than one); the publisher (this may be given in shortened form, dropping all but the first name named); the year of publication or of most recent copyright; and the page number. The following example correctly combines textual with parenthetical documentation.

> In "Home Burial," Frost has a husband complain, "A man must partly give up being a man / With women-

```
folk" (The Poetry of Robert Frost, ed. Edward Con-
nery Latham [New York: Holt, 1969] 52).
```

PD2. For your principal primary source, after the first reference, only a page number is required. For long poems, however, it may be more useful, if easily available, to give line numbers or stanza numbers rather than page numbers. If the poem is short, line numbers are unnecessary and should be omitted, nor is there any need to cite a page number after the first documentation. For plays in verse also, citation by line number (preceded by act and scene number) will often be more useful than by page; for example, *Othello* (5.2.133).

PD3. Documentation for run-in quotations always follows the quotation marks. If the quotation ends with a period, move it to the end of the documentation. If it ends with an exclamation point or question mark, leave it, but put a period after the documentation as well. The following examples are from "Home Burial":

```
"She moved the latch a little. 'Don't—don't go'"
   (56).
"'There you go sneering now!'" (67).
```

PD4. With block quotations, parenthetical documentation follows the last mark of punctuation without further punctuation after the parentheses:

```
He saw her from the bottom of the stairs
Before she saw him. She was starting down,
Looking back over her shoulder at some fear. (1-3)
```

PD5. Avoid cluttering your paper with excessive documentation. When possible, use one note to cover a series of short quotations. (See example, Q1.) Remember that short poems need no parenthetical documentation at all after the first reference. Do not document well-known sayings or proverbs that you use for stylistic purposes and that form no part of the substance of your investigation (and of course be wary of including hackneyed commonplaces in your formal writing).

PD6. It is customary in a formal paper to document all quoted materials. Do not, however, fall victim to the too frequent delusion that *only* quotations need documentation. The first purpose of documentation (see page 361) implies that any major or possibly controversial assertion concerning interpretation may need documentation. If you declare that the climax of a long poem occurs with an apparently insignificant passage that you choose not to quote for full analysis, it may be more important for the reader to have line numbers for that passage than for any quotations from the poem. Judgment must be exercised.

> `The vividness with which Amy recalls her husband's remark the morning of the burial is evidence that the words have been preying on her mind (92–93).`

VIII. Grammar, Punctuation, and Usage: Special Problems

1. Grammar

G1. In discussing the action of a literary work, rely primarily on the present tense (even when the work itself uses the past), keeping the past, future, and perfect tenses available for prior or subsequent actions; for example,

> `When Amy withdraws from her husband and slides downstairs "beneath his arm / That [rests] on the banister" (31–32), the references to sliding, a staircase, and a banister create an ironic allusion to what will be revealed as their central concern, the dead child.`

G2. Do not let pronouns refer to nouns in the possessive case. Antecedents of pronouns should always hold a strong grammatical position: a possessive is a mere modifier, like an adjective.

WRONG	`In Frost's poem "Home Burial," he writes . . .` (Antecedent of "he" is in possessive case.)

RIGHT	`In his poem "Home Burial," Frost writes . . .` (Antecedent of "his" is the subject of the sentence.)

2. Punctuation

P1. Do not set off restrictive appositives with commas. A "restrictive" appositive is one necessary to the meaning of the sentence; a "nonrestrictive" appositive could be left out without changing the meaning.

WRONG	`In his book, A Boy's Will, Robert Frost . . .` (Without the title we do not know which of Frost's books is referred to. As punctuated, the sentence falsely implies that Frost wrote only one book.)
RIGHT	`In his book A Boy's Will, Robert Frost . . .`
RIGHT	`In his first book, A Boy's Will, Robert Frost . . .` (The adjective "first" identifies the book. The title simply supplies additional information and could be omitted without changing the meaning.)

P2. Words used simply as words should be either underlined or put in quotation marks.

WRONG	`The sixth word in "The Road Not Taken" is yellow.` (This statement is false; all the words in the poem are black.)
RIGHT	`The sixth word in "The Road Not Taken" is "yellow."`

Since the word "yellow" is quoted from the poem, it has here been put in quotation marks. However, if you list a series of words from the poem, you may prefer underlining for the sake of appearance. Whichever system you choose, be consistent throughout your paper.

3. Usage

U1. Though accepted usage changes with time, and the distinctions between the following pairs of words are fading, many instructors will bless you if you try to preserve them.

convince, persuade *Convince* pertains to belief (conviction); *persuade* pertains to either action or belief. The following sentences observe the distinction. "In 'To His Coy Mistress' the speaker tries to persuade a young woman to sleep with him." "In 'To His Coy Mistress' the speaker tries to convince a young woman that she has nothing to lose by sleeping with him." "I persuaded him to have another drink though he was convinced he ought not to."

disinterested, uninterested A disinterested judge is one who has no "stake" or personal interest in the outcome of a case and who can therefore judge fairly; an uninterested judge goes to sleep on the bench. A good judge is interested in the case but disinterested in its outcome. An uninterested reader finds reading boring. A disinterested reader? Perhaps one who can enjoy a good book whatever its subject matter.

imply, infer A writer or speaker implies; a reader or listener infers. An implication is a meaning hinted at but not stated outright. An inference is a conclusion drawn from evidence not complete enough for proof. If you imply that I am a snob, I may infer that you do not like me.

sensuous, sensual *Sensuous* normally pertains to the finer senses, *sensual* to the appetites. Good poetry is sensuous: it appeals through the imagination to the senses. A voluptuous woman, an attractive man, or a rich dessert makes a sensual appeal that stirs a desire for possession.

quote, quotation *Quote* was originally used only as a verb. Today the use of "single quotes" and "double quotes" in reference to quotation marks is almost universally accepted; but, although the use of "quote" for "quotation" is common in informal speech, it is still unacceptable in formal writing.—Note also that quoting is an act performed by the writer about literature, not by the writer of literature.

WRONG	`Shakespeare's famous quotation "To be or not to be" . . .`
RIGHT	`The famous quotation from Shakespeare, "To be or not to be" . . .`
RIGHT	`Shakespeare's famous line "To be or not to be" . . .`
BETTER	`Hamlet's famous line "To be or not to be" . . .`
BEST	`Probably the most-quoted line by Shakespeare is Hamlet's "To be or not to be" . . .`

U2. Other words and phrases to be avoided:

center around A geometrical impossibility. A story may perhaps center *on* a certain feature, but to make it center *around* that feature is to make the hub surround the wheel.

lifestyle An over-used neologism, especially inappropriate for use with older literature.

what the author was trying to say was The implication of this expression is that the author failed to say what he meant, and its use puts you in the patronizing position of implying that you could have done a much better job of it—to which the only proper rejoinder is "If you're so smart, why ain't you famous?"

Others suggested by your instructor:

_______________ _______________

_______________ _______________

_______________ _______________

IX. A Sample Explication

"A Study of Reading Habits"

The first noteworthy feature of Philip Larkin's "A Study of Reading Habits" (reprinted in Laurence Perrine and Thomas R. Arp, Sound and Sense, 8th ed. [San Diego: Harcourt, 1992] 23) is the ironic discrepancy between the formal language of its title and the colloquial, slangy, even vulgar language of the poem itself. The title by its tone implies a formal sociological research paper, possibly one that samples a cross section of a population and draws conclusions about people's reading. The poem presents, instead, the confessions of one man whose attitudes toward reading have progressively deteriorated to the point where books seem to him "a load of crap." The poem's real subject, moreover, is not the man's reading habits but the revelation of life and character they provide.

The poem is patterned in three stanzas having an identical rime scheme (abcbac) and the same basic meter (iambic-anapestic trimeter). The stanzaic division of the poem corresponds to the internal structure of meaning, for the three stanzas present the speaker at three stages of his life: as schoolboy, adolescent, and adult. The chronological progression is signaled in the first lines of the stanzas by the words "When," "Later," and "now." The "now" is the present out of which the adult speaks, recalling the two earlier periods.

The boy he remembers in stanza 1 was unhappy, both in his home and, even more so, at school. Perhaps small and bullied by bigger boys, probably an indifferent student, making poor grades, and scolded by teachers, he found a partial escape from his miseries through reading. The books he read -- tales of action and adventure, pitting good guys against bad guys, full of physical conflict, and ending with victory for the good guys -- enabled him to construct a fantasy life in which he identified with the virtuous hero and in his imagination beat up villains twice his size, thus reversing the situations of his real life.

In stanza 2 the speaker recalls his adolescence, when his dreams were of sexual rather than muscular prowess. True to the prediction of "ruining [his] eyes" in stanza 1, he had to wear spectacles, which he describes hyperbolically as "inch-thick" -- a further detriment to his social life. To compensate for his lack of success with girls, he envisioned himself as a Dracula-figure with cloak and fangs, enjoying a series of sexual triumphs. His reading continued to feed his fantasy life, but, instead of identifying with the virtuous hero, he identified with the glamorous, sexually ruthless villain. The poet puns on the word "ripping" (the speaker "had ripping times in the dark"), implying both the British slang meaning of "splendid" and the violence of the rapist who rips the clothes off his victim.

In stanza 3 the speaker, now a young adult, confesses that he no longer reads much. His accumulated experience of personal failure and his long familiarity with his shortcomings have made it impossible for him to identify, even in fantasy, with the strong virtuous hero or the viciously potent villain. He can no longer hide from himself the truth that he resembles more closely the weak secondary characters of the escapist tales he picks up. He recognizes himself in the undependable dude who fails the heroine, or the cowardly storekeeper who knuckles under to the bad guys. He therefore has turned to a more powerful means of escape, one that protects him from dwelling on what he knows about himself: drunkenness. His final words are memorable -- so "unpoetical" in a traditional sense, so poetically effective in characterizing this speaker. "Get stewed," he says, "Books are a load of crap."

It would be a serious mistake to identify the speaker of the poem, or his attitudes or his language, with the poet. Poets, writers of books themselves, do not think that "books are a load of crap." Philip Larkin, moreover, an English poet and a graduate of Oxford, was for many years until his death a university librarian (James Vinson, ed., Contemporary Poets, 3rd ed. [New York: St. Martin's, 1980] 877). "A Study of Reading Habits" is both dramatic and ironic. It presents a first-person speaker who has been unable to cope with the reality of his life in any of its stages and has therefore turned toward various means of escaping it. His confessions reveal a progressive deterioration of values (from good to evil to sodden indifference) and a decline in reading tastes (from adventure stories to prurient sexual novels to none) that reflect his downward slide.

Comments

The title of this paper is enclosed in quotation marks because the writer has used the title of the poem for the title of the paper. The paper uses textual and parenthetical documentation. Line numbers for quotations from the poem are not supplied, because the poem is too short to require them: they would serve no useful purpose. Notice that in quoting from stanza 1, the writer has changed the phrase "ruining my eyes" to fit the essay's syntax, but has indicated the alteration by putting the changed word within brackets. The paper is written for an American audience; if it had been written for an English audience the writer would not have needed to explain that "ripping" is British slang or to have made it a point that the poet is English. The paper is documented for an audience using this textbook. If it were directed toward a wider audience, the writer would want to refer for the text of the poem not to a textbook or anthology but to the volume of Larkin's poetry containing this poem (*The Whitsun Weddings* [London: Faber, 1964] 31). Also, the writer would probably wish to include the poet's name in his title: Philip Larkin's "A Study of Reading Habits" (or) An Examination of Larkin's "A Study of Reading Habits." Since Larkin's nationality and his profession as a librarian are not common knowledge, the paper documents a biographical source where that information is found.

Glossary of Poetic Terms

The definitions in this glossary sometimes repeat and sometimes differ in language from those in the text. Where they differ, the intention is to give a fuller sense of the term's meaning by allowing the reader a double perspective on it. Page numbers refer to discussion in the text, which in most but not all cases is fuller than that in the glossary.

Accent In this book, the same as *stress*. A syllable given more prominence in pronunciation than its neighbors is said to be accented. 177–87

Allegory A narrative or description having a second meaning beneath the surface one. 88–89

Alliteration The repetition at close intervals of the initial consonant sounds of accented syllables or important words (for example, *m*ap-*m*oon, *k*ill-*c*ode, *p*reach-ap*p*rove). Important words and accented syllables beginning with vowels may also be said to alliterate with each other inasmuch as they all have the same lack of an initial consonant sound (for example, "*I*n*e*bri*a*te of *a*ir am *I*"). 164–68

Allusion A reference, explicit or implicit, to something in previous literature or history. (The term is reserved by some writers for implicit references only, such as those in "On His Blindness," 125, and "In the Garden," 130; but the distinction between the two kinds of reference is not always clear-cut.) 120–24

Anapest A metrical foot consisting of two unaccented syllables followed by one accented syllable (for example, un-der-stand). 178

Anapestic meter A meter in which a majority of the feet are anapests. (But see *Triple meter*.) 178, 185–86

Apostrophe A figure of speech in which someone absent or dead or something nonhuman is addressed as if it were alive and present and could reply. 65

Approximate rime (also known as *imperfect rime*, *near rime*, *slant rime*, or *oblique rime*) A term used for words in a riming pattern that have some kind of sound correspondence but are not perfect rimes. See *Rime*. Approximate rimes occur occasionally in patterns where most of the rimes are perfect (for example, arrayed-said in "Richard Cory," 318), and sometimes are used systematically in place of perfect rime (for example, "Mr. Z," 115). 165

Assonance The repetition at close intervals of the vowel sounds of accented syllables or important words (for example, h*a*t-r*a*n-*a*mber, v*ei*n-m*a*de). 164–67

Aubade A poem about dawn; a morning love song; or a poem about the parting of lovers at dawn. 52, 301

Ballad A fairly short narrative poem written in a songlike stanza form. Examples: "The Two Ravens" (The Twa Corbies), 12–14; "Ballad of Birmingham," 14; "Edward," 229; "La Belle Dame sans Merci," 294; "Ettrick," 325. Also see *Folk ballad*.

Blank verse Unrimed iambic pentameter. 187

Cacophony A harsh, discordant, unpleasant-sounding choice and arrangement of sounds. 200–201

Caesura See *Grammatical pause* and *Rhetorical pause*.

Connotation What a word suggests beyond its basic definition; a word's overtones of meaning. 37–43

Consonance The repetition at close intervals of the final consonant sounds of accented syllables or important words (for example, boo*k*-pla*que*-thi*ck*er). 164–67

Continuous form That form of a poem in which the lines follow each other without formal grouping, the only breaks being dictated by units of meaning. 214–15

Couplet Two successive lines, usually in the same meter, linked by rime. 219

Dactyl A metrical foot consisting of one accented syllable followed by two unaccented syllables (for example, mer-ri-ly). 178

Dactylic meter A meter in which a majority of the feet are dactyls. (But see *Triple meter*.) 178, 186

Denotation The basic definition or dictionary meaning of a word. 37–43

Didactic poetry Poetry having as a primary purpose to teach or preach. 235–36

Dimeter A metrical line containing two feet. 178

Dipodic foot The basic foot of *dipodic verse*, consisting (when complete) of an unaccented syllable, a lightly accented syllable, an unaccented syllable, and a heavily accented syllable, in that succession. However, dipodic verse accommodates a tremendous amount of variety, as shown by the examples in the text. 192

Dipodic verse A meter in which there is a perceptible alternation between light and heavy stresses. See *Dipodic foot*. 192

Double rime A rime in which the repeated vowel is in the second last syllable of the words involved (for example, politely-rightly-spritely); one form of *feminine rime*. 171 (Question 5)

Dramatic framework The situation, whether actual or fictional, realistic or fanciful, in which an author places his or her characters in order to express the theme. 25–26

Dramatic irony See *Irony*.

Duple meter A meter in which a majority of the feet contain two syllables. Iambic and trochaic are both duple meters. 178

End rime Rimes that occur at the ends of lines. 165

End-stopped line A line that ends with a natural speech pause, usually marked by punctuation. 187

English (or *Shakespearean*) *sonnet* A sonnet riming *ababcdcdefefgg*. Its content or structure ideally parallels the rime scheme, falling into three coordinate quatrains and a concluding couplet; but it is often structured, like the Italian sonnet, into octave and sestet, the principal break in thought coming at the end of the eighth line. 219–220 (Exercise 1)

Euphony A smooth, pleasant-sounding choice and arrangement of sounds. 200–201

Expected rhythm The metrical expectation set up by the basic meter of a poem. 184

Extended figure (also known as *sustained figure*) A figure of speech (usually metaphor, simile, personification, or apostrophe) sustained or developed through a considerable number of lines or through a whole poem. 69–70

Feminine rime A rime in which the repeated accented vowel is in either the second or third last syllable of the words involved (for example, ceiling-appealing, hurrying-scurrying). 164, 171 (Question 5)

Figurative language Language employing figures of speech; language that cannot be taken literally or only literally. 61–68, 79–89, 100–108

Figure of speech Broadly, any way of saying something other than the ordinary way; more narrowly (and for the purposes of this book), a way of saying one thing and meaning another. 61–68, 79–89, 100–108

Fixed form Any form of poem in which the length and pattern are prescribed by previous usage or tradition, such as *sonnet*, *limerick*, *villanelle*, *haiku*, and so on. 217–21

Folk ballad A narrative poem designed to be sung, composed by an anonymous author, and transmitted orally for years or generations before being written down. It has usually undergone modification through the process of oral transmission. 13–14

Foot The basic unit used in the scansion or measurement of verse. A foot usually contains one accented syllable and one or two unaccented syllables, but the *monosyllabic foot*, the *spondaic foot* (*spondee*), and the *dipodic foot* are all modifications of this principle. 177–78

Form The external pattern or shape of a poem, describable without reference to its content, as *continuous form*, *stanzaic form*, *fixed form* (and their varieties), *free verse*, and *syllabic verse*. 214–221, 223. See *Structure*.

Free verse Nonmetrical verse. Poetry written in free verse is arranged in lines, may be more or less rhythmical, but has no fixed metrical pattern or expectation. 186–87

Grammatical pause (also known as *caesura*) A pause introduced into the reading of a line by a mark of punctuation. Grammatical pauses do not affect scansion. 184–85

Haiku A three-line poem, Japanese in origin, narrowly conceived of as a fixed form in which the lines contain respectively five, seven, and five syllables (in American practice this requirement is frequently dispensed with). Haiku are generally concerned with some aspect of nature and present a single image or two juxtaposed images without comment, relying on suggestion rather than on explicit statement to communicate their meaning. 223

Heard rhythm The actual rhythm of a metrical poem as we hear it when it is read naturally. The heard rhythm mostly conforms to but sometimes departs from or modifies the *expected rhythm*. 184

Heptameter A metrical line containing seven feet. 178

Hexameter A metrical line containing six feet. 178

Hyperbole See *Overstatement*.

Iamb A metrical foot consisting of one unaccented syllable followed by one accented syllable (for example, $\breve{\text{re}}$-$\overline{\text{hearse}}$). 178

Iambic meter A meter in which the majority of feet are iambs. The most common English meter. 178, 185–86

Iambic-anapestic meter A meter that freely mixes iambs and anapests, and in which it might be difficult to determine which foot prevails without actually counting. 186

Imagery The representation through language of sense experience. 49–52

Internal rime A rime in which one or both of the rime-words occur *within* the line. 164–65

Irony A situation, or a use of language, involving some kind of incongruity or discrepancy. 104. Three kinds of irony are distinguished in this book:

Verbal irony A figure of speech in which what is meant is the opposite of what is said. 104–106

Dramatic irony A device by which the author implies a different meaning from that intended by the speaker (or by *a* speaker) in a literary work. 106–107

Irony of situation (or *situational irony*) A situation in which there is an incongruity between actual circumstances and those that would seem appropriate or between what is anticipated and what actually comes to pass. 107–108

Italian (or *Petrarchan*) *sonnet* A sonnet consisting of an octave riming *abbaabba* and of a sestet using any arrangement of two or three additional rimes, such as *cdcdcd* or *cdecde*. 218–19, 220 (Exercise 1)

Limerick A fixed form consisting of five lines of anapestic meter, the first two trimeter, the next two dimeter, the last line trimeter, riming *aabba*; used exclusively for humorous or nonsense verse. 217–18, 221–22

Masculine rime (also known as *single rime*) A rime in which the repeated accented vowel sound is in the final syllable of the words involved (for example, dance-pants, scald-recalled). 164, 171 (Question 5)

Metaphor A figure of speech in which an implicit comparison is made between two things essentially unlike. It may take one of four forms: (1) that in which the literal term and the figurative term are *both named*; (2) that in which the literal term is *named* and the figurative term *implied*; (3) that in which the literal term is *implied* and the figurative term *named*; (4) that in which *both* the literal and the figurative terms are *implied*. 61–64

Meter Regularized rhythm; an arrangement of language in which the accents occur at apparently equal intervals in time. 176–87

Metonymy A figure of speech in which some significant aspect or detail of an experience is used to represent the whole experience. In this book the single term *metonymy* is used for what are sometimes distinguished as two separate figures: *synecdoche* (the use of the part for the whole) and *metonymy* (the use of something closely related for the thing actually meant). 65–66

Metrical pause A pause that supplies the place of an expected accented syllable. Unlike *grammatical* and *rhetorical pauses*, metrical pauses affect scansion. 193

Monometer A metrical line containing one foot. 178

Monosyllabic foot A foot consisting of a single accented syllable (for example, shine). 178

Octameter A metrical line containing eight feet. 178

Octave (1) An eight-line stanza. (2) The first eight lines of a sonnet, especially one structured in the manner of an Italian sonnet. 218

Onomatopoeia The use of words that supposedly mimic their meaning in their sound (for example, boom, click, plop). 198

Onomatopoetic language Language employing *onomatopoeia*.

Overstatement (or *hyperbole*) A figure of speech in which exaggeration is used in the service of truth. 101–104

Paradox A statement or situation containing apparently contradictory or incompatible elements. 100–101

Paradoxical situation A situation containing apparently but not actually incompatible elements. The celebration of a fifth birthday anniversary by a twenty-year-old man is paradoxical but explainable if the man was born on February 29. The Christian doctrines that Christ was born of a virgin and is both God and man are, for a Christian believer, paradoxes (that is, apparently impossible but true). 100

Paradoxical statement (or *verbal paradox*) A figure of speech in which an apparently self-contradictory statement is nevertheless found to be true. 100

Paraphrase A restatement of the content of a poem designed to make its *prose meaning* as clear as possible. 23–24

Pentameter A metrical line containing five feet. 178

Personification A figure of speech in which human attributes are given to an animal, an object, or a concept. 64–65

Petrarchan sonnet See *Italian sonnet*.

Phonetic intensive A word whose sound, by an obscure process, to some degree suggests its meaning. As differentiated from *onomatopoetic words*, the meanings of phonetic intensives do not refer to sounds. 198–99

Prose Nonmetrical language; the opposite of *verse*. 176

Prose meaning That part of a poem's *total meaning* that can be separated out and expressed through paraphrase. 131–34

Prose poem Usually a short composition having the intentions of poetry but written in prose rather than verse. 187

Quatrain (1) A four-line stanza. (2) A four-line division of a sonnet marked off by its rime scheme. 219

Refrain A repeated word, phrase, line, or group of lines, normally at some fixed position in a poem written in stanzaic form. 166, 175, 215–17

Rhetorical pause (also known as *caesura*) A natural pause, unmarked by punctuation, introduced into the reading of a line by its phrasing or syntax. Rhetorical pauses do not affect scansion. 184

Rhetorical poetry Poetry using artificially eloquent language, that is, language too high-flown for its occasion and unfaithful to the full complexity of human experience. 235

Rhythm Any wavelike recurrence of motion or sound. 176–87

Rime (or *rhyme*) The repetition of the accented vowel sound and all succeeding sounds in important or importantly positioned words (for example, old-cold, vane-reign, court-report, order-recorder). The above definition applies to *perfect rime* and assumes that the accented vowel sounds involved are preceded by differing consonant sounds. If the preceding consonant sound is the same (for example, manse-romance, style-stile), or if there is no preceding consonant sound in either word (for example, aisle-isle, alter-altar), or if the same word is repeated in the riming position (for example, hill-hill), the words are called *identical rimes*. Both *perfect rimes* and *identical rimes* are to be distinguished from *approximate rimes*. 164–67

Rime scheme Any fixed pattern of rimes characterizing a whole poem or its stanzas. 215–17

Run-on line A line which has no natural speech pause at its end, allowing the sense to flow uninterruptedly into the succeeding line. 187

Sarcasm Bitter or cutting speech; speech intended by its speaker to give pain to the person addressed. 104

Satire A kind of literature that ridicules human folly or vice with the purpose of bringing about reform or of keeping others from falling into similar folly or vice. 104

Scansion The process of measuring verse, that is, of marking accented and unaccented syllables, dividing the lines into feet, identifying the metrical pattern, and noting significant variations from that pattern. 178–83

Sentimental poetry Poetry aimed primarily at stimulating the emotions rather than at communicating experience honestly and freshly. 234–35

Sestet (1) A six-line stanza. (2) The last six lines of a sonnet structured on the Italian model. 218

Shakespearean sonnet See *English sonnet*.

Simile A figure of speech in which an explicit comparison is made between two things essentially unlike. The comparison is made explicit by the use of some such word or phrase as *like*, *as*, *than*, *similar to*, *resembles*, or *seems*. 61

Single rime See *Masculine rime*.

Situational irony See *Irony*.

Sonnet A fixed form of fourteen lines, normally iambic pentameter, with a rime scheme conforming to or approximating one of two main types—the *Italian* or the *English*. 139, 218–21

Spondee A metrical foot consisting of two syllables equally or almost equally accented (for example, trūe-blūe). 178

Stanza A group of lines whose metrical pattern (and usually its rime scheme as well) is repeated throughout a poem. 178, 215–17

Stanzaic form The form taken by a poem when it is written in a series of units having the same number of lines and usually other characteristics in common, such as metrical pattern or rime scheme. 215–17

Stress In this book, the same as *Accent*. But see 177 (footnote).

Structure The internal organization of a poem's content. See *Form*.

Sustained figure See *Extended figure*.

Syllabic verse Verse measured by the number of syllables rather than the number of feet per line. 196. Also see *Haiku*.

Symbol A figure of speech in which something (object, person, situation, or action) means more than what it is. A symbol, in other words, may be read both literally and metaphorically. 80–87

Synecdoche A figure of speech in which a part is used for the whole. In this book it is subsumed under the term *Metonymy*. 65–66

Terza rima An interlocking rime scheme with the pattern *aba bcb cdc*, etc. 228

Tetrameter A metrical line containing four feet. 178

Theme The central idea of a literary work. 23–24

Tone The writer's or speaker's attitude toward his subject, his audience, or himself; the emotional coloring, or emotional meaning, of a work. 145–49

Total meaning The total experience communicated by a poem. It includes all those dimensions of experience by which a poem communicates—sensuous, emotional, imaginative, and intellectual—and it can be communicated in no other words than those of the poem itself. 131–34

Trimeter A metrical line containing three feet. 178

Triple meter A meter in which a majority of the feet contain three syllables. (Actually, if more than 25 percent of the feet in a poem are triple, its effect is more triple than duple, and it ought perhaps to be referred to as triple meter.) Anapestic and dactylic are both triple meters. 178

Triple rime A rime in which the repeated accented vowel sound is in the third last syllable of the words involved (for example, gainfully-disdainfully); one form of *feminine rime*. 171 (Question 5)

Trochaic meter A meter in which the majority of feet are trochees. 178, 185–86

Trochee A metrical foot consisting of one accented syllable followed by one unaccented syllable (for example, bār-tĕr). 178

Understatement A figure of speech that consists of saying less than one means, or of saying what one means with less force than the occasion warrants. 102–104

Verbal irony See *Irony*.

Verse Metrical language; the opposite of *prose*. 176

Villanelle See 221 (Exercise 2).

COPYRIGHTS AND ACKNOWLEDGMENTS

W. H. AUDEN "The Unknown Citizen," "That night when joy began," and "Musée des Beaux Arts" from *W. H. Auden: Collected Poems*, Edward Mendelson, editor. Copyright © 1976 by Edward Mendelson, William Meredith, and Monroe K. Spears, Executors of the Estate of W. H. Auden. Reprinted by permission of Random House, Inc.

D. C. BERRY "On Reading Poems to a Senior Class at South High" reprinted from *Poet Lore* magazine, 1966, by permission of *Poet Lore*.

ELIZABETH BISHOP "One Art" from *The Complete Poems, 1927–1979* by Elizabeth Bishop. Copyright © 1976 by Elizabeth Bishop. Copyright © 1979, 1983 by Alice Helen Methfessel. Reprinted by permission of Farrar, Straus and Giroux, Inc.

PHILIP BOOTH "Stefansson Island" from *Weathers and Edges* by Philip Booth. Copyright © 1959, 1961, 1962, 1963, 1964, 1965, 1966 by Philip Booth. Used by permission of Viking Penguin, a division of Penguin Books USA Inc.

GWENDOLYN BROOKS "We Real Cool" © Gwendolyn Brooks. Reprinted from *Blacks*, (The David Company: 1987) by permission of the author.

STERLING A. BROWN "Southern Cop" from *Black Voices*, ed. Abraham Chapman. Published by New American Library © 1968.

WILLIAM BURFORD "A Christmas Tree" from *Man Now* by William Burford. Reprinted by permission of the author.

LUCILLE CLIFTON "Good Times" from *Good Times* by Lucille Clifton. Copyright © 1969 by Lucille Clifton. Reprinted by permission of Random House, Inc.

ELIZABETH COATSWORTH "Song of the Rabbits outside the Tavern" reprinted with permission of Macmillan Publishing Company from *Away Goes Sally* by Elizabeth Coatsworth. Copyright 1934 by Macmillan Publishing Company, renewed 1962 by Elizabeth Coatsworth Beston.

MARTHA COLLINS "The Story We Know" first appeared in *Poetry*, December 1980. Copyright © by the Modern Poetry Association. Subsequently published in *The Catastrophe of Rainbows* © 1985 by Martha Collins and published by Cleveland State University Poetry Center. Reprinted by permission of the Editor of *Poetry* and Martha Collins.

FRANCES CORNFORD "The Guitarist Tunes Up" reprinted by permission of Grosset Press and Barrie & Jenkins Ltd.

MALCOLM COWLEY "The Long Voyage" from *Blue Juniata: A Life*, by Malcolm Cowley. Copyright Malcolm Cowley 1941, renewed © 1969 by Malcolm Cowley. Reprinted by permission of Viking Penguin, Inc.

COUNTEE CULLEN "Incident" from *On These I Stand* by Countee Cullen. Copyright © 1925 by Harper & Brothers; copyright renewed 1953 by Ida M. Cullen. Reprinted by permission of GRM Associates, Inc., agents for the Estate of Ida M. Cullen.

E. E. CUMMINGS "the greedy the people," "if everything happens that can't be done," and "in Just-" are reprinted from *Complete Poems, 1913–1962*, by e. e. cummings, by permission of Liveright Publishing Corporation. Copyright © 1923, 1925, 1931, 1935, 1938, 1939, 1940, 1944, 1945, 1946, 1947, 1948, 1949, 1950, 1951, 1952, 1953, 1954, 1955, 1956, 1957, 1958, 1959, 1960, 1961, 1962 by the Trustees for the e. e. cummings Trust. Copyright © 1961, 1963, 1968 by Marion Morehouse Cummings.

WALTER DE LA MARE "The Listeners" from *The Collected Poems of Walter de la Mare*. Copyright © 1970 by Walter de la Mare. Reprinted by permission of the literary trustees of Walter de la Mare and the Society of Authors as their representative.

JAMES DICKEY "The Lifeguard" © 1961 by James Dickey. Reprinted from *Drowning with Others* by permission of Wesleyan University Press and University Press of New England.

EMILY DICKINSON "There's a certain slant of light," "I taste a liquor never brewed," "Because I could not stop for Death," "If you were coming in the fall," "I heard a fly buzz when I died," "I like to see it lap the miles," "As imperceptibly as grief," "'Twas warm at first like us," "One dignity delays for all," "Apparently with no surprise," "Alter! When the hills do.," "Abraham to kill him," "An altered look about the hills," "Much madness is divinest sense," "Our journey had advanced," "I felt a funeral in my brain," "It sifts from leaden sieves," "A narrow fellow in the grass," "There is no frigate like a book," "There's been a death in the opposite house," "We outgrow love," reprinted by permission of the publishers and the Trustees of Amherst College from *The Poems of Emily Dickinson*, Thomas H. Johnson, ed., Cambridge, Mass.: The Belknap Press of Harvard University Press, copyright 1951, © 1955, 1979, 1983 by the President and Fellows of Harvard College. "'Twas warm at first like us" from *The Complete Poems of Emily Dickinson*, edited by Thomas H. Johnson. Copyright 1929 by Martha Dickinson Bianchi. Copyright © renewed 1957 by Mary L. Hampson. By permission of Little, Brown and Company.

KEITH DOUGLAS "Vergissmeinnicht" from *Collected Poems* by Keith Douglas. Reprinted by permission of Editions Poetry London.

RICHARD EBERHART "For a Lamb" from *Collected Poems* by Richard Eberhart. Copyright © 1960, 1976, 1987 by Richard Eberhart. Reprinted by permission of Oxford University Press, Inc.

T. S. ELIOT "The Love Song of J. Alfred Prufrock" from *Collected Poems 1909–1962*, copyright 1936 by Harcourt Brace Jovanovich, Inc., copyright © 1963, 1964 by T. S. Eliot. Reprinted by permission of the publisher.

MARI EVANS "When in Rome" by Mari Evans from *I Am a Black Woman*, published by William Morrow & Company, 1970. Reprinted by permission of the author.

GAVIN EWART "Ending" from *Collected Poems 1933–1980* by Gavin Ewart. Reprinted by permission of Hutchinson Publishing Group Ltd.

LAWRENCE FERLINGHETTI "Constantly risking absurdity" from *A Coney Island of the Mind* by Lawrence Ferlinghetti. Copyright © 1958 by Lawrence Ferlinghetti. Reprinted by permission of New Directions Publishing Corporation.

CAROLYN FORCHÉ "The Colonel" from *The Country Between Us* by Carolyn Forché. Copyright © 1980 by Carolyn Forché. Reprinted by permission of HarperCollins Publishers.

ROBERT FRANCIS "The Hound" reprinted from *Robert Francis: Collected Poems, 1936–1976* (Amherst: University of Massachusetts Press, 1976), copyright © 1936, 1964 by Robert Francis.

ROBERT FROST "After Apple-Picking," "Never Again Would Birds' Song Be the Same," "Mending Wall," "Desert Places," "Birches," "Home Burial," "Happiness Makes Up in Height for What It Lacks in Length," "Acquainted with the Night," "The Span of Life," "The Aim Was Song," "It takes all sorts," "Nothing Gold Can Stay," "Design," "Stopping by Woods on a Snowy Evening," "'Out, Out—,'" "Departmental," "Dust of Snow," "Fire and Ice," "The Road Not Taken," "Bereft," from *The Poetry of Robert Frost*, edited by Edward Connery Lathem. Copyright 1923, 1928, 1930, 1939, © 1969 by Holt, Rinehart and Winston. Copyright 1936, 1942, 1951, © 1956, 1958, 1962 by Robert Frost. Copyright © 1964, 1967, 1970 by Lesley Frost Ballantine.

ISABELLA GARDNER "In the Museum" by Isabella Gardner. Copyright 1952, copyright © renewed 1980 by Isabella Gardner McCormick Tate. This poem appeared in *Birthdays in the Ocean*, published in 1955 by Houghton Mifflin Company. Reprinted by permission of Houghton Mifflin Company.

CHRISTOPHER GILBERT "Pushing" from *Across the Mutual Landscape* by Christopher Gilbert. Copyright © 1984. Reprinted by permission of Graywolf Press.

ROBERT GRAVES "The Naked and the Nude" from *Robert Graves: Collected Poems*, 1975. Reprinted with permission of the Executors of the Estate of Robert Graves and A. P. Watt Ltd.

R. S. GWYNN "Snow White and the Seven Deadly Sins" from *Texas Poets in Concert: A Quartet*, copyright © 1990 by University of North Texas. Reprinted by permission of University of North Texas Press.

DONALD HALL "Names of Horses" from *Kicking the Leaves* by Donald Hall. Copyright © 1978 by Donald Hall. Reprinted by permission of HarperCollins.

ROBERT HAYDEN "Those Winter Sundays" and "The Whipping" are reprinted from *Angle of Ascent, New and Selected Poems* by Robert Hayden, by permission of Liveright Publishing Corporation. Copyright © 1966, 1970, 1972, 1975 by Robert Hayden.

WILLIAM HEYEN "Riddle" from *Erika: Poems of the Holocaust*, copyright © 1991 by Timeless Press, Inc., St. Louis. Reprinted by permission of Timeless Press, Inc.

M. CARL HOLMAN "Mr. Z" copyright © 1967 by M. Carl Holman. Reprinted by permission.

A. E. HOUSMAN "Epitaph on an Army of Mercenaries" and "Eight O'Clock" from *Last Poems* by A. E. Housman. Copyright 1922 by Holt, Rinehart and Winston. Copyright 1950 by Barclays Bank Ltd. "Loitering with a vacant eye," "The Immortal Part," "Is my team plowing," "Loveliest of Trees," "Terence, this is stupid stuff," "To an Athlete Dying Young," and "Bredon Hill" from "A Shropshire Lad," authorized edition, from *The Collected Poems of A. E. Housman*. Copyright 1939, 1940, © 1965 by Holt, Rinehart and Winston. Copyright © 1967, 1968 by Robert E. Symons. Permission to reprint granted by Henry Holt and Company, Inc. "Oh who is that young sinner" by A. E. Housman, reprinted with permission of Charles Scribner's Sons, an imprint of Macmillan Publishing Company from *My Brother*, by Laurence Housman. Copyright 1937, 1938 by Laurence Housman, renewed 1965, 1966 by Lloyds Bank Ltd.

LANGSTON HUGHES "Cross" from *Selected Poems of Langston Hughes* by Langston Hughes, copyright © 1959 by Langston Hughes. Reprinted by permission of Alfred A. Knopf, Inc. "Dream Deferred" from *The Panther and the Lash* by Langston Hughes, copyright © 1967 by Arna Bontemps and George Houston Bass. Reprinted by permission of Alfred A. Knopf, Inc.

TED HUGHES "Thistles" from *New Selected Poems* by Ted Hughes. Copyright © 1961 by Ted Hughes. Reprinted by permission of HarperCollins Publishers.

RICHARD HUGO "The Freaks at Spurgin Road Field" is reprinted from *Making Certain It Goes On, The Collected Poems of Richard Hugo*, by permission of W. W. Norton & Company, Inc. Copyright © 1984 by the Estate of Richard Hugo.

RANDALL JARRELL "The State" and "The Death of the Ball Turret Gunner" from *The Complete Poems* by Randall Jarrell. Copyright © 1945, 1972, 1973 by Mrs. Randall Jarrell. Reprinted by permission of Farrar, Straus and Giroux, Inc.

ELLEN KAY "Pathedy of Manners" from *A Local Habitation*, originally published by Ohio University Press.

GALWAY KINNELL "Blackberry Eating" from *Mortal Acts, Mortal Words* by Galway Kinnell. Copyright © 1980 by Galway Kinnell. Reprinted by permission of Houghton Mifflin Company.

ETHERIDGE KNIGHT "The warden said to me" from *Poems from Prison* © 1968 by Broadside Press. Reprinted by permission of Broadside Press.

MAXINE KUMIN "The Sound of Night" copyright © 1961 by Maxine Kumin. Reprinted by permission of Curtis Brown, Ltd.

PHILIP LARKIN "A Study of Reading Habits" from *The Whitsun Weddings* by Philip Larkin. "Aubade" from *Collected Poems* by Philip Larkin. Reprinted by permission of Faber and Faber Ltd. "Church Going" and "Toads" by Philip Larkin are reprinted from *The Less Deceived* by permission of the Marvell Press, England.

PHILIP LEVINE "The Fox" by Philip Levine from *One for the Rose*, Atheneum, 1981. Reprinted by permission of the author.

JANET LEWIS "Remembered Morning" from *Poems Old and New 1918–1978*. Reprinted with the permission of Ohio University Press/Swallow Press, Athens.

ROBERT LOWELL "Watchmaker God" from *History* by Robert Lowell. Copyright © 1973 by Robert Lowell. Reprinted by permission of Farrar, Straus and Giroux, Inc.

GEORGE MACBETH "Bedtime Story" from *The Broken Places* by George MacBeth (Scorpion Press, 1963). Reprinted by permission of the author.

KATHARYN HOWD MACHAN "Leda's Sister and the Geese" from *Sometime the Cow Kick Your Head: Light Year '88/9* (Cleveland: Bits Press, 1988). By permission of the author.

ARCHIBALD MACLEISH "You, Andrew Marvell" and "Ars Poetica" from *New and Collected Poems 1917-1982* by Archibald MacLeish. Copyright © 1985 by the Estate of Archibald MacLeish. Reprinted by permission of Houghton Mifflin Company.

NAOMI LONG MADGETT "Offspring" from *Pink Ladies in the Afternoon* (Detroit: Lotus, 1972, 1990). By permission of the author.

JOHN MASEFIELD "Sea-Fever" from *Collected Poems* (Macmillan: 1938) by John Masefield. By permission of the Society of Authors as the literary representative of the Estate of John Masefield.

CLEOPATRA MATHIS "Getting Out" from *Aerial View of Louisiana* by Cleopatra Mathis. Copyright 1980 by Sheep Meadow Press and Cleopatra Mathis. Reprinted by permission of the author.

PHYLLIS MCGINLEY "The Adversary," copyright 1937, renewed 1965 by Phyllis McGinley. "Trinity Place" copyright © 1959 by Phyllis McGinley, from *Times Three* by Phyllis McGinley. Used by permission of Viking Penguin, a division of Penguin Books USA Inc.

ALICE MEYNELL "Summer in England, 1914" reprinted with permission of Charles Scribner's Sons, an imprint of Macmillan Publishing Company, from *The Poems of Alice Meynell: Complete Edition*. Copyright 1923 by Wilfred Meynell, renewed 1951 by Viola Meynell.

JOSEPHINE MILES "Oedipus" from *Poems 1930–1960* by Josephine Miles. Reprinted by permission of Indiana University Press.

EDNA ST. VINCENT MILLAY "Counting-Out Rhyme" by Edna St. Vincent Millay. From *Collected Poems*, Harper & Row. Copyright © 1928, 1955 by Edna St. Vincent Millay and Norma Millay Ellis. Reprinted by permission of Elizabeth Barnett, Literary Executor.

MARIANNE MOORE "Nevertheless" reprinted with permission of Macmillan Publishing Company from *Collected Poems* by Marianne Moore. Copyright 1944, and renewed 1972, by Marianne Moore. "What Are Years?" reprinted with permission of Macmillan Publishing Company from *Collected Poems* by Marianne Moore. Copyright 1941, and renewed 1969, by Marianne Moore.

OGDEN NASH "The Turtle" from *Verses from 1929 On* by Ogden Nash. Copyright 1940. By permission of Little, Brown and Company.

HOWARD NEMEROV "The Amateurs of Heaven" and "Grace to Be Said at the Supermarket" from *Trying Conclusions: New and Selected Poems*, 1991, University of Chicago Press. Reprinted by permission of the author.

SHARON OLDS "The Victims" from *The Dead and the Living* by Sharon Olds, copyright © 1983 by Sharon Olds. Reprinted by permission of Alfred A. Knopf, Inc.

MARY OLIVER "Through Ruddy Orchards" from *No Voyage and Other Poems*. Copyright Molly Malone Cook Literary Agency Inc. By permission of the Molly Malone Cook Literary Agency Inc.

SIMON J. ORTIZ "Speaking" from *New Worlds of Literature*, eds. Jerome Beaty and J. Paul Hunter. Permission given by author, Simon J. Ortiz.

WILFRED OWEN "Dulce et Decorum Est" and "Anthem for Doomed Youth" from *Collected Poems of Wilfred Owen* by Wilfred Owen. Copyright © 1963 by Chatto & Windus, Ltd. Reprinted by permission of New Directions Publishing Corporation.

GRACE PALEY "The Sad Children's Song" from *Leaning Forward* © 1985 by Grace Paley. Reprinted by permission of Tilbury House, Publishers, Gardiner, Maine.

LINDA PASTAN "The Imperfect Paradise" is reprinted from *The Imperfect Paradise, Poems by Linda Pastan*, by permission of the author and W. W. Norton & Company, Inc. Copyright © 1988 by Linda Pastan. "The Hat Lady" is reprinted from *Heroes in Disguise, Poems by Linda Pastan*, by permission of the author and W. W. Norton & Company, Inc. Copyright © 1991 by Linda Pastan.

SYLVIA PLATH "Metaphors" from *The Collected Poems of Sylvia Plath*, edited by Ted Hughes. Copyright © 1960 by Ted Hughes. Reprinted by permission of HarperCollins Publishers. "Mirror" from *The Collected Poems of Sylvia Plath* edited by Ted Hughes. Copyright © 1963 by Sylvia Plath. Reprinted by permission of HarperCollins Publishers. "Spinster" from *The Colossus and Other Poems* by Sylvia Plath. Copyright © 1961 by Sylvia Plath. Reprinted by permission of Alfred A. Knopf, Inc.

DUDLEY RANDALL "Blackberry Sweet" from *New Black Poetry*, edited by Clarence Major. Copyright 1969 by International Publishers Co., Inc. Reprinted by permission of International Publishers Co., Inc. "Ballad of Birmingham" and "To the Mercy Killers" from *After the Killing* (Chicago: Third World Press, 1973).

JOHN CROWE RANSOM "Bells for John Whiteside's Daughter" and "Parting, without a Sequel" from *Selected Poems*, 3rd ed., revised and enlarged by John Crowe Ransom. Copyright 1927 by Alfred A. Knopf, Inc. and renewed 1955 by John Crowe Ransom. Reprinted by permission of the publishers.

HENRY REED "Naming of Parts" from *A Map of Verona* by Henry Reed. Reprinted by permission of Jonathan Cape Ltd.

ISHMAEL REED "Turning Pro" reprinted with permission of Atheneum Publishers, an imprint of Macmillan Publishing Company, from *New and Collected Poems* by Ishmael Reed. Copyright © 1988 by Ishmael Reed.

ALASTAIR REID "Curiosity" from *Passwords* by Alastair Reid. Copyright © 1959 by Alastair Reid; originally published in *The New Yorker*. Reprinted by permission of the author.

CARTER REVARD "Discovery of the New World" from *New Worlds of Literature*, ed. Jerome Beaty and J. Paul Hunter. Copyright © Carter Revard. Reprinted by permission of the author.

ADRIENNE RICH "Living in Sin" is reprinted from *The Fact of a Doorframe, Poems Selected and New, 1950–1984*, by Adrienne Rich, by permission of W. W. Norton & Company, Inc. Copyright © 1984 by Adrienne Rich. Copyright © 1975, 1978 by W. W. Norton & Company, Inc. Copyright © 1981 by Adrienne Rich.

ALBERTO RÍOS "Nani" from *Whispering to Fool Wind*, copyright © 1982 by Alberto Ríos. Reprinted by permission of the author.

ELISAVIETTA RITCHIE "Sorting Laundry" reprinted from *Poetry*, February, 1989, by permission of the author.

EDWIN ARLINGTON ROBINSON "The Sheaves" reprinted with permission of Macmillan Publishing Company from *Collected Poems* by Edwin Arlington Robinson. Copyright 1925 by Edwin Arlington Robinson, renewed 1953 by Ruth Nivison and Barbara R. Holt.

THEODORE ROETHKE "I knew a woman" copyright 1954 by Theodore Roethke. From *The Collected Poems of Theodore Roethke* by Theodore Roethke. Used by permission of Doubleday, a division of Bantam Doubleday Dell Publishing Group, Inc.

CARL SANDBURG "Splinter" from *Good Morning, America*, copyright 1928 and renewed 1956 by Carl Sandburg. Reprinted by permission of Harcourt Brace Jovanovich, Inc.

SIEGFRIED SASSOON "Base Details," copyright 1918 by E. P. Dutton, renewed 1946 by Siegfried Sassoon. From *Collected Poems* by Siegfried Sassoon. Used by permission of Viking Penguin, a division of Penguin Books USA Inc.

PHILIP SCHULTZ "I'm Not Complaining," copyright © 1982 by Philip Schultz from *Deep within the Ravine* by Philip Schultz. Used by permission of Viking Penguin, a division of Penguin Books USA Inc.

KARL SHAPIRO "The Fly" from *Selected Poems* (Random House, Inc: 1968). Copyright © 1968 Karl Shapiro by arrangement with Wieser & Wieser, Inc., 118 25th St., New York, NY 10010.

ROBERT B. SHAW "Shut In" by Robert B. Shaw, from *Poetry*, March 1990. Copyright © 1990 by the Modern Poetry Association. Reprinted by permission of the editor of *Poetry*, with the consent of the author.

MARTIN BRISTOW SMITH "A goat on a stroll near a brook" from *Five-Line Frolics* © 1982 by Exposition Press. Reprinted with permission of Exposition Press of Florida, Inc.

W. D. SNODGRASS "Powwow" from *The New Yorker*, June 29, 1962. Copyright W. D. Snodgrass. Reprinted by permission of the author.

GARY SOTO "Small Town with One Road" first appeared in *Poetry*. Copyright © November 1985 by The Modern Poetry Association. Reprinted by permission of the Editor of *Poetry* and Gary Soto.

WILLIAM STAFFORD "Traveling through the dark" from *Stories That Could Be True* (Harper & Row: 1960). Copyright © 1960 by William Stafford. Reprinted by permission of the author.

ANN STANFORD "The Beating," copyright © 1969 by Ann Stanford, from *The Descent* by Ann Stanford. Used by permission of Viking Penguin, a division of Penguin Books USA Inc.

MAURA STANTON "Comfort" from *Cries of Swimmers* (Salt Lake City: Utah University Press, 1984). Reprinted by permission of the author.

WILL D. STANTON "Dandelions" copyright © by Will D. Stanton. Originally published in *The New Yorker Magazine*, 1960. Reprinted by permission of John Hawkins & Associates.

WALLACE STEVENS "The Death of a Soldier," "Sunday Morning," "The Snow Man," "The Poems of Our Climate," and "Disillusionment of Ten O'Clock" from *The Collected Poems of Wallace Stevens* by Wallace Stevens. Copyright 1954 by Wallace Stevens. Reprinted by permission of Alfred A. Knopf, Inc.

WILLIAM L. STIDGER "A Day" reprinted from *I Saw God Wash the World* (Rhodeheaver-Hall-Mack Co., Philadelphia, PA).

BARTON SUTTER "Shoe Shop," first appeared in *Poetry*, February 1980. Copyright © 1980 by the Modern Poetry Association. Reprinted by permission of the editor of *Poetry*, with the consent of the author.

MAY SWENSON "On Its Way," by May Swenson. Copyright © 1970 by May Swenson and reprinted with the permission of The Literary Estate of May Swenson.

SARA TEASDALE "Barter" reprinted with permission of Macmillan Publishing Company from *Collected Poems* by Sara Teasdale. Copyright 1917 by Macmillan Publishing Company, renewed 1945 by Mamie T. Wheless.

DYLAN THOMAS "Do Not Go Gentle into That Good Night," "Poem in October," and "Fern Hill" from *Poems by Dylan Thomas* by Dylan Thomas. Copyright 1945 by the Trustees for the Copyrights of Dylan Thomas, 1952 by Dylan Thomas. "Poem in October" was first printed in *Poetry*. Reprinted by permission of New Directions Publishing Corporation.

JEAN TOOMER "Reapers" is reprinted from *Cane* by Jean Toomer, by permission of Liveright Publishing Corporation. Copyright 1923 by Boni & Liveright. Copyright renewed 1951 by Jean Toomer.

DEREK WALCOTT "The Virgins" from *Sea Grapes* by Derek Walcott. Copyright © 1976 by Derek Walcott. Reprinted by permission of Farrar, Straus and Giroux, Inc.

C. WEBSTER WHEELOCK "Divorcée" reprinted by permission of the author.

JOHN HALL WHEELOCK "Earth" reprinted with permission of Charles Scribner's Sons, an imprint of Macmillan Publishing Company, from *The Gardener and Other Poems* by John Hall Wheelock. Copyright © 1961 by John Hall Wheelock.

RICHARD WILBUR "The Writer" from *The Mind Reader*, copyright © 1971 by Richard Wilbur. Reprinted by permission of Harcourt Brace Jovanovich, Inc. "Mind" from *Things of This World*, copyright © 1956 and renewed 1984 by Richard Wilbur. Reprinted by permission of Harcourt Brace Jovanovich, Inc. "A Late Aubade" from *Walking to Sleep*, copyright © 1968 by Richard Wilbur. Reprinted by permission of Harcourt Brace Jovanovich, Inc.

ARTHUR WILKINS "A cannibal said to her mate" from *Mortal Taste* (Exposition Press: 1965). Copyright 1965 by A. N. Wilkins. Reprinted by permission of the author.

WILLIAM CARLOS WILLIAMS "The Widow's Lament in Springtime," "The Red Wheelbarrow," "To Waken an Old Lady," and "Poem" from *The Collected Poems of William Carlos Williams, 1909–1939*, vol. I. Reprinted by permission of New Directions Publishing Corporation. "The Dance" from *The Collected Poems of William Carlos Williams, 1939–1962*, vol. II by William Carlos Williams. Copyright © 1962 by William Carlos Williams. Reprinted by permission of New Directions Publishing Corporation.

SUSAN WOOD "Eggs" reprinted by permission of Louisiana State University Press from *Campo Santo* by Susan Wood. Copyright © 1991 by Susan Wood.

IVAN LEONARD WRIGHT "The Want of You" reprinted from *The Best Loved Poems of the American People*, edited by Hazel Felleman (Doubleday & Company, Inc., 1936).

JUDITH WRIGHT "Portrait" from *Collected Poems 1942–1970* by Judith Wright. Reproduced by kind permission of Angus & Robertson Publishers, London and Sydney.

WILLIAM BUTLER YEATS "Sailing to Byzantium" and "Leda and the Swan" reprinted with permission of Macmillan Publishing Company from *The Poems of W. B. Yeats: A New Edition*, edited by Richard J. Finneran. Copyright 1928 by Macmillan Publishing Company, renewed 1956 by Georgie Yeats. "The Second Coming" reprinted with permission of Macmillan Publishing Company from *The Poems of W. B. Yeats: A New Edition*, edited by Richard J. Finneran. Copyright 1924 by Macmillan Publishing Company, renewed 1952 by Bertha Georgie Yeats. "The Wild Swans at Coole" reprinted with permission of Macmillan Publishing Company from *The Poems of W. B. Yeats: A New Edition*, edited by Richard J. Finneran. Copyright 1919 by Macmillan Publishing Company, renewed 1947 by Bertha Georgie Yeats. "Down by the Salley Gardens" and "The Coming of Wisdom with Time" from *The Poems of W. B. Yeats: A New Edition*, edited by Richard J. Finneran (New York: Macmillan, 1983).

Index of Authors, Titles, and First Lines

Authors' names appear in capitals, titles of poems in italics, and first lines of poems in roman type. Numbers in roman type indicate the page of the selection and italic numbers indicate discussion of the poem.